DATE DUE

#16			

DEMCO 38-296

Fulbright Papers

PROCEEDINGS OF COLLOQUIA

SPONSORED BY THE
UNITED STATES–UNITED KINGDOM
EDUCATIONAL COMMISSION:
THE FULBRIGHT COMMISSION, LONDON

Volume 15

Penal theory and practice

Looking from a transatlantic, interdisciplinary perspective, this book examines the crisis in penal policy facing the governments of both Britain and the United States.

Sentencing guidelines, the organisation of prisons and their function, the use of non-custodial sentences and 'informal justice', women and the criminal justice system: these are just some of the issues addressed here by a group of distinguished theorists and practitioners. The contributors include criminologists, sociologists, lawyers and philosophers; judges, civil servants involved with penal policy, and those with practical experience in prisons and in other aspects of penal practice and reform.

At a time when criminal justice systems are increasingly perceived as failing the societies they serve, this book makes a major contribution to the debate on crime and punishment.

The Fulbright Programme of Educational Exchanges, which has been in operation since 1946, aims to promote mutual understanding between the United States of America and other nations. It now operates in more than 120 countries, with forty-three bi-national commissions involved in its administration. In the United Kingdom the Commission aims to offer qualified British and American nationals the opportunity to exchange significant knowledge and educational experience in fields of consequence to the two countries, and thereby to contribute to a deeper mutual understanding of Anglo-American relations and to broaden the means by which the two societies can further their understanding of each other's cultures. Amongst its activities the Commission promotes annual colloquia on topics of Anglo-American interest; the proceedings are published in this series.

Penal theory and practice

Tradition and innovation in criminal justice

edited by

ANTONY DUFF, SANDRA MARSHALL,
REBECCA EMERSON DOBASH
AND RUSSELL P. DOBASH

MANCHESTER
UNIVERSITY PRESS

IN ASSOCIATION WITH
THE FULBRIGHT COMMISSION, LONDON

DISTRIBUTED EXCLUSIVELY IN THE USA AND CANADA
BY ST MARTIN'S PRESS

COPYRIGHT © THE US–UK EDUCATIONAL COMMISSION, 1994

Published by Manchester University Press
Oxford Road, Manchester M13 9NR, UK
and Room 400, 175 Fifth Avenue,
New York, NY 10010, USA

*Distributed exclusively in the USA and Canada
by* St. Martin's Press, Inc.,
175 Fifth Avenue, New York, NY 10010, USA

British Library Cataloguing-in-Publication Data

A catalogue record for this book is available from the British Library

Library of Congress Cataloging-in-Publication Data

Penal theory and practice : tradition and innovation in criminal
  justice / edited by Antony Duff ... [et al.].
      p.   cm. – (Fulbright papers : v. 15)
    "Proceedings of the Fulbright Colloquium on Penal Theory and Penal
Practice ... held at the University of Stirling from 1 to 4
September 1992"–Foreword.
    Includes index.
    ISBN 0–7190–3821–9
      1. Punishment–Great Britain–Congresses. 2. Punishment–United
States–Congresses. 3. Corrections–Great Britain–Congresses.
4. Corrections–United States–Congresses. I. Duff, Antony.
II. Fulbright Colloquium on Penal Theory and Penal Practice (1992 :
University of Stirling) III. Series.
HV9642.P46   1994
364.6'0941–dc20   93–50559
ISBN 0–7190–3821–9 *hardback*

Phototypeset by Intype, London
Printed in Great Britain
by Biddles Ltd, Guildford and King's Lynn

Contents

Figures and tables

Notes on contributors

Ian Brownlee is Senior Lecturer in the Department of Law, University of Leeds

Michael Cavadino is Lecturer in Law at the Centres for Criminological and Legal Research, University of Sheffield.

James Dignan is Lecturer in Law at the Centre for Criminological and Legal Research, University of Sheffield.

Rebecca Dobash is Professor in the School of Social and Administrative Studies, University of Wales College of Cardiff.

Russell Dobash is Senior Lecturer in the School of Social and Administrative Studies, University of Wales College of Cardiff.

Antony Duff is Professor in the Department of Philosophy, University of Stirling.

Marjory D. Fields is a Judge of the Family Court of New York State.

Barbara A. Hudson is Director of the Centre for Criminal Justice Studies, and Senior Lecturer in the Department of Social Work and Social Policy, University of Northumbria at Newcastle.

Gill McIvor is a Research Fellow in the Social Policy Research Centre, University of Stirling.

Bill McWilliams is a Visiting Scholar at the Institute of Criminology, University of Cambridge.

Sandra Marshall is Lecturer in the Department of Philosophy, University of Stirling.

Tony Marshall is Vice-Chair of Mediation UK.

Rod Morgan is Professor of Criminal Justice in the Faculty of Law, University of Bristol.

David Morran is joint Co-ordinator of the CHANGE Project at the University of Stirling.

Paul H. Robinson is Professor in the Faculty of Law, Northwestern University.

Andrew Rutherford is Reader in the Faculty of Law, University of Southampton, and is Chairman of the Howard League.

Joe Sim is Reader in Sociology, Institute of Crime, Justice and Welfare Studies, Liverpool John Moores University, Liverpool.

Hans Toch is Professor in the School of Criminal Justice, University of Albany.

Michael Tonry is Sonosky Professor of Law and Public Policy, University of Minnesota.

Andrew von Hirsch is Professor at the School of Criminal Justice, Rutgers University, and Senior Research Fellow at the Institute of Criminology, University of Cambridge.

Monica Wilson is joint Co-ordinator of the CHANGE Project at the University of Stirling.

Ed Wozniak is a Senior Researcher in the Central Research Unit at the Scottish Office.

Peter Young is Senior Lecturer in the Center for Criminology and the Social and Philosophical Study of Law, University of Edinburgh, and Director of the Centre.

Foreword

This volume records the proceedings of the Fulbright Colloquium on Penal Theory and Penal Practice which was held at the University of Stirling from 1 to 4 September 1992. The relationship of punishment to crime, always a subject of hot debate, needs continual reassessment as beliefs, attitudes and values change. The University of Stirling's initiative in bringing together experts from both sides of the Atlantic to discuss this subject in an Anglo-American context was much welcomed by the Fulbright Commission, which was pleased to give its warm support.

In meeting its aim of promoting Anglo-American cultural understanding, the Commission sponsors at least one, and sometimes two, colloquia each year on subjects of mutual interest and importance to the USA and the UK. These meetings of distinguished scholars and practitioners in specialist fields augment the Commission's traditional awards of studentships, scholarships and fellowships to British and American citizens for study, teaching, research or work experience in the other's country. Over 11,000 such exchanges have been supported in this way by the Commission since it was established in 1948.

The Colloquium at Stirling covered a wide range of topics affecting criminal justice. Penal theory and practice in the United Kingdom and the United States were contrasted and compared in the light of recent experience and valuable conclusions were reached.

The opinions expressed are, of course, personal to the contributors and do not necessarily reflect the views of the Commission. Nevertheless, the Commission believes that publication of the proceedings will be greatly valued by all those concerned with how penal theory and practice are changing to meet the needs of society in Britain and America. The subject is of vital importance to the effective running of both democracies and the Fulbright Commission is pleased to have been able to contribute to its discussion at this time.

John E. Franklin, *Executive Director*
United States-United Kingdom Educational Commission
The Fulbright Commission, London

Acknowledgements

We would like to express our gratitude to the Fulbright Commission, whose generous grant made possible the Fulbright Colloquium at which these papers were read; to Captain John Franklin, Executive Director of the Fulbright Commission, for his help and encouragement; to the University of Stirling, where the Colloquium was held, for financial support and organisational assistance; to University of Wales, College of Cardiff, and to the Scottish Office, for further financial support; to Yvonne McClymont, for her invaluable help in organising and running the Colloquium, and in the process of editing the papers for publication; and to all the participants in the Colloquium, who made it the stimulating and productive occasion that it was.

R. A. D.
S. E. M.
R. E. D.
R. P. D.

Introduction

ANTONY DUFF, SANDRA MARSHALL, REBECCA EMERSON
DOBASH AND RUSSELL P. DOBASH

The provision, application and administration of punishment, the realm of what might be called 'practical penality',[1] is one of the contexts in which abstract theory, research and concrete practice are brought most obviously and sharply into contact with each other. Philosophers and legal theorists discuss 'the justification of punishment': they ask what general aims the institution of punishment should serve if it is to be justified, what values or principles should govern it; their shelves are full of more or less sophisticated 'theories of punishment'. Social scientists – sociologists and criminologists – often address similar questions. Their central concern, however, is to investigate, to analyse and to explain the operation of criminal justice; to critically evaluate the way 'justice' and 'punishment' are embodied in institutional practices, and how these affect offenders and victims.

Practitioners of various kinds grapple with the business of punishment. Legislators and policy makers must decide what kinds of conduct should be criminalised, and thus rendered subject to punishment; what kinds of punishment should be available to the courts; what kinds of principle or policy should guide the courts in their sentencing decisions. Judges must decide what sentence to impose on each convicted offender – and, in so far as they have either formal or effective power over sentencing policy, what principles and policies should guide such decisions. Those, like probation officers, whose task it is to advise the courts must decide what kind of advice to offer. Prison governors and officers must administer the most dramatic kind of punishment imposed by the courts: they, and the service of which they are part, have to form some view of what their job is – of what prisons are for, and of how they should be organised and governed. Probation officers have to administer other sentences imposed by the courts, most obviously probation itself and Community

Service Orders: they require some conception of what they are (or should be) doing. And then there are, of course, the offenders themselves (sometimes, the offenders *our*selves): how do, or can, or should they conceive the punishments which are imposed on them?

Academic theorists and researchers have an obvious responsibility to policy makers and practitioners. They should remind themselves constantly of the challenge of practice – of various versions of the question 'But what use is all this to my friend the Governor of Barlinnie Prison?', which a summer school student asked after listening to two philosophers discussing the standard theories of punishment. This is not, of course, to say that theorists should be in the business of offering detailed practical guidance to practitioners – they are unlikely to have either the expertise or the experience which that requires. Just what their role should be has been a subject of considerable debate; should they act, for instance, as 'detached scholars', as 'state counsellors', or as 'critical sympathisers' (Weiss, 1982; Dobash and Dobash, 1990)? Each of these possible roles suggests different relationships between theoretical research and practical policy. Specific research results rarely, if ever, bring about specific transformations in policies and practices, but recent investigations of the impact of research on social policy (Weisss, 1982; Dobash and Dobash, 1990) suggest that one important role for academic researchers is to formulate new ideas and concepts: new analytical formulations of problems, novel ways of seeing and conceptualising issues.

Whatever the specific position of academics, however, the role of theory and research should be critical rather than necessarily consoling: to articulate conceptions of what punishment *ought* to be (if it ought to be at all), against which existing practices can be measured, and will no doubt be found to be more or less seriously defective. But theorists and researchers do at least have some responsibility to show how theory and research *could* be applied to practice. The route from a theoretical account of the justification of punishment to a decision about what particular kinds of punishment should be available to the courts, or about the application and administration of particular kinds of punishment, is neither clear nor short; the route from research to practical policy is a circuitous process involving a number of complex, multi-layered and sometimes unpredictable steps. Theoretically- or empirically-minded scholars cannot be expected to map out every detail of that route, but they should at least be able to give some indication of how it could be mapped. It is a justified complaint against some (too many) academics that they fail to recognise or to discharge this responsibility.

Practitioners themselves also have some responsibility to think theoretically, and to grapple with the implications of research results. Even when their job is more concerned with applying policies made by others than with making policy themselves, they need some conception of what they should be doing: of the point of the particular enterprise in which they are engaged, of the values or principles that should structure it, and of how they should conceive their relationship with the offenders with whom they have to deal. These conceptions should play a critical, and not merely a consoling or rationalising, role in their practical lives – as a standard against which they can assess what they do or are asked to do, as an ideal towards which they should aspire. But to articulate any such conception requires them to understand their practice in the context of relevant theory and knowledge about the nature of, and the possible justifications for, punishment. The same is more obviously true of those whose job it is to make penal policy: how can policy be adequately made without a clear conception of its proper aims, and without a basis in relevant research results? It is a justified complaint against some (too many) practitioners that they fail to take this responsibility seriously enough: they pay inadequate attention to normative theory or to relevant research results, and so bind themselves to limited or over-simplified conceptions that ignore the significant values and possibilities to be found in penal theory and research.

This way of talking about the practical responsibilities of theorists and researchers, and the theoretical responsibilities of practitioners, might suggest a simple hierarchy which sets theory above practice. In such an elite system, theorists are seen as 'detached scholars' who must help practitioners by telling them what ends they should be pursuing, what principles they must respect – providing them with critical standards for the conduct of their practical tasks; practitioners should look (look up) to academics for this necessary assistance. But that would be a distortion, which conceals the extent to which theorists and researchers can and should learn from practice. Good practice not only provides the problems and issues which form the raw material of theory and research, but can often itself embody (albeit implicitly) ways of understanding punishment and its aims, which constitute, if not an articulated 'theory of punishment', at least a conception of punishment which theorists and researchers should take seriously. One task of theory is not merely to bring to bear on practice a set of aims, principles and values whose foundation and articulation is independent of the concrete practices to which they are then applied, but also to try to render more explicitly articulate the theoretical conceptions that practice itself can embody.

All of this suggests (which should hardly be surprising) that the distinctions between 'theory' and 'practice', or between 'theorists/ researchers' and 'practitioners', should not be drawn too sharply. Good theory and research is sensitive to practice, and learns from it as well as providing a basis for its critical assessment. Good practice is sensitive to theoretical analysis and to research results, and is informed by a critical understanding of its own endeavours.

A similar point applies to the distinctions amongst theorists and researchers fostered by the orthodox specialisations of modern academia. Punishment and criminal justice are topics in philosophy, in legal theory, in criminology and sociology, as well as in psychology, literature, history . . . It is obvious, for instance, that any adequate philosophical account of punishment must be sensitive both to the empirical actualities of the penal institutions whose rationale is to be examined, and to the social and political contexts from which particular theories of punishment emerge. It is equally obvious that any adequate sociology of punishment must attend to those normative questions about the meaning and justification of punishment with which philosophers are concerned. Academics must talk and listen to each other as well as to practitioners; it is a justified complaint against some (too many) academics of various disciplines that they are insufficiently aware of, and insufficiently sensitive to, the work being done in other disciplines.

One of the aims of the Fulbright Colloquium, at which the papers in this volume were initially presented, was to bring together theorists, researchers, policy makers and practitioners from different disciplines, backgrounds, and countries (Scotland, England, Wales, and the United States), in the hope that they could talk usefully to each other. The participants included legal theorists, sociologists, criminologists, philosophers, and psychologists; civil servants, judges, probation officers, and prison governors. We have been able to publish only a selection of the thirty-four papers which were given at the Colloquium (see Appendix 1 for a full list); not even publication of all the papers would do justice to the varied and fruitful exchanges generated by the Colloquium (both within and outwith the formal sessions). But apart from their intrinsic interest, the papers do give some indication of how fruitfully practice and theory can interact.

SENTENCING AND 'JUST DESERTS'

Recent discussions of sentencing theory and practice in the United Kingdom have inevitably focused to some degree on the background to, and the provisions and likely effects of, the Criminal Justice Act 1991 (see *von Hirsch, Cavadino*, and *Hudson**; also Wasik and Taylor, 1991). One central feature of the Act is its focus on 'just deserts': as the White Paper which preceded the Act put it, 'the aim of the Government's proposals is better justice through a more consistent approach to sentencing, so that convicted criminals get their "just desserts"[sic]' (Home Office, 1990, para. 1.6).[2] Another feature is the concern to reduce the courts' reliance on imprisonment, in favour of greater use of non-custodial 'punishments in the community', whose 'punitive' character is to be emphasised in order to ensure that they are taken seriously as punishments. These concerns provide the topics of several of the papers in this volume.

In its contemporary form the 'justice model' of punishment marked a reaction against the consequentialist orthodoxies that had dominated penal theory in the post-war period; a reaction provoked in part by the perceived failure of consequentialist approaches (most notably the rehabilitative approach in which California had led the way) to achieve their crime-preventive aims, but partly too by a renewed concern, in penal theory as in other areas of political and social thought, with rights as opposed to utility – in particular the rights of the guilty as well as those of the innocent. Criminals should not be treated merely as 'objects' who needed to be subjected to 'treatment' to remedy their criminal behaviour – a subjection that might involve indeterminate 'rehabilitative' sentences, and denied their status as responsible agents. Rather, they must be respected as rational and autonomous agents, whose wrongdoing deserved condemnation and punishment.[3]

Liberal advocates of the 'justice model' have typically seen it as *limiting* the punitive power of the state. Criminals are to be punished *no more* severely than they deserve (they are not to be subjected to extended or indefinite sentences for the sake of prevention); the state's intrusion into their lives, while still dramatically coercive (especially in the case of imprisonment) should be limited to ensuring that they receive their 'just deserts' – it may not extend to attempts to 'cure' or 'reform' them. But 'just deserts' can also clearly serve as

*Italics indicate chapters in this volume.

a slogan for those who want to emphasise *punishment*, as the infliction of deserved suffering, as against other apparently 'softer' responses to crime; whilst 'just deserts' theorists have hoped that the adoption of this model would lead to lower levels of prison sentences, to a general reduction in penal coercion, the model can also be (ab)used by those who want to increase the severity of punishment (see Hudson, 1987; in response, see von Hirsch, 1993, ch. 10).

A concern for 'just deserts' generates the principle of proportionality in sentencing: the severity of the punishments imposed on offenders should be proportionate to the seriousness of their offences. This raises various questions, a number of which are addressed in this volume.

First, just how is the principle of proportionality to be articulated? To turn it into a practicable sentencing principle we need a scale of crimes which will render crimes commensurate with each other in terms of their relative seriousness, and a scale of penalties which will render the different types and levels of punishment commensurate with each other in terms of their relative severity. We then need to 'anchor' the top and bottom points of the penalty scale: to specify the heaviest and the lightest penalties that should be available to the courts. And we then need to bring the two scales together, so that we can assign particular levels or types of penalty to particular types of crime (and, in the end, to particular instances of each type). One problem here is that of the commensurability of penalties: how far can we render different kinds of punishment commensurable, for instance by expressing the 'punitive bite' of each in terms of 'units of punishment' (*Robinson*)? Another is that of the range of penalties to be allowed: how far would this approach, in order to ensure practicable commensurability, allow only a limited range of non-custodial 'community-based' punishments (see Wasik and von Hirsch, 1988; contrast Morris and Tonry, 1990)? Another is that of the factors to be attended to in assessing the seriousness of a crime or the severity of a penalty: how far, for instance, should such factors as prior record be allowed to aggravate, or social deprivation to mitigate, the seriousness of a crime? How far should courts be allowed or required to attend to the particularities of the offender's situation and background, and to the actual effect that a particular penalty is likely to have (see *Tonry*, pp. 69–74 on 'like-situated offenders, comparable crimes, and generic punishments')?

Second, just how is the principle of proportionality to be institutionalised as a guide for judicial practice? What should the roles of the legislature, of the courts, of sentencing councils be? Should the norms of sentencing be expressed in numerical tables, or in more discursive principles? These questions have particular force in relation to the Criminal Justice Act 1991. Given the vagueness of the guidance that the Act provides for courts, how far can we expect that courts will in fact take the insistence on proportionality seriously, or apply the concept consistently, or impose fewer or shorter prison sentences? Can we hope that the Act will produce 'progress toward a somewhat fairer sentencing system' (*von Hirsch*, p. 40); or should we rather fear that it will not 'provide the solution to the prison numbers crisis', and 'will overall serve to compound rather than alleviate the crisis of legitimacy' in the British penal system (*Cavadino*, pp. 46,47)?

Third (and most fundamentally), how should the principle of proportionality figure in a sentencing system? Von Hirsch wants to make it *the* central principle of sentencing, in the hope that this will make sentencing decisions 'somewhat (and let me emphasise the "somewhat") fairer' (*von Hirsch*, p. 28). Paul Robinson argues that we can respect it, by insisting that the *amount* of punishment an offender receives (as measured in 'units of punishment') be proportionate to the seriousness of her or his offence, whilst also allowing considerable scope to other, roughly utilitarian, considerations of crime prevention in determining the *method* by which that amount should be imposed. But should the requirements of strict proportionality ever be relaxed or overridden, either to allow harsher sentences, for instance to deal with violent and predictably dangerous offenders (see *von Hirsch*, pp. 31–2, and *Cavadino*, pp. 45–6, on the provisions of the 1991 Act), or to allow lighter sentences for reasons of humanity or parsimony? The latter possibility is one that especially concerns Tonry, who is sceptical about any demand for strict proportionality. He argues that the application of such a strict principle to the actual world of contemporary crimes and punishments will be a source of injustice rather than greater justice, and that it needs to be balanced against a principle of parsimony which sometimes requires sentences lighter than strict proportionality would require. The principle of proportionality should set 'presumptive maximum sentences' for offences, but a 'parsimony presumption' should require judges 'to impose the least severe sentence consistent with the governing purpose *at* sentencing' (*Tonry*, pp. 80–1; see Morris and Tonry, 1990; for criticism see *Brownlee, von Hirsch*, pp. 36–7).

Andrew von Hirsch and Michael Tonry both insist on the importance of parsimony in punishment, but von Hirsch seeks to achieve

this by means of a 'parsimonious scale' which accords with the requirements of proportionality (*von Hirsch*, p. 33), whereas Tonry sees parsimony as a principle which conflicts with, and may qualify, the demand
for proportionality (*Tonry*, pp. 77–81).

Both also favour a wider use of non-custodial punishments, although
von Hirsch is more concerned than Tonry to ensure that they are
imposed in accordance with the demands of strict proportionality. But
both also recognise that imprisonment will still be necessary as a
punishment for some offences and some offenders, whether because
only imprisonment can do justice to the seriousness of their crime,
or because only thus can the public be protected.

IMPRISONMENT

The use of imprisonment, however, has been central to what has been
perceived as the 'penal crisis' in the United Kingdom (and if the
United Kingdom is in such a crisis, so too is the United States).
Michael Cavadino and others have identified a number of problems
and issues – unlawful arrests, unsound convictions, an expanding
prison population, prison overcrowding, prison riots, disorders and
hostage taking, staff disruption in prisons, disaffection of those subject
to the criminal justice system – which taken together constitute a
continuing, indeed growing crisis in the criminal justice system in the
United Kingdom (see Fitzgerald and Sim, 1982; Woolf and Tumim,
1991; Cavadino and Dignan, 1992). Though Cavadino talks of the
' "crisis of legitimacy" which affects not only prisons but the entire
penal enterprise', the 'characteristics and symptoms' of the 'penal
crisis' which he picks out are all features of the prison system
(*Cavadino*, p. 42).

It is a mistake to take imprisonment as the *paradigm* of punishment,
if this means regarding it either as the most *usual* mode of punishment, or as the presumptively appropriate punishment for most
offences, so that non-custodial punishments must be justified as 'alternatives' to the imprisonment which would otherwise be appropriate
(see *Young*). But the central role of imprisonment in discussions of
punishment generally, and of the 'penal crisis' in particular, is hardly
surprising. Imprisonment is the most dramatically coercive form of
sentence typically imposed by the state.[4] The difference in imprisonment rates between Britain and other Western European countries,
and between the United States and Western Europe,[5] raises acutely
the question of why we rely on imprisonment as heavily as we do. And

it is in our prisons that the failures of the penal system are made most obvious.

But though all can and do agree both that our prisons are in crisis, and that they are the most dramatic manifestation of a more general 'penal crisis', they do so from very different points of view, which generate very different conceptions of the character of that 'crisis'. Is the central objection to imprisonment, for all but the most serious kinds of offence, that it is an unduly harsh punishment, that it is inconsistent with any acceptable version of the principle of proportionality (see *von Hirsch*, p. 30, on persistent petty property offenders); or that it is relatively ineffective as a means of preventing future offending; or that it is too expensive?[6] Should we seek to resolve the 'crisis' by building more prisons to accommodate the number of criminals who should be imprisoned, or by sharply reducing our use of imprisonment? Any answer to such questions will need to involve an account of the proper use of imprisonment as a punishment. Should the problems *within* prisons – problems manifested in prison disturbances and in industrial action by prison staff – be understood as reflecting the lack of effective discipline and order among prisoners, and the unreasonable demands of staff unions; or rather as the natural result of the inhumanity and injustice with which prisoners are typically treated, and of the unreasonable and conflicting demands which the system makes of prison officers? Any answer to these questions will need to involve an account of the proper internal organisation of prisons: what should the status of the prisoners be; how far should the organisation of prisons be aimed at securing simply 'order', or at justice, or rehabilitation?

Hans Toch's paper in this volume addresses further questions. He is primarily concerned with exploring the ways in which prison policy is actually arrived at, and the ways in which a properly informed and articulated public opinion could and should influence policy. His discussion of prison policies in the United States, especially the use of 'shock incarceration' and of 'Intensive Discipline Units', is a salutary reminder of the gulf that divides theoretical argument from political practice, of the conflicting pressures and aims which in fact determine policy developments, and of the gap between official rhetoric and actual practice. His conclusions, however, are surprisingly (if relatively) optimistic: the penal 'machine becomes a strange assortment of pulleys and rubber bands, serendipitously arrived at' (*Toch*, p. 120), and if public opinion were to be taken seriously, it would point towards a more flexible, less harsh, and potentially rehabilitative use of imprisonment. Furthermore, listening to the views of the public reduces alienation, democratises the process of policy making, and, whilst not perfect, is better than a system of elite planners and 'politics as usual'.

Rod Morgan, a member of the Woolf inquiry into the English prison disturbances of 1990 (see Woolf and Tumim, 1991), is concerned with the internal organisation and operation of prisons. He notes that, in Britain at least, there is now general agreement on the limited aims of imprisonment, as being imposed for the sake of 'denunciation, retribution and/or public protection . . . not reform or narrowly conceived deterrence' (*Morgan*, p. 130); that this strengthens the idea that the imprisonment itself constitutes the punishment; and that this gives support to the principle of 'normalisation' for which he and King had argued – the idea that 'the same general standards which govern the life of offenders in the community should be held to apply to offenders in prison'(*Morgan* , p. 131; see King and Morgan, 1980). The two key notions which he draws from this are that of 'just prisons' (prisons whose regimes respect non-consequentialist requirements of justice in their dealings with prisoners), and that of 'responsible prisoners' (prisons which treat their inmates as responsible agents); and he explores the ways in which such notions might be given substance in our actual prisons (see also *Cavadino*, on the crisis within our prisons, and on the Woolf Report and responses to it; and *Wozniak* on developments within Scottish prisons).

Morgan and Toch describe complex processes associated with the creation and implementation of penal innovations. Many such innovations in prisons emerge after important, sometimes sustained, periods of prison unrest and disorder. A common historical pattern involves the introduction of stringent measures and/or a gradual reduction in the living standards and rights of prisoners, followed by disruption and disorder. English, Welsh and Scottish prisons have recently undergone such a period; indeed, it has been unprecedented in its ferocity and the level of damage to property (Cavadino and Dignan, 1991; for the United States, see, for example, Colvin, 1992). Such periods are then followed by commissions, public inquiries and, usually although not always, new policies and initiatives. Morgan is concerned about how such reforms will be achieved, but is basically enthusiastic about the possibility of 'achieving decent prison conditions' (*Morgan*, p. 143). Cavadino and Joe Sim are much more pessimistic. Whatever the final outcome of these developments, it is rare in the United Kingdom for the penal system to attempt to monitor and assess the implementation of innovations following such a period.

Ed Wozniak's paper in this volume describes just such a process of implementing change, in which there is an attempt to combine policy formulation, management and research with the goal of improving standards in Scottish prisons. Like the penal estate in England and Wales, the Scottish penal system has undergone a period of unprecedented unrest followed by a lengthy period of assessment and innovation. The Scottish Prison Service appears to have committed itself to the ideal of the responsible prisoner, by seeking to create an enabling and facilitating environment. Wozniak's role in this process is to monitor and evaluate these efforts by carrying out periodic surveys of the attitudes and opinions of prisoners and staff. Surprisingly, in the light of the recent history of unrest, he finds that most staff and prisoners agree on a number of important issues, and that there is a reasonably high level of satisfaction about the relationships between prisoners and staff. Prisoners complain about prison conditions, but their greatest concerns are the problems of maintaining links with their families. What most prisoners appear to want is a reasonable standard of living, better visiting facilities for families, and improved relationships with staff. The Scottish Prison Service's intention to continue to monitor these reactions, to directly assess staff and prisoners' evaluations of innovations, and to use the results in assessing the performance of specific establishments, seems to signal a genuine commitment to translating ideals not just into policy but also into practice.

FINES, PROBATION AND COMMUNITY SERVICE

Imprisonment is the narrow apex of the penal pyramid: below it lie the wide range of non-custodial penalties, including Community Service Orders, fines and probation (to which a range of conditions may be attached). These lack the dramatically coercive character of imprisonment; they do not present themselves as central aspects of the 'penal crisis' (indeed those who think that the crisis consists largely in the problem of imprisonment may see them as part of the solution to it): but we need at least to ask what role they can properly play in a penal system.

One role which fines (at a fairly low level) and probation (without stringent demands attached to it) play is that of a presumptive penalty for obviously minor offences for which there is clearly no question of imprisonment. However, the combination of concerns about effective crime-control with the growing recognition of the problems of imprisonment has led in the last decade to an increased interest in 'intermediate sanctions': in penalties falling between the two perceived extremes of imprisonment (for a significant period) and relatively small fines or undemanding probation.[7]

Such sanctions (or suitable combinations of them, designed to be manifestly punitive or 'tough') have been seen by many as practicable, economic and effective alternatives to imprisonment. Thus one of the aims of the Criminal Justice Act 1991 was to beef up the range and the demanding character of such non-custodial sanctions so as to make them acceptable as alternatives to imprisonment (see Home Office, 1988; Home Office, 1990). One danger with this strategy is that of 'recruitment from the shallow end' (see *von Hirsch*, p. 34; Cohen, 1985): the danger that such sanctions will be imposed not instead of imprisonment, but on those who would not otherwise have received a custodial sentence at all. Another problem is that of 'breach sanctions' (see *von Hirsch*, p. 34): the danger that the use of more stringent forms of such sanctions might actually increase the use of imprisonment, if imprisonment is the penalty for breaches of them. A third, perhaps deeper, problem is that so long as such sanctions are seen simply as 'alternatives to imprisonment', their character and their possible value will be distorted; punishment will still be understood as consisting paradigmatically in imprisonment, and these sanctions will be structured and presented in that light – as lesser (and cheaper) kinds of punishment which must be compared with imprisonment. Hence the significance of the Canadian Sentencing Commission's recommendation that 'community sanctions be defined and applied as sanctions in their own right' (1987; reproduced in von Hirsch and Ashworth, 1992, p. 339). Of course, this might serve to increase the danger of 'recruitment from the shallow end'. But if we should follow the Commission in resisting 'the indiscriminate application of principles relevant to custody to assess the merits of community sanctions' (*ibid.*), we must ask what principles *are* relevant to assessing their merits. How should such sanctions figure in the practice of sentencing; what are their proper aims; how should they be administered, and how should breaches of them be dealt with, if not by imprisonment?

In England, at least, probation was not historically viewed as a *punishment* at all: it grew out of the early police court missions, whose aim was to save offenders from imprisonment by persuading the court to release them on recognizance to the supervision of a police court missionary (see King, 1969; McWilliams, 1983). This view of probation as an alternative to punishment was given statutory expression in the requirement that courts should make a probation order 'instead of sentencing' the offender (Powers of Criminal Courts Act 1973, s.2). In his contribution to this volume Bill McWilliams sketches the changes in the probation service's view of its task – and in its conception of the offenders with whom it has to deal – since its inception, but focuses on the problems it now faces, problems arising in part from the growth of the 'managerial' ethos, and in part from the 1991 Act. The Act presents a probation order as a 'community sentence', and it was the government's clear intention that probation should be recognised as a punishment (see Wasik and von Hirsch, 1988, p. 569; Duff, 1992, pp. 44–5). Probation officers have reacted with hostility to what they see as a radical change in the character of their task: these new provisions, by emphasising 'punishment rather than positive influence', make 'a clear break with the established role and values of the probation service' (Beaumont, 1989, p. 101). McWilliams shares this distrust, although his conception of probation (as it used to be) as a way of 'cooling the mark out' is far less ambitious (some would say more cynical) than that of many traditional probation officers, but one might ask whether probation could be conceptualised in a more fruitful way (see Bottoms and McWilliams, 1979; Duff, 1992, pp. 56–9).

Community service was, unlike probation, introduced explicitly as a punishment (Powers of Criminal Courts Act 1973, ss. 14–17; see Pease and McWilliams, 1980). As Gill McIvor notes, however, there has been no agreement on the 'primary penal objective' of community service (*McIvor*, p. 171): should it be understood primarily in reparative, or rehabilitative, or retributive terms? It might be suggested that one advantage of such a sentence is that it 'could appeal to a variety of philosophies and fulfil . . . a number of sentencing aims' (*ibid.*); one might also argue that there need be no sharp distinction between these aims – that 'retribution', properly understood, could consist precisely in some reparative endeavour that will rehabilitate the offender by repairing the communal bonds damaged by the crime (see Duff, 1992, pp. 55–6). Courts do need to be clear, however, whether community service should be seen as an alternative to imprisonment (to be reserved for those who would otherwise have received a custodial sentence), or as a sentence in its own right, which might be imposed on those who would not otherwise have been liable to imprisonment. We must ask too whether their main concern should be to find a kind of community service which would be in its substantive character appropriate to the particular offender and her or his situation, or to impose a kind of order which could be readily ranked (as a strict proportionality principle requires) in terms of its severity relative to other kinds of punishment (see the doubts expressed in Wasik and von Hirsch, 1988, and von Hirsch, Wasik and Greene, 1989, about the extent to which community service should be used). McIvor's paper, based on the research she has been doing, explores the positive prospects for, and the problems faced by, Community Service Orders after the 1991 Act.

Imprisonment, probation and community service have all received extensive discussion in the literature. However, as Peter Young notes in his paper in this volume, 'the fine is by far the most commonly used of all penal sanctions in most western penal systems' (*Young*, p. 185), but it is also one of the most infrequently discussed in the penal literature. His general project (see Young, forthcoming) is to remedy this lack: to engage not only in an empirical inquiry into the ways in which fines are used (for instance, the kinds of crime for which they are seen as a possible or appropriate penalty), but also in a theoretical inquiry into the significance of the fine as a punishment. The use of fines puts 'a monetary price on harm' (*Young*, p. 186), that is, in using fines we imply that the crimes for which they are imposed can be adequately 'paid for' by a monetary payment. In some cases, however (Young's example is rape), we regard a fine as inappropriate. Young suggests that this is not merely because rape is too 'serious' a crime to be paid for in this way, but because the 'harm' involved in rape is not a *kind* of harm for which monetary 'compensation' could be appropriate. One question then is whether we can draw any clear distinction between the kinds of crime for which fines are, and those for which they are not, appropriate; another is whether we should continue to see fines (as they are typically now seen) simply as relatively minor penalties on a scale which is topped by (and whose penal significance is thus interpreted in the light of) imprisonment. Perhaps indeed there are more (essentially moral) questions to be asked about the current use of fines: how far does their accepted use for a wide range of crimes reflect and foster a (morally) distorted conception both of those crimes (as crimes which could be 'paid for' monetarily), and of the meaning of punishment itself?

The topics touched on so far have been central to what might be called orthodox penal theory and practice. They take for granted the existence of a system roughly similar to those with which we are familiar in the western world: a penal system through which offenders will typically be dealt with by a range of familiar legal dispositions. Though theorists disagree about the proper aims of the system, about the principles (or their relative weighting) by which it should be structured, about the proper role of the familiar range of penalties, they typically agree about the kind of system which needs to be justified, and about the kinds of justification which could plausibly be offered for it. They agree, we may say, that the provision of an adequate 'theory of sentencing' is a central and proper task of penal theory.

But there are other topics which must be raised, other voices which must be heard – voices that in different ways and to different degrees cast doubt on the enterprise of developing a general theory of sentencing which will rationalise and justify something like our existing formal, institutional modes of responding to crime, and that seek to question some of the assumptions on which such theories and practices are typically based.

WOMEN'S VOICES

Some of these voices are those of women: of women as victims of crime, and also of women as offenders (a topic not covered in this volume, but see Carlen, 1983; Heidensohn, 1985; Dobash, Dobash and Gutteridge, 1986; Morris, 1987). In the last two decades the penal establishment has experienced unprecedented challenges from the community. Feminist activists, legal practitioners and theorists have been at the forefront of these efforts. They have challenged the legacy of indifference in criminal justice responses (Dobash and Dobash, 1980), and demanded more meaningful reactions to women and children who have experienced physical and sexual assault. In Great Britain, the United States and elsewhere, the battered women's and rape crisis movements have lobbied legislatures, policy makers, legal practitioners and criminal justice functionaries to change policy and practice in order to provide better protection for the victims of male violence. For some, greater assistance for victims should be linked with more assertive actions against offenders which demonstrate the seriousness of their acts and treat them as equivalent to other violent acts. In contrast to many abolitionists who argue for the dismantling of criminal justice, feminists and others have argued for an increased reliance on the police, prosecution and courts as a means of deterring male violence and protecting victims; new legislation, policies and practices created in both countries have apparently been meant to challenge violence and offer greater protection to victims.

Marjory Fields begins her paper in this volume by comparing the legal reforms concerning rape with those concerning violence against women in the home. She concludes that meaningful reforms relating to rape have been hampered by a number of technical problems, as well as by continued resistance associated with patriarchal assumptions about rape. By contrast, she argues that reforms in the area of violence against women have been far-ranging and meaningful (see also Schecter, 1982; Dobash and Dobash, 1992). New laws, policies and practices have made an important difference in criminal justice responses to violence in the home, yet there are continuing and persistent problems in the implementation of these reforms. Fields shows how judicial reluctance and ignorance mean that civil law remedies such as 'orders of protection' (injunctions/interdicts in the United Kingdom) are not being issued and enforced, leaving many women who are victimised by their male partners with little or no protection (see Barron, 1990; Dobash and Dobash, 1992, for the situation in Britain). The preferred remedy in many jurisdictions in the United States continues to be diversion into programmes of mediation and couple conciliation. However, Fields argues, the evidence shows that such interventions are rarely successful in stopping violence or protecting victims; diversion and mediation rarely work in situations in which one of the parties is fearful of the other and the aggressor is in a dominant and controlling position – the usual circumstances when men use violence against women in the home. Fields concludes that arrest, prosecution and sentencing of violent men constitute more appropriate remedies for such violence.

The use of diversion, couple mediation and conciliation, often through family courts, has a long history in the United States. In the last ten years, alternative responses have emerged to deal with men who assault their female partners. There are now well over 300 of these programmes for violent men in the United States and Canada, and similar programmes have begun in the United Kingdom, Europe, Australia and New Zealand. Such programmes are not usually concerned with mediation and conciliation: instead, they concentrate on the man, his violent behaviour, and the need for him to change his behaviour and attitudes. Some such programmes are rooted in therapeutic orientations, others take an educational approach, and a significant number claim to operate in a 'pro-feminist' manner by challenging and confronting men, and seeking to educate and shame them into taking responsibility for their actions and attitudes towards women and violence. Pro-feminist approaches are critical of therapeutic orientations which, it is argued, fail to deal with the violence, to confront men or to instil responsibility (Dobash and Dobash, 1992). The therapeutic orientation sees violence as the presenting problem, to be skirted round in search of 'deeper' sources of understanding. Pro-feminist approaches deal in a direct way with the violence as *the* problem to be addressed. Many of the North American programmes are directly linked to criminal justice; men sent onto these programmes are often on probation to the courts. In the United Kingdom, the only such programmes are linked to criminal justice; one is CHANGE, which is described in detail in this volume by David Morran and Monica Wilson.

The CHANGE programme works with and through the criminal justice system: courts refer men to the programme after conviction for a violent act, as a condition of a probation order; the programme insists on the criminality of the men's conduct, and aims to bring them to take responsibility for their violence, as *intentional* conduct which they *chose* and can therefore change. These aims accord with some of the official rhetoric that preceded the Criminal Justice Act 1991. The programme does not talk the language of retribution (though participation in the programme may be seen as a burden the men are required to assume because of their offence, which could be said to constitute it as a retributive punishment; see Duff, 1992; Dobash and Dobash, 1992, pp. 240–50), but it aims to 'increas[e] the offender's sense of responsibility and understanding of the need to avoid [such] crime in future' (Home Office, 1988, para. 1.2); to 'bring home to [them] the effect of their actions on others', and 'get them to face up to what they have done, and to see how they can avoid offending in future' (Home Office, 1990, paras. 2.6, 4.12). On the other hand, the programme is clearly a radical alternative to other and more traditional kinds of punishment – most obviously, to imprisonment and fines (the most usual sanction). It might thus also be seen as belonging with a range of other experiments and proposals which aim to undermine the dominance of the criminal justice system as traditionally conceived, or to change our understanding of its proper aims.

INFORMAL JUSTICE

James Dignan's contribution to this volume focuses on other examples of penal experiments – on 'reparation' schemes which aim, either by direct discussion between offenders and victims or by indirect negotiations through project staff, to reach agreement on some way in which the offender can make reparation to the victim. One problem faced by such experiments has been the lack of any agreement on just what their aim(s) should be. Dignan argues that they should be understood in the light of Braithwaite's theory of 'reintegrative shaming' (Braithwaite, 1989; Braithwaite and Pettit, 1990); that this points the way towards a more general 'restorative' rather than 'retributive' conception of the aims of the criminal justice system, and that we can identify practicable ways of moving towards a radical transformation of criminal justice along these lines. Tony Marshall also looks towards a transformation of criminal justice from 'retribution' towards 'restoration'.

Marshall proposes innovations in responses to crime which go beyond the formal, established mechanisms, and which take very seriously the idea of 'community' (an idea which figured rhetorically in the British government's approach to the 1991 Act; see Home Office, 1988). He points out how many of these experimental schemes have been introduced in the United States and Great Britain as a means of diverting offenders away from formal systems of punishment in order to reduce expenditure. The way forward, he argues, is to strengthen and extend existing community reactions to crime in order to return the 'conflicts' associated with crime to the community (see Christie, 1977). New structures and processes would be primarily based on 'informal' reactions grounded in the principles of restorative and reparative justice; these require denunciation, reparation and reintegration. What he seeks is a mediating and normalising species of social control which would reconcile the offender to the victim and the community. Whilst this clearly reflects some of the ideals of abolitionists, Marshall rejects their programme of radical non-intervention and deconstruction: 'non-intervention has major costs in failing to denounce wrong-doing and ... victims' needs are ... ignored' (*Marshall*, p. 251).

Dignan and Marshall propose community-based responses which offer more benign methods of dealing with crime, and claim to benefit victims, offenders and the community. However, doubts have been raised about such proposals. As Barbara Hudson points out, the North

American experience with informal community-based systems suggested that it was the poor and dispossessed 'who were denied access
to "proper" justice' and 'fobbed off' with informal responses (*Hudson*,
p. 294). Research has confirmed that Neighbourhood Dispute Centres
in the United States and Law Centres in Great Britain often, although
not always, fail to resolve many of the 'conflicts' with which they deal
(Lerman, 1986; Marshall and Merry, 1990). Other critics argue that
such informal mechanisms merely result in recruiting more people
into the criminal justice system's net. Feminists, particularly in the
United States, have made various criticisms of such community-based
programmes. Violence against women and sexual assaults on children
are, they note, often identified as the types of offence best suited for
diversion from the formal criminal justice system – a reflection of the
seriousness that the system accords these problems. Informal reactions, they argue, send inappropriate messages to the offender, the
victim and the community: that this is not a serious problem (a crime)
requiring formal intervention and sanctions. Once within the informal
networks, the women and children who are the victims of such crimes
are required to subordinate their concerns and fears to the exigencies
of reparation and reconciliation. And if crime is merely a 'relationship
problem', equally involving offender, victim and the community, how
can the violent and sexually abusive man be held accountable and
responsible for his behaviour? Such objections might raise doubts
about the appropriateness of purely informal, 'restorative' responses
to other types of crime as well. Can we (or should we try to) do
without the formal denunciatory or condemnatory processes of the
criminal justice system (both Dignan and Marshall emphasise the need
for 'denunciation' or 'shaming')? Is it a distortion to portray all crimes
as 'conflicts'? Do we live in the kinds of community which are necessary for such 'reparative' justice to become a reality? But such ideas
sketch an alternative ideal of community justice which must be taken
very seriously.

ABOLITIONISM

Attempts to improve, reform and develop criminal justice, however
benign, are rejected by adherents of a strong abolitionist agenda.
European abolitionists, primarily Norwegian and Dutch social scientists and legal theorists, seek to deconstruct the rhetoric of punishment, and to dismantle the pillars of penality (Bianchi and van
Swaaningen, 1986; de Haan, 1990; and see *Rutherford*, pp. 286–7): for

them, all justice developments are inherently and inevitably repressive and coercive. Most abolitionists seek at least to abolish imprisonment, 'within a framework of decriminalisation, depenalisation, destigmatisation, decentralisation and deprofessionalisation' (de Haan, 1991, quoted by *Sim*, p. 266); some go further, to propose the elimination of the police and courts. In his paper in this volume, Joe Sim describes the ideals, theoretical arguments and political tactics of abolitionists in the United Kingdom, who differ markedly from their continental counterparts.

In the United Kingdom abolitionist thinking has been apparent in many organisations, most notably, according to Sim, in the Radical Alternatives to Prison group (RAP). Sim seeks to show how the political efforts of RAP around such issues as women in prison, objections to 'control units' in prisons, the expansion of the penal estate, and an ongoing critique of the 'penal crisis', have made important contributions to penal developments in the United Kingdom. Unlike most continental abolitionists, RAP argued for improvements in penal conditions, and pointed to the Barlinnie Special Unit in Scotland as a way forward (Boyle, 1977), whilst recognising the inherent contradiction between this approach and any strong abolitionist argument: lobbying for the improvement of prisons, and other reforms and developments *within* the penal system, appear to constitute distinct departures from continental abolitionist thinking. Sim tells how RAP, particularly through the journal *The Abolitionist*, accepted the challenge of feminist thinking about sexual violence, and consequently argued for a 'policy of exemplary or retributive punishment' in response to *some* crimes (*Sim*, p. 271). Embracing feminist arguments about sexual and physical assaults on women, and demanding criminal justice intervention for such crimes, constitutes a serious and radical departure from most abolitionist thinking (see Dobash and Dobash, 1992, p. 210).

Andrew Rutherford questions Sim's insistence on the importance of abolitionist arguments in the formulation of penal policy in the United Kingdom. Dutch abolitionists, he argues, were able to influence the course of penal affairs in the Netherlands because they had important, direct links with policy makers and criminal justice officials. Such connections were impossible in the United Kingdom. He claims, however, that significant successes of an abolitionist type have been achieved in the United Kingdom, specifically a dramatic reduction in the incarceration of juveniles.

Hudson, whilst 'not arguing for an abolitionist agenda as such', agrees with abolitionists in questioning 'the prevailing assumption that legal reasoning is necessarily the framework within which the response to crimes should be decided' (*Hudson*, p. 292). She is especially concerned with the recent (re-)growth of 'legal hegemony': the expansion of legal reasoning and legal discourse into contexts from which it had been excluded, for example the reaction against 'informal justice', the 'transfer [of] criminal justice discretion from non-legal professionals back to lawyers' and judges (*Hudson*, p. 295). Like abolitionists, she advocates the language of social problems and social policy over the discourse of legal reasoning, with its stress on crime and penality. Legal reasoning, she argues, is inherently linked to the 'drift to a law and order society', and in such a society social policies wither or disappear while more law and more prisons is the order of the day (*Hudson*, p. 296).

As the discourse of social problems recedes, it is replaced by legal discourse which emphasises, for instance, 'just deserts' and 'proportionality'. But the principle of proportionality, like most legal discourse, is premised on the supposed universality and impartiality of law, whereas, Hudson argues, law is in fact inherently ideological, riddled with class, race and gender biases. Like Tonry, Hudson is suspicious of abstract principles, and argues that principles such as proportionality are biased because they ignore the social and economic inequalities which constitute the foundation for so much crime. A principle of proportionality might be defensible 'as a setter of upper limits to punishment', and 'desert' can work 'as a limiting factor . . . making sure that no new legal injustices are added to the social injustices already suffered by impoverished and powerless offenders' (*Hudson*, pp. 301, 304): but within those limits she wants to expand the space available for 'discourses which are centred on helping offenders refrain from reoffending, which insist on feasible as well as fair penalties, which reveal the offender's individuality and difference from other offenders, which appreciate constraints on choice and which understand the disadvantages which not only play their part in people's likelihood of wrong-doing but also of having their wrong-doing dealt with by the penal system' (*Hudson*, p. 304).

Thus we come full circle, back to 'just deserts' and proportionality and the role that such concepts should play in our normative understanding of penality. For some theorists, these concepts are absolutely crucial to an adequate normative account of punishment and sentencing: they help to define the proper aims of punishment, and generate the central principles of sentencing. For others, they have an important but far more limited role as penal principles; and for yet others, a focus on concepts such as these serves only to distract our attention from the real problems of criminal justice.[8]

Notes

1   See Garland, 1985: 'penality' refers 'to the whole of the penal complex, including its sanctions, institutions, discourses and representations' (p. x).

2   The Government's printed concern was unfortunately to ensure 'just desserts' [sic] for criminals; its actual concern to ensure 'just deserts' marked a shift in emphasis from the earlier Green Paper (Home Office, 1988; see Duff, 1992).

3   Von Hirsch, 1976, the report of the American Committee on the Study of Incarceration, was one of the most significant early advocates of this argument; for an initial critical response see Gardner, 1976.

4   This ignores the death penalty, but we agree with von Hirsch and Ashworth that '[a] civilized state . . . should not have this vile sanction at all – so there should be no occasion for the courts to have to decide when and why it should be imposed' (von Hirsch and Ashworth, 1992, p. x).

5   See Ashworth, 1992, pp. 218–20: in 1989 the number of prisoners per 100,000 population was 97 in the UK, 57 in Sweden, and 45 in the Netherlands – and 350 in the United States. As Ashworth also points out, however, such statistics must be used with caution: the rankings within Western Europe are quite different if, for instance, we ask about the rate of custodial sentences per 100,000 recorded crimes.

6   The latter two points figured in the Green and White Papers which preceded the Criminal Justice Act 1991: see Home Office, 1990, para. 2.7; Home Office, 1988, Part I. Cynics might suggest that the consideration of expense has loomed large for a government desperate to reduce public spending.

7   See *Tonry*, p. 61; more generally, see Morris and Tonry, 1990; von Hirsch and Ashworth, 1992, ch. 6; Ashworth, 1992, ch. 10; von Hirsch, 1993, ch. 7.

8   All the papers in this volume, as well as this Introduction, were written in 1992 or early in 1993 – before the full flowering of judicial hostility to certain aspects of the Criminal Justice Act 1991 (notably the provisions concerning unit fines and the relevance of prior record in sentencing), which led to the Criminal Justice Act 1993; and before the revival of a strident 'law and order' rhetoric amongst government ministers during the latter part of 1993, which threatens to encourage an increase, rather than a decrease, in the use of imprisonment.

References

Ashworth, A. J. (1992), *Sentencing and Criminal Justice*, Weidenfeld and Nicholson, London.

Barron, J. (1990), *Not Worth the Paper . . .?*, Women's Aid Federation England, Bristol.

Beaumont, W. (1989), 'Professional reactions and comments', in H. Rees and E. Hall Williams (eds.), *Punishment, Custody and the Community*, London School of Economics, London, pp. 87–111.

Bianchi, H., and van Swaaningen, R. (1986), *Abolitionism: Towards a Non-Repressive Approach to Crime*, Free University Press, Amsterdam.

Bottoms, A. E., and McWilliams, W. (1979), 'A non-treatment paradigm for probation service', *British Journal of Social Work*, IX, pp. 159–202.

Boyle, J. (1977), *A Sense of Freedom*, Pan Books, London.

Braithwaite, J. (1989), *Crime, Shame and Reintegration*, Cambridge University Press, Cambridge.

Braithwaite, J., and Pettit, P. (1990), *Not Just Deserts: A Republican Theory of Criminal Justice*, Oxford University Press, Oxford.

Canadian Sentencing Commission (1987), *Sentencing Reform: A Canadian Approach*, Canadian Government Publishing Centre, Ottowa.

Carlen, P. (1983), *Women's Imprisonment: A Study in Social Control*, Routledge & Kegan Paul, London.

Cavadino, M., and Dignan, J. (1992), *The Penal System: An Introduction*, Sage, London.

Christie, N. (1977), 'Conflicts as property', *British Journal of Criminology*, XVII, pp. 1–15.

Cohen, S. (1985), *Visions of Social Control*, Polity Press, Cambridge.

Colvin, M. (1992), *The Penitentiary in Crisis: From Accommodation to Riot*, State University of New York Press, Albany.

de Haan, W. (1990), *The Politics of Redress*, Unwin Hyman, London.

de Haan, W. (1991), 'Abolitionism and crime control: a contradiction in terms', in K. Stenson and D. Cowell (eds.), *The Politics of Crime Control*, Sage, London, pp. 203–17.

Dobash, R. E., and Dobash, R. P. (1980), *Violence Against Wives*, Free Press, New York; Macmillan, London.

Dobash, R. E, and Dobash., R. P. (1990), 'How research makes a difference to policy and practice', in D. Besharov (ed.), *Family Violence: Research and Public Policy Issues*, The AEI Press, Washington DC, pp. 185–204.

Dobash, R. E, and Dobash., R. P. (1992), *Women, Violence and Social Change*, Routledge, London.

Dobash, R. P., Dobash, R. E., and Gutteridge, S. (1986), *The Imprisonment of Women*, Blackwell, Oxford.

Duff, R. A. (1992), 'Alternatives to punishment – or alternative punishments?', in W. Cragg (ed.), *Retributivism and Its Critics* (ARSP Beiheft No. 47), Franz Steiner, Stuttgart, pp. 43–68.

Fitzgerald, M., and Sim, J. (1982), *British Prisons*, 2nd edn., Basil Blackwell, Oxford.

Gardner, M. (1976), 'The renaissance of retribution: an examination of "Doing Justice" ', *Wisconsin Law Review*, pp. 781–815.

Garland, D. (1985), *Punishment and Welfare*, Gower, Aldershot.

Heidensohn, F. (1985), *Women and Crime*, Macmillan, Basingstoke.

Home Office (1988), *Punishment, Custody and the Community*, HMSO, London.

Home Office (1990), *Crime, Justice and Protecting the Public*, Cm. 965, HMSO, London.

Hudson, B. (1987), *Justice through Punishment: A Critique of the 'Justice' Model of Corrections*, Macmillan, London.

King, J. F. S. (ed.) (1969), *The Probation and After-Care Service*, 3rd edn., Butterworth, London.

King, R., and Morgan, R. (1980), *The Future of the Prison System*, Gower, Aldershot.

Lerman, L. G. (1986), 'Mediation of wife abuse cases: the adverse impact of informal dispute resolution on women', *Harvard Women's Law Journal*, VII, pp. 57–113.

McWilliams, W. (1983), 'The mission to the English police courts 1876–1936', *Howard Journal*, XXII, pp. 129–47.

Marshall, T. F., and Merry, S. D. (1990), *Crime and Accountability: Victim/Offender Mediation in Practice*, HMSO, London.

Morris, A. (1987), *Women, Crime and Criminal Justice*, Blackwell, Oxford.

Morris, N., and Tonry, M. (1990), *Between Prison and Probation: Intermediate Punishments in a Rational Sentencing System*, Oxford University Press, New York.

Pease, K., and McWilliams, W. (1980), *Community Service by Order*, Scottish Academic Press, Edinburgh.

Schecter, S. (1982), *Women and Male Violence*, Southend Press, Boston.

von Hirsch, A. (1976), *Doing Justice – The Choice of Punishments*, Hill and Wang, New York.

von Hirsch, A. (1993), *Censure and Sanctions*, Oxford University Press, Oxford.

von Hirsch, A., and Ashworth, A. J. (eds.) (1992), *Principled Sentencing*, Northeastern University Press, Boston (UK edn 1993, Edinburgh University Press, Edinburgh).

von Hirsch, A., Wasik, M., and Greene, J. (1989), 'Punishment in the community and the principles of desert', *Rutgers Law Journal*, XX, pp. 595–618.

Wasik, M., and Taylor, R. D. (1991), *Blackstone's Guide to the Criminal Justice Act of 1991*, Blackstone Press, London.

Wasik, M., and von Hirsch, A. (1988), 'Non-custodial penalties and the principles of desert', *Criminal Law Review*, pp. 555–72.

Weiss, C. (1982), 'Policy research in the context of diffuse decision-making', in D. B. P. Kallen *et al.* (eds.), *Social Science Research and Public Policy-Making: A Reappraisal*, NFER-Nelson, Windsor, pp. 289–315.

Woolf, H., and Tumim, S. (1991), *Prison Disturbances April 1990*, Cm. 1456, HMSO, London.

Young, P. (forthcoming), *Punishment, Money and Legal Order*, Edinburgh University Press, Edinburgh.

PART ONE

Crisis and reform

1

Sentencing reform: its goals and prospects

ANDREW von HIRSCH

This is an opportune time for the present volume, as a major piece of legislation regulating sentencing has come into force – the Criminal Justice Act of 1991. The Act applies a guiding principle, that of proportionality, to sentencing decisions. Considering that only a few years ago there was almost no interest in sentencing reform in the United Kingdom, this is a remarkable step. In this introductory essay, I would like to address the aims and prospects of sentencing reform: that is, what we can and cannot reasonably expect from sentencing reform, including the reforms embodied in the 1991 Act.

INCREASED CRIME CONTROL NOT THE GOAL

The belief that sentencing reform can achieve significantly reduced crime rates is, I think, a dangerous delusion. There was a wave of that kind of thinking in the US in the early 1980s: the rise, and subsequent fall, of 'selective incapacitation'. A number of criminologists, including Peter Greenwood (1982) and James Q. Wilson (1983), proposed targeting certain 'high risk' offenders, deemed likely to commit frequent felonies, for substantially increased prison sentences. Restraining these individuals, it was said, would produce a significant reduction in such crimes. Such a strategy, however, is not particularly fair, as the indicia of risk to be relied upon – prior arrests and certain social factors – have so little relation to the blameworthiness of the offender's conduct (von Hirsch, 1985, ch. 11). And when the probable effects were looked at more carefully, the numbers did not add up: the strategy cannot target a sufficient proportion of active offenders to make much of a dent on crime rates (National Academy of Sciences, 1986; von Hirsch, 1988).

The lesson of selective incapacitation can be generalized: sentencing strategies that emphasize crime control tend to be inequitable, and their effectiveness is likely to be rather limited. Once controlling crime becomes the overriding aim, moreover, escalating the response becomes too easy: if a strategy is tried and does not work, why not apply more drastic medicine? Nowhere has this phenomenon been more visible than in the US drug war – where American legislatures and judges got tough on drugs without visible success, so they got still tougher – with no effect on crime rates but a dramatic one on rates of imprisonment.

I thus regard it as a virtue of the 1991 Act that it does not set the reduction of crime rates as its primary goal. The 1990 White Paper (Home Office, 1990) made it still clearer that this cannot be a realistic aim for sentencing legislation.

PROPORTIONALITY

If enhanced prevention is not to be the goal, what should be? Our objective should, I think, be to try to make sentencing decisions somewhat (and let me emphasise the 'somewhat') fairer. Whatever the defects of the 1991 Act, it has the virtue of making a fairness objective – that of proportionality – the guiding rationale.

Proportionality and fairness
Why should sentences be proportionate with the gravity of offenses? Elsewhere (most recently, in von Hirsch 1993, ch. 2), I have tried to suggest why; the reasons, in a nutshell, concern the censuring implications of punishment. Since the criminal sanction conveys blame, its amount should comport with the degree of blameworthiness of the conduct. Behind these arguments lies a strong intuition shared by ordinary people in their everyday lives, that penalties should reflect the blameworthiness of the behavior. Even children demand parity in punishments for similar acts of misbehavior. In the law, disparate sentences – disparate, that is, in the sense of visiting unequal sanctions for equally reprehensible conduct – also strike us as morally troublesome.

If proportionality has this central role as a requirement of fairness, then the concept needs explicit articulation in the standards for sentencing. It is precisely such an explicit articulation that has been lacking in traditional English sentencing doctrine, and which the 1991 Act tries, for the first time, to introduce. The Act uses the term 'proportionality' in a rather undifferentiated fashion, and does not supply much in the way of criteria for the concept's application. However, a considerable body of theory has developed concerning the criteria for proportionality, namely, on the distinction between 'ordinal' proportionality and the fixing of the anchoring points of a penalty scale (von Hirsch, 1985, ch. 4); on the role of the prior record (von Hirsch, 1985, ch. 7; Wasik, 1987; von Hirsch, 1991) and on gauging the seriousness of crimes (von Hirsch and Jareborg, 1991).

'Perfect' fairness not the aim

How well can a sentencing system achieve proportionality? The standards used to implement this aim are likely to be rough-and-ready ones. In Minnesota, an attempt was made to spell those standards out in detail through the use of numerical guidelines (von Hirsch, Knapp and Tonry, 1987, ch. 5). But the more one tries to be explicit, the more the anomalies will become apparent. Norms for sentencing – whether couched as numerical guidelines, or as statutory principles implemented through appellate courts' precedents – will lump together cases that might be distinguishable.

One can try to alleviate such imperfections: one of the attractions of statutory principles over numerical guidelines is, for example, that they more easily permit the courts to differentiate among conduct of different degrees of gravity within the same statutory offense classification. Even such efforts, however, will not fully succeed. Any workable system of rules will have to be at least somewhat aggregative. When one considers how rough-and-ready legal standards have to be, the political compromises that have to go into any sentencing law, and the vagaries of court application of the standards, it is clear that perfectly equitable results are unlikely to be achieved.

It is a mistake, however, to take a perfectionist view: that unless proportionality can be achieved completely, it should not be sought at all. Even an imperfect application of ideas of proportionality may be more equitable than a scheme which relies on no guiding rationale, or emphasises some other goal such as crime control. With all the defects of the Minnesota guidelines outlined by Michael Tonry in his essay (this volume, ch. 3), I doubt that fairer results would have been achievable merely by broadening the ranges and leaving more to unguided discretion, or by basing the ranges on another set of objectives.

The same point – of resisting perfectionist objections – holds for another issue, that of 'just deserts in an unjust society'. Societies in which access to the means for a good life are skewed by class (as is true in the UK, and more starkly so in the US) make it harder to devise standards which are fair. One can try to alleviate this difficulty in various ways, for example, by making the more extreme forms of social deprivation a culpability-related mitigating factor (see Gardner, 1976; von Hirsch, 1993, epilogue). Treating deprived offenders as less culpable does, however, create the risk of making them seem more suitable for incapacitative approaches (Ward, 1992). And even if it were decided nevertheless that social deprivation should be mitigating, there will be cases on the margin: the person who is deprived but not quite enough so to qualify. We must bear in mind that the solutions cannot be perfect, but that even an imperfect proportionality-based scheme may be preferable, in terms of equity, to a scheme based on other aims.

What changes in sentencing practice can be hoped for as a result of an increased emphasis on proportionality? Perhaps the most striking change may be in the treatment of repetitive property offenders. Prior to 1992, such offenders – including even persistent petty offenders – were often imprisoned. Imprisonment, it was thought, would either help deter repetitive offending in others, or else incapacitate this offender from further violations. A proportionalist rationale makes the gravity of the current offense the primary determinant of the sentence. Where the current offense is not serious, the severe sanction of incarceration is not appropriate. The White Paper explictly contemplates a reduction in rate of incarceration in such cases, and the 1991 Act's requirement that the current offense be 'serious' before a custodial sentence is invoked is designed to have this effect. Paul Cooper (1992) suggests that the Act should have at least some success in reducing incarceration rates for repetitive lesser offenders.

Deviations from proportionality
Sentencers wish to achieve multiple aims. To what extent, then, does a proportionalist standard permit pursuit of ulterior purposes?

Deviating upward or downward from the normal sentence on account of aggravating or mitigating circumstances is no derogation from proportionality at all. As long as those deviations relate to the degree of blameworthiness of the conduct – that is, its harmfulness or culpability – they are actually called for by the principle of proportionality. The individual who has done less-than-typical harm through his offense, or shows reduced culpability, deserves less punishment.

Substituting among penalties of comparable severity also does not infringe desert requirements, even when the reason for substitution is something other than desert. Suppose crime X is of intermediate gravity and is ordinarily punished by a period of community service. If a particular offender has a drug or alchohol problem that could be alleviated by period of supervision and treatment, substituting that sanction does not infringe the parity requirements of desert – so long as the latter penalty is of roughly the same onerousness (Wasik and von Hirsch, 1988; von Hirsch, 1993, ch. 7). The 1991 Act requires that community sanctions should be both commensurate with the seriousness of the criminal conduct and 'suitable' for the offender. To make that provision comport with proportionality principles, the sanction's severity should be determined by the gravity of the conduct, but – among possible penal measures of equivalent severity – the choice of which measure may be made on the ground of suitability (Ashworth, 1992, ch. 10). Such an approach carries with it the danger that the severity-equivalence criterion may erode, so that risk- and treatment-considerations lead to penalties of quite different onerousness. But the principle should be apparent.

What, however, of real deviations from proportionality? The 1991 Act contemplates extending durations of confinement in exceptional cases where the offender has been convicted of a violent or sexual offense and is deemed likely to engage in conduct that inflicts 'serious' physical or psychological injury. Literally, such a provision does not fit proportionality requirements, as it expressly contemplates a sanction more severe than the gravity of the current offense warrants. How, then, can it be reconciled with proportionalist sentencing aims?

Paul Robinson (1987) has pointed out that a distinction can be made between the principles normally applicable to sentencing decisions, and those that might apply when exceptional degrees of harm are involved. As a requirement of fairness, proportionality ordinarily ought to be observed in sentencing decisions. Where extraordinary harms are involved, however, fairness might be permitted to give way to concerns about public protection. A. E. Bottoms and Roger Brownsword (1983) have suggested applying this kind of principle to permit extensions of confinement for extraordinarily dangerous individuals.

Are such exceptional measures desirable? There are cases of extraordinary social harm where most of us would be prepared to sacrifice fairness constraints. Justice demands that persons who have done no wrong ought not to lose their liberty, yet most of us would endorse quarantining persons who are carriers of deadly epidemic diseases. Cholera, however, is a much greater threat to community survival than dangerous offenders are. It is, as I have recently elaborated elsewhere (von Hirsch, 1993, ch. 6), debatable whether high-risk offenders constitute a danger of sufficient magnitude, and whether they can be identified with sufficient assurance, to make departures from normal proportionality constraints justified. And the dangerousness provisions of the 1991 Act are drawn more loosely than the Bottoms/Brownsword proposal would suggest – particularly, in those provisions' failure to define what degree of likelihood of serious bodily injury is required (ibid.; Ashworth, 1992, ch. 9).

But whatever conclusion one reaches on this particular issue, the distinction that Robinson (1987) draws is a vital one. There is a great difference in principle between (1) a system which ordinarily observes proportionality constraints, and departs from them only in exigent situations, and (2) a system which permits routine derogations from desert of a substantial nature. The former system is fair and proportionate in the main, in a way that the latter is not. Provided that the dangerousness provisions of the 1991 Act are not unduly expanded in practice, the reform can still be a basically proportionalist one.

Robinson's distinction is also worth bearing in mind when critics challenge proportionality requirements by singling out special situations where a deviation might seem intuitively attractive. Michael Tonry, for example, cites in his essay (in this volume, ch. 3) what he considers a particularly sympathetic case – that of a poor offender who is working hard to attain a skill – and argues that firm proportionality constraints should be rejected because they cannot accommodate such situations. I shall consider Tonry's case in more detail later, but one point is worth making here: if this case cannot be accommodated within proportionality constraints, and if Tonry is right that it really warrants special sympathy, why not invoke an exceptional (in this case, downward) departure? This, at least, would assure proportionate sanctions in more run-of-the-mill cases less worthy of special sympathy.

PROPORTIONALITY AND PARSIMONY

Punishment deprives those punished of their liberty or of other important rights. If such other rights are given the importance they should have, quanta of punishments should be constrained: a principle of parsimony in the infliction of penal suffering should be observed. The importance of parsimony is not universally acknowledged – some penologists pay it little heed (see Wilson, 1983). But the contributors to this volume seem largely in agreement that punishments should be parsimoniously inflicted. This raises the question I shall try to deal with next: how parsimony relates to the principle of proportionality.

Parsimony and selectivity

Most penal aims can be implemented in more or less parsimonious fashion. This is clearly the case with a desert model. Proportionality imposes more stringent constraints on the ordinal ranking of punishments than on a scale's anchoring points. The leeway permitted in anchoring the scale permits one to devise an array of penalties that is more, or less, sparing in the use of substantial punishments. I have recently suggested that there are reasons of principle for preferring a more parsimonious scale (see von Hirsch, 1993, ch. 5), but my solution for anchoring the scale is admittedly not the only conceivable one. The same leeway exists, however, for other sentencing rationales. Consider selective incapacitation again. Those who believe that sentencing policy should emphasize segregating dangerous offenders may still differ on how likely and how harmful future offending should be in order to qualify for incapacitative measures. Those differences could lead to a more, or less, severe penalty scale.

The goal of parsimony raises the question of parsimony for *whom?* A proportionalist sentencing rationale seeks to achieve parsimony across the board, by making reductions in penalties *pro rata*. The more proportionality is downgraded in favor of other sentencing rationales, the more selective the reductions will be: some people convicted of a given offense will benefit, but others not. Indeed, relaxing proportionality constraints may mean that the disfavored offenders will receive significant *increases* in punishment. This is the familiar evil trade-off: you, the reformer, can have your favored defendants for gentle treatment so long as we, the guardians of law and order, can have ours for tough sanctions. The more selective the system becomes, the more that evil materializes. (It is interesting that Peter Greenwood's selective-incapacitation scheme is actually quite lenient with 'low risk' robbers: they would only receive a year in prison. It is the bad risks, under his proposals, that would receive eight years (see Greenwood, 1982).)

Parsimony and non-custodial penalties

Concerns about the excessive use of imprisonment have led to a new interest in 'intermediate sanctions' – those less severe than imprisonment but more substantial than small fines or routine probation. The 1991 Act provides for expanded authority to employ such sanctions, and applies the proportionality principle to their use. The intent is to have such sanctions used for crimes in the middle level of seriousness, which are often now dealt with by incarceration.

There are, however, two problems, and any scheme for intermediate penalties that does not address them is likely to fail. One problem is that of recruitment from the 'shallow' end of the offender pool. The judge or magistrate who imposes a non-custodial sanction likes to see the offender comply with its terms. Compliance is made more likely by recruiting tractable offenders, who tend to be those with lesser crimes and modest criminal records. These, however, are people who up to now have received small fines or other lesser sanctions. Such recruitment practice, therefore, does not diminish the use of imprisonment, but merely raises the severity of the non-custodial sanctions which are imposed on the least serious cases in court dockets. An analysis by Todd Clear and Patricia Hardyman (1990) of intensive-supervision probation in several US jurisdictions suggests that it is precisely lesser offenders that are recruited for ISP, with little or no effect on the use of imprisonment.

The other problem is that of breach sanctions. The person put on routine probation in a large case-load was given little scrutiny, so that technical breaches were unlikely to come to light. The new intermediate sanctions tend to make breaches more apparent: failure to pay an installment of a unit fine, or to abide by the terms of an intensive-supervision program, will come more swiftly to the attention of the authorities. To make such programs credible to the public, it is tempting to take a stance of toughness towards violators, i.e. a policy of imprisoning for breaches. The difficulty is, of course, that such a policy may end up sending more people to prison than would be the case had the intermediate sanction not been invoked.

One of the attractions of a proportionalist sentencing rationale is that it helps deal with these two problems. If sentence severity must be graded according to the gravity of the offense, then intermediate sanctions should be targeted at crimes of middling gravity, not lesser crimes; nor is imprisonment an appropriate sanction for breaches not involving significant criminal harm (Wasik and von Hirsch, 1988; von Hirsch, 1993, ch. 7). The 1991 Act has provisions that attempt to deal with these issues (see Ashworth, 1992, ch. 9), and the question that remains is whether they will prove adequate when applied in practice. We need to watch carefully whether, after the Act, intermediate sanctions are used chiefly for middle-level offenses rather than minor ones, and whether imprisonment is used more sparingly as the breach penalty.

Political constraints

How severe or lenient a penalty system becomes is much influenced by the political environment of the jurisdiction, particularly by the extent of 'law and order' politics. The more officials feel they must urge harsh sanctions as a way of reassuring the public of their determination to fight crime, the more likely it becomes that penalties will rise.

To see the effects of this phenomenon, consider Sweden today. Traditionally, that country employed modest penalty levels. In 1988 Sweden adopted legislation that is a more complicated version of England's 1991 Criminal Justice Act. It sets forth a principle of proportionate sanctions, and supplies a number of criteria for the principle's application (von Hirsch and Ashworth, 1993, pp. 292–307). At the time of enactment the Social Democrats were the ruling party. The statute was explicitly designed to be 'neutral' in its impact on rates of imprisonment.

In 1991 Sweden had elections. A conservative coalition, then in opposition, made getting tough with criminals a major theme in its campaign. Since Swedish conservatives could not be as vocal as their American counterparts in attacking social programs, they needed to find other themes to emphasize, and law-and-order came readily to hand. As a result, the election campaign gave much more emphasis to punishment issues than had previous elections. The conservatives won the election, have been proposing increases in levels of imprisonment, and have secured enactment of changes in parole-eligibility rules that will make some increase likely. However, large increases do not seem in prospect, for there remains an important practical obstacle: sending more people to prison is expensive, and the government is short of money.

What if, for the reasons just stated, Sweden does raise its prison populations? Critics of proportionalist sentencing theory, or some of them, are likely to seize upon that fact to 'prove' that proportionality leads to harsher punishments. But the fallacy in such reasoning is apparent enough. What may lead to somewhat harsher punishments in Sweden is not the adoption of the proportionalist sentencing reform in 1988, but the electoral success three years later of former opposition parties that have made toughness on crime a priority. Trends towards severity or leniency are influenced not so much by sentencing theory as by political developments such as these.

The political factors that influence punishment levels are largely outside the control of sentencing reformers. One cannot stop increases in punishment brought about by strong law-and-order pressures by waving a book or pointing to a sentencing doctrine. The best that reformers can do is to adopt a rationale that does not justify or provide support for penalty increases. In this regard, proportionalism is preferable to traditional utilitarian theories – because, as noted previously, it does not make reductions in crime its primary aim.

Where law-and-order pressures are present, proportionalism has another advantage: that of distributing any penalty increases more ratably. Suppose that, in Jurisdiction X, prison populations increase by ten per cent. Were the increase distributed proportionately, any prisoner would receive a comparatively limited increase in his term of confinement. The more one deviates from proportionality, however, the more certain targeted groups of offenders may suffer disproportionately large increases. Much as an overall ten-per-cent increase would disturb me, I would be much more uncomfortable to see that population increase occurring through a small percentage of prisoners suffering a doubling of their prison terms. In short, it is not just aggregate levels of imprisonment that count, but who suffers any increase and by how much.

Can parsimony be a guiding rationale?
In his essay in this volume, Michael Tonry criticizes proportionalism as allowing insufficient scope for penalty reductions, and seems to urge that parsimony be the primary guiding rationale for sentencing policy. (More precisely, he urges that proportionality concerns set only the upper limit on permissible punishment, with parsimony objectives permitting reductions below these limits whenever feasible.) Does this claim stand analysis?

Parsimony emphasizes the reduction of penal suffering. It points to a lowering of penalty levels – something that proportionate sanctions can achieve, by moving the penalty scale's anchoring points downward. What parsimony alone does not tell us is who should benefit from penalty reductions and by how much. But the 'who?' and 'how much?' questions are, precisely, those crucial to sentencing policy. To answer those questions of distribution of sentences, some rationale is needed – either proportionality or something else.

Consider Professor Tonry's previously mentioned example of the young offender from a deprived background who has learned to be a mechanic and seems to be making serious efforts to escape the cycle of poverty and crime. Why not, Tonry asks, reduce this individual's punishment in the name of parsimony? Parsimony, however, does not tell us why this individual should be selected for penalty reductions rather than some other. Why not choose, instead, the offender who has made no effort to learn a trade or otherwise improve his lot? Or the offender who offends despite a privileged background? There must be some guiding reason for the selection. One possibility might be risk concerns: our mechanic might be less likely to return to crime. This, however, raises the familiar problems of incapacitation as a basis for sentence (von Hirsch, 1985, ch. 11). Another possibility might be that of personal merit: we have more sympathy for the mechanic because of his efforts to improve himself despite the obstacles of his background. In this case, we need some account of when personal merit is an appropriate criterion. Is it appropriate, for example, to review the entire course of the offender's life for indications of virtue or vice? If not, why should our mechanic be entitled to the penalty reduction, but not (say) the wealthy offender who has given substantial sums to charity? If the fairness and appropriateness of the selection criterion is at issue, then there is no avoiding addressing the merits of the proportionality criterion: when, if ever, is it proper to deviate from proportionality to favor certain offenders? Just invoking parsimony will not help.

PROSPECTS FOR SUCCESS OF THE REFORM

The American experience

The prospects for success of sentencing reforms depend on the setting in which they are undertaken. The American experience makes that clear. During the 1970s and early 1980s the US was active in reform efforts. A number of states – most notably Minnesota – adopted guidelines designed to limit increases in prison populations and achieve greater proportionality of sentence. In Minnesota the reform achieved considerable success during its first years (von Hirsch, Knapp, and Tonry, 1987, ch. 8). The experience in America of the last half-decade, however, has been less happy. Concerns about fairness and predictability of sentence have given way to a policy of escalated sanctions. Symptomatic of that policy is the 'war against drugs', with its campaign for sharply increased penalties for drug offenses at both state and federal levels. Another symptom has been the draconian character of the federal sentencing guidelines, adopted in 1987 and applicable to infringements of federal criminal statutes. Those guidelines, which lack any coherent sentencing rationale, were designed to double the use of imprisonment in federal cases and halve the use of probation (von Hirsch, 1989). Even more sophisticated state guideline systems, such as Minnesota's, have not been exempt from such pressures.

Why this change? The answer lies in a change in the political environment. The 1980s saw an extraordinary shift to the right in American politics, and that conservatism has made higher criminal penalties one of its primary objectives. There has been much writing in the United Kingdom about 'moral panics', but one has not seen a real moral panic until one has witnessed the American response to the supposed crack-cocaine epidemic. The harsh federal sentencing guidelines were preceded by Congressional adoption of extraordinarily severe mandatory minimum sentences for drug crimes, and the federal sentencing commission took its cues on penalty levels from those provisions. The substantial recent increases in drug penalties in Minnesota's guidelines were the result of legislative pressures for a tougher stance against drugs.

American sentencing reformers have preferred numerical guidelines as the vehicle of reform. Numerical guidelines have the advantage of greater clarity and comprehensiveness. Because penalties for various crimes are fixed simultaneously, consistency is easier to achieve. And such guidelines are more readily enforceable: the judge must apply the guideline penalty or penalty-range in the grid, unless he or she can cite special circumstances of aggravation or mitigation. Numerical guidelines are, however, particularly vulnerable to political pressures. American reformers have favored having a rule-making commission, rather than the legislature itself, set the presumptive sentences, because a commission is comparatively more sheltered from law-and-order politics. But 'comparatively' must be emphasized: as a rule-making commission obtains its powers from the legislature and its members are appointed by the jurisdiction's chief executive, it cannot long resist demands to raise penalties. And penalties can readily be raised by changing the numbers on the grid.

The British setting

The setting for sentencing reform seems somewhat more propitious (or less unpropitious) in the United Kingdom. Prior to 1993, the political pressures for escalated punishments have been less. The Thatcher government did periodically make fierce statements about crime, but law and order was not one of its priorities (see Cavadino, this volume, ch. 2). No ambitious proposals to raise penalties were put forward; indeed, the White Paper (which appeared at the end of the Thatcher years) explicitly endorsed reducing the use of imprisonment for property offenders. The conservatism (indeed, ferocious conservatism) of Thatcherite policies focused on other areas such as economic policy, union rights, and local government. That the UK has lower rates of violent crime, and somewhat less social and racial polarization, than the US may contribute to this difference.

Since early 1993, the atmosphere has changed – with the current government making increasingly strident pronouncements on law and order. Nevertheless, criminal justice remains less a matter of populist politics in the UK than in America. Legislators and ministers move more gingerly when proposing measures to alter the practice of judges and magistrates. One does not hear political spokesmen urging the appointment of judges with sterner attitudes about crime, nor does one hear senior officials denouncing judges whose judgments they deem too lenient – both, alas, common practice in the States. The mode of guidance that has been chosen in the 1991 Act is also less vulnerable to politically-inspired changes in penalty levels, for the Act deals in principles, not specific quanta of sentence.

Certain traditions in English thinking about sentencing may also make the shift to proportionalism easier. One is the tradition of the sentencing tariff: that sentences should ordinarily be graded, in a manner that in some degree reflects their seriousness. The rationale for the tariff was the doubtful one of deterrence, and the criteria for deciding where various offenses should fit in the tariff were underdeveloped. But given the basic idea of a scale of graded penalties, it is not so difficult to alter its guiding rationale to one of proportionality, and to make more explicit the norms for ranking crimes.

Also helpful has been the more limited scope of the dangerousness debate. The famous Floud report (Floud and Young, 1981) urged extended sentences for specially dangerous offenders, but did not propose that risk considerations should determine sentencing policy generally. This made it easier, in the 1991 Act, to combine a general rule of proportionate sentences with an exception dealing with specially dangerous offenders.

Prospects of success of the 1991 reforms

If the setting for the recent reforms is more propitious than in the US, what are the prospects? Here, any optimism must be much qualified. One difficulty is that judges and magistrates – particularly the former – are not accustomed to receiving guidance in their sentencing decisions, and may resist the reforms to a greater or lesser degree. Overcoming that resistance may require further persuasive efforts, as well as the active co-operation of the Court of Appeal. This difficulty is compounded by the loose drafting of the 1991 Act. The Act does not spell out its criteria of proportionality much, and crucial provisions – such as those governing the role of prior criminal record – read rather obscurely (see, more fully, Wasik and von Hirsch, 1994). Paul Cooper (1992), in a thoughtful essay on the probable impact of the Act, warns of those difficulties, as does Andrew Ashworth (1992).

Nevertheless, at least some progress may be anticipated. Cooper is right, I think, in suggesting that the Act will make it more difficult to incarcerate repetitive property offenders. More fundamentally, the Act may induce sentencers to begin to think of 'proportionality' as a basic concept that they need to apply when deciding sentences, much as judges now know that they need to understand the basic principles of criminal intent when instructing a jury before verdict. If judges and magistrates become used to thinking in this fashion, then progress towards a somewhat fairer sentencing system will have been made. But let me emphasize the 'somewhat': hopes for dramatic changes, either in reduced punishment levels or in increased predictability in sentencing decisions, are likely to be disappointed.

References

Ashworth, A. (1992), *Sentencing and Criminal Justice*, Weidenfeld and Nicolson, London.

Bottoms, A. E., and Brownsword, R. (1983), 'Dangerousness and rights', in J. W. Hinton, (ed.), *Dangerousness: Problems of Assessment and Prediction*, George Allen & Unwin, London, pp. 9–22.

Cavadino, M. (1994), 'The UK penal crisis: where next?', this volume, ch. 2.

Clear, T., and Hardyman, P. (1990), 'The new intensive supervision movement', *Crime and Delinquency*, XXXVI, pp. 42–60.

Cooper, P. (1992), 'Commensurability after the Criminal Justice Act', paper prepared for Fulbright International Colloquium 1992, Penal Theory and Penal Practice, University of Stirling, September 1992.

Floud, J., and Young, W. (1981), *Dangerousness and Criminal Justice*, Heinemann, London.

Gardner, M. (1976), 'The renaissance of retribution: an examination of "Doing Justice" ', *Wisconsin Law Review*, pp. 781–815.

Greenwood, P. W. (1982), *Selective Incapacitation*, RAND Corporation, Santa Monica, California.

Home Office (1990), *Crime, Justice and Protecting the Public*, CM 965, HMSO, London.

National Academy of Sciences, Panel on Research on Criminal Careers (1986), *Report*, in Blumstein, A. *et al.*, *Criminal Careers and 'Career Criminals'*, National Academy Press, Washington, DC, I, pp. 1–209.

Robinson, P. (1987), 'Hybrid principles for the distribution of criminal sanctions', *Northwestern Law Review*, LXXXII, pp. 19–42.

Tonry, M. (1994), 'Proportionality, parsimony, and interchangeability of punishments', this volume, ch. 3.

von Hirsch, A. (1985), *Past or Future Crimes: Deservedness and Dangerousness in the Sentencing of Criminals*, Rutgers University Press, New Brunswick, NJ.

—— (1988), 'Selective incapacitation reexamined: the National Academy of Sciences' Report on Criminal Careers and "Career Criminals" ', *Criminal Justice Ethics*, VII, pp. 19–35.

—— (1989), 'Federal sentencing guidelines: do they provide principled guidance?', *American Criminal Law Review*, XXVII, pp. 367–90.

—— (1991), 'Criminal record rides again', *Criminal Justice Ethics*, X, pp. 2, 55–7.

—— (1993), *Censure and Sanctions*, Oxford University Press, Oxford.

von Hirsch, A., and Ashworth, A. (eds.) (1993), *Principled Sentencing*, Edinburgh University Press, Edinburgh.

von Hirsch, A., and Jareborg, N. (1991), 'Gauging criminal harm: a living-standard analysis', *Oxford Journal of Legal Studies*, XI, pp. 1–38.

von Hirsch, A., Knapp, K., and Tonry, M. (1987), *The Sentencing Commission and Its Guidelines*, Northeastern University Press, Boston.

Ward, T. (1992), 'Dangerousness, insanity, and indeterminate detention', paper prepared for Fulbright International Colloquium 1992, Penal Theory and Penal Practice, University of Stirling, September 1992.

Wasik, M. (1987), 'Guidance, guidelines, and criminal record', in M. Wasik and K. Pease (eds.), *Sentencing Reform: Guidance or Guidelines?*, Manchester University Press, Manchester, pp. 104–25.

Wasik, M., and von Hirsch, A. (1988), 'Non-custodial penalties and the principles of desert', *Criminal Law Review*, pp. 555–72.

—— (1994), 'Section 29 revised: previous convictions in sentencing', *Criminal Law Review*, forthcoming.

Wilson, J. Q. (1983), *Thinking About Crime*, rev. edn., Basic Books, New York.

2

The UK penal crisis: where next?

MICHAEL CAVADINO

THE CRISIS CONTINUES

If we accept that it is appropriate to call the recent state of the penal system in the United Kingdom[1] one of 'penal crisis'[2], then there can be little dispute that the crisis is continuing. The crisis has been described and analysed in a variety of ways (Cavadino and Dignan, 1992, ch. 1; Evans, 1980; Bottoms, 1980; Fitzgerald and Sim, 1982), but its characteristics and symptoms include the following: high and rising prison populations; overcrowding and poor conditions within prisons; unrest among prison staff and inmates, culminating in industrial disputes on the one hand and riots and disturbances on the other. To simplify somewhat, it can be said that there are two interacting aspects to the crisis: on the one hand there is a material '*crisis of penological resources*', and on the other an ideological '*crisis of legitimacy*' which affects not only prisons but the entire penal enterprise. In all these respects little or no improvement was in evidence by the summer of 1992.

As regards the material crisis of resources and the key issue of the size of the prison population, some recent green shoots of hope are withering rapidly. The daily average population of the prisons in England and Wales peaked in 1988 at 49,949 and declined significantly in the next two calendar years to a figure of 45,636 in 1990, reflecting both a fall in the remand population and a decrease in the number of offenders sentenced to custody. This decline appeared to fuel optimism within the Home Office that the long-running 'prison numbers crisis' was close to being solved. For at the same time as the prison population was declining, prison capacity was rising as the prison building programme initiated by the Conservative government in the early 1980s was approaching completion, with the result that the system as a whole started to become less overcrowded. As a result it was forecast that the certified normal accommodation (CNA) of prisons in England and Wales would exceed the number of inmates by 1992. This prediction led Lord Justice Woolf in his report on the English prison system and the riots of 1990 to suggest that after 1992 prison overcrowding should be 'a thing of the past' (Woolf and Tumim, 1991, para. 1.189).

However – as had indeed been predicted by a statistical bulletin issued by the Home Office itself in May 1991 (Home Office, 1991a, para. 11) – it was not long before this downturn began to show signs of being reversed, just as previous such trends had in the past. The prison population rose steadily from March 1991 onwards and although the daily average population for the calendar year of 1991 was (at 45,897) only 261 higher than the 1990 figure, by 31 December the figure was 2,000 greater than it had been 12 months earlier (Home Office, 1992a). Perhaps most disturbingly, this figure appeared to reflect reversals in some of the most encouraging trends which had emerged in the previous years. Both magistrates' and Crown Courts seemed to be imposing a greater number and a higher proportion of custodial sentences; moreover, this development also affected young offenders, who had represented something of a success story in 1989 and 1990. It looked as if the government-approved thrust to divert offenders (especially young offenders) from custody had run out of steam somewhat in 1991, as sentencing practice slipped back into a more punitive pattern. The custodial remand population also increased, reflecting an increase in cases awaiting trial in the Crown Court. This suggests that the National Mode of Trial Guidelines for magistrates' courts,[3] issued in October 1990, have not had the effect of reducing the number of committals for Crown Court trial and nor are hopes of increasing the granting of bail as yet being fulfilled. In the long term the prison population picture looks even bleaker. The Home Office's official statistical projections show the total rising by 25 per cent by the year 2000, to a figure of 57,500 (Home Office, 1992b).

If these projections turn out to be accurate, the effect will be that prison overcrowding, far from being a thing of the past, will persist well into the 21st century. The certified normal accommodation of the entire prison system, which is only expected to reach about 54,000 when the prison building programme is completed in the mid-1990s, will be exceeded by the total number of prisoners from 1996 onwards. In the meantime there could technically be some excess capacity over population, but this by no means ensures that there will be no overcrowding during this period, because a large margin of excess capacity is needed to eliminate overcrowding to compensate for available prison places being in the wrong type of establishment or in the wrong part of the country for the inmates. (This problem is exacerbated by the policy of shielding training and dispersal prisons from overcrowding, which ensures that local prisons and remand centres routinely suffer from gross overcrowding even when overall capacity and population are in near-equilibrium.) A further indication of the persistence of the numbers problem is the number of remand prisoners being kept in police cells at a time when pressure on the system as a whole was supposed to be reduced. The number rose from a daily average of 119 in 1986 to 1,088 in 1991 (peaking at over 1,800), and on 23 June 1992 was 1,357 – this in the year which, Woolf was assured, would see the end of prison overcrowding[4].

Nor has the penal system's crisis of legitimacy abated. James Dignan and myself have argued elsewhere (Cavadino and Dignan, 1992, ch. 1) that this is a threefold crisis. The system lacks legitimacy with the general public and the 'chattering classes' of politics and the media, giving rise to political problems for the system, those who run it and the government whose responsibility it is; it lacks legitimacy for those who work in it, giving rise to chronic industrial relations problems and a general malaise within the probation service; and it lacks legitimacy with penal subjects, whose sense of injustice is, as the Woolf report recognised, the key factor in inducing them to engage in riots and disorder. Regular blows at the system's legitimacy with the general public continue to be struck, including a highly-publicised spate of suicides at Feltham Young Offenders' Institution in 1991–2 and a succession of reports by various bodies,[5] including Her Majesty's Chief Inspector of Prisons, Judge Tumim,[6] further exposing the squalor of conditions inside establishments such as Dartmoor and Risley. Malaise among penal staff continues, with officers at Brixton and the governor of Feltham threatening recently to refuse to admit new inmates. And the sense of injustice among prisoners which Woolf identified seems also to remain, leading to several incidents of prison disorder in 1991 and 1992.

On the face of it, then, the penal crisis seems likely to persist and indeed deepen. The question is whether government criminal justice strategy can alter this gloomy scenario over the coming years. Some elements of the government's strategy are already in place, while some are perhaps only beginning to develop and some may be yet to be conceived. I now proceed to consider these strategies and assess their chances of success.

THE CRIMINAL JUSTICE ACT 1991

On the legislative front, the main measure to deal with the penal crisis in England and Wales is the Criminal Justice Act 1991, whose provisions (implemented in October 1992) have been dubbed the 'just deserts' package of reforms by ministers. However, this is something of a misnomer. It is true that one thrust of the reforms is that offenders should receive punishment of an amount proportionate to the seriousness of their current offences, but another contrasting theme is that violent and sexual offenders should receive longer custodial sentences than hitherto. The reforms could equally well be termed 'punitive bifurcation': 'bifurcation' because they continue the policy trend to treat more minor offenders in the community rather than in custody while simultaneously treating more serious offenders more harshly, and 'punitive' because even the treatment of offenders in the community is to take on a more punitive and controlling aspect, with tougher penalties and combinations of penalties being made available as sentencing options.

Although the Act contains a wide variety of important reforms, for example to the law on fines and parole, its primary focus is on sentencing. Section 1 provides statutory criteria which the courts must consider are satisfied before they pass custodial sentences, the theory being that these, combined with the availability of tougher community sentences, will encourage sentencers to divert more offenders from custody. The potential Achilles' heel of this strategy is that the criteria remain vague and their interpretation is left to the same judicial discretion which bears the major responsibility for creating the prison numbers crisis in the first place (Cavadino and Dignan, 1992, ch. 4). Thus, for example, a court may pass a custodial sentence if of the opinion that the current offence is too 'serious' to justify a non-custodial penalty. The word 'serious' is left undefined, with no guidance as to its interpretation. While it will rule out custody for obviously trivial property offences it may have only a very limited effect on the overall number of offenders who are diverted from custody, unless there is a radical shift in courts' attitudes to custodial sentencing of a kind that seems unlikely given the latest trends in sentencing.

These criteria do nothing in themselves to reduce the *lengths* of custodial sentences, which are at least as important a factor in generating prison numbers as is the 'custody-or-not' decision. Here section 2 of the Act states that (except for violent and sexual offenders from whom the public is deemed to need protection) sentences should be 'commensurate with the seriousness of the offence'. Again it is left to sentencers to decide what is 'commensurate'. The avowed intention is that sentencers should scale down their sentencing tariff in response to changes to the parole system, which will ensure that time served in custody for many prisoners bears a closer relationship to that passed by the courts, but there can again be no guarantee of this.

The effects of other facets of the Act are equally uncertain. The juvenile court (renamed the 'youth court') is to deal with seventeen-year-olds as well as the ten-sixteen age group, but it remains to be seen whether this has the effect of extending the juvenile court's more lenient sentencing tradition to seventeen-year-olds or, conversely, to infect the sentencing of sixteen-year-olds with a greater punitiveness. Again, the tougher community sentences mean that offenders subject to them will be at greater risk of ending up in custody as a result of breaching the tighter requirements of these orders. Something similar is also true of parolees, who will have longer periods when they are at risk of being returned to prison and subjected to a longer stretch in custody if they reoffend while on parole.

The Home Office's latest prediction (1992b, para. 15) is that the Criminal Justice Act and associated changes will reduce the sentenced prison population by 3,500 by 1995. This guesstimate, which could well prove to be over-optimistic, was incorporated into the discouraging predictions of overall prison numbers mentioned earlier. Clearly, therefore, the Criminal Justice Act is unlikely to provide the solution to the prison numbers crisis.

Nor does the Act seem likely to solve the crisis of legitimacy, despite its attempt to provide a more coherent legitimating ideology for sentencing in the form of 'just deserts'. Although the notion that punishments should be proportionate to the seriousness of offences is an attractive and popular one, the coherence of the Act is vitiated by the fact that this principle is combined with the inconsistent one of bifurcation. Bifurcation is particularly likely to exacerbate the sense of injustice of those on the wrong end of it, namely those prisoners who find themselves serving longer sentences as a result. Nor can other prisoners realistically be expected to start viewing their treatment as less unjust because of the abstract assurance that sentencing is now on the basis of just deserts. Perhaps to the contrary, for the introduction of new rules regarding sentencing and parole will throw up many anomalies visible to prisoners themselves, whereby those sentenced after October 1992 will find themselves either advantageously or disadvantageously placed compared with those sentenced earlier. Resentful feelings caused by this kind of relative injustice have proved potent factors in the genesis of prison disorders in the past. And if the Act will do little to increase the penal system's legitimacy with penal subjects it may achieve even less *vis-à-vis* penal staff. Probation officers in particular, although seeking to take advantage of some of the opportunities provided by the Act, are generally unhappy about their enforced involvement with tougher and more punitive community penalties. It could be, therefore, that the Act will overall serve to compound rather than alleviate the crisis of legitimacy.

THE RESPONSE TO WOOLF

Although it did not use the word 'legitimacy', the Woolf report (Woolf and Tumim, 1991) effectively acknowledged the existence of a crisis of legitimacy (alias a widespread 'sense of injustice') among prisoners and put forward a wide-ranging set of recommendations aimed at alleviating it. These included proposals to ameliorate physical conditions and regimes within prisons, and placed a particular emphasis on the need to improve grievance and disciplinary conditions in the prison system. The government responded to Woolf by announcing on the day of the report's publication in February 1991 a set of immediate reforms, which included an accelerated programme to provide integral sanitation for all cells by the end of 1994. This package was followed in September by a White Paper on prisons, *Custody, Care and Justice* (Home Office, 1991b), which accepted the great majority of Woolf's recommendations. However, it left largely uncertain the time-scale over which they would be implemented, while at the same time the Home Secretary was saying publicly that no extra resources would be made available for implementation, which could take up to twenty-five years. A year after Woolf reported, a survey by the Prison Reform Trust (1992) found a picture of patchy progress: for example, while two-thirds of prisons had increased provision for visits, there had been little improvement concerning the timing and quality of meals, and local prisons tended to trail badly when it came to the improvement of physical conditions and facilities. The general picture was that prison governors were committed to reform but had so far only been able to introduce resource-neutral reforms. Several emphasised to the Prison Reform Trust that further improvements would require increased resources.

For its part, the government has accepted (in *Custody, Care and Justice*) Woolf's recommendation that there should be a Code of Standards for prison conditions and regimes, and an official steering group is working towards the publication of a code in December 1993. Issues yet to be resolved concerning this code include how minimal the minimum standards will turn out to be, whether they will be enforceable, and (again) what input of resources can be expected to enable establishments to meet the standards. On enforceability, it seems unlikely that the government will follow Woolf's proposal that the standards should eventually become legally enforceable via judicial review procedure; a sufficient input of resources 'to ensure prisons are decent places for all who live and work in them and all who visit them', to quote the steering group (Dunbar, 1992, para. 2), seems equally unlikely in the short or medium term. The danger is that the code will serve merely to raise hopes only to disappoint them, exacerbating rather than mitigating the crisis of legitimacy.

Clearly there are some legitimising reforms that cannot be successfully undertaken without alleviating the crisis of resources, either by supplying greater resources to the penal system or by reducing demands placed on it by reducing prison numbers. Other reforms, as prison governors have found, have fewer resource implications. In this respect, Woolf's key proposal for the creation of an independent Complaints Adjudicator is of particular interest. This recommendation – again accepted by the government in *Custody, Care and Justice* – was for a single independent body to act as the final avenue of appeal in the prison disciplinary system, and also to 'recommend, advise and conciliate' at the final stage of the prison grievance procedure (Woolf and Tumim, 1991, para. 14.349). An Independent Complaints Adjudicator for Prisons (ICAP) is due to be appointed in 1993. In theory, the existence of the ICAP could have a substantial impact on the legitimacy of the prison system for its inmates, both by guaranteeing them a fair hearing for their complaints or appeals against disciplinary findings and by deterring staff misbehaviour towards prisoners. In practice, however, there is again a risk that these new arrangements could serve to raise hopes only to dash them. Prisoners will need to have exhausted all internal appeal procedures before reaching the ICAP, who will be heavily dependent on information received from prison staff in making his or her decisions. (Both Woolf and the government rejected the idea of a Prisons Ombudsman to whom prisoners could take their complaints at any stage (Woolf and Tumim, 1991, para. 14.352).) Thus the ICAP will occupy a role analogous to that of the Police Complaints Authority, which although independent still relies on police officers to undertake investigations against other police officers and suffers as a result from severely reduced credibility. The legitimacy of the prison could turn out to be as little enhanced by the ICAP as that of the police is by the PCA.

THE END OF LAW AND ORDER?

One potent factor which has made a major contribution to the current penal crisis is 'law and order ideology' (Cavadino and Dignan, 1992, ch. 1; Hall, 1980; Reiner and Cross, 1991). This punitive ideology – espoused and promoted by the Conservative Party under Margaret Thatcher, most notably in her first victorious general election campaign of 1979 – helped to bring about the prison building programme of the 1980s, contributed to an increase in the severity of sentencing in the mid-80s and fostered the punitive aspects of bifurcation policy. However – and despite an increase of 87 per cent in public spending on 'law and order' in real terms between 1979 and 1992 – it failed notably to reduce the amount of officially recorded crime, which continued to rise apart from brief downturns in 1983 and 1988.

Since the middle of the decade the volume of law and order rhetoric emanating from government has been toned down, with ministers taking a more eclectically pragmatic line. 'Law and order' has been combined with other themes and approaches to dealing with crime and punishment such as voluntarisation, privatisation and a new emphasis on the role of the 'community' in schemes such as neighbourhood watch (Reiner and Cross, 1991). Particularly prominent in this new pragmatic mix has been the theme of *managerialism* (Bottoms and Stevenson, forthcoming). This approach, favoured within the Home Office, is based on the notion that modern managerial techniques can be successfully applied to the problems of crime and punishment, as exemplified by the achievements of the 'systems management' school in juvenile justice during the 1980s. Managerialism encompasses this type of systems management, which employs interagency co-operation and monitoring to pursue the diversion of offenders from court and custody, as well as other trends such as situational crime prevention.

One interesting aspect of this new managerialism is a gradual swing back of the pendulum in terms of philosophies of punishment. Following the 'collapse of the rehabilitative ideal' (Bottoms, 1980) in the 1970s – encapsulated in the notion that 'nothing works' to reform offenders – dominant schools of thought such as the 'Justice Model' and 'law and order ideology' held that punishment had to be justified in retributive terms. The managerialist approach rejects blanket rehabilitative pessimism, holding instead that 'something works'. Systematic experimentation, research and monitoring, it is now believed, can identify methods of penal training which will 'work' to reform offenders and thereby make criminal justice expenditure more cost-effective (Pitts, 1992).

For a while during the run-up to the 1992 general election it seemed as if 1979-style law and order might re-emerge onto the political agenda as Home Secretary Kenneth Baker declared war on motor offenders and 'bail bandits' (offenders who commit further crimes while on bail) and launched posters claiming that 'Labour's Soft On Crime'. However, in the event law and order played no great part in the election campaign proper, the Conservatives presumably calculating that the rise in crime and the legitimacy crisis in the criminal justice system made them too vulnerable in this area.

The future direction of penal policy under Mrs Thatcher's successor as Prime Minister, John Major, is by no means clear. But so far 'Majorism' has tended to continue Thatcherite policies of financial stringency and privatisation while assuming a gentler and less authoritarian image which would not gel easily with a returned to strident law and order rhetoric. Since the general election returning the Conservatives to power in April 1992, the picture emerging from Whitehall in the present recessionary economic climate is of Treasury pressure to ensure that it gets value for money in spending on criminal justice,[7] a factor which can be expected to encourage further the trend away from punitive rhetoric and towards the managerial approach. But this is unlikely on its own to solve the crises of resources and legitimacy – indeed, financial restrictions may well exacerbate the former, which may then in turn worsen the latter.

Although the influence of law and order ideology seems to have passed its peak, certainly its peak of popularity with government, it has by no means disappeared. Indeed, the Criminal Justice Act of 1991 could paradoxically serve to give it a new lease of life. For on the one hand courts are to be given new and tougher community sentences and encouraged to employ them primarily for the purpose of inflicting what is expressly 'punishment' on offenders, while on the other hand the new restrictions on sentencing could provoke a backlash from the judiciary against what may be portrayed as the unwarranted softness of the new legislation.[8]

Another Conservative ideology still seems to be on the rise within penal politics: that of privatisation. Britain's first privately-run prison, Wolds Remand Prison, opened in April 1992,[9] with a second (Blakenhurst) due to open in 1993, and ministers have floated the idea that as many as half of Britain's prisons could subsequently be privatised. The government presumably hopes that the privatisation strategy will assist the crises of legitimacy and resources, as well as easing industrial relations problems by undermining the bargaining power of the Prison Officers' Association (Wolds is staffed by non-POA labour), but in all these respects the strategy could prove counterproductive. The inherently controversial nature of privatisation means that private status is likely to be at least as delegitimising as legitimising to a prison. Much is likely to depend on the quality of the regimes which are in fact offered by privatised institutions. Initially it may well be that the first private prisons may score well overall in this regard, as was the case in the United States, where commercial concerns first opened showpiece institutions as 'loss leaders', but – as critics of the US experience claim – this could change over time as the private companies seek to maximise profits by cutting costs (Porter, 1990). On the overall resource front, the gamble of privatisation is that, despite the need to generate profits for shareholders, competition will produce much greater efficiency than in the public sector, leading to an alleviation of the crisis of resources, but in the medium and long term this is very much a gamble. Finally, even if the spectre of privatisation does cow the POA – and does not contribute to provoking a more militant backlash from it – there could well be deleterious effects on the morale, attitude and recruitment of prison staff in the remaining state-run prisons, whose crises could deepen as a result.

CONCLUSION

If the trajectory of current policies and trends continues over the next five to ten years, the likely end result will be a further worsening of the penal crisis. The best that can be hoped for is that the Criminal Justice Act, the implementation of Woolf, managerialism and privatisation will all prove to be modest successes. But even if this is the case, there is every reason to believe that prison numbers will still continue to rise and outstrip the extra accommodation provided by the prison building programme, and that the crisis of legitimacy and its attendant problems will also persist. Although the government seems to be locked on course for the time being, until it becomes clear how well or badly present policies will work, the time could well arrive before long when some major event – such as a return to peak levels of overcrowding, a fresh round of serious rioting or a national industrial dispute – forces it to accept that the crisis is not being solved and that a further change of direction is necessary.

Regarding the crisis of resources, the options will then essentially be twofold: to persuade the Treasury to release substantial extra sums for a new prison building programme and to improve physical conditions within existing prisons, or to take effective action to reduce prison numbers. The former seems implausible at a time when 'law and order' spending is under particular threat from a Treasury keen to reduce expenditure and demand verifiable 'value for money' for any extra funds provided.[10] Substantial further spending for the purpose of locking up even more people to little obvious good effect within a prison system which already holds a higher proportion of the population than does any other in Western Europe should not logically endear itself to the cost-conscious. But the alternative, limiting the demand for rather than the supply of penal resources, is of course also easier said than done.

The problem is that the Criminal Justice Act 1991 represents the very end-point of a strategy that has been developing and taking shape ever since the 1970s, arguably since the Criminal Justice Act of 1967 introduced the suspended sentence, or even since the Probation of Offenders Act 1907. This is the policy of trying to limit the prison population by *encouraging* (but in general not *requiring*) sentencers to employ non-custodial rather than custodial sentences and to keep most of the custodial sentences they do pass as short as possible. This has been pursued by creating a proliferation of 'alternatives to custody', and by trying to make these as attractive to sentencers as possible whether by stressing their rehabilitative potential, their justice or (in the case of 'punitive bifurcation') their toughness and the fact that they are 'not a soft option'. Guidance on sentence lengths has been left largely to the Court of Appeal and the 'guideline judgements' it has increasingly issued for various types of offence.

Typically, the introduction of an important new 'alternative to custody' sentence such as community service has had some effect in diverting offenders from custody but has at the same time diverted a roughly equal number of offenders from other non-custodial penalties (e.g. Pease *et al.*, 1977). As the number of such penalties increases (and Britain already has appreciably more than most countries), one would expect diminishing returns to set in as the non-custodial sector reaches saturation point. The Criminal Justice Act 1991 seeks to add further impetus to the diversionary effects of its new penalties by prescribing that an (undefined) threshold of 'seriousness' must be surpassed by the current offence before custody is selected. Even so, and as we have seen, its effects are expected to be limited and it seems unlikely that any substantial further steps down this particular diversionary road are possible. It is perhaps not a hopeful sign for this strategy that one of the new penalties provided for in the Criminal Justice Act was the surreally Orwellian one of curfews enforced by electronic tagging, implementation of which has been delayed for the time being following an at times farcically discouraging pilot experiment with bailees (Mair and Nee, 1990).

If any real progress is to be made on prison numbers (further to any that may be effected by the 1991 Act) it will necessitate a shift away from mere persuasion of the judiciary towards legislation that represents a substantial intrusion on the discretion they have hitherto enjoyed in making decisions about not only sentencing, but also remands in custody and trial venues. It is these decisions that are the 'crux of the penal crisis' (Cavadino and Dignan, 1992, ch. 4) since it is they which create prison numbers. To date governments have fought shy of attacking the citadel of 'judicial independence' – and have at times come off worst merely skirting its environs – yet if the Criminal Justice Act fails, or succeeds insufficiently well, there will be little else to try short of such an assault. One theory has it that only a Conservative government could 'take on the judges' – on the 'only Nixon could go to China' principle – but one suspects that even a determined Home Secretary would think twice about engaging in such a struggle, especially as the government would find itself ranged against the powerful 'law and order' lobby within the ranks of its own party. For its part, the judiciary would be sure to fight its corner keenly. In 1992 a new Lord Chief Justice was appointed, Lord Taylor, who may be much less inflexible than his predecessor but who seems equally convinced of the inviolability of 'judicial independence'. This being so, the government looks to be heading towards a situation which, if not insoluble, admits of no easy or painless solution.

It will probably be even harder to solve the crisis of legitimacy. Legitimacy is a fragile flower which is easy to destroy but takes time and careful nurturing – and resources – if it is to grow. It will also require a skilful balancing act, not only (as Woolf said) between security, control and justice, but also between the different audiences for whom the penal system's legitimacy is suspect. It may be difficult, for example, to assuage the sense of injustice felt by prisoners without running the risk of exacerbating fears among the general public that the penal system is 'too soft', or encouraging prison staff to believe that their superiors care more for inmates than for themselves.

The best, though not the easiest, strategy for building lasting legitimacy must be to attempt to ensure that the system is as genuinely just as possible. Indeed, this was the conclusion Lord Justice Woolf expressed in declaring: 'If there is an absence of justice, prisoners will be aggrieved . . . If a proper level of justice is provided in prisons, then it is less likely that prisoners will behave in this way [i.e. riot]' (Woolf and Tumim, 1991, para. 1.151). In the long term, the penal system needs to be transformed from one which routinely infringes human rights to one which, as consistently as is possible in a human institution, respects and upholds them. The experiences of other countries such as the former West Germany and the Netherlands suggest that paying serious attention to upholding and enforcing the human rights of prisoners does indeed have a significant effect in reducing their sense of injustice and contributing to order within the prison system (Cavadino and Dignan, 1992, p. 258).

The ramifications of such a human rights approach are manifold. One concerns the nature of relationships between penal staff and penal subjects, and indeed the entire prison officer occupational culture. To his credit, the Director General of the English Prison Service, Mr Joe Pilling, has taken to saying (*The Guardian*, 12 June 1992) that prison staff must show sincere respect for prisoners' basic human dignity and sense of worth. However, this is less likely to happen if prison officers feel that the government shows them little respect in their handling of industrial relations within the prison system and in privatising parts of it. Equally essential if human rights are to be taken seriously is the effective enforcement of basic standards of decency in the physical conditions of prisoners. And perhaps most fundamentally, it needs to be recognised that every single day that an individual is imprisoned unnecessarily represents a grave infringement of human rights.

At this point the twin crises of legitimacy and resources converge. Staffing problems, physical conditions and the 'numbers crisis' do not merely represent the difficulties of finding, allocating and stretching scarce resources – they are serious moral issues. It is morally as well as practically imperative for government both to provide the resources which will improve conditions for penal subjects and increasingly to deny those resources (notably places within prison) which worsen them. Such a denial would necessitate the crucial political battle with the judiciary which governments have so far shirked. There is, alas, as yet no hint that this will change in the foreseeable future. As long as this remains the case, the penal crisis looks set to continue and to deteriorate further.

Notes

1 This paper is primarily concerned with the penal system of England and Wales, with which I am most familiar. Scotland suffers from similar problems, while many of the Northern Ireland penal system's problems are largely *sui generis*.

2 Doubts about the appropriateness of using the word 'crisis' are considered but ultimately dismissed in Cavadino and Dignan (1992, ch. 1).

3 [1990] 3 All E.R. 979 (issued as a Practice Direction).

4 The number of prisoners presently in police cells has been partially attributed by some to the decision by an earlier Home Secretary, Kenneth Baker, (responding to the Woolf report in February, 1991) to accelerate the provision of integral sanitation for all cells by 1994. This decision necessitated the temporary or permanent decommissioning of many cells, increasing the pressure on the system.

5 These reports included one by the torture committee of the Council of Europe in December 1991, which described conditions in some prisons as 'inhuman and degrading treatment', and another by the US-based human rights monitoring organisation Helsinki Watch in June 1992, which called them 'abhorrent'.

6 The position of Judge Tumim as an officially licensed critic of prisons is an interesting one, illustrating the interactions between the crises of legitimacy and resources and the political difficulties involved in trying to manage both simultaneously. Carvel (1992) reports that Home Secretaries and senior Home Office civil servants have valued Tumim's work in delegitimising prisons in the hope that it will add political weight to their strategy of diverting offenders from custody and increasing the prisons budget (thereby easing the crisis of resources). But on the other hand Tumim's reports obviously have a negative effect in helping to fuel the crisis of legitimacy.

7 It has been reported that in April 1992 the Treasury sent a stiff memorandum to the Home Office warning that continued expenditure on police and the penal system would be conditional on rigorous scrutiny of its cost-effectiveness (*The Guardian*, 8 May 1992). Subsequently the Home Office has initiated what is said to be a radical review of policing in which little is to be held sacred. These developments could indicate the writing on the wall for expenditure on the penal system.

8 The main text of this essay was written in the summer of 1992. Since then, developments have very much tended to confirm the least optimistic versions of my prognostications, with the Major government tilting dramatically towards a punitive 'law and order' programme during 1993.

9 By July 1992 Wolds had already attracted criticism from some sections of the

press on the grounds that its conditions and facilities were luxurious compared with those in state prisons. Although it is of course early days, this does not bode well for privatisation as a strategy for legitimising the penal system with the general public.

10 See note 7 above.

References

Bottoms, A. E. (1980), 'An introduction to "The Coming Crisis" ', in A. E. Bottoms and R. H. Preston (eds.), *The Coming Penal Crisis: A Criminological and Theological Explanation*, Scottish Academic Press, Edinburgh, pp. 1- 24.

Bottoms, A. E., and Stevenson, S. (forthcoming) ' "What went wrong?": Criminal justice policy in England and Wales, 1945–70', in D. Downes (ed.), *Unravelling Criminal Justice*, Macmillan, London, pp. 1–45.

Carvel, J. (1992), 'Crusader with a stir role', *The Guardian*, 8 June.

Cavadino, M., and Dignan, J. (1992), *The Penal System: An Introduction*, Sage, London.

Dunbar, I. (chairman) (1992), *A Code of Standards for the Prison Service: A Discussion Document Produced by the Code of Standards Steering Group*, Prison Service, London.

Evans, P. (1980), *Prison Crisis*, George Allen and Unwin, London.

Fitzgerald, M., and Sim, J. (1982), *British Prisons*, 2nd edn., Basil Blackwell, Oxford.

Hall, S. (1980), *Drifting into a Law and Order Society*, Cobden Trust, London.

Home Office (1991a), *Projections of Long-Term Trends in the Prison Population to 1999*, Home Office Statistical Bulletin 10/91.

Home Office (1991b), *Custody, Care and Justice: The Way Ahead for the Prison Service in England and Wales*, Cm 1647, HMSO, London.

Home Office (1992a), *The Prison Population in 1991*, Home Office Statistical Bulletin 8/92.

Home Office (1992b), *Projections of Long-Term Trends in the Prison Population to 2000*, Home Office Statistical Bulletin 10/92.

Mair, G., and Nee, C. (1990), *Electronic Monitoring: The Trials and their Results*, Home Office Research Study No. 120, HMSO, London.

Pease, K., Billingham, S., and Earnshaw, I. (1977), *Community Service Assessed in 1976*, Home Office Research Study No. 39, HMSO, London.

Pitts, J. (1992), 'The end of an era', *Howard Journal of Criminal Justice*, XXXI, pp. 133–49.

Porter, R. G. (1990), 'The privatisation of prisons in the United States: a policy that Britain should not emulate', *Howard Journal of Criminal Justice*, XXIX, pp. 65–81.

Prison Reform Trust (1992), *Implementing Woolf: The Prison System One Year On*, Prison Reform Trust, London.

Reiner, R., and Cross, M. (1991), 'Introduction: beyond law and order – crime and criminology into the 1990s', in R. Reiner and M. Cross (eds.), *Beyond Law and Order: Criminal Justice Policy and Politics into the 1990s*, Macmillan, Basingstoke, pp. 1–17.

Woolf, H., and Tumim, S. (1991), *Prison Disturbances April 1990*, Cm 1456, HMSO, London.

PART TWO

Proportionality and parsimony

[3]

Proportionality, parsimony, and interchangeability of punishments

MICHAEL TONRY

If intermediate punishments are to be used more widely, procedures and principles governing their use must be developed. Although new intermediate punishments are often conceived in large part for use in lieu of incarceration, experience on three continents shows that many judges prefer to impose such penalties on offenders who would not otherwise be bound for prison. Working out procedures governing intermediate punishments will be hard enough. Working out principles governing imposition of penalties in individual cases may be harder and will require consideration of finer-grained issues than writing on the philosophy of punishment traditionally addresses. Most philosophical writing on punishment deals with broad issues of justification. Insofar as questions of distribution are considered, attention focuses on prison sentences. Because prison sentences can be expressed in seemingly objective units of months or years, and since 'disparity' in prison terms looks prima facie to be a bad thing, recent writing on the distribution of punishment celebrates what Andrew von Hirsch (1992) calls 'the principle of proportionality.'

The theses of this essay are that strong proportionality constraints in the distribution of punishments generally are likely to cause more injustice than they prevent, and that application of strong proportionality constraints to intermediate sanctions will stifle their development, circumscribe their use, and produce avoidable injustices.

There are three fundamental problems with a strong proportionality principle. First, by celebrating equality in suffering for 'like-situated' offenders, it often requires imposition of more severe and intrusive punishments than are required by prevailing social norms and political values. Second, it misleadingly objectifies punishment, by allocating punishments in terms of 'like-situated offenders' and generic penalties. Third, it ignores the problem of 'just deserts in an unjust society'. Most offenders committing common law crimes come from disadvantaged backgrounds, and disproportionately they come from minority groups. Arguments for a highly proportional system of deserved punishments evade the question of whether offenders from deeply deprived backgrounds deserve the same penalties as do other, less deprived, offenders.

A punishment system permitting interchangeability of roughly equivalent penalties is likely, overall, to be more just, less harsh, and more sensitive to problems of social injustice than a punishment system predicated on desert-based proportionality. 'Like-situated offenders' convicted of comparable crimes can justly receive quite different sentences including financial penalties for some, incarceration for others, and community-based sanctions for still others.

This essay attempts to demonstrate and defend the preceding observations. Part I describes policy developments that make consideration of the applied philosophy of intermediate sanctions timely. Part II reviews philosophical writings on punishment and argues that principles of proportionality and parsimony are in stark conflict in general and in many specific cases. Part III examines in some detail Andrew von Hirsch's arguments for a strong principle of proportionality and his proposals for devising a punishment scheme premised on proportionality concerns. Part IV offers a critique of von Hirsch's proposals and Part V sketches a counter-proposal that reconciles concerns for proportionality and parsimony.

WHY INTERMEDIATE PUNISHMENTS?

Policy makers in the United Kingdom and the United States are considering how to incorporate intermediate punishments into comprehensive sentencing policies.[1] Passage in the UK of the Criminal Justice Act 1991 with its increased emphasis on non-custodial penalties has drawn attention to the subject.

In the United States, historically high and growing prison populations, severe pressures on public budgets, and the evolution of the American sentencing reform movement have combined to focus interest on non-custodial (or partly custodial) penalties, and on the integration of non-custodial penalties into comprehensive systems of sentencing guidelines.

American incarceration rates have risen steadily since 1970 but startlingly since 1980, when the number of sentenced offenders held in state prisons (that is, disregarding those in county jails serving sentences of one year or less) stood at 330,000. By 30 June 1992, that number had increased to 856,000. The combined prison and jail incarceration rate in 1990 was 455 per 100,000 population, a level five to ten times that of most developed countries. On 31 December 1991, state prisons were on average operating at 131 per cent of rated capacity and federal prisons at 146 per cent.

Competition for scarce public funds, coupled with a continuing federal commitment to a 'war on drugs' and an ever-toughening crime control strategy, produced great interest in the 1980s in a wide range of intermediate punishments, including house arrest, intensive (sometimes fifteen to twenty-five contacts per month) probation, day-reporting centers, restitution, community service, electronic monitoring, residential drug treatment, day fines, and boot camps.

Many intermediate punishment programs have failed to achieve their objectives. Initiated in hopes of reducing prison crowding (by diverting less serious offenders from prison), reducing recidivism (by enhancing surveillance and some services), and reducing costs (by shifting offenders from more-expensive prisons to less-expensive community programs), in many programs none of these goals are being realised. When tested, these programs generally achieve no worse, but no better, recidivism rates than do prisons when comparable groups of offenders are compared. Many judges order intermediate punishments for offenders who otherwise would receive probation. This increases costs. Moreover, because intermediate sanctions are more intensive and structured than probation, more condition violations and new offenses are observed and acted upon; in many programs 40 to 50 per cent of offenders are ejected for misconduct and sent to prison or jail as punishment. Since many of these offenders would in past years have received probation, they are in effect shifted twice upwards, first to an intermediate sanction and then to prison. This also increases costs. If intermediate punishments are to achieve their goals, it has become clear that standards are needed both for assigning offenders to particular penalties and for setting 'back-up' penalties for violations of program conditions.

A few states have taken tentative steps toward standards for use of intermediate sanctions. Washington allows for modest interchangeability of punishments (e.g., day-for-day substitution of community service days for up to thirty days confinement). Oregon, in addition to setting presumptive sentencing ranges in months, specifies 'punishment units' for each cell in its guidelines grid, to provide a generic coin to permit (an as yet uncompleted task) convertibility of sanctions. Pennsylvania includes the words 'intermediate punishments' in the lower levels of its guidelines, although no other guidance is offered. Many Minnesota counties, and some individual judges across the country, use local guidelines for non-custodial penalties.

There are, however, no well-established models for devising comprehensive systems of structured sentencing discretion that incorporate intermediate punishments. Both mechanics and normative rationales need development. Unusually, policy makers are interested in learning what theorists and philosophers can tell them, and if the advice makes sense, policy makers are likely to pay attention.

Two broad, albeit not fully developed, approaches have been proposed. One, associated with Andrew von Hirsch, Martin Wasik, and Andrew Ashworth, among others, calls for stacking of punishments: prison terms scaled to offense severity for the most serious crimes, restrictive community sanctions for the next-most-serious, large financial penalties for the next-most-serious, and so on, allowing relatively little latitude for imposition of different kinds of punishment on like-situated offenders (Wasik and von Hirsch, 1988; Ashworth, 1992). A second, proposed by Norval Morris and me, allows for much greater substitution and interchangeability of punishments and proportions maximum penal vulnerability to offense severity but allows substantial discretion to impose less severe sentences (Morris and Tonry, 1990).

Increased interest in intermediate sanctions has sharply posed the conflict between principles of proportionality and parsimony. Concern for proportionality calls for like treatment of like-situated offenders. Concern for parsimony, a Hippocratic criminal justice prescription to do least harm, calls for imposing the least severe punishment that meets legitimate social purposes.

The tension between proportionality and parsimony has always existed below the surface in indeterminate sentencing systems, and is likely to survive silently in recent Swedish and English schemes that rely on principles rather than numbers for guidance to judges. Without guidelines, judges can balance concerns for deserved punishments and parsimony in individual cases. Lip service can be paid to concern for horizontal equity, avoiding disparity, and treating like cases alike. Without concrete criteria of proportionate sentencing, individual sentences cannot easily be assessed for their consistency with proportionality principles.

The tension between proportionality and parsimony, however, became apparent when American jurisdictions began to develop sentencing guidelines for prison sentences and it became acute when policy makers began to work on standards for non-custodial penalties. American sentencing guidelines to date mostly set standards for prison sentences calibrated to measures of current and past criminality. Proportionality is a prominent feature. Guidelines derive in part from concern to alleviate sentencing disparities; once offenses are scaled for severity, some proportionality between penalties for different offenses inexorably follows. In effect, sentencing guidelines for prison sentences prefer proportionality over parsimony. If some sentences are harsher than judges believe appropriate, the harshness is said to be justifiable because the punishment is no more or less severe than that suffered by 'like-situated' offenders.

JURISDICTION AND DISTRIBUTION

The tension between proportionality and parsimony and the problem of just deserts in an unjust world are the fundamental problems facing an applied philosophy of punishment concerning intermediate sanctions. This section attempts to frame these issues by considering how Bentham and Kant might address proportionality in distribution and then looking at how modern writers have addressed it.

Proportionality based on justification
Neither classical utilitarian punishment theories in principle nor classical retributive theories in practice provide convincing explanations of why punishment should (or can) observe strict proportionality conditions.

Proportionality is presumably a value for utilitarians only to the extent that its non-observance produces net dissatisfaction. For utilitarians, invoking Bentham, punishment itself is an evil and should be used as sparingly as possible: 'upon the principle of utility, if [punishment] ought at all to be admitted, it ought only to be admitted in as far as it promises to exclude some greater evil' (Bentham, 1948 [1789], p. 281, quoted in Pincoffs, 1966, p. 20).

No doubt utilitarian concerns require some observance of proportionality in punishment. Punishments completely divorced from community notions of fairness – in our time, perhaps, to refuse to punish child abusers, or to sentence two of three equally culpable participants in a crime to five years imprisonment and the third to a $50 fine – would produce unacceptable levels of dissatisfaction and indicate, on utility grounds, that some greater acknowledgement of the importance of violated community values is required; however, that imposes at most only a weak proportionality condition, relating punishment not to notions of desert but to notions of social consequences.

Thoroughgoing retributivists, for whom a retributive justification of punishment entails retribution in distribution, might prefer a system of perfectly proportioned punishments, but in practice such a system is unrealizable. Kant's principle of equality, the Right of Retaliation, 'the mode and measure of punishment which public justice takes as its principle and standard', has practical limits. It may be that 'the principle of equality ... may be rendered by saying that the undeserved evil which anyone commits on another is to be regarded as perpetrated on himself' (Kant, 1887 [1797], pp. 195–7), but it is far from clear what that means. Capital punishment for murder, a $500 penalty for a $500 theft, perhaps (squeamishly) a beating for an assault; these crimes and punishments satisfy the test. But how to punish an attempted murder, a rape, emotional abuse of the elderly, securities fraud, environmental crimes? No doubt systems of scaled punishment can be devised, but only with formidable working out of details. Does Kant's principle of equality require punishment scaled to the offender's culpability, to the offender's benefit, to the victim's harm? What of villainous attempts that serendipitously produce no harm? What of venial crimes that unforeseeably produce great harm? Is the offender's evil-doing to be assessed as the Recording Angel would, taking account of his weaknesses, the pressures to which he was subject, his motives, or primarily as measured by the objective evil his offense embodies?

Proportionality in distribution
The normative conflict concerning proportionality in distribution is between those (e.g., Ashworth, 1992; von Hirsch, 1992) who believe that equality and proportion in distribution are overridingly important and those (Hart, 1968; Honderich, 1989, pp. 237–41; Morris and Tonry, 1990, ch. 4; Walker, 1991, ch. 15) who do not.

There are at least three major categories of writers on punishment who argue for weak proportionality conditions. First, writing in a utilitarian framework, and positing that punishment has principally preventive purposes, H. L. A. Hart writes of 'the somewhat hazy requirement that 'like cases be treated alike'' (1968, p. 24). Hart's argument for this modest recognition of proportionality is, however, not retributively premised but derives from concern for the adverse social effects of divorcing punishment too greatly from common morality: 'for where the legal gradation of crime expressed in the relative severity of penalties diverges sharply from this rough scale, there is a risk of confusing common morality or flouting it and bringing the law into contempt' (p. 25).

Second, proponents of hybrid theories, including Morris (1974) and Honderich (1989), argue that principled systems of punishment must take account of both preventive and retributive considerations. Honderich (1989), for example, argues that retribution, in James Fitzjames Stephens' sense of revenge and satisfaction of grievance, and deterrence, each have roles to play (1989, pp. 233–7). Morris (1974) argues for a system of limiting retributivism in which punishment's primary purposes are preventive but subject to the desert constraint that punishments be 'not undeserved' and, within the range of not undeserved punishments, the parsimonious constraint that no punishment be imposed that is more severe than is necessary to achieve legitimate social purposes.

Third, proponents of a variety of ideal punishment theories reject their policy implications on 'just deserts in an unjust world' grounds but presumably would allow room for distributive echoes of their ideal rationales. R. A. Duff, for example, rejects his own retributive/ expressive ideal theory in favor of deterrent approaches for social injustice reasons. This is my own view as well: in the abstract I have some sympathy for a retributive scheme with strong proportionality conditions; in practice, observing that the vast preponderance of common law offenders are poor, ill-educated, often mentally subnormal, and often from minority groups, I believe that punishment strongly committed to proportionality will exacerbate social injustice and further disadvantage the already disadvantaged.

THE PRINCIPLE OF PROPORTIONALITY

Andrew von Hirsch has, over the last fifteen years (e.g., 1976, 1985, 1992), shown how a punishment system can be devised and justified that has equality and proportionality as central elements. For many people, there is strong intuitive appeal in a punishment system that attaches high value to equality and proportionality. Public opinion surveys have repeatedly demonstrated strong public support for the maxim 'treat like cases alike and different cases differently' (e.g., Doble, Immerwahr, and Richardson, 1991).

Von Hirsch acknowledges both the limits of Kant's 'principle of equality' and human incapacity to specify the single ideally appropriate punishment for any individual offender who has committed a particular offense, but nonetheless offers a comprehensive scheme for assuring proportionality. He distinguishes between ordinal and cardinal magnitudes of punishments (1985, ch. 4). The cardinal magnitude is the unknowable, single deserved penalty. Ordinal magnitude indicates a crime's seriousness relative to other crimes. In von Hirsch's scheme, cardinal magnitudes can be approximated or negotiated for use in setting the 'anchoring points' of a punishment scale, the most and (possibly) the least severe punishments that can appropriately be imposed on offenders. Within these anchoring points, punishments can be scaled in terms of relative severity of offenses. Assuming, for example, that crimes were divided into fifteen severity categories, level 8 offenses should, all else being equal, be punished more severely than level 7 offenses and less severely than level 9 offenses. Thus, the combination of cardinal anchors with ordinal rankings celebrates equality (all level 8 offenses receive similar punishments) and proportionality (less serious offenses receive less severe punishments, more serious offenses receive more severe punishments). Some subsidiary issues remain a bit vague, including specification of anchoring points, the step problem (how many severity categories), and the interval problem (are the severity differences between offense levels the same throughout the scale, or may it be that, for example, level 10 offenses are only 10 per cent more serious than level 9 offenses while level 5 offenses are twice as serious as those at level 4?). In a work in progress, von Hirsch is addressing these and other questions.

Rationale
The overall premise of von Hirsch's argument is that punishment is an exercise in blaming, and proportionality is a necessary implication. Persons committing relatively more severe offenses are relatively more blameworthy and deserve relatively more severe punishments.

Prior record
Von Hirsch's punishment scheme is based principally on *offenses*, with only minor adjustments to take account of prior criminality. Some writers on just deserts (Fletcher, 1978; Singer, 1979) argue that prior criminality should have no effect on punishment for a new crime; prior penalties have 'paid for' prior crimes.

Von Hirsch allows some increases of penalty for past crimes on the rationale that penalties for a first offense should be somewhat less than is deserved. Because a first offense may be out of character and result from extenuating situational conditions, first offenders may be less blameworthy than it appears and should be given the benefit of the doubt. For some number of subsequent offenses, a gradually disappearing discount may be appropriate. Thereafter each offense should receive its full, deserved, proportionate punishment.

Measure of offense
Although von Hirsch has written about concepts of scaling crime severity, his proportionality analysis takes criminal codes more or less as given. Thus, answers to classical, substantive law harm-versus-culpability arguments – whether attempts should be punished as seriously as completed crimes, whether fortuitous harm (the picked pocket containing the unexpected thousand-dollar coin, the assault that unforeseeably results in death) is relevant to punishment, whether there should be a general defense of necessity – do not shape the scale.

Measure of culpability
Von Hirsch's scheme is premised on legal, rather than moral, assessments of blameworthiness (although the rationale for leniency for first offenders shades into character assessment). The offender is to be blamed for the *offense,* not for the moral culpability it expresses. If Jean Valjean and Leona Helmsley are both convicted of stealing bread, they are to be blamed for stealing bread and identically punished accordingly. Although von Hirsch coined the phrase 'just deserts in an unjust society' in *Doing Justice* (1976), he argues that, on balance, disadvantaged offenders will be better served under a desert scheme than under a utilitarian scheme: they will be punished no more severely than others for a given offense (as they might under predictive [more likely to reoffend] or deterrent [more likely to be tempted] systems). And if they are stigmatised by conviction and punishment, at least the resulting 'disabilities are the consequence of the person's own actions in having violated the law' (1976, p. 148).

Standard punishments
Just as offenses are considered generically for purposes of scaling and punishment, punishments are designed to deal with 'standard cases' and the 'characteristic onerousness of various sanctions' (von Hirsch, 1990, p. 10). One contrary view, as with the contrary view of offender culpability, would be to consider the subjective impact of the sanction

on the offender. Another would be to take account of the objective conditions of different kinds of institutions, different probation regimes, and so on.

Von Hirsch notes these possibilities but responds in three ways. First, the 'law generally works with standard cases', and why not here? Second, in special (limited) circumstances, such as illness or advanced age, there might be deviations from the standard case. Third, although sanction severity depends in part on subjective painfulness, it also depends on 'the moral importance of the rights taken away' (1990, p. 10) and prison deprives crucial liberty rights of free movement and association.

Von Hirsch's scheme could provide a comprehensive desert-based system of punishment. The question is whether such a system offers a just and practicable system for punishing convicted offenders.

CRITIQUE OF PRINCIPLE OF PROPORTIONALITY

Efforts to apply philosophers' distinctions to policy-makers' decisions necessarily raise different concerns than do disagreements among philosophers. Current initiatives to increase use of 'non-custodial' penalties in the United Kingdom and 'intermediate' sanctions in the United States necessarily require translation of theorists' distinctions into practitioners' realities.

It is at this point of translation that the case for strong proportionality conditions breaks down. There are at least five major difficulties. First, strong proportionality conditions require objectification of categories of offenders and offenses that are oversimplified and overinclusive. Second, proportionality arguments are often premised on objective legal measures of desert, typically current and past crimes, rather than on the subjective degree of moral culpability expressed by the offender, under particular circumstances and conditions. Third, strong proportionality conditions run head-on into 'just deserts in an unjust society'. Fourth, strong proportionality conditions violate notions of parsimony by requiring imposition of unnecessarily severe punishments in individual cases in order to assure formal equivalence of suffering. Fifth, strong proportionality conditions presuppose that imposition of offenders' deserved punishments is an overriding moral imperative rather than one of several competing ethical considerations.

The illusion of 'like-situated offenders'

If recent efforts in the United Kingdom and the United States to increase use of intermediate sanctions are to succeed, the appropriateness of different punishments for 'like-situated offenders' must be recognised.

'Like-situated offender' is nested in quotation marks to express the artificiality of notions of like-situated offenders, comparable crimes, and generic punishments. A strong proportionality-in-punishment argument insists on equal treatment of like-situated offenders and proportionately different treatment of differently situated offenders. A fundamental difficulty is that this assumes that offenders can conveniently and justly be placed into a manageable number of more-or-less desert categories and that standard punishments can be prescribed for each category. Unfortunately, neither side of the desert-punishment equation lends itself to standardization.

Neither offenders nor punishments come in standard cases. The practice of dividing offenders and punishments into generic categories produces much unnecessary suffering and provides only illusory proportionality. A look at Minnesota's sentencing guidelines shows why.

Figure 3.1 sets out the original 1980 Minnesota sentencing guidelines grid, which was expressly premised on 'modified just deserts'.[2] Offenses are divided on the vertical axis into ten categories and on the horizontal axis into seven categories of criminal history. An offender's presumptive sentence is determined by consulting the cell at which the row containing his conviction offense meets the column expressing his criminal history. Cases falling in cells below the bold black line are presumed bound for state prison for a term of months within the narrow range specified. Cases falling above the line are presumed not bound for prison (the number in the above-the-line cells represents the prison sentence to be imposed if the offender fails satisfactorily to complete a nonprison sentence).

Because the guidelines attach high value to proportionality, 'departures' are discouraged. Either party may appeal a departure which, to be upheld, must be found to have been based on 'substantial and compelling' reasons. Rules set out illustrative bases for departures and forbid some. For example, the original rules prohibited departures based on offenders' educational, vocational, family, or marital circumstances and also forbade departures based on predictions of dangerousness or 'amenability' to treatment.[3] The reasons behind these prohibitions are not unattractive – to prevent judges from favoring more advantaged, often white, offenders over more disadvantaged,

Figure 3.1 Minnesota sentencing guidelines grid (in months)

Severity levels of conviction offense		Criminal history score						
		0	1	2	3	4	5	6
Unauthorised use of motor vehicle Possession of Marijuana	I	12*	12*	12*	15	18	21	24
Theft-related crimes ($150–2,500) Sale of marijuana	II	12*	12*	14	17	20	23	27 25–29
Theft crimes ($150–2,500)	III	12*	13	16	19	22 21–23	27 25–29	32 30–34
Burglary – felony intent Receiving stolen goods ($150–2,500)	IV	12*	15	18	21	25 24–26	32 30–34	41 37–45
Simple robbery	V	18	23	27	30 29–31	38 36–40	46 43–49	54 50–58
Assault, 2nd degree	VI	21	26	30	34 33–35	44 42–46	54 50–58	65 60–70
Aggravated robbery	VII	24 23–25	32 30–34	41 38–44	49 45–53	65 60–70	81 75–87	97 90–104
Assault, 1st Degree Criminal sexual conduct, 1st degree	VIII	43 41–45	54 50–58	65 60–70	76 71–81	95 89–101	113 106–120	132 124–140
Murder, 3rd degree	IX	97 94–100	119 116–122	127 124–130	149 143–155	176 168–184	205 195–215	230 218–242
Murder, 2nd degree	X	116 111–121	140 133–147	162 153–171	203 192–214	243 231–255	284 270–298	324 309–339

Notes:
* one year and one day
Italicised numbers within the grid denote the range within which a judge may sentence without the sentence being deemed a departure.

Source: Minnesota Sentencing Guidelines Commission (1980)

often black or Indian, offenders, to prevent imposition or prolongation of prison sentences on rehabilitative or incapacitative grounds, and to prevent judges from departing from presumptive prison sentences for middle-class offenders because they are especially amenable to non-incarcerative sentences.

Minnesota's tidy system, whatever its abstract merits, overaggregates offenders in at least four ways. First, consider Table 3.1, which shows the offenses that fall within offense severity levels five and six, and Table 3.2, which shows the rudiments of the scheme for calculating criminal histories. Persons convicted of solicitation of some forms of prostitution are considered equally as culpable as people convicted of robbery or second degree manslaughter, and persons convicted of four minor property misdemeanors are considered as culpable as people convicted of a violent felony. A person convicted of solicitation with four prior misdemeanor convictions is thus, for Minnesota sentencing purposes, like-situated to a person convicted of manslaughter or robbery with a prior robbery conviction. Similarly, a person convicted of sale of marijuana with four misdemeanor convictions is like-situated to a person convicted of forcible rape with a prior rape conviction. There are plausible arguments for why offenders were grouped and criminal history scores calibrated as they were. The Minnesota commission was serious and idealistic in making these decisions. Nonetheless, at day's end, offenders classified by Minnesota as like-situated will in many peoples' eyes look very unlike indeed.

Table 3.1 Offense levels V and VI, Minnesota sentencing guidelines (1 January 1980 version)

Level V

Vehicular homicide
Criminal sexual conduct (3rd degree) – statutory rape, offender more than 2 years older
Manslaughter (2nd degree)
Perjury – in felony trial or firearms permit application
Possession of incendiary device
Robbery
Solicitation of prostitution
Tampering with a witness

Level VI

Arson (2nd degree) – with over $2,500 loss
Assault (2nd degree) – with a deadly weapon
Burglary of a dwelling while armed
Crimial sexual conduct (2nd degree) – statutory rape
Criminal sexual conduct (4th degree) – forcible rape or incompetent victim
Escape – with violence or threat
Kidnapping – victim released unharmed
Receipt of stolen goods – over $2,500
Sale of hallucinogens
Sale of heroin
Sale of other narcotics

Source: Minnesota Sentencing Guidelines Commission (1980).

Second, Minnesota's guidelines are based on *conviction offenses*,[4] which are at best imperfect and inconsistent measures of culpability. Because of ubiquitous plea bargaining in the United States, one of two equal participants in a robbery may be convicted of robbery and the other of aggravated robbery. Similarly, one may plead guilty to

Table 3.2　Criminal history score, Minnesota sentencing guidelines (1 January 1980 version)

Each previous felony conviction	1 point
Current offense committed while on probation or parole, in jail or prison, or released pending sentencing for prior crime	1 point
Four prior misdemeanor convictions	1 point
Two prior gross misdemeanor convictions	1 point

Source: Minnesota Sentencing Guidelines Commission (1980).

the reduced charge of robbery while the other is convicted at trial of aggravated robbery. Of two otherwise comparable robbers, one might be charged in a rural county where prosecutorial policy requires guilty pleas to the full offense (aggravated robbery), whilst another is allowed to plead to robbery in an urban county where aggravated robberies are common and office policy routinely permits acceptance of pleas to lesser offenses. For reasons of local prosecution priorities, or limited manpower, or concern with evidentiary problems, one offender may be convicted of a greatly reduced offense while another comparable offender not affected by those considerations will be convicted of the full offense. The point is not to challenge the legitimacy of the considerations that lead to convictions of particular crimes in particular cases, but to point out that offenders convicted of the same offense may have committed very different acts reflecting very different culpability and, conversely, that offenders convicted of different crimes may have committed comparable acts with similar culpability.

Third, looking behind the grid, Minnesota allows little play for non-criminal-record factors to influence penalties. Consider a minority offender who grew up in a single-parent, welfare-supported household, who has several siblings in prison and who was formerly drug-dependent but who has been living in a common-law marriage for five years, has two children whom he supports, and has worked steadily for three years at a service station – first as an attendant, then an assistant mechanic, and now a mechanic. In Minnesota, none of these personal characteristics are supposed to influence the sentencing decision, and certainly not to justify imposition of a non-custodial sentence on a presumed prison-bound offender. For people who believe in individualised sentences, on either utilitarian or retributive grounds, Minnesota's refusal to consider my hypothetical offender's promising features will seem regrettable. For people concerned by the gross over-representation in courts, jails, and prisons of deeply disadvantaged people, Minnesota's refusal to consider evidence that my hypothetical offender is overcoming the odds will seem deeply regrettable.

Fourth, Minnesota attaches no significance to the collateral effects of a prison sentence on the offender, or on the offender's family or children, what Nigel Walker (1991, pp. 106–08) calls incidental (on the offender) and obiter (on the offender's dependents and associates) effects of punishment. Incarceration for a drug crime for a woman raising children by herself may result in the break-up of her family and placement of her children in foster homes or institutions, or in homes of relatives who will not be responsible care-providers. Incarceration of an employed father and husband may mean loss of the family's home and car, perhaps the break-up of a marriage, perhaps the creation of welfare dependency by the wife and children. To ignore that incidental and obiter effects of punishments vary widely among seemingly like-situated offenders is to ignore things that most people find important.

Thus, for a wide diversity of reasons, offenders whom Minnesota's sentencing guidelines treat as like-situated often are not. A similar analysis could be offered of the punishment side of the crime and punishment equation. Objectively, punishments valued in the generic coin of imprisonment can be very different. In most American jurisdictions, a prison sentence means 'placed in the custody of the department of corrections', which in turn can mean anything from placement in a fear-ridden, gang-dominated maximum security prison under lock-up twenty-three hours a day, through placement in a minimum security camp or campus, to home confinement. Objectively, a sentence to twenty-four months probation can mean anything from living normally and mailing a bi-monthly postcard to the probation office to being contacted ten to twenty-five times a month, reporting to the probation office three times a week, observing a curfew, and being subject to frequent unannounced urinalyses.

Subjectively, three years' imprisonment may mean very different things to a twenty-three-year-old gang member, for whom it is a rite of passage; a forty-year-old employed husband and father, for whom it will likely destroy the material conditions of his and his family's lives; a frightened, effeminate twenty-year-old middle-class student, for whom it may result in sexual victimization; or a seventy-year-old, for whom it may be life imprisonment.

Problems of objectification of crimes, offenders, and punishments are especially stark in a numerical guidelines system. In systems that feature written policy guidelines, they lurk beneath the surface. The Minnesota illustration is generally relevant to analysis of proportionality in punishment, however, because it makes real world implications of strong proportionality conditions starkly apparent. If proportionality is an, or the, overriding principle in the distribution of punishment in practice, then the imperfections of objectification that I describe are presumably regrettable but acceptable costs to be paid for a principled punishment system. If they appear unacceptable, the problem may be that the principle of proportionality offers less helpful guidance than its proponents urge.

Objective measures of responsibility

Von Hirsch's proportionality argument relies on objective measures of penal deservedness. This is curious. Desert theories, especially blaming theories, are premised on notions of individual blameworthiness, which seem inexorably linked to particularised judgments about moral responsibility. Objective measures of harm are seldom sufficient for conviction in the criminal law: that is why doctrines of competency, *mens rea*, and affirmative defense exist and why doctrines like strict liability and felony-murder are disfavored. If individualised moral judgments are germane to conviction, it is not obvious why they are not also germane to punishment.

If punishment is principally about blaming, surely it is relevant whether the offender was mentally impaired, socially disadvantaged, a reluctant participant, or moved by humane motives. Surely it is morally relevant, whatever the path to conviction, what the offender did, with what *mens rea*, and under what circumstances. Surely it is morally relevant whether a particular punishment will be more intensely experienced by one person than by another. In other words, the three subjective considerations that Minnesota's guidelines ignore – what did he really do, what will the conditions of his sanction really be, will he suffer more intensely than others – are relevant to moral judgments of blameworthiness and proportionate punishments. Nigel Walker expresses this when he observes: 'Retributive reasoning would lead instead to a 'personal price list' which would take into account not only gradations of harm but offenders' culpability and sensibility' (1991, p. 103).[5]

The failure of von Hirsch's arguments to take account of individualised differences in culpability and individual effects of punishment looks strange when we recall that von Hirsch's is a retributive theory. Utilitarian theories reject interpersonal comparisons of utility, as Lionel Robbins' classic essay (1938) explains, either on measurement grounds (variable intensity of satisfactions, utility monsters, and so on), or on normative grounds (no individual's satisfactions *should* count for more). However, utilitarian theories are concerned with general policies and aggregate social measures and not with fine-tuned moral judgments.

An unjust society

Punishment schemes that attach high value to proportionality necessarily ignore the differing material conditions of life, including poverty, social disadvantage, and bias, in which human personalities and characters take form. The substantive criminal law rejects motive for intention and in the English-speaking countries allows no formal excusing or mitigating defense of social disadvantage. Yet in both the United Kingdom and the United States, most common law offenders are products of disadvantaged and deprived backgrounds and in both countries vastly disproportionate numbers of alleged, convicted, and imprisoned offenders are members of racial and ethnic minorities. The likelihood, for example, that a black American male is in prison today is eight times greater than that a white American male is in prison.

The problem of 'just deserts in an unjust world' is a fundamental problem for a strong proportionality constraint. Whether retributive theories are rationalised in terms of benefits and burdens, or equilibrium, or blaming, or condemnation, or penance, they must presume equal opportunities for all to participate in society. When some are disabled from full participation by discrimination, disability, or exclusion, by denial of access to public goods, by the burdens of social and economic disadvantage, it is difficult to claim that they enjoy the benefits of autonomy that produce obligation. To take just one example, proponents of benefits and burdens theories are hard pressed to explain how a person who is denied society's benefits deserves to be burdened by social obligation.

Many writers on the philosophy of punishment from both retributive and utilitarian premises recognise this problem. R. A. Duff, after developing an ideal theory of expressive punishment based on social condemnation and individual penance, rejects his own proposals in favor of a deterrence-premised system because: 'punishment is not justifiable within our present legal system; it will not be justifiable unless and until we have brought about deep and far-reaching social, political, legal, and moral changes in ourselves and our society' (1986, p. 294).

Jeffrey Murphy, after developing an ideal punishment theory deriving from a Rawlsian original-position analysis of benefits and burdens, rejects it on grounds that it will not serve justice until 'we have restructured society in such a way that criminals genuinely do correspond to the only model that will render punishment permissible – i.e., make sure that they are autonomous and that they do benefit in the requisite sense' (1973, p. 110).

Even Andrew von Hirsch, arguing that a desert-based system of distribution will achieve less additional disadvantage to the disadvantaged than a utilitarian system, concludes nonetheless: 'as long as a substantial segment of the population is denied adequate opportunities for a livelihood, any scheme for punishing must be morally flawed' (1986, p. 149).

Not surprisingly, proponents of utilitarian and mixed punishment theories acknowledge the same problem. H. L. A. Hart, for example, in explaining the role of excuses in the substantive criminal law, notes in respect of deeply disadvantaged people, 'The admission that the excusing condition may be of no value to those who are below a minimum level of economic prosperity may mean, of course, that we should incorporate as a further excusing condition the pressure of gross forms of economic necessity' (1968, p. 51).

Ted Honderich, who argues for a hybrid punishment theory, observes: 'there is nothing that can be called the question of [punishment's] moral justification which is left to be considered if one puts aside the great question of the distribution of goods in society' (1989, pp. 238–9).

In the United States, giving lip service to concern for offenders from disadvantaged backgrounds, most sentencing commissions have forbidden judges to 'depart' from sentencing guidelines on grounds of offenders' personal circumstances. The putative rationale for such policies is that judges would favor middle-class offenders in mitigating sentences. This rationale is empirically misconceived and perverse; only an insignificant proportion of common law offenders are from middle- and upper-class backgrounds. The normal range of socio-economic backgrounds of common law offenders ranges from the deeply disadvantaged to the merely deprived. The chimerical middle-class offender is conspicuous by his absence. The perversity of such policies is that they forbid special treatment of offenders from deprived backgrounds who have achieved some personal successes. The minority offender from a broken home and a devastated neighborhood who has nonetheless managed a reasonably stable domestic life, achieved some educational success, and found secure employment is as unentitled to a mitigated sentence as a middle-class offender. Thus, policies designed to prevent unfair treatment of disadvantaged offenders as a class have the likely effect of unfair treatment of disadvantaged offenders as individuals.

A proponent of proportionality might respond by noting that loosening proportionality conditions to permit mitigation of sentences for 'deserving' disadvantaged offenders also permits aggravation of sentences for the 'undeserving,' especially those who appear likeliest to offend again. This is a different problem and one that can be addressed by placing strict proportionate limits on maximum sentences and by establishing stringent standards to guide decisions to aggravate punishments.

Parsimony

Proponents of strong proportionality conditions necessarily prefer equality over minimization of suffering. For nearly two decades in the United States, Andrew von Hirsch and Norval Morris have been disagreeing over the role of parsimony in punishment. Von Hirsch (1985) has argued for strong desert limits on punishment and high priority to pursuit of equality and proportionality in punishment. Morris (1974) has argued that desert is a limiting, not a defining, principle of punishment and that policy should prescribe imposition of the least severe 'not undeserved' sanction that meets legitimate policy ends. Within these outer bounds of 'not undeserved' punishments Morris has consistently argued for observance of a principle of parsimony.

To some extent Morris and von Hirsch have argued past each other. Morris argues that a desert approach is unnecessarily harsh and von Hirsch responds by noting that he personally favors relatively modest punishments and, in any case, desert schemes are not inherently more severe than other schemes. In turn, von Hirsch argues that Morris's 'not undeserved' proportionality constraints are vague, the breadth of allowable ranges of sentencing discretion is never specified, and Morris responds by noting that absolute measures of deserved punishment are unknowable and that his aim is to minimise imposition of penal suffering within bounds that any given community finds tolerable.

The problem is that they start from different major premises – von Hirsch's is the 'principle of proportionality', Morris's the 'principle of parsimony'. The difference between them can be seen by imagining a comprehensive punishment scheme, perhaps resembling Minnesota's (see Figure 3.1). Imagine that policy makers have conscientiously classified all offenders into ten categories and, using von Hirsch's ordinal/cardinal magnitude and anchoring points approach, have decided that all offenses at level VII deserve twenty-three- to twenty-five-month prison terms. Imagine further that reliable public opinion surveys have shown that 90 per cent of the general public would find a restrictive non-custodial punishment 'not unduly lenient' and a 36-month prison term 'not unduly severe' for level VII offenses.

Von Hirsch would, I presume, argue that for non-exceptional cases concern for proportionality requires that persons convicted of level VII crimes receive at least a twenty-three-month prison term, even though public opinion would support much less severe punishments. To achieve greater proportionality, von Hirsch would punish some offenders much more severely than is socially or politically required.

Morris, by contrast, would presumably argue that imposing twenty-three-month terms on all level VII cases would be unjust because it would constitute imposition of punishment that is not required by public attitudes or preventive considerations. Morris would argue that, barring exceptional circumstances, no level-VII offender should receive more than twenty-five months' incarceration but that many should receive less than twenty-three months. To achieve less aggregate suffering, Morris would punish some offenders much less severely than concern for proportionality would suggest.

The preceding hypothetical is overstated. Von Hirsch would, at least for exceptional cases, approve departures from the twenty-three to twenty-five-month range or perhaps approve a wider range (for example, eighteen to twenty-eight months). Morris would almost certainly want to establish a normal upper bound lower than thirty-six months and would want to devise some system for assuring that level VII offenders receive roughly equivalent punishments.

Sorting out principles
Disagreements about just punishments, like disagreements about the death penalty or abortion, are often in the end disagreements about powerful intuitions or deeply embedded values. It may be that differences in view between those who give primacy to proportionality and those who give primacy to parsimony cannot be bridged.

The burden of persuasion should rest, however, it seems to me on those who reject Isaiah Berlin's observations that 'not all good things are compatible, still less all the ideals of mankind' (1969, p. 167) and that 'the necessity of choosing between absolute claims is then an inescapable characteristic of the human condition' (1969, p. 169).

Punishment raises at least two important conflicts between ideals – between the principles of proportionality and parsimony, between the quests for criminal justice and social justice.

Punishment is not unique in this respect. *Justice, Equal Opportunity, and the Family* (1983) by James Fishkin shows similar irreconcilable conflicts in ideals that are posed by family policy. Even in ideal theory, he argues, values inherent in support for equal opportunity conflict with values inherent in support for family autonomy. Notions of equal opportunity, he argues, must include a 'principle of merit', that 'there should be a fair competition among individuals for unequal positions in society' (p. 19), and a 'principle of equal life chances specifying roughly equal expectations for everyone regardless of the conditions into which they are born' (p. 20). Without equal life chances, both common experience and modern sociology instruct, scarce social goods will not be distributed according to merit. As Fishkin observes, 'if I can predict the outcomes achieved by an individual merely by knowing his or her race, sex, ethnic origin, or family background, then equality of life chances has not been realised' (p. 34).

If we were single-mindedly devoted to equal opportunity, then, we should view equalization of life chances as an overriding goal of social policy. However, Fishkin argues, efforts to equalize life chances run head on into another powerful principle, that the value of autonomy in a private sphere of liberty encompasses a principle of family autonomy, of non-intrusion by the state into the family's sphere of private liberty.

In other words, equal opportunity and family autonomy conflict fundamentally. Full respect for equal opportunity would involve intrusion into the family that would widely be seen as objectionably intrusive. Full respect for family autonomy would widely be seen as cruel disregard for children's basic needs.

And so it may be with punishment. Principles of proportionality and parsimony may simply conflict, with resolutions between them necessarily partial and provisional.

RECONCILING PROPORTIONALITY AND PARSIMONY

A middle ground exists on which a punishment scheme can be built that honors both proportionality and parsimony – development of sentencing guidelines that establish presumptive sentencing ranges in which the upper bounds are set in accordance with the proportionality principle and the lower bounds are sufficiently flexible to honor the parsimony principle. This would discourage disparately severe punishments, including aggravation of sentences on predictive or rehabilitative grounds beyond what would otherwise be deemed appropriate. If von Hirsch is correct as a social psychologist of punishment when he insists that desert schemes are not necessarily more severe than other schemes, use of proportionality constraints to set upper bounds (within higher statutory maxima) should result in upper-bound penalties that are no harsher than would occur in a scheme with narrow ranges. Below those upper bounds, however, judges could set sentences not premised on 'standard cases' or 'standard punishments'.

The challenge is not to decide between proportionality and parsimony, but to balance them in ways that preserve important elements of each. This is not the place to discuss mechanics at length. A reconciliation can be sketched.[6]

Use proportionality to establish presumptive maximum sentences
Much of von Hirsch's proportionality analysis can be used in setting maximum bounds of sentencing authority for ordinary cases. By using standardized measures of offense severity, proportionate maximum sentences can be specified, the gap between those upper bounds and statutory maxima to be reserved for extraordinary cases subject to the provision of reasons and the possibility of appellate sentence review. The Advisory Council on the Penal System (1978) proposed such a scheme, albeit not in the vocabulary of guidelines. The worst injustices in sentencing and the worst disparities are those suffered by people who receive aberrantly long or severe penalties. Presumptive guidelines for maximum sentences scaled to proportionality could both lessen the likelihood of aberrantly severe penalties and achieve proportionality among those offenders receiving the most severe presumptive sentences.

Parsimony presumption

Within the authorised bounds, judges should be directed to impose the least severe sentence consistent with the governing purposes *at* sentencing (e.g., Morris and Tonry, 1990, pp. 90–2). Within, for example, any category of offenses encompassed in an offense severity level in Minnesota's sentencing guidelines grid, judges should be directed to consider monetary penalties or their equivalents (e.g., community service) when retribution or deterrence is the governing purpose, stringent community controls when incapacitation is at issue, and community controls with treatment conditions when sex or drug or alcohol treatment is called for, reserving incarcerative sentences only for cases when deterrence, public attitudes, or incapacitation seem to dictate. If the parsimony presumption favored the least restrictive alternative, judges would have to devise particularised reasons for doing otherwise – including imposition of sentences for incapacitative or deterrent reasons.

Rough equivalence

Efforts to devise ways to make punishments interchangeable have foundered on proportionality's shoals. If prison is used as the norm, and all other penalties must be converted to carceral coin, interchangeability soon collapses. Almost inexorably, one day in prison equals two or more days of house arrest equals two or more days of community service. Something about the process seems to force literal thinking. If sentences must be proportionate in incarceration time, the scope for use of non-custodial penalties necessarily is limited.

Thinking about equivalences becomes easier if proportionality constraints are loosened. If any prison sentence up to twenty-four months can be imposed in a given case, then the range for substitution is broadened immensely.

Thinking about equivalences also becomes easier if prison is replaced by money, say a day's net pay, as the basic unit from and to which sanctions are converted.

Thinking about equivalences becomes easier if we think about different purposes to be served *at* sentencing in a given case. If the goals are retribution and deterrence, then prison and financial penalties ought to be fully interchangeable, as might also, for the indigent, a combination of residential controls, community service, restitution, and supervision.

If, for normative reasons, sentencing guidelines and guidance are to be scaled proportionately to the severity of crime, objectively measured, and expressed in standardized units of incarceration, objectively characterised, the scope for non-custodial penalties will necessarily be slight. It is not easy to devise non-custodial penalties that are objectively equivalent to twenty-three months' incarceration.

If non-custodial penalties are to be widely adopted and used, proportionality constraints must be loosened to take account of the almost infinite variety of offender circumstances, offense contexts, and punishment dimensions. If ways can be devised to institutionalise principles both of proportionality and parsimony in punishment, we are likely to do less injustice than if we establish systems that seek an illusion of equality of suffering for offenders in whose lives equality in most other things has been conspicuously absent.

Notes

1 Citations of sources for empirical assertions in this section can be found in Morris and Tonry (1990).

2 Since the guidelines took effect in 1980, law-and-order political pressures have influenced statutory changes and policy decisions by the commission that have selectively but substantially increased penalties for controversial crimes and made the system's claims for principled scaling and proportionality weaker (Frase, 1991).

3 Appellate decisions have since recognised limited 'amenability to probation' and 'non-amenability to prison' criteria for departures (see Frase, 1991).

4 The US Sentencing Commission, to avoid problems described in this paragraph, based its guidelines on 'relevant conduct', by which it refers to the defendant's actual behavior and its consequences. In practice, prosecutors manipulate the federal guidelines extensively but use more ingenious subterfuges (Federal Courts Study Committee, 1990).

5 Walker defines 'sensibility': 'the intensity of the suffering, hardship, or inconvenience which a given penalty will inflict depends on the individual: on sex, age, social position, and so on' (Walker, 1991, p. 99).

6 Among the issues that might be discussed: the strengths and weaknesses of the punishment units approach; whether sentencing grids should have two, three, four or more 'bands' representing different presumptions concerning the appropriate type of sentence; at what offense severity level the normal offense is so serious that only incarceration sentences should be authorised; the widths of bands of authorised sentences for categories of cases; whether equivalences should be conceptualised in terms of suffering, intrusiveness, or some other measure. There is little literature on any of these subjects and this essay does not add to it.

References

Advisory Council on the Penal System (1978), *Sentences of Imprisonment – A Review of Maximum Penalties*, HMSO, London.

Ashworth, A. (1992), 'Non-custodial sentences', *Criminal Law Review*, pp. 242–51.

Bentham, J. (1948) [1789], *Introduction to the Principles of Morals and Legislation*, edited by W. Harrison, Oxford University Press, Oxford.

Berlin, I. (1969), *Four Essays on Liberty*, Oxford University Press, Oxford.

Doble, J., Immerwahr, S., and Richardson, A. (1991), *Punishing Criminals – The People of Delaware Consider the Options*, The Public Agenda Foundation, New York.

Duff, R. A. (1986), *Trials and Punishments*, Cambridge University Press, Cambridge.

Federal Courts Study Committee (1990), *Report*, Administrative Office of the US Courts, Washington, DC.

Fishkin, J. S. (1983), *Justice, Equal Opportunity, and the Family*, Yale University Press, New Haven.

Fletcher, G. (1978), *Rethinking Criminal Law*, Little Brown, Boston.

Frase, R. (1991), 'Sentencing reform in Minnesota: ten years after', *Minnesota Law Review*, LXXV, pp. 727–54.

Hart, H. L. A. (1968), *Punishment and Responsibility: Essays in the Philosophy of Law*, Oxford University Press, Oxford.

Honderich, T. (1989), *Punishment – The Supposed Justifications*, Polity, Cambridge.

Kant, I. (1887) [1797], *Rechtslehre*, Part Second, 49, trans. by W. Hastie, T. & T. Clark, Edinburgh.

Minnesota Sentencing Guidelines Commission (1980), *Report to the Legislature – January 1, 1980*, Minnesota Sentencing Guidelines Commission, St. Paul, Minnesota.

Morris, N. (1974), *The Future of Imprisonment*, University of Chicago Press, Chicago.

Morris, N., and Tonry, M. (1990), *Between Prison and Probation: Intermediate Punishments in a Rational Sentencing System*, Oxford University Press, New York.

Murphy, J. (1973), 'Marxism and retribution', *Philosophy and Public Affairs*, II, pp. 217–43.

Pincoffs, E. L. (1966), *The Rationale of Legal Punishment*, Humanities Press, New York.

Robbins, L. (1938), 'Interpersonal comparisons of utility: a comment', *The Economic Journal*, XLVIII, pp. 635–41.

Singer, R. G. (1979), *Just Deserts: Sentencing Based on Equality and Desert*, Ballinger, Cambridge, MA.

von Hirsch, A. (1976), *Doing Justice – The Choice of Punishments*, Hill and Wang, New York (rev. edn. 1986, Northeastern University Press, Boston).

von Hirsch, A. (1985), *Past or Future Crimes – Deservedness and Dangerousness in the Sentencing of Criminals*, Rutgers University Press, New Brunswick, NJ.

von Hirsch, A. (1990), 'Scaling intermediate punishments: a comparison of two models', unpublished manuscript, Rutgers University Department of Criminal Justice, Rutgers, NJ.

von Hirsch, A. (1992), 'Proportionality in the philosophy of punishment', *Crime and Justice – A Review of Research*, XVI, edited by M. Tonry, University of Chicago Press, Chicago, pp. 55–98.

Walker, N. (1991), *Why Punish?*, Oxford University Press, Oxford.

Wasik, M., and von Hirsch, A. (1988), 'Non-custodial penalties and the principles of desert', *Criminal Law Review*, pp. 555–72.

[4]

Hanging judges and wayward mechanics: reply to Michael Tonry

IAN BROWNLEE

In his essay in this volume, 'Proportionality, parsimony, and inter-changeability of punishments', Michael Tonry gives us a succinct and closely argued synopsis of his opposition to theories of punishment and procedures for the distribution of punishments that are based on what he characterises as principles of strong proportionality. His opposition rests on two concerns for social justice. First, he expresses a conviction that a system based on strong proportionality constraints can (and in most places and times *will*) result in the imposition of unnecessarily severe punishments by pursuing formal equality at the expense of permissible leniency. Secondly, he cautions that those unnecessarily severe punishments will come to be borne dispro-portionately. Given the unjust circumstances of our social world, they will fall most often upon the economically marginal groups of society who currently contribute the overwhelming majority of persons at risk of punishment in the criminal justice systems of both the United States and, to a lesser but measurable extent, the United Kingdom.

CRIMINAL JUSTICE AND SOCIAL JUSTICE

The central contention of Tonry's paper is not that proportionality schemes cannot be made to work in practice. Certainly, given the elusiveness of the concept of 'harm', there are enormous practical difficulties in assessing the seriousness of offences and in ranking them on that measure. Problems, no less taxing, arise too from the attempt to devise graduated scales of punishments from which to choose appropriate responses. And, even if one succeeds in construct-ing two more-or-less generally acceptable tables on either side of the harm/response dichotomy, the relationship between the two is by no means obvious. But von Hirsch's general scheme, it is conceded, could eventually provide a comprehensive desert-based system of punishment. What is denied is that such a system would be wise and just, or possessed of more objective validity than a contending system that aimed to promote the principle of restraint or 'parsimony' above the application of equality before the law. For Tonry, it is no justification, either, if aberrant severity is experienced universally; if punishments are 'wrong' because they are too severe, they are not 'right' merely because they are equally severe between different recipients.

The cornerstone of this argument is an attack upon the desirability of fixing objective measures of culpability in order to determine the level of 'penal deservedness'. This notion of objectively determinable culpability lies at the heart of retributive or blaming theories of punishment: punishment is a 'desert' because culpable harm has been done, and for the former to be quantifiable the latter must be measurable. In von Hirsch's scheme, as is well known, the seriousness of a crime, conceptually, has two elements: the degree of harmfulness of the conduct and the extent of the actor's culpability when committing the conduct (von Hirsch, 1986). The conceptual framework itself is not at issue in the present debate but, centrally, the desirability of measuring the level of culpability on 'standard case' criteria is.

HUMAN DIFFERENCE AND DIFFERING CULPABILITY

Explicitly, the position advanced in Tonry's essay negates the existence of 'like-situated' offenders. That phrase, and the expression 'comparable crimes', are both 'artificial notions... Neither offenders nor punishments come in standard cases' (Tonry, ch. 3, p. 69). Remembering that the yardstick in this debate is the likelihood of an accretion in social justice arising from a particular mode of distributing punishment, we may ask not only whether this proposition is true, but also whether devising a system of punishment on the basis that it might be true, will actually result in a net gain in social justice.

Of course, on a purely anthropological level, the first part of that proposition is undoubtedly true. The issue for sentencers (and for those who seek to guide them) is to determine which of the myriad symbols of human diversity should properly influence the sentencing decision, and to what extent. Substantive criminal law principles supply some limited guidance on this by providing, for instance, that certain degrees of mental illness or varieties of automatism excuse from guilt altogether. However, as Tonry notes, substantive common

law concepts like *mens rea* are not particularly attuned to the differing
material conditions of life. Culpability is clearly a wider concept than
intention (at least in the sense in which that latter term is employed
by criminal lawyers in common law jurisdictions). As a consequence,
a finding of guilt based upon a determination of criminal intention
still leaves open most of the essential issues involved in determining
culpability; it is this latter determination which, both sides of this
particular debate would agree, should properly influence the choice
of punishment.

To examine this issue further, it may be helpful to consider the
hypothetical mechanic, Tonry's figure, not so much of straw, as of
grease, oil and sweat. Certainly, there is much about his character
which, in the absence of his most recent court appearance, would
commend him. But the question remains: is the judge, who must now
deal with him for his transgression of the criminal law, at fault if he
or she does not mitigate his sentence to reward the defendant's
struggles up to the point of that offence? In other words, is the level
of his culpability (which, together with a measure of the harmfulness of his act, will determine his penal blameworthiness) to be dis-
counted *because of the sort of person he is*? The assertion that it should
is, in essence, the core of Tonry's critique of desert theories, but in
condemning schemes like the Minnesota guidelines for their refusal
to consider the personal characteristics of the once wayward mechanic,
Tonry, it may be argued, has opened the door to a labyrinth of
personal preferences and judicial dislikes.

The mechanic in this story has been what might be called, perhaps
patronisingly, a 'born loser'. For several years he has fulfilled society's
low expectations of him but, of late, he has reformed, struggled,
achieved. But let us suppose that six months ago he raped a woman at
knife-point, after he had been called out to her broken-down vehicle.
Despite a not-guilty plea, which necessitated a long and harrowing
trial, he has been convicted of the offence.

The evidence has determined his responsibility, but what is to determine his culpability? Or to ask that question in a more practical way,
how is the judge to 'see' him when she determines what sentence is
appropriate? As an 'uppity nigger'? As a potential danger to women?
As a person who has tried against all the odds, and temporarily failed?
Or as a rapist, *simpliciter*? The first view offends any objective notion
of justice, even if it does reflect a very visible symbol of human difference. The second would go against our hypothetical rapist, presumably, on the questionable ground of predictability of dangerousness.

The third, on the other hand, might resound to his favour, but may leave his victim feeling 'doubly victimised'. It is the fourth characterisation of the offender which, it may be argued, is the most appropriate, since it imparts the greatest level of neutrality to the assessment. Sentencing on the factual basis of proven offence leads, by definition, to the defendant being sentenced on the basis of what he has done, rather than who he is, has been, or might become. Such a claim, of course, is explicitly at odds with Tonry's own position.

If a further resort to hypothetical cases is permissible, let us imagine that the wayward mechanic took with him an assistant from the garage. This other young man is from the 'right side of the tracks', and is reasonably well educated. In short, he really has no social disadvantage to plead in mitigation. Despite an initial reluctance, he succumbed to his colleague's inducements and he also raped the stranded motorist.

The point is not to suggest that people from socially disadvantaged backgrounds make more willing rapists than those who come from homes higher up the social scale. The purpose in drawing the example in this way is to question the assertion, which one may deduce from Tonry's position, that the minority offender from a broken home and a devastated neighbourhood who has nonetheless managed a reasonably stable domestic life and so on, should be entitled to a mitigated sentence *on those grounds alone.* In the further hypothetical example he is the instigator of the second rape, and is responsible in a sense for more than half of the victim's suffering. Why he should carry anything less than half the total punishment awarded is by no means clear. If in this case the principles of proportionality and of parsimony are in conflict and if, as Tonry suggests, neither principle can claim anything more than a conditional objective validity, then can we say that reducing the severity of the punishment of one of the rapists below that of the other, merely on the grounds of prior disadvantage, is a demonstrably more just outcome?

ECONOMIC CRIME AND SOCIAL DISADVANTAGE

Of course, it might be objected that rape has been chosen as the offence in these examples because it is an emotive crime for which few objective commentators can find much mitigation. A louder and, arguably, stronger case can usually be made on these grounds in respect of economic crimes. After all, common sense alone seems to suggest that the urge to steal is going to prove less resistible the more poverty-stricken one is. One does not have to adopt a full-blown determinism in order to draw links between certain conditions of relative economic deprivation and criminal behaviour.

Suppose for the sake of the present discussion that some such link, short of out-and-out determinism (which would, of course, undermine legal responsibility), can be demonstrated between social disadvantage and involvement in economic crime. Would such a circumstance demand that proportionality constraints be loosened so that the disadvantaged were inevitably to be treated more leniently than the better-off for equal amounts of dishonesty? Tonry argues this case strongly, asserting that a failure to adjust assessment of culpability to reflect social disadvantage merely serves to perpetuate the vast over-representation of the economically marginal in the custodial system. However, in both its moral and practical dimensions, this argument leaves some further avenues for the sceptic to explore.

UNDERSTANDING AND BLAMING: THE VICTIMS' PERSPECTIVE

To deal with the moral dimension first. By virtue of their office, judges are in the business of blaming. In other words, a judge in his or her public role has a duty to reflect the expectations of society and of offenders' victims, at least in as far as these do not stray over legitimate boundaries of revenge and vindictiveness. The legitimate interests of victims impose limits on the extent to which culpability may be reduced for the purposes of sentencing, and not only for pragmatic or utilitarian reasons. Indeed, as Tonry reminds us, Morris's parsimony principle calls for less severe punishments only in as much as they meet legitimate social purposes.

To take this argument further, if we are to believe the evidence of numerous victim surveys, it is not only the prison population that is disproportionately drawn from the economically marginal sections of society; the direct effects of much crime also fall disproportionately on the already disadvantaged. And if this is so, then the law's denunciatory function belongs as much to the poor and the disadvantaged as to the rich. On these grounds, therefore, the moral superiority of parsimony over proportionality in respect of socially disadvantaged offenders is not as clear-cut as Tonry's paper suggests. If the problem of 'just deserts in an unjust world' is as much of a problem for strong proportionality theories as Tonry contends, then perhaps, in turn, the comparative absence of the victim's perspective from his paper permits the moral superiority of his own position to be overstated.

CHALLENGING SOCIAL JUSTICE: THE 'HANGING JUDGE' AS SOCIAL REFORMER

This is not necessarily to argue that social disadvantage should be ignored altogether when culpability is in issue. Clearly, there must be room for some recognition of motive in general as well as exceptional cases, and proponents of strict proportionality will do well to address this thorny issue in their continuing work. However, as a generality, the question of how society is structured, and the possible consequences of the unequal distribution of opportunities within that structure, are essentially political issues. It may well be true that, within a capitalist division of labour, certain groups of people are more likely to engage in activity that is at odds with the prevailing criminal code; it may be equally true that within existing conditions certain, readily identifiable sections of the population are disproportionately susceptible to law enforcement and criminalisation. The combination of these two factors will undoubtedly lead to the sort of skewed distribution of classes and races within the prison population that now appears. It does not necessarily follow from this that it is for judges in their sentencing function to redress, on a piecemeal basis, the social inequities of the capitalist order.

In addition to these moral and political considerations, there are real practical difficulties in equipping judges with wide discretion to fix sentences on a subjective 'type of person' assessment. Tonry's paper seems to work on the premise that, in Minnesota's case for example, if the guidelines did not prohibit the practice, judges would invariably attribute the appropriate culpability discounts to the right sorts of personal characteristics. This may or may not be so, but the fact that Tonry sees the need to establish stringent standards to circumscribe the aggravation of sentences for 'the undeserving' suggests that he may have his own reservations about the progressiveness of some, at least, of the judges.

The image of the 'hanging judge' may be a crude stereotype, but the influence of hardline opinions among influential members of the judiciary would, surely, minimise the reductive effect of purely subjective sentencing. Clearly, as Tonry's 'sketched reconciliation' suggests, it is reasonable to expect that in order to make parsimony more certain, directions will have to be issued to the judges. Practical difficulties may then be envisaged in drafting such directions, particularly in jurisdictions with strict separation of powers notions in their constitutions. In addition, if the reported experience of reductionism in

Germany is representative (Feest, 1988), in order to achieve any major reductions one would also have to regulate and change the behaviour of other agents within the criminal justice system, particularly the prosecutors. The criminal justice process is multi-layered and interdependent, and interventions for change are more likely to succeed if they are also 'multi-faceted'.

So, it is contended that, when practicalities are considered, there is at least room to query whether the loosening of proportionality constraints on sentencers would necessarily bring about the increase in social justice that underpins the claims of opponents of desert theory to some sort of moral or ethical superiority.

RE-THINKING THE TARIFF

Tonry's critique of strong proportionality contains a third concern, less central to the thesis but still of great importance to abolitionists and other penal reformers. This is the assertion that strong proportionality constraints limit and even exclude the use of non-custodial sentences, and it is predicated on the invariable linking of notions of proportionality with the seemingly inevitable use of 'carceral coin' as the standard unit by which to measure sentence severity. As many sentencing systems are presently constructed, the observation that 'alternatives' are invariably conceived of as alternatives to custody seems sustainable. And if proportionality inevitably means equal amounts of custody, at least at the 'heavy end' of the spectrum of offences, then perhaps the criticism that strict proportionality constraints are inherently inimical to non-custodial sentences is made out. But one may query whether this is an a priori or merely an empirical criticism.

Proponents of desert theory have argued to the contrary that proportionate punishments can be exacted without increasing severity levels, provided that one observes the difference between ordinal and cardinal proportionality. While the demands of ordinal magnitude must be considered inviolable if the principle of treating unlike offenders differently is to have any meaning, the limits imposed by notions of cardinal magnitude may be treated largely as a matter of convention. As such, cardinal magnitude may be subject to revision downward provided only (it may be a large proviso) that conventional modes of judicial thought can be persuaded to change. On this rationale, what prevents the use of, say, intensive probation to punish house burglars is not the constraints of strong proportionality as such, so much as the existence of a 'tariff' that views probation as outside the range of punishments appropriate to that type of offence.

Tariffs like this evolve over many years, 'bolstered', to borrow Andrew Ashworth's phrase, by arguments from analogy and swayed by occasional moral panics (Ashworth, 1992, p. 91). Given this sort of origin, they are susceptible to change, although the mechanics of change may vary from jurisdiction to jurisdiction and rapid change cannot always be expected, judicial character being what it is. But once the tariff is revised, pro rata changes in all the available punishments are effected without offending principles of proportionality. After all, in Britain we still punish murderers more severely than sheep rustlers, although nowadays we hang very few of either.

Changes in judicial thinking of the kind required to effect a change in the ordering of punishments can be assisted by meaningful communication between those who sentence and those who provide disposals outside the custodial regime. The aim of this communication is not to persuade sentencers away from the view that offences of house burglary or of violence against the person are worthy of heavier punishment than, say, offences of minor damage. Rather, the re-education is aimed at demonstrating that this or that particular form of non-custodial disposal is commensurate with serious offending.

In a sense, this kind of strategy for expanding the use of non-custodial sentencing reverses the order of logic employed in Tonry's scheme. Here, the method is to 'up-tariff' the severity of the punishment (at least in the perception of the sentencer), rather than to 'down-grade' the level of culpability of the offender and, as a consequence, the seriousness of the offence. This is clearly the approach implicit in the arguments offered in the British government's White Paper (Home Office, 1990) for increasing the use of community penalties, although that is hardly surprising given that government's conversion to desert theory (*ibid.*, para. 2.9). Such an approach places the principle of proportionality at the heart of official justifications for punishment, while at the same time committing it to a reduction, rather than an expansion, in the use of custodial sentencing. Tonry's argument would suggest that these two aims are irreconcilable. The success or failure of the 1991 Act on the measure of percentage use of imprisonment will provide a good test of his critique.

References

Ashworth, A. (1992), *Sentencing and Criminal Justice,* Weidenfeld & Nicolson, London.

Feest, J. (1988), *Reducing the Prison Population: Lessons from the West German Experience,* National Association for the Care and Resettlement of Offenders, London.

Home Office (1990), *Crime, Justice and Protecting the Public,* Cmd 965, HMSO, London.

von Hirsch, A. (1986), *Past or Future Crimes – Deservedness and Dangerousness in the Sentencing of Criminals,* Manchester University Press, Manchester.

5

Desert, crime control, disparity, and units of punishment

PAUL H. ROBINSON

A distribution of punishment according to principles of desert frequently conflicts with a distribution according to utilitarian principles of crime control. One can blamelessly cause a harm or evil prohibited by the criminal law. While little or no punishment may be deserved, the offender may be dangerous and his punishment may be an effective means of deterring others. Yet, in determining criminal liability, the criminal law most frequently bars liability in the absence of blameworthiness, deferring to the civil commitment system to provide needed protection from dangerous blameless offenders. But this preference for desert, even at the expense of crime control, is tested again at the time of sentencing. No matter what the offender's assigned liability, deterrent, incapacitative, or rehabilitative goals may suggest a greater (or a lesser) degree of punishment than does an actor's blameworthiness. And in every instance where the criminal law takes the utilitarian course in assessing liability, it passes the conflict between desert and crime control on to the sentencing judge. Should the offender's sentence more closely match what he deserves, or what will minimize future crime, or is there a compromise between the two?

The clash is inevitable because the primary concern of desert is punishment for the offense at hand. In the pursuit of crime control, in contrast, factors that have little or nothing to do with the offense at hand may be highly relevant. What is the predicted likelihood of recidivism for this kind of offender? What is the reliability of the predictor used? What is the past successful rehabilitation rate for offenders of this kind? Is the offender well known, has the prosecution received much publicity, such that a severe punishment would provide a particularly cost-effective means of sending a general deterrence message? What is the cost of the sentence that would minimize future criminality and how does it compare to the cost of the predicted crimes?[1]

Because of this natural tension between desert and crime control, it is understandable that much of the current sentencing theory debate focuses on the claimed virtues of desert over crime control or vice versa. But all of the arguments lead to results that are necessarily less than satisfying because we ultimately are asked to determine whether we prefer to sacrifice justice or to suffer more crime (crime that could be avoided by full reliance upon utilitarian principles). Neither of these alternatives is attractive. One naturally wonders whether there are means by which both desert and crime control can be accommodated rather than both compromised. My conclusion is, sadly, no . . . but. It may be possible to fully accommodate desert and, at the same time, accommodate much if not most of the crime control goals.

PUNISHMENT AMOUNT VS. PUNISHMENT METHOD

The potential for accommodation exists because, I will argue, notions of desert concern primarily the *amount* of punishment. Its focus is on whether the amount of punishment is more or less than deserved. The particular method by which a given amount of punishment is imposed is not a desert concern, as long as the total 'bite' of the punishment imposed is that which is deserved. Admittedly, different methods of sanctioning – for example, imprisonment, house arrest, weekend jail, close community supervision with restriction of liberty and privacy, fines, community service – have different punitive effects. But if one could accurately measure and take account of the relative 'bite' of each method, one could give the total punitive 'bite' deserved through any of a number of methods. I will have more to say later on the practical difficulties of adjusting for the relative punitive effect of different sanctioning methods.

The implication of the desert focus on amount rather than method is significant. It means that once the total punitive 'bite' is set according to what is deserved – quantified as 'units of punishment' – one can leave decisions on method of punishment to strictly utilitarian calculations to maximize crime control. As I shall discuss in a moment, while amount of punishment may be relevant in a utilitarian calculus, the method of sanction and a number of other variables in the criminal justice system may be considerably more important to utilitarians. Thus is created the possibility for accommodation.

In 1987 I noted the possibility of a system based on the amount-method distinction and the 'units of punishment' concept (Robinson, 1987a, pp. 39–41; 1987b, pp. 41–61). Several states have adopted or are testing sentencing systems that rely in part upon the concept.[2] It has been suggested that I ought to say more about what I had in mind with regard to these matters, which I shall take this opportunity to do. Other writers have taken up the idea, and developed it in different ways.[3] A reader might profitably look to these variations.

DESERVED UNIFORMITY AND EFFECTIVE DISCRETION

The amount-method distinction provides the opportunity to accommodate rather than compromise another sticky conflict – between the need for uniformity between similar cases and judicial discretion to individualize sentences. A potential for accommodation exists because the uniformity-discretion conflict, I will argue, is a form of the desert-crime control conflict.

Just as a sentence may be undeserved because it is disproportionate to an actor's blameworthiness, so too may it be undeserved because it is disproportionate to the severity of sentences given other offenders of similar blameworthiness. Von Hirsch's distinction between the cardinal and ordinal components of desert illustrates the point (von Hirsch, 1985, ch. 4). Specifically, desert requires punishment within a certain range of severity corresponding to the actor's degree of blameworthiness: the death penalty for theft is undeserved. This is the cardinal issue of desert. But desert also requires that an actor receive less punishment than more blameworthy offenders and more punishment than less blameworthy offenders. This is the ordinal issue of desert.

The breadth of the range of cardinal desert is in dispute. I take Norval Morris's claim that desert operates only to introduce broad ranges within which a sentence must fall (Morris, 1974, pp. 73–6) to be a disagreement only as to the cardinal question. No matter who is right on this score, the ordinal requirement significantly narrows the range of deserved punishment for a given case because the large number of distinguishable degrees of blameworthiness must be accounted for on a limited scale of punishments.

If it is true that desert principles are violated where an actor receives a punishment noticeably more or less severe than other offenders of similar blameworthiness, desert cannot exist in a system of unjustified sentencing disparity. By unjustified disparity, I mean sentences whose severity depends in any significant part on the judges who impose them rather than upon the actor's degree of blameworthiness. Different judges have different sentencing philosophies and different values. If a judge takes his or her sentencing responsibilities seriously, as most judges do, that sincerity will mean judicial soul-searching that inevitably brings philosophy and values into play. Thus, even among the most thoughtful and most conscientious judges, there is likely to be disparity in sentences for similar offenders committing similar offenses. The unfortunate result is a sentence inconsistent with desert because it will depend in part on which judge does the sentencing.

One obvious solution to such sentencing disparity is to eliminate or restrict the sentencing discretion of judges, to have judges simply apply articulated sentencing rules. Eliminating judicial sentencing discretion would have other, largely unacceptable, effects, however. Most obviously, it is more difficult to prevent future crimes by offenders without allowing judicial discretion to shape a sentence to the particular offender at hand. Every offender and every offender's situation is slightly different. A sentence that will effectively minimize the likelihood of recidivism or maximize the likelihood of deterrence in one case may not do so in another case, even where the offender has committed the same offense under similar conditions. Does the offender have a job? Has he committed a previous offense? Does he use drugs? What is his family situation? What treatment programs are available? Do they work for this kind of an offender? Does he have the money to pay a fine? Is this particular offense a growing problem? Is this the kind of offense for which people calculate the potential risks and gains before they commit it? The answer to these and many other questions can determine the kind of sentence – prison, weekend jail, community service, fine, house arrest, curfew, or combination of these – that best minimizes the chance of future crimes. But this tailoring of a unique sentence based upon the particular facts of each case requires a significant degree of judicial discretion. Such is the source of the tension: to permit such discretion is to risk sentencing disparity; to forbid such discretion is to suffer avoidable crimes.

This aspect of the uniformity-discretion tension is a subspecies of the more general conflict between desert and crime control. Desert requires uniformity in application that will assure similar punishment for similar blameworthiness. Crime control requires judicial discretion to fashion the most effective sentence, given the facts of each offender's situation. As with the general conflict between desert and crime control, the most common approach to the conflict to date is to strike a compromise between the competing goals: reduce and structure discretion in the hopes of reducing disparity, while preserving some ability to individualize the sentence. As with the more general conflict, however, under the compromises neither goal is dismissed but neither is satisfied. 'In/out' sentencing grids, for example, the most common form of structured sentencing in the United States, eliminate or significantly reduce judicial authority in deciding whether to imprison but otherwise leave discretion intact. This means that judges lose the ability to individualize sentences with regard to the imprisonment decision. At the same time, the in/out grids do little or nothing to reduce disparity with regard to sentencing decisions other than in/out, such as the length of prison term within sentencing range, the conditions of probation, whether to fine, the amount of fine, and so on.

Is there a means of accommodating the goals of uniformity and individualization without compromising both? The amount-method distinction and the 'units of punishment' concept suggests that there is. Our concern for uniformity is primarily a concern for uniformity in the *amount* of punishment, while our need for individualization stems in large part from our desire to individualize the *method* of sanction. If this is true, one might be able to fashion a superior sentencing system by providing uniformity in assessing the amount of punishment through articulated sentencing rules, yet allowing extensive judicial discretion in determining the sanctioning method or combination of methods that seem most effective in preventing future crime given the particular characteristics of the offense or the offender.

Is it true that the demands of desert and uniformity concern only the amount of punishment? Is it true that the individualization need of crime control resides in large measure with the selection of sanctioning method?

DESERT: IS CONTROL OVER PUNISHMENT AMOUNT BUT NOT METHOD ENOUGH?

Imagine two offenders who commit the same offense under similar circumstances such that the community sees equal blameworthiness. The first offender is judged to be a good candidate for probation; all indications are that he will not commit another offense if released. For the second offender there is not the same assurance against recidivism if released and, in any case, he has no money to pay a fine as a means of non-incarcerative punishment. This is a common situation. If the first offender gets probation, community service, and a fine, while the second gets imprisonment, will we see the different sentences as unfair? Perhaps. We may see the fined offender as receiving less punishment than the imprisoned offender, while they deserve the same amount. But if the first offender is fined an amount equal to six months of his annual salary and ordered to do 340 hours of community service (equivalent to two months of 8-hour-day work) while the second offender is given ten days in jail, would we come to the same conclusion? Perhaps not. Some might even suggest that the first offender is receiving more punishment than the second, although the method of imposition is non-incarcerative. If given the choice between the two sentences, the first offender might prefer to serve the ten days in jail than to pay the heavy fine and perform the substantial community service.

In other words, a sentencing system can inflict a given amount of punishment through any number of sanctioning methods, incarcerative and non-incarcerative. Presumably, either of the two sentences above could be adjusted so that at some point the incarcerative and the non-incarcerative sentences have the same *punitive bite*. If this were done, it seems unlikely that one would say that unfair disparity exists. This suggests that when we say that similar offenders deserve 'similar' sentences, we mean that they deserve a similar *amount* of punishment, without insisting on a particular kind of sanctioning method. The example also suggests that the sanctioning method that will best prevent future offenses might be different in different cases, even if the offense is the same. While the total punishment 'bite' may be the same for the two sentences, and they may each provide the same deterrent effect, an incarcerative sentence provides more effective incapacitation of an immediately dangerous offender.

If desert can be satisfied through setting the total amount of punishment and as long as this total amount is imposed, judges can be given broad discretion in fashioning an individualized sentence. Judges can be let loose to individualize each sentence in a way that minimizes recidivism and maximizes deterrence, taking account of the unique factors of each case, without our worrying that such discretion will cause unwanted sentencing disparity. An important implication of this is that such a system permits a reduction in the use of incarceration while continuing to give the punishment deserved. Given the current financial difficulties of most governments and the problems of prison overcrowding, this may present an attractive program. Perhaps most importantly, such a program might gain wide political support, and thus be a genuinely plausible reform, because it does not solve the financial and overcrowding problem by settling for giving offenders less punishment than they deserve.

EFFECTIVE CRIME CONTROL: IS CONTROL OVER SANCTIONING METHOD BUT NOT AMOUNT ENOUGH?

It seems likely that unimpeded utilitarian control over the selection of sanctioning method can do much to control crime. The sanction can target the factors that most strongly predict future criminality, be it drug dependence, lack of job skills, poor interpersonal skills, or lack of appreciation for the devastating effect an offense can have on a victim, the victim's family, and the community generally. Drug treatment programs, job training, personal and family counselling, victim restitution, and service to the community are just some of the possible sanctioning methods that can be combined with one another, with other sanctions, or with imprisonment. For dangerous offenders, imprisonment may be the preferred method. For non-dangerous offenders, non-incarcerative methods may be equally effective yet much less expensive. In a world of limited (or decreasing) correctional resources, the imposition of punishment with equal deterrent value through less expensive methods means that more of such deterring punishment can be imposed and, presumably, more deterrence effected.

It is probably not true, however, that crime control concerns can be fully satisfied by having complete control over the method of sanctioning, in the way that desert concerns can be fully satisfied by having desert as the primary principle in determining the amount of punishment. The single constraint on judges – that the total punitive bite of all sanctions must add up to the total amount of punishment that the offender deserves – admittedly may rule out some sentences that might more effectively prevent future crimes. For example, if the offense is sufficiently serious, it simply may not be possible for the offender to satisfy the total punishment called for through the low-impact mechanisms of non-incarcerative methods. Only the high-impact sanction of incarceration may be able to provide the total punishment deserved. Similarly, less serious offenses may not generate sufficient punishment units to incarcerate a dangerous offender for the period of his predicted dangerousness. By assessing amount of punishment according to desert alone, then, some crime control possibilities are lost.

On the other hand, crime control goals can be furthered through a host of mechanisms, including many unrelated to the sentencing process. Modified rules governing search and arrest, greater investigative resources, speedier trials, revised trial procedures, all could increase the crime control effectiveness of the current criminal justice system. Indeed, crime control goals can be furthered through a host of mechanisms entirely outside the criminal justice process, as through a change in social conditions such as educational and job opportunities, as well as a change in social values such as work ethic and inter-class tolerance.

There may be good reason to resist some of these non-sentencing reforms. Each reform may incur some cost, either in additional financial expenditure or in its detrimental effect to societal interests, such as privacy or personal autonomy. But it nonetheless is true that crime control can be achieved through a variety of mechanisms. Desert concerns, in contrast, focus almost exclusively on amount of punishment imposed by the criminal justice system. No other mechanisms for satisfying desert are available. Before desert is sacrificed in determining the amount of punishment to be imposed, one ought to be persuaded that no other mechanism, of the many available, would be as efficient in achieving the same crime control effect that the undeserved punishment would achieve.

In calculating whether a crime control mechanism other than the amount of punishment may be equally or more efficient than giving an undeserved sentence, utilitarians cannot disregard the value of doing justice. That is, it is not just out of deference to the arguments of desert advocates that utilitarians ought to prefer other crime control strategies. The fact is there is disutility in imposing undeserved sentences. The imposition of sentences more than or less than deserved has an effect broader than simply the abstract injury of injustice to the offender at hand. The criminal justice system can operate as efficiently as it currently does only because of the acquiescence and co-operation of the participants, offenders and suspects as well as officials. Acquiescence and co-operation exist because the system is viewed as legitimate, as having some moral credibility that subverts the urge of those sanctioned to revolt and to seek and expect the help of others similarly sanctioned (see Seidman, 1984).

Perhaps even more important to the utilitarian calculus is the confirmation by recent social science research that the criminal law's power in gaining compliance is a direct function of its moral credibility with the general public[4]. Most people obey the law, the studies suggest, not because they fear the pain of criminal sanction but because they want to do what is right. They are driven in large part by their perceptions of themselves as honest law-abiding people. But the effectiveness of the law in this role is a function of its credibility with the community for doing justice. If the law closely matches people's shared intuitive notions of justice, it grows in its power to affect their conduct. If the law is seen as being unjust, its power as a moral force is diminished. Having an offender's punishment disproportionate to his blameworthiness or having it depend in any part upon who the offender gets as a sentencing judge can only undercut the law's moral credibility and, thereby, its power to gain compliance. This suggests that even a purely utilitarian analysis would cede the issue of amount of punishment to an exclusively desert determination, reserving desert-free calculations for setting the method of sanction and for non-sentencing reforms.

IMPLEMENTING A UNITS OF PUNISHMENT SYSTEM

Can such a 'units of punishment' sentencing system be implemented? It clearly presents some challenges. Three parts are needed: (1) a relatively sophisticated and fully articulated set of rules that set the amount of punishment deserved by an offender given his offense, (2) a range of sanctioning methods with information for judges on which, from a pure crime prevention point of view, are most effective for what kinds of offenders and offenses, and (3) a table of 'conversion' or 'equivalency' ratios that accurately reflect the relative punitive bite of each sanctioning method.

Sentencing rules to establish the amount of punishment
There does not yet exist a sophisticated system of articulated rules that can assess the amount of punishment deserved by a particular offender for a particular offense. Criminal codes provide only a rough estimate, classifying offenses into grades, setting the conditions that will give complete exculpation and, in a few instances, providing mitigations and aggravations that move offenses between grades. One difficulty in creating this part of the system is that many things go into our assessment of the degree of punishment that an offender deserves. Desert takes account of such things as the kind and extent of harm caused or risked, the actor's culpable state of mind as to its occurrence, his degree of contribution in bringing about the offense where multiple offenders are involved, as well as special mitigating conditions – short of a complete excuse – that reduce our assessment

of blame and special aggravating conditions that increase it. Even if the relevant factors are identified, a second and more difficult challenge is to quantify each and to take account of its interaction with other factors.

While the task of quantifying the amount of deserved punishment is difficult, there is every indication that it is feasible. Many existing sentencing guidelines, such as those of the United States Sentencing Commission, pick up where the criminal code leaves off, to articulate more refined judgments on the amount of punishment deserved. The federal guidelines take account of, among other things, the specific characteristics of the offense, the offender's role in the offense, the nature of the victim, other offenses to be sentenced for, and the offender's willingness to accept responsibility for his offense. They use these factors to determine where the offender fits among the forty-three sanction 'levels' that the guidelines provide (United States Sentencing Commission, 1992, s. 1B1.1).

Some attempts at using statistical models to quantify blameworthiness have been developed in the context of the death penalty (see for example, New Jersey Proportionality Review Project, 1989; Baldus and Woodworth, forthcoming). Several studies use past death-penalty-eligible cases to statistically determine the factors that influence juries toward giving or withholding the death penalty. The factors and their relative effect are used to produce a statistical model that sets each case at a given 'culpability level'. The level on which a case falls is used by a reviewing court to help determine whether use of the death penalty in that case would be 'disproportionate to the penalty imposed in similar cases, considering both the crime and the defendant', in violation of constitutional requirements.[5] This kind of analysis could be applied more broadly to generate culpability levels for offenses beyond capital offenses.

One danger in developing a relatively sophisticated system of desert assessment is the potential for unworkable complexity in application. This has been a criticism of the federal sentencing guidelines, which many people feel are not sophisticated enough. Some thought has been given to drafting techniques and system structures that would maximize the potential for sophistication while keeping a system workable (see for example, Robinson, 1987b). It is realistic to conclude that presently we are capable of producing a workable system that can accurately quantify an actor's blameworthiness.[6] No doubt additional study and experience would be required before such a system is both sophisticated and simple.

Sentencing options to maximize crime prevention

There is little benefit in judicial discretion to select a sanctioning method or combination of methods if sentencing judges have few options. The growing recognition of the costs of incarceration and the increasingly difficult financial condition of many governments have created an incentive for finding new, cheaper, non-incarcerative sanctioning methods. The two most sought-after characteristics of a non-incarcerative sanction have been crime prevention potential and low cost. Thus, innovations have included, for example, community service assignments, weekend custody that allows the offender to hold a job, electronic wrist bracelets to monitor an offender's location at home and enforce an evening curfew, periodic drug testing, the administration of drugs that will make the offender physically ill if he uses a narcotic, and so on.

The units of punishment system described here suggests another desirable characteristic, beyond effective crime prevention and low cost, that we ought to try to cultivate in non-incarcerative sanctions: a high punitive value ('bite'). The higher its punishment value, the more effective a sanction is as a substitute for prison in satisfying the required units of punishment. Thus, one might wish to add to the sanction options such things as fine limits set according to percentage of assets or percentage of income rather than a fixed limit, publication of offender names and the details of their offenses, and work furlough from spartan half-way houses for which offenders have to pay the costs rather than from an offender's home. For similar reasons, one might use non-incarcerative sanctions already on the list in a way that increases their punitive bite. Thus one might use a wrist bracelet to compel full-time house arrest when not at work, rather than just to enforce a curfew; one might make community service assignments to more unpleasant jobs; or one might add more onerous and more intrusive conditions to release to community supervision. The more punitive the non-incarcerative sanction the more frequently it can serve as a substitute for an incarcerative sanction.

Conversion ratios among sanctioning methods

Some preliminary work suggests that it is feasible to establish the relative punitive value of different sanctioning methods (Erikson and Gibbs, 1979; Sebba 1978; Sebba and Nathan, 1984). The studies also suggest that there is some consistency in perceptions of the relative bite of various sanctions. Additional research more directly designed to set sanctioning method ratios for a units of punishment system is underway but is as yet incomplete.[7]

Constructing this important piece of a units of punishment system has some difficult hurdles. The technical difficulties are surmountable. Considerable work has been done on the most reliable means of testing perceived scales such as that needed here (see for example, Erikson and Gibbs, 1979, p. 106; Sebba and Nathan, 1984, pp. 226–9). The conceptual questions are not so easily answered. Whose view ought to be measured in judging the relative punitive effect? If the point of the ratios is to assure the community that less severe sanctioning methods do not necessarily mean less punishment, then the community's views of the relative punitive values ought to be used.[8] On the other hand, there is good evidence that the public has a poor idea of the actual conditions and punitive effect of different sanctions, especially non-incarcerative sanctions. One solution may be to do closely controlled studies, rather than surveys, in which the test subjects are given a good deal of detail about each sanctioning method before testing their perceptions of relative punitive effect.

What if people have different views of the relative punitive effect of different sanctions, as seems likely? Some people may value their freedom more than their money, or vice versa. What if identifiable groups of people have different views? Should the system try to individualize the punishment equivalencies? I think not. This marks the realistic limit of a criminal justice system's refinement in giving deserved punishment. Empirical research will tell us how much consensus there is on relative punitive effect. If the deviation is within tolerable limits, we ought simply to attempt to set ratios that represent the norm for the jurisdiction, whether that is a municipality, a state, or an entire country, whoever holds law-making authority for the offense being sentenced. Differences among jurisdictions might be reflected in different ratios: New York's ratios might be different than Montana's, which might be different than the federal system's, which might be different than Scotland's. This is desirable. If the ratios are to reflect the community's perceptions, they ought to be different if different communities have different perceptions.

SUMMARY AND CONCLUSION

A sentencing system built around the distinction between amount of punishment and method of punishment may have the potential for satisfying both desert and crime prevention goals. The grading assessments made by the criminal code provide a starting point for a more refined analysis by the sentencing system. If this analysis looks exclusively to the actor's blameworthiness in setting the amount of punishment, it can fully satisfy the demands of desert. If desert demands are satisfied by articulated sentencing rules in determining the amount of punishment, the system also avoids improper sentencing disparity.

While crime control advocates might wish to influence the amount of punishment, both desert and utilitarian arguments exist in support of limiting crime control efforts to selecting the method of sanction and to reform efforts outside the sentencing process and outside the criminal justice process. By doing so, by assuring that the amount-of-punishment determination satisfies desert requirements untainted by crime control concerns, the system gains moral credibility that increases its power as a mechanism for gaining public compliance.

A system that allows desert to determine the amount of punishment and crime prevention strategies to determine the method of punishment requires three distinct pieces. First, it must provide a set of articulated sentencing rules that will assign the quantum of punishment deserved, 'units of punishment', for a given offense and offender, taking account of the full range of factors that can affect our assessment of an actor's blameworthiness. This is within our power to do, although further work and experience is required if the system is to be as sophisticated and workable as ultimately we will want. Second, the system must give sentencing judges a wide range of sentencing options, preferably sanctions that can prevent future crimes and inflict a substantial punitive bite at low cost. Also needed is advice for judges as to situations in which each sanctioning method is most effective. Finally, the system must provide a measure of the relative punitive effect of the various sanctioning methods and take account of this relative punitive effect in gauging whether a contemplated sanction or combination of sanctions satisfies the amount of punishment deserved. Under such a system, there is the potential not simply to compromise desert and crime control but to accommodate them both.

Notes

1 For a more detailed account of the potential conflicts among different distributive principles, see Robinson, 1987a, pp. 19–28.

2 See e.g. New Jersey Supreme Court Committee on Sanctioning, 1992; New Jersey Supreme Court Sentencing Pathfinders Committee, 1992; Jackson, 1989;

> Louisiana Sentencing Commission, 1989a, 1989b; Oregon Criminal Justice Council, 1989, pp.96–107; Oregon, 1989, ss. 253–05–011 et seq..

3   See Wasik and von Hirsch, 1988; von Hirsch, Wasik and Greene, 1989; Morris and Tonry, 1990, pp. 73–81; von Hirsch, 1993, chs. 5–6.

4   See Tyler, 1990, chs. 3–4. Tyler cites a number of other studies that suggest similar conclusions (pp. 30–9).

5   See e.g., *Furman* v. *Georgia* 408 US 238 (1972); *Sochor* v. *Florida* 112 S.Ct. 2114 (1992).

6   It would be easiest to produce a system that mirrored the community's views of blameworthiness. Of course, this is not necessarily a system that moral philosophers would approve of. It could be modified as necessary to meet their objections, but then might not serve the utilitarian's purpose of maximizing the system's credibility with the general public.

7   By Professor John Darley of Princeton University Department of Psychology.

8   One might be tempted to set the ratios to maximize the crime prevention effects on offenders, in which case one might use offenders or likely offenders as the relevant test population. But this would undercut the value of the ratios in assuring the general public that offenders are receiving the punishment that they deserve. Until empirical data is available to tell us whether these two populations perceive the relative punitive bite of sanctions differently, we will not know whether this is an issue that we need be concerned about.

References

Baldus, D. C., and Woodworth, G. A. (forthcoming), 'Proportionality review of death sentences: New Jersey's options', *Chance Magazine.*

Erikson, M. L., and Gibbs, J. P. (1979), 'On the perceived severity of legal penalties', *Journal of Criminal Law and Criminology*, LXX, pp. 102–116.

Jackson, C. L. (1989), *Briefing Paper on Sanction Structure*, Louisiana Sentencing Commission, Louisiana.

Louisiana Sentencing Commission (1989a), *Initial Presentation of Sanction Structure Report*, Louisiana Sentencing Commission, Louisiana.

Louisiana Sentencing Commission (1989b), *Guidelines*, Louisiana Administrative Code, 22:IX(1), s.403, Louisiana.

Morris, N. (1974), *The Future of Imprisonment*, University of Chicago Press, Chicago.

Morris, N., and Tonry, M. (1990), *Between Prison and Probation: Intermediate Punishments in a Rational Sentencing System*, Oxford University Press, New York.

New Jersey Proportionality Review Project (1989), *Homicide Case Data Collection Instrument*, New Jersey.

New Jersey Supreme Court Committee on Sanctioning (1992), *Report*, New Jersey Supreme Court Judicial Conference on Sanctioning and Provision, New Jersey.

New Jersey Supreme Court Sentencing Pathfinders Committee (1992), *Interim Report*, New Jersey Supreme Court, New Jersey.

Oregon Criminal Justice Council (1989), *Oregon Sentencing Guide Implementation Manual*, Portland, Oregon.

Oregon (1989), *Oregon Administrative Rules*, Office of the Secretary of State, Portland, Oregon.

Robinson, P. H. (1987a), 'Hybrid principles for the distribution of criminal sanctions', *Northwestern Law Review*, LXXXII, pp. 19–42.

Robinson, P. H. (1987b), 'A sentencing system for the 21st century?', *Texas Law Review*, LXVI, pp. 1–61.

Sebba, L. (1978), 'Some explorations in the scaling of penalties', *Journal of Research in Crime and Delinquency*, XV, pp. 247–62.

Sebba, L., and Nathan, G. (1984), 'Further exploration in the scaling of penalties', *British Journal of Criminology*, XXII, pp. 221–49.

Seidman, L. M. (1984), 'Soldiers, martyrs and criminals: utilitarian theory and the problem of crime control', *Yale Law Journal*, XCIV, pp. 315–49.

Tyler, T. (1990), *Why People Obey the Law*, Yale University Press, New Haven.

United States Sentencing Commission (1992), *Federal Sentencing Guidelines Manual*, West Publishing, St Paul, Minnesota.

von Hirsch, A. (1985), *Past or Future Crimes: Deservedness and Dangerousness in the Sentencing of Criminals*, Rutgers University Press, New Brunswick, NJ.

von Hirsch, A. (1993), *Censure and Sanctions*, Oxford University Press, Oxford.

von Hirsch, A., Wasik, M., and Greene, J. (1989), 'Punishments in the community and the principles of desert', *Rutgers Law Journal*, XX, pp. 595–618.

Wasik, M., and von Hirsch, A. (1988), 'Non-custodial penalties and the principles of desert', *Criminal Law Review*, pp. 555–72.

PART THREE

The role of imprisonment

6

Catering to the public: prison policy in the nineties

HANS TOCH

Those who look for philosophical consistency in prison policies are apt not to find it. There are several reasons for this fact. The first is that sentencing provisions can be enacted as political statements. The second is that the public to whom such statements are addressed can be ambivalent about the way prisons are deployed.

Politics as it affects policy is the art of compromise, presaged by Solomon when he resolved a custody dispute by offering half a child to each parent. Compromise can occur between corollaries of diametrically opposed values or goals, by allocating a portion of the pie to each. A prison system that evolves in this way can embody responses by legislative factions to divergent constituencies that demand escalating efforts to 'lock 'em up and throw away the key'; they may also know of welfare-oriented constituencies who want different approaches, such as prevention and treatment of offenders. Some groups of citizens are envisioned as opposed to spending money; others are seen to have competing uses for the money they want to spend.

The combinatory political formula for arriving at prison policy today requires legislators to be tough on crime and kinder and gentler to people with problems. But offenders are often people with problems that our toughness exacerbates. Our actions spawn problems that we solve through crisis management. Instead of tempering justice with mercy, we temper retributive overkill with safety nets of hasty remedial services that ameliorate the consequences of retributive policy. To take an example, it is an inconsistent policy to incarcerate women on a large scale and make gargantuan efforts to find placements for children, to open co-operative nurseries in prisons and to worry about reunion and visiting programs. Clients of dissonant policies sense the dissonance, and we cannot keep a young mother from asking whether our welfare concerns could be better reconciled with our punitive dispositions if we punish her in the community.

SEED AND SWEEP

I do not suggest here that combinatory formulas intrinsically preclude coherent approaches. The criterion of coherence would be an underlying commonality of goal. A tough-and-kind approach can have a purpose. One example is the 'sweep and seed' of drug-infested communities (US Department of Justice, 1992), which is a 'left hook-right hook' sequence that makes conceptual sense. The communities are intimidated, paralyzed and emasculated by endemic drug dealing. The prescribed first step is a massive enforcement drive – a sweep – that closes drug bazaars and clears away the drug merchants who have conducted intrusive business at the expense of law-abiding citizens. But drug merchants are replenishable, and sweeps provide evanescent respite from community disorganization and decay.

The answer is the 'seed' phase, which denotes follow-up interventions that empower community residents to recapture their neighborhoods. Seeding provides for organizing residents so they can address conditions in their communities that underlie drug addiction and crime. Seeding is symbiotically related to sweeping. Sweeps offer short-term solutions that are preconditions to long-term solutions. Community responses could not be initiated until citizens are free from intimidation; arrests would make no sense unless prevention efforts follow. Other conceptual links can be appended to taste. One such link is that of police reform. Community policing approaches make sweeping-officers the partners of seeding efforts. Prisons do seeding by subjecting swept addicts to rehabilitative interventions before reintegrating them into the community.

But the model in practice is not driven by logic. It results from the need to compromise between perceived short-term and long-term concerns of diverse constituencies. This compromise also governs the allocation of resources to long-term and short-term components as programs are implemented. Recent allocation of federal funds in the United States' war on drugs, for example, runs 68 per cent for enforcement. This allocation buys much more sweeping than seeding, given the relative cost of these efforts.

PRISONS AND DUSTBINS

Prisons are the congested repositories of sweeps, but are also the beneficiaries of draconian sentences that are aimed at the recidivist-ically swept. As a combined result, prison populations over-represent young, addicted property offenders, mostly under two- to three-year sentences, and non-violent recidivists sentenced for inordinate periods of time. Prisons face this influx while operating under politically-inspired mandates that vary in detail from jurisdiction to jurisdiction.

Many mandates are originated by conservative legislators, and con-ceded by liberals as a trade-off. This includes building as many prison cells as it takes to accommodate intake populations, given escalating sentencing policies and practices. A second goal of conservatives is to ensure that the imprisoned inmates are exposed to hard work and no-nonsense discipline. The counterpart liberal thrusts – conceded by conservatives in exchange for tough sentencing provisions and run-away construction funds – provide for treatment aimed at addiction, and due process in administrative proceedings.

Legislators, of course, may see logic where it does not exist for non-legislators. In this sense, consistency may be the hobgoblin of persons caught in cross-pressures from their constituents. Consider the follow-ing sentiments that were recently expressed by legislators in the state of New York, in response to a survey (Flanagan, Brennan and Cohen, 1991): eight out of ten who answered this study (82%) opined that 'unless we do something about the root causes of crime such as poverty and unemployment, the crime rate will remain high'; three out of four (73%) said 'it would be better to treat drug abuse as a disease rather than punish it as a crime', and a comparable proportion (72%) argued that 'the best way to reduce crime in America is to expand social programs that will give disadvantaged people better education, job training and equal employment opportunities' (pp. 24–25).

Two-thirds of the same group (67%), however, responded that 'stif-fer jail sentences are needed to show criminals that crime does not pay'; nine out of ten (85%) said that 'even if prisons can't deter or rehabilitate criminals, long prison sentences are needed so that we can keep habitual and dangerous offenders off of [sic] our streets', and two-thirds (64%) felt that 'punishing criminals more harshly would reduce crime by setting an example and showing others that crime does not pay' (p. 26). Yet four out of five legislators (79%) indicated in the survey that 'rehabilitation programs in our prisons should be expanded', and three of four (74%) argued that 'rehabilitating a criminal is as important as making a criminal pay for his or her crime' (p. 27). It is difficult offhand to see how beliefs such as these can cohere philosophically, and how they could inspire legislation that one could call a 'policy' relating to imprisonment.

This picture is discouraging enough, but incomplete. Ultimately, more discordant developments can occur as non-policies are enacted or implemented, and expenses and population pressures mount. Chaos can begin to threaten as components of the system fight each other to fend off the onrush of bodies with intersecting lawsuits and other forms of internecine warfare. The response requires economy-inspired legislative retreat that can only be effected at the expense of residual consistency, blunting thrusts painfully arrived at through compromise.

The Great American Prison Crisis – or 'The Crunch', as it is known in the profession – climaxed in the early eighties, when it had become obvious that we could not stuff more offenders into oversubscribed prisons that were bulging at the seams, but that construction could not keep pace with the demand for additional cell space. The realization that Something Had to be Done sparked a search for politically acceptable solutions to the problem. I shall center on one clear-cut example of such solutions, because it highlights the difference between politically-inspired acts and genuine responses to public opinion.

SHORT SHARP SHOCKS

In a report issued by the Georgia Department of Corrections (Flowers, Carr and Ruback, 1991, p. 3) it is noted that 'by the early 1980s, jail/prison overcrowding was universally recognized as the single most serious problem facing Georgia's criminal justice system'. In one twelve-month period (1983), for example, the state's prison population increased from 14,057 to 15,504. Not coincidentally, in November of that year Georgia began use of what it called 'Special Alternative Incarceration', or SAI (much effort is usually expended in reform on exercises of innovative nomenclature to arrive at acronyms).

An early description of the Georgia program in a *New York Times* article (Clendinen, 1985) opens with the following vignette: 'Five young men – three burglars, an arsonist and a car thief – arrived at the Dodge Correctional Institute two hours southeast of here by car last month with long hair, designer jeans, tattoos and an attitude of independent swagger. In short order, the swagger was gone.'

The *New York Times* accentuates the harshness of the offenders' reception in the camp, and describes it as an integral program ingredient. The Georgia Corrections Department acknowledged that 'the appeal to the media of a military-style prison program in terms of its "filmability" . . . cannot be underestimated. The media vividly captured the image of young men who have broken the law being verbally disciplined and marched through their daily activities of hard work and calisthenics' (Flowers, Carr and Ruback, 1991, p. 1). The routine in the Georgia camp called for head-shaving, delousing, and barked stentorian commands. 'That', writes the *New York Times'* reporter, 'was their welcome to a Georgia program meant to give young criminals a tough 90-day experience of prison life that they will never wish to repeat. The program, which the state describes as "shock incarceration", is one of a number of new measures being taken across the South to keep criminals out of overcrowded and increasingly expensive prisons.'

The *New York Times* reporter quotes an official who described the *sine qua non* of prison reform as follows: 'It's got to be safe, it's got to be tough – or punitive – and it's got to be inexpensive'. The dominant message to be conveyed to young inmates as they entered the Georgia program was clearly that of 'toughness'. A second reporter, who covered the opening of an SAI institution in another state (Michigan), highlights the same emphasis:

> The booming commands of a drill sergeant echo through the halls of Camp Sauble, where beginning this week convicts will trade a year or more in prison for 90 days of hard labor, intense physical training and intimidation . . .
>
> Pool tables, television sets and other means of recreation have been moved out of Camp Sauble . . .
>
> The 156 inmates will have little time for recreation. The inmates will rise at 5 a.m. and prepare for an inspection of bunks and uniforms. After breakfast they will fall in for a workout before heading out in eight-man crews for about seven hours of unpaid work in and around Mason County.
>
> Military protocol will be strictly enforced. Inmates will be required to stand at attention when in the presence of an instructor. They will receive demerits for violations.
>
> (Associated Press, 1988)

One corollary of the theme in this second state was that some constituents concluded that prisons should emulate the regime. The

Prosecuting Attorneys Association of Michigan, a lobbying group, released a policy paper in which they proclaimed:

> We are deeply concerned that many young offenders view the prison experience as 'easy' . . . Earlier this year the Department of Corrections reported that 40% of convicts eligible to repay their debt to society with only 90 days in SAI chose instead to spend 2 ½ years in a state penitentiary. Doubtless, this disturbing trend is partly due to an attitude reflected in the report, which says, 'SAI is tough, as well it ought to be, as it is an alternative to prison'.
>
> Why should 'tough' only be found in 'alternatives to prison?' . . . Legislative action should be taken now to remove the layers of prison freedoms and amenities . . . Only under an in-prison routine of demanding exertion and actively earned privileges can the prison system move toward more limited periods of rehabilitative punishment instead of long, facility-glutting periods of room, board and idleness at taxpayer expense.
>
> (Prosecuting Attorneys, 1989)

In New York, shock incarceration began on a somewhat inauspicious note. The first group of young volunteer prisoners changed their minds after arriving at the camp. According to one account:

> Nine inmates at the state's first military-style prison camp have been sent to Attica and Elmira state prisons after they injured two guards while protesting against the harsh and regimental treatment.
>
> The six-month programs of militaristic treatment, modeled after some prisons in the South, started Sept. 10 . . . two inmates became upset Monday morning about the rigorous training method imposed at the camp. One of the inmates struck a guard and a fight ensued between two guards and the two inmates . . . After the fight broke up, six more inmates started to complain about the harsh treatment.
>
> 'They didn't like the shock training.'
>
> (New York Times, September 20 1987)

New York offered shock incarceration to 225 youthful offenders on an 'experimental basis'. But only a year later, with no research returns available, that population was doubled. A 1989 legislative package provided for an increase to 1,200 shock incarceration beds. It also raised eligibility age standards and made the program available to women. Similar expansions occurred on the national scene. Starting with Georgia in 1983, the number of states using shock incarceration totaled 11 in 1989, 14 in 1990, and 17 in 1991, with five camps due to open in 1992. A federal omnibus crime bill called for federal camps. Urban detention centers showed parallel interest. In covering the mayoral election campaign in New York in 1989, the *New York Times* reported that 'the program of choice for most candidates appears to be establishing work camps, which combine boot-camp discipline with drug treatment and education. The idea allows candidates to talk tough, but convey a hint of sensitivity as well' (Barbanel, 1989). The winning candidate, Mayor David Dinkins, proclaimed that 'this is one marine who believes in the value of discipline and respect . . . and I'm going to make sure that some young guys get a whole lot of it early on'. An opponent wanted it understood by the press that the offenders under his administration would lead more spartan lives: 'They would do calisthenics at 5:30 in the morning,' he said, 'mow the grass in 95-degree heat or shovel snow at 15 degrees below zero'. New York's retired mayor, Edward Koch, joined by claiming intellectual primacy. He observed that 'the Governor and I have been way out in front on this a long time ago. The others are wrapping themselves in the boot camp. I would like to give them the boot' (Barbanel, 1989).

INGREDIENTS OF A WINNING RECIPE

Shock incarceration is instructive because it is an example of a politically acceptable alternative selected out of a range of truly intermediate punishments (Morris and Tonry, 1990). Georgia, which had opened the first shock camp with its prison population at 15,500 in 1983, expected to imprison 39,257 people by 1993. An emergency Early Release Program had to be instituted, but a governor was elected in 1990 after promising to rescind it. The Georgia Corrections Department pointed out that 'It soon became apparent that early releases could only be discontinued if another program was initiated that would keep the backlog from becoming prohibitively high and would provide a publicly acceptable degree of punishment for offenders' (Flowers, Carr and Ruback, 1991).

The result of this discovery was a more intense interest in shock incarceration. This interest sparked a number of variations on the theme, which had varying political advantages. One part of the Georgia package was the original garden-variety SAI model, in which young, non-previously-imprisoned offenders undergo a thirty-day military-type experience as a condition of probation. The candidates are selected by judges from a pool of convicted offenders who are eligible for up to five-years' imprisonment. This eligibility requirement was dropped along the way, making boot camps a potential corrective for draconian sentences. An obscure amendment that thus gives judges the power to de-escalate punishments makes it possible for the legislature to advertise its punitiveness with impunity. On the other hand, it also makes it possible for judges to become punitive (and risk-aversive) by placing would-be probationers in boot camps. There is evidence, however, that this is not what judges have done in Georgia. They have used their discretion – as judges use any discretion – to 'tailor-make' dispositions, gratefully escaping from silly, politically-motivated determinacy. Flowers, Carr and Ruback (1991) touchingly report that 'the judges like SAI because it gives them "a sense of being respected" in their sentencing practices' (p. 47).

The second part of the package are honest-to-God boot camps, introduced in July 1991 for Georgia prison inmates. In this program the selection of campers is made by the parole board, which also exercises considerable discretion. Age of eligibility for the candidates has become higher (thirty years), and sentence length is generous (ten years), but there is a provision that inmates with draconian sentences must be nonviolent offenders.

Boot-camp graduates are placed on intensive parole, with a proviso for mandatory treatment participation. The concept of mandating involvement has become an important theme in the nineties, and it is politically critical. Making treatment available to offenders sounds mushy and uninviting, but mandating treatment sounds hard-nosed and responsive to the problem (drug-related crime) that is of concern. Moreover, the no-nonsense premise is appealing: irresponsible people are not entitled to be bums – or drug-addicted bums – at public expense; society is entitled to create incentives that make chronic irresponsibility unattractive. The ethos is non-libertarian, but constraints are designed to produce volitional behavior in the long run, when the non-irresponsible person is ready for it. Discipline produces self-discipline, and the freedom to exercise it. Freedom for irresponsible people produces irresponsibility.

The parole board's selection of boot camp candidates provides early release without early release. The parole board does not 'release' inmates, but changes the modality of their confinement. It also does not 're-sentence' inmates because sentences hypothetically remain in force. The systems remains *de jure* as it is, but *de facto* has diluted determinacy and has defused advertised punitiveness through selective de-escalated punishment.

The third part of the Georgia package are SAI/Probation boot camps, to which offenders are sentenced as a condition of probation. These camps provide an intermediate punishment for nonrecidivistic drug offenders and for probation violators. The latter would otherwise end up in prison, but prisons can also expect the former (ultimately), unless War on Drug fever is somehow appeased. Provisions made in Georgia for returning unsuccessful graduates to boot camps make the prison a truly last resort.

FUNCTIONAL EQUIVALENTS OF SIBERIA

The fourth component of the Georgia package is called Intensive Discipline Units, and is reserved for inmates who have trouble adjusting to prisons. The IDU program is Georgia's version of the 'maxi-maxi' prison that has been sweeping the country. 'A 'maxi-maxi' prison is a segregation facility. Viewed in administrative terms, it is a consolidated, centralized way of dealing with prison infractors. The process is one that takes prisoners out of disciplinary segregation cells in various prisons, and collects them in a composite punishment setting.

One argument for the maxi-maxi system is economy. If one has a segregation prison it makes it possible to build modular prisons that have dormitories and no segregation cells. IDU is also a specialized setting in which staffing is less rich – therefore less expensive – because inmates stay in cells. The defenders of the concept also contend that the IDU makes conventional prisons more relaxed because these prisons no longer take turns accommodating recalcitrant offenders.

One risk in creating IDU-equivalents is that a less-than-attractive aspect of imprisonment – punitive isolation or segregation – acquires a visibility it does not normally enjoy. Citizens who have no preconception of prison read about men who are 'kept isolated, shackled at the waist and wrists when allowed out of their 6-by–10-foot cells and made to spend their daily recreation hour in newly built cages' (*New York Times*, February 20 1991). They also read about these men fed tepid food in cells, and about the solidity of doors needed to protect the guards from the excrement thrown by the helplessly angry inmates. Public relations officials do not enjoy such accounts, nor do they like the civil libertarian critics they invite.

There is no cause for concern. A typical editorial notes in passing, 'critics have argued that locking an inmate in solitary for 23 hours a day is no way to encourage social skills', and rejoins, 'That is not a self-evident proposition. It might just be that a period of quiet and lonely reflection on crime as a way of life is just what many of these men need. Moreover, it shouldn't be forgotten that those inmates . . . had already demonstrated quite clearly that their personalities were more than a little disordered. Many of them are simply sociopaths' (Albany *Times Union*, June 7 1991).

One feature of this argument is that, though the dichotomy that it proposes between sociopaths and decent people is sharp, the conclusion it draws is not retributive. 'Discomfort', the argument goes, 'can be a regenerative experience. It can be particularly regenerative for irresponsible hedonists who have done what they like at other people's expense, and who must learn to control themselves'. The 'pain-is-good-for-them' formula converts a setting self-consciously designed to lack rehabilitative programs into a rehabilitative enterprise. The view seems to be, 'we can rehabilitate you the hard way or the easy way'. Hard cases are not hopeless, but invite more austere regenerative approaches. The tough-but-optimistic stance is typified by a provision of the Georgia and New York maxi-maxi settings which lets inmates earn their way out of segregation before their sentences expire, by behaving in exemplary ways.

Elsewhere, as I pointed out, there is stress on compulsory participation in regenerative experiences. Prisoners across the US and in Canada are told that they must work or partake of educational experiences, and that the length of their stay hinges on their compliance. Drug-related offenders are assigned to drug programs under similar injunctions. Boot-camp residents return from forced marches to non-optional-but-benevolent group therapy experiences. The composite experience is an incoherent composite. A similar incoherence characterizes the Mutt-and-Jeff interplay of determinacy and diversion. Draconian sentences – embodying 'retributionist' policy – feed offenders into a system that must shorten sentences because it cannot afford to retain the offenders for the full length of their terms.

In other words, logically inconsistent perspectives prop one another up through their cohabitation. We wage a retributive war featuring wholesale arrests and hefty determinate sentences. This congests prisons and strains budgets to an impossible degree. It also punishes many non-violent addicts, who return to prison to be punished again. We discover that this is too expensive and senseless, so we opt for a hard-nosed version of rehabilitation tied to reductions of time. We reintroduce discretion in a system in which we have forced judges to sentence offenders in harshly punitive ways. The machine becomes a strange assortment of pulleys and rubber bands, serendipitously arrived at.

THE PUBLIC AND PRISON POLICY

In 1958, S. I. Hayakawa wrote an article called 'Why the Edsel laid an egg'. The Edsel was a large, ungainly, chromium-plated car that consumers refused to buy. The auto maker (Ford) said they had based the car's design on consumer survey responses. Ford blamed the recession for the debacle, but Hayakawa (1962) wrote, 'one wonders . . . whether the recession itself is not partly to be blamed on carmakers who, in defiance of all rational consumer interests – economy, convenience, safety, maneuverability and beauty – have been trying to foist on the *majority* of the public fabulously overpriced jukeboxes such as only people of deprived origins or the neurotic would want to buy and only the prosperous can afford to maintain' (p. 171). Hayakawa pointed to a 'doctrine' which 'implies that if you hold the key to people's irrationality, you can exploit and diddle them to your heart's content and be loved for it' (p. 172).

Hayakawa talked of irrationality because he suspected Ford of succumbing to the 'phallic symbolism school' of design, while others reported that Ford's consultants had used more pedestrian approaches. They had surveyed female consumers and male consumers, and pooled the desiderata of the groups into a hermaphrodite composite.

Whichever version one accepts, the lesson applies to the way in which prison policy has been formulated in recent times. The problem does not lie with the desire to enact a consumerist criminology (Wilkins, 1985), but with the way consumers are stereotyped in efforts to assess what they want. Legislators segmentalize publics into predefined interest groups (as did Ford with Edsel customers), to which they seek to appeal. They are also attuned to the voices of constituents who approach legislatures with strongly worded predilections and sentiments. Such constituents are often self-selected, but are hard to ignore.

The fear of crime issue illustrates the problem of assessing citizen input. The issue is volatile (disappears in wartime or becomes displaced by economic concerns), but politicians know that it is risky to discriminate between long-term and short-term public apprehensions. Fear, in particular, can never be adjudged illegitimate. If the threat is crime, something must be done about the perception of crime. Prison construction responds to fear of crime, even if prisons remain after fear is dissipated.

Fear can be admittedly less than rational. Constituents who demand more prisons tend to live in small towns or suburbs. They fear – but rarely experience – crime. Urban citizens live with crime. But they are less apt to demand wars on crime, because they know better from experience. The drug dealers arrested in last night's raid stand replaced; gang wars (in which innocents are shot) are fought to name successors. Urban citizens know a great deal, but can be superseded by the sentiments of suburbanites.

Citizens in general are also better at detailing needs than at spelling out solid, long-term solutions to needs. This does not mean that politicians are better at this. Nor does it mean that one needs experts to do the job. But one has to find some way to translate raw sentiments into solutions responsive to problems the public perceives. One must find a way to explore public opinion in depth, and consider the consequences and ramifications of solutions that are proposed. This includes expectations or hypotheses to be tested through evaluations of outcomes.

The process needs nurturing and patience. People with strong needs (such as fears) start by ranting and raving, or doing magical, top-of-the-head thinking: 'We need lots of executions'. Why? 'It would teach criminals a lesson.' After they are dead? 'We must think of the victims.' How do victims benefit from execution? 'They feel vindicated.'

All right, a first try. Are there other things we could do? 'We could make the offender help the victim.' (Great. The Anglo-Saxons did it centuries ago. They called it bot.) 'You have the offender indentured to the victim, who'd get everything he earns.' Until they are even? 'That's not enough. You could add punitive compensation, like they do in civil trials.'

That sort of thinking (or something like it) is called planning. Legislators and administrators do it, but worry needlessly about what the public might accept – the public being presumably vindictive and bloodthirsty. (The public may in turn feel inhibited by inaction they expect from officials.) Stereotypes inhibit thinking and rational policy development. They can also provide officials with the wrong premises for things that they do. In New York, for example, officials appropriately stress work for inmates. Why should a prison system do this? An official is quoted by the press: ' "I've been troubled for years by the public perception that inmates sit around all day watching TV or pumping iron while the average guy is trying hard to make ends meet", said Thomas A. Coughlin III, Commissioner of the State Department of Correctional Services. "We fully intend to change the perception of inmates getting a free ride" ' (Sullivan, 1992). As it happens, the public perception exists, but work should not be provided to ease suspicions about the good life prisoners lead, nor should boot camps be set up for their 'filmability'. Such rationales keep the public from centering on sound justifications for policy development.

EXPLORING PUBLIC OPINION

In a recent analysis of opinion poll data, the Edna McConnell Clark Foundation (1992) concluded that 'when asked, citizens reveal that they are afraid of crime. But perhaps unexpectedly, they show that they are not nearly as punitive as some of their leaders think' (p. 23). Citizens (unlike academic criminologists) favor rehabilitation as the 'primary purpose of criminal sanctions'; citizens also like a system which gives judges 'the flexibility to make the punishment fit the crime'. If we give citizens a forced choice between prison and probation, they more often than not opt for imprisoning the offender. They do this because they (correctly) equate probation with freedom. But if provided with a choice of intermediate options, most survey respondents favor their use with non-violent offenders, assuming that rules are enforced and back-up options exist.

These conceptions are better highlighted when citizen opinions are explored in more detail. Two studies by the Clark Foundation (Doble and Klein, 1989; Doble, Immerwahr and Richardson, 1991) transcend explorations that relied on spontaneous focus groups. In these studies, a philosopher was used to feed information to citizens and supervise discussion of issues. Groups were filmed to ensure their dispassionateness and fairness. Pre/post-instrumented surveys asked the groups to suggest sanctions for contrasting types of offenders.

The most salient finding is that the citizens studied hold coherent positions which become articulated as information is assimilated. The citizens favor imprisonment because it is closer than nothing (i.e. probation) to what they want. They basically want offenders to be changed. They are unhappy with prisons in this regard – even as they opt for sending people to prison – because prisons don't do the job. For the public, rehabilitation means that you move from undisciplined hedonism to self-control and disciplined work. One sends people to a setting that provides the ingredients of such change, which are (1) work, (2) supervision, (3) discipline, and (4) a modality of self-improvement, such as education, vocational training, and therapy for offenders with problems (e.g. addicts or sex offenders).

The public does not want to see an offender imprisoned unless the offender is violent and poses a threat. It wants to see offenders engage in serious toil under strict supervision, repaying victims if possible. It wants to see effective rehabilitative experiences imposed on offenders in a disciplined setting. It wants serious sanctions to back up less serious sanctions for recalcitrant offenders.

How does this view differ from stereotypes of public opinion on which legislation is based? For one, the public is not retributionist and desirous of 'throwing the book' at offenders, nor is it dividing into 'soft' and 'hard-nosed' factions. The public thinks that prisons are appropriate repositories for hardened violent criminals. But prisons are not envisioned as places of storage and idleness. For the public, prisons belong on a continuum of stern rehabilitative efforts that range from enforced labor in the community through institutional programs that require disciplined activity. The public likes work-as-restitution sentences. The public also favors shock incarceration, but does not see boot camps as safety valves of congested prisons.

The public is not in the pain-amelioration or time-shortening business; it does not care that prisons may be crowded. The public, however, is not in the discomfort-inflicting business, as the 'filmability' school implies; it does not want boot camps because they are 'rough'. The public's view of corrections is consistent, and quite remarkably consistent over time. It is a secular version of the puritan ethic that envisages redeemability through works, and reassimilation into the community. It is an optimistic, anyone-can-make-it, never-give-up stance which observers (including de Tocqueville) have dubbed the American ethic.

The public thinks that offenders can progress in the same way others should progress – through hard work, discipline and unflagging dedication. It thinks of sentences as incentives to change, and punishment as an indentured change experience. Deprivation is seen as the means to an end. Citizens see intermediate punishments as appropriately targeted change modalities for offenders who do not need to be sequestered to protect the community.

Lawmakers who respond to this view of dispositions would not ask themselves 'how much deprivation does the offender deserve?' but 'how substantial is the compulsory rehabilitative experience we are entitled to exact, given the nature of the offender's transgression?'.

Fortuitously, a politically attractive development in American corrections – the shock incarceration setting – encapsulates desiderata that

citizens want highlighted in correctional experiences. Other intermediate punishments would similarly have popular appeal to the
extent that they feature similar combinations of work, discipline and
self-improvement options. Within the prison, trends such as compulsory drug treatment, work and educational involvement are congruent
with this consumer sentiment.

The public opposes draconian sentences for non-violent recidivists,
but sees prison as a back-up for offenders who do not comply with
intermediate punishment regimes. And the public does not like the
use of unadulterated probation on a large scale. Citizens endorse
determinate sentencing as a concept (equivalent dispositions for comparable offenders for the sake of fairness) but like flexibility to permit
judges to individualize dispositions.

If citizens had their way, the pendulum of correctional policy would
swing to rehabilitation and individual deterrence as a goal. Dispo-
sitional options would proliferate, drug offenders would be treated,
and the prison population and probation would shrink. Communities
would see offenders in substantial numbers in public service projects,
and short-term confinement settings, including half-way houses, work-
release institutions and prison camps, would be opened in large
numbers.

Academic observers could argue that the system the public seems
to want lacks coherence. Determinacy-cum-flexibility sentencing looks
hopelessly eclectic. The range of punishments citizens suggest seems,
in turn, too tough or lenient. The public's assumptions about refor-
mation (liberation through discipline) sound utopian and ethically
suspect.

But if we end up doing what the public wants, we acquire a goal –
rehabilitation – against which we can test outcomes. We free legislators
from having to prove how tough they are. We permit offenders to be
constructively engaged and let them contribute to their communities.
We experiment with new modalities of treatment. And we ease prison
crowding and rethink the use of prisons.

Such gains are worthy, but if we do what citizens want, we also
reduce their alienation: by conveying to people that we are listening
to them, we persuade them to take more of an interest in improving
the system. And if we get the public to plan, to offer more than top-
of-the-head (or gut) reactions, we get democracy-in-action, which is
responsive-but-rational government. Such government may be imperfect, but is better than a government of elite planners or one of
politics as usual.

References

Associated Press (1988), 'In Michigan: shock versus prison', *News Release*, March 12.

Barbanel, J. (1989), 'Accord in mayoral race: boot camps for criminals', *New York Times*, July 19.

Clendinen, D. (1985), 'Crowded prisons in South lead to tests for other punishments', *New York Times*, December 18.

Doble, J., Immerwahr, S., and Richardson, A. (1991), *Punishing Criminals: The People of Delaware Consider the Options*, Edna McConnell Clark Foundation, New York.

Doble, J., and Klein, J. (1989), *Punishing Criminals: The Public's View. An Alabama Survey*, Edna McConnell Clark Foundation, New York.

Edna McConnell Clark Foundation (1990), *Americans Behind Bars*, Edna McConnell Clark Foundation, New York.

Flanagan, T. J., Brennan, P. G., and Cohen, D. (1991), *Attitudes of New York Legislators Toward Crime and Criminal Justice: A Report of the State Legislator Survey, 1991*, University of Albany, Albany, NY.

Flowers, G. T., Carr, T. S., and Ruback, R. B. (1991), *Special Alternative Incarceration: Evaluation*, Georgia Department of Corrections, Atlanta, GA.

Hayakawa, S. I. (1962), 'Why the Edsel laid an egg: motivational research versus the reality principle', in Hayakawa, S. I. (ed.), *The Use and Misuse of Language*, Fawcett World Library, New York.

Morris, N. (1974), *The Future of Imprisonment*, The University of Chicago Press, Chicago.

Morris, N. and Tonry, M. (1990), *Between Prison and Probation: Intermediate Punishments in a Rational Sentencing System*, Oxford University Press, Oxford.

New York Times, September 20 1987.

New York Times, February 20 1991.

President's Commission on Law Enforcement and Administration of Justice (1967), *The Challenge of Crime in a Free Society*, US Government Printing Office, Washington, DC.

Prosecuting Attorneys Association of Michigan (1989), *Comprehensive Corrections Policies in Michigan*, East Lansing, Michigan, September 18.

Rothman, D. J. (1980), *Conscience and Convenience: The Asylum and its Alternatives in Progressive America*, Little, Brown and Company, Boston.

Sullivan, R. (1992), 'In New York, state inmates work or else', *New York Times*, January 27.

Times Union (Albany, NY) (1991), 'Editorial: why not a maxi-maxi?', June 7.

US Department of Justice Operation (1992), *"Weed and Seed": Reclaiming America's Neighborhoods*, US Government Printing Office, Washington, DC.

Wilkins, L. T. (1985), *Consumerist Criminology*, Heinemann, London.

7

Just prisons and responsible prisoners

ROD MORGAN

BACKGROUND

The administration of prisons in Britain in the last two decades has been repeatedly subject to major disruptions. In Scotland, England and Wales there was a litany of prison disorders throughout the 1970s and 1980s (Home Office, 1984, Appendix A; Scraton, Sim and Skidmore, 1991). In England controlling staff has been as much a problem as controlling prisoners: industrial disputes have been perennial.[1] There have been a series of inquiries into these events, several of them involving high profile reviews of prisons policy, most recently by Lord Justice Woolf in his report on the events at Strangeways Prison in Manchester and other prisons in April 1990 (Woolf, 1991). As a result of these reviews major changes in the organisation of prisons and the decision-making procedures of those responsible for their management have been introduced. In England and Wales, for example, a prisons inspectorate, independent of the Prison Department, was created in 1981; significant innovations were made in management information systems during the 1980s; 'Fresh Start', an initiative involving the phasing out of routine staff overtime working, was implemented between 1987–90; the regional and headquarters organisation of prisons was radically changed in 1990; a new prisoner complaints system was introduced in 1991; and prisoner disciplinary proceedings were fundamentally altered in 1992.[2]

The administrative disruptions are to continue. In early 1992 the first prison under privatised management opened, another opened in 1993 and the Home Secretary has stated his intention to contract out many more institutions (including Strangeways Prison) in the near future. In 1993 – in both Scotland, England and Wales – the prison services are becoming government agencies separated from the ministries of which they have been a part. In England, a Chief Executive without previous experience of prisons has been appointed to head the new agency, plans are in hand to appoint an independent Prison Ombudsman, pilot projects to introduce prisoner contracts are under way and the Minister has referred to the possibility of introducing market-type mechanisms so that prisons compete with each other for the provision of different services. He has suggested that trusts, on the lines adopted in the educational and health services, might be set up.

Given the welter of change that has occurred and is planned to happen, it is vital that the Prison Service develop a coherent vision of its purpose and practice and the values that should underpin that practice. It has repeatedly been observed, most recently in the Woolf Report, that in the wake of the loss of confidence in rehabilitative purposes which took place in the 1970s, the prison services lost their way and, perhaps as a corollary, suffered from a lack of leadership and a lowering of morale that was integrally related to the disturbances of the 1970s and 1980s. The Woolf Report has suggested a conceptual framework within which prison managers might operate and has outlined a series of operational signposts to guide future practice. Those proposals – in the formulation of which I was closely involved – have been widely discussed and I have elaborated on their meaning elsewhere (Morgan, 1992a, pp. 713–23; Morgan, 1992d, pp. 231–50). However, in considering the future for prisons policy we should begin with an even more fundamental question – namely, the relationship between prison and sentencing objectives. Of course, the two are not the same. There is a clear distinction between the purposes informing sentencing decisions and the purposes which guide those who administer particular sentences, including imprisonment. But the two are likely to be related and ideally should be grounded on the same principles (Wood, 1991). How consistent are or might they now be? It is worth reflecting that in 1966 the *Royal Commission on the Penal System* was abandoned because its members could not get beyond first base. After two years of deliberations six of the eighteen members resigned, convinced that no set of general principles for the foundation of penal policy could be found – the only Royal Commission in English constitutional history never to produce a report. As a result the Advisory Council on the Penal System was established to deal on a piecemeal and pragmatic basis with whatever issues the Minister might refer to it. Were a Royal Commission reappointed today to address the same questions would the outcome be similarly inconclusive? I think not. Let me summarise briefly how I think things now stand.

SENTENCING OBJECTIVES AND THE AIMS OF IMPRISONMENT

Cursory scrutiny of the various Government papers which preceded the English Criminal Justice Act 1991 suggests there is substantial agreement on the following points.

First, that the prison is not the best place in which to encourage citizens to act responsibly and live in a law-abiding manner.

> Imprisonment restricts offenders' liberty, but it also reduces their responsibility; they are not required to face up to what they have done and to the effect on their victim or to make recompense to the victim or the public. If offenders are not imprisoned, they are more likely to be able to pay compensation to their victims and to make some reparation to the community . . . their liberty can be restricted without putting them behind prison walls. Moreover, if they are removed in prison from the responsibilities, problems and temptations of everyday life, they are less likely to acquire the self-discipline and self-reliance which will prevent re-offending in future.
>
> (Home Office, 1988, para 1.1)

Further: 'It is better that people . . . exercise self-control than have controls imposed upon them . . . however much prison staff try to inject a positive purpose into the regime . . . prison is a society which requires virtually no sense of personal responsibility for prisoners' (Home Office, 1990, para 2.6–2.7).

Second, it is doubted whether sentences of imprisonment always serve generally to deter. What the Home Office refers to as the 'attrition rate' – the low likelihood that those responsible for a given category of offence will be caught, convicted and sentenced to a particular punishment – has upset Beccaria's 'four certainties' of offence, detection, conviction and punishment.[3] As a consequence, though:

> Deterrence is a principle with much immediate appeal. Most law-abiding citizens understand the reasons why some behaviour is made a criminal offence, and would be deterred by the shame of a criminal conviction or the possibility of a severe penalty. There are doubtless some criminals who carefully calculate the possible gains and risks. But much crime is committed on impulse, given the opportunity presented by an open window, etc. . . . It is unrealistic to construct sentencing arrangements on the assumption that most offenders will weigh up the possibilities in advance and base their conduct on rational calculation.
>
> (Home Office, 1990, para 2.8)

Third, it is now fully accepted that although, arguably, prison administrators should do what they can to encourage the rehabilitative process, imprisonment should never be imposed in order to make offenders in some sense better. 'It was once believed that prison, properly used, could encourage a high proportion of offenders to start an honest life on their release. Nobody now regards imprisonment, in itself, as an effective means of reform for most prisoners' (Home Office, 1990, para 2.7). Indeed, it is emphatically asserted that if improvement is the sentencer's objective then the prison is not the place to which the offender should be dispatched. 'Offenders are not given sentences of imprisonment by the courts for the purpose of ensuring their rehabilitation. Most offenders are usually likely to have a better prospect of reform is they stay in the community' (Home Office, 1991, para 1.28).

Fourth, denunciation, retribution and/or public protection is what is held to justify a sentence of imprisonment, not reform or narrowly conceived deterrence.

> The Government's proposals therefore emphasise the objectives which sentencing is most likely to meet successfully. The first objective for all sentences is denunciation of and retribution for the crime; depending on the offence and the offender, the sentence may also aim to achieve public protection, reparation and reform of the offender, preferably in the community.
>
> (Home Office, 1991, para 2.9)

This proposition is enshrined in the Criminal Justice Act 1991 s.1. Custodial sentences should not be passed except where the offence is 'so serious that only such a sentence can be justified' or 'where the offence is a violent or sexual offence, that only such a sentence would be adequate to protect the public from serious harm'.

What follows from this? I suggest that quite apart from the pressure for parsimony in the use of imprisonment, there is now a reasonable basis for arguing that Paterson's dictum – offenders are sent to prison *as* a punishment not *for* punishment (Ruck, 1951) – is no longer merely penological rhetoric but has at long last come into its own as a statement of what prisons are used for. Paterson's dictum now represents a new realism in sentencing theory. What remains to be seen is whether sentencing practice is equally realistic. The Criminal Justice Act 1991 offers little guidance as to how seriously different offences should be regarded and what the balance should be between proportionate denunciation and protection of the public from future harm. Moreover it has to be conceded that the sentencing objective of denunciation will continue to give scope for the doctrine of less eligibility, with all the consequences that may have for depressing standards of provision in prisons relative to those in the community (Webb and Webb, 1932; Garland, 1990). Nevertheless, there is nothing in sentencing theory which leads offenders to be imprisoned which now justifies making conditions in prisons more restrictive or punitive than the fact of loss of liberty necessarily means they are. It follows that what Roy King and I rather inelegantly described back in 1980 as the principle of *normalisation* should now be applied to prison conditions. Namely, that as resources allow, and consistent with the constraints of secure custody, the same general standards that govern the life of offenders in the community should be held to apply to offenders in prison (King and Morgan, 1980, p. 37). This is the backcloth for thinking about the characteristics of the just prison.

JUST PRISONS

It is a commonplace that although prisons represent the ultimate creation of the criminal justice system they are all too often separated from the other institutions that make up that system, and their operation is frequently ill-informed by the principles which allegedly underpin the system. In 1978, at a time when the English and Welsh courts had adopted a virtual 'hands off' policy in relation to the judicial review of conditions and decision-making in prisons, Zellick baldly asserted that 'the law stops at the prison gates' (Zellick, 1978). In 1980 the analysis of prison management and prison officers' working conditions undertaken by the May Committee revealed a relatively isolated and inward-looking service. In 1991 Lord Justice Woolf reached the same conclusion, though he found that the fault was not peculiar to the prison service: it was characteristic of criminal justice agencies generally. Indeed, it was precisely because the criminal justice system lacked the qualities of a system that Woolf recommended the formation of a criminal justice consultative council in order to promote the development of agreed and common purposes (Woolf Report, 1991, paras. 10.157–10.158.C). What should just prisons comprise?

Many commentators are likely to find Woolf's discussion of the 'tasks of the Prison Service' disappointing. Woolf does not review – as the Scottish Prison Service document *Opportunity and Responsibility* did (Scottish Prison Service, 1990) – the origins and nature of the critique of treatment and training (King and Morgan, 1980), nor did he set

out the case for the so-called 'justice' approach or consider the argu-
ments for and against 'humane containment' (Bottoms, 1990).
Indeed, contrary to critical received wisdom Woolf finds merit in the
May Committee's statement of 'positive custody' and, with two caveats,
endorses the Prison Service's current 'Statement of Purpose' (Woolf
Report, 1991, paras. 10.1–10.44). The caveats are critical, however.
They would, if adopted, significantly shift the balance of prison
priorities.

Woolf came to the conclusion that the disorders he was investigating
had no single cause nor would they be prevented by a simple remedy.
Their origins, he argued, lay in an imbalance between three elements
in the running of prisons – *security, control* and *justice*. It is the third of
these three elements that Woolf can fairly claim to have added to the
official agenda for prison reform. What does he mean by it?

Woolf's use of the term justice is more complex than that of *security*
or *control.* By *security* he means any prison service's primary obligation
to keep in custody those persons committed into custody by the courts.
By *control* he means order within prison though, as I have argued
elsewhere (Morgan, 1992a, p. 235), order would have been the better
term since order is not necessarily the product of control: quite the
contrary. By *justice,* however, Woolf means several things which, ideally,
might have been separated by employing several terms. It is worth
considering these different meanings in turn. First, Woolf appears to
suggest that we can infer what a just prison should comprise from an
analysis of sentencers' objectives. Without spelling out what the proper
uses of imprisonment are or should be in the manner that I have
attempted above, Woolf takes it for granted that sentencers intend by
a sentence of imprisonment that an offender should lose his liberty,
but no more than that. He assumes that it is no part of sentencers'
purpose that prisoners should be subject to punitive conditions
beyond those consistent with the fact of custody. Moreover, Woolf
argues that when sentencing offenders to prison sentencers do so
guided by the Statement of Purpose formulated by the Prison Service.
They expect prisoners to be held in conditions consistent with the
Statement of Purpose – that is, looked after 'with humanity' and
helped to 'lead law abiding and useful lives in custody and after
release'. This seems a reasonable proposition even if it is a legal
fiction: it is very doubtful that most sentencers are aware of the Prison
Service's Statement of Purpose, let alone the statutory Prison Rules
from which, ultimately, it is derived. Thus Woolf is able to conclude:

If the Prison Service contains that prisoner in conditions which are unhumane or degrading, or which are otherwise wholly inappropriate, then a punishment of imprisonment which was justly imposed, will result in injustice. It is no doubt for this reason, as well as because any other approach would offend the values of our society, that the Statement of Purpose acknowledges that it is the Prison Service's duty to look after prisoners with humanity. If it fulfils this duty, the Prison Service is partly achieving what the Court must be taken to have intended when it passed a sentence of imprisonment. This must be that, while the prisoner should be subject to the stigma of imprisonment and should be confined in a prison, the prisoner is not to be subjected to inhumane of degrading treatment.

(Woolf report, 1991, para. 10.19)

It follows that prison regimes inconsistent with either the 'new realism' in sentencing theory or the Prison Service's own Statement of Purpose will render the experience of imprisonment unjust.

Of course this begs a number of questions, not least as to what is to count as 'inhumanity' and what constitutes degrading treatment. As the recent interchange between the Council of Europe Committee for the Prevention of Torture and Inhuman and Degrading Treatment or Punishment (CPT) and the British Government (arising out of the CPT's inspection and condemnation of prison conditions in England and Wales) illustrates, there is a good deal of room for disagreement on this issue (Council of Europe, 1991a, 1991b). Woolf adopts a relatively pragmatic approach to the question, both analytically and substantively. For Woolf the proof of the pudding is largely in the eating. If the experience of imprisonment results in 'a deterioration in the ability of the prisoner to operate effectively and lawfully within society', or if prisoners are treated 'in a way which is likely to leave them in an embittered and disaffected state on their release' then the overall purpose of the criminal justice system – the prevention of crime – will have been prejudiced (Woolf report, 1991, paras. 14.8–14.9). It follows that to the extent that injustice in the form of unfairness and lack of due process within prisons leads prisoners to feel embittered and disaffected then this form of injustice must also be eradicated. Woolf's case is consequentialist:

we are not seeking to achieve more comfortable surroundings, greater luxuries or increased privileges for prisoners for their own sakes. To think of that would be fundamentally to misconceive the argument. We are seeking to ensure that a prisoner serves his sentence in a way which is consistent with the purpose behind the court's decision to take away

his liberty and his freedom of movement, while ensuring he is treated
with humanity and justice.

(Woolf Report, 1991, para. 14.5)

In the Woolf Report, therefore, justice as fairness within prisons is
pressed into consequentialist service partly to support a neo-rehabilitative position. Woolf categorically disavows the proposition that prisons should be used in order that prisoners be rehabilitated. But just
prisons, it is implicitly suggested, are more likely to provide the positive
environment within which rehabilitative efforts may successfully be
made. Moreover, according to the Woolf analysis justice in prisons is
a pre-condition for order in prisons, and it can reasonably be concluded that disorderly and insecure prisons will provide an arid terrain
in which positive custody leading to law-abiding and useful lives on
release will be unlikely to flourish.

My own view is that Woolf's argument that improved conditions
should not be provided for prisoners 'for their own sake' is mistaken
on two counts. First, though prisons might be more orderly were
prisoner conditions improved, and if prisons were more orderly then
more prisoners might take more positive advantage of whatever facilities were offered – this would be to throw into reverse what I have
elsewhere referred to as a prison disorder amplification spiral
(Morgan, 1992a, pp. 233–4) – there is nevertheless no evidence that
prisons would become more effective in the sense that fewer prisoners
would be re-convicted on release (Brody, 1976). It follows that justice
delivered on the basis of this fragile premise is unlikely to rest secure.
Second, as already argued, no matter what realism and parsimony in
the use of custody comes to inform sentencing policy, we should not
underestimate the continued potency of 'less eligibility' thinking. To
the extent that this view continues to be held it follows that if improved
prison conditions cannot easily or safely be justified on the utilitarian
grounds of crime reduction, then Woolf's rationale will not hold and
some other justification must be sought.

An alternative justification is readily available. It has been eloquently
advanced by Richardson (1985). It rests on prisoners' peculiar vulnerability. It is precisely because prisoners are shut away, lacking legal,
moral and political credibility, held at the mercy of and dependent
on the goodwill of the state, that a case can be made out for vesting
special positive rights in prisoners against the authorities. In my judgement this is the route through which improved prison conditions and
procedural justice, consistent with the new realism in sentencing

policy, will best be made a practical reality. Further, it is on this foundation that I think Woolf's welcome recommendations, *inter alia*, for: active regimes; community prisons; the establishment of an independent element in the prisoner grievance system; statutory limitations to crowding; and, in the long run, the establishment of legally enforceable prison standards, are likely best to be achieved.

RESPONSIBLE PRISONERS

What I have described as the new realism in sentencing – the proportionate denunciation of offenders for the seriousness of their offences – emphasises their culpability. This has led to new emphasis on the responsibility of prisoners. What does it mean to say prisoners are responsible and should be treated accordingly?

First, it means carrying over the logic of criminal culpability into the management of the prison. Prisoners are responsible for their criminal acts, that is the essence of guilt, and the onus of addressing and changing criminal behaviour rests fundamentally on prisoners themselves. They are the key actors. If they do not wish to change it will not happen. The staff do not have available to them expertise enabling them to impose change and they do not have the right to make the attempt by coercive means. The new realism in sentencing requires, to use Morris's terminology, a shift from the paradigm of 'coerced cures' to one of 'facilitated changes' (Morris, 1974). This should be the new neo-rehabilitative ideal. We are not justified in sending offenders to prison in order to make them better because the evidence suggests that is a fruitless mission. Moreover, the prison may be the least promising environment imaginable in which attempts at positive change might be undertaken. It may be true, as the Home Office has argued, that 'however much prison staff try to inject a positive purpose into the regime . . . prison is a society which requires virtually no sense of personal responsibility from prisoners' (Home Office, 1991a, p. 31). Nevertheless, prisons can be more or less conducive places for prisoners to try to help themselves. Prison managers are able to maximise the degree to which prisoners are able to retain responsibility for their lives on a day-to-day basis and in the long term, and, given that prisons are part of the criminal justice system, the overall purpose of which is to reduce crime, then arguably it is the duty of the Prison Service to create an environment for prisoners which minimises the likelihood that they will be harmed by the experience and maximises their opportunity to benefit.

It may be argued that the latter proposition represents a departure on my part from the doctrine of humane containment which, with Roy King, I commended to the May Committee in 1980 (King and Morgan, 1980). This is not the place in which to engage in self-indulgent justification and I will not attempt it. I would merely point out that nothing in our exposition of humane containment suggested that we did not value prisoners' opportunities to make positive use of their time in custody. What we argued was that merely intoning the phrase 'positive custody' would prove to be mere rhetoric and I believe, in retrospect, that that explains the dismal fate of the May formula. The dignity of prisoners, and prisoners' will to face up to their position, is more likely to be promoted by establishing basic rights, due process procedures and minimum standards. What I will concede is that if the framework for the achievement of basic standards and due process procedures is in place then, to the extent that staff are motivated by it, there may be a case for adding to the Prison Rules some statement to the effect that it is part of the duty of the Prison Service to assist prisoners to become law-abiding members of society on their release.

This does not mean the prison authorities pretending to know what is best for prisoners or taking decisions on their behalf in an authoritarian or paternalistic manner. But it may mean providing prisoners with programmes – such as those of a cognitive behavioural nature currently being introduced in England for sex offenders and the CHANGE programme in Scotland discussed by Morran and Wilson in this volume ch. 13 – in which they can opt to participate, with trained staff engaging with them to address their offending behaviour. In the case of sex offenders, particularly those judged to be at greatest risk of re-offending, this involves getting prisoners to acknowledge their criminal acts, facing up to the consequences of their behaviour for their victims, and learning to recognise the warning signs that they are once again moving into a situation where further offences may occur, in the hope that they will develop the will to take evasive action (Prison Service, 1991).

The concept of the responsible prisoner also involves recognising that the commission of an offence does not imply irresponsibility in all aspects of life, nor dies it wipe out the social responsibilities which prisoners retain. Prisoners remain fathers or sons, mothers or daughters, partners or friends, householders or tenants, employers or employees, debtors or creditors, neighbours and so on. Moreover, the fact that the vast majority of prisoners in prison at any one time are serving medium- or long-term sentences should not blind us to the fact that most persons who experience custody, over 80 per cent if all legal categories of prisoners are taken into account, are in prison for relatively short periods, weeks or months rather than years. Custody is for most prisoners a relatively brief interlude and their responsibilities and duties in the community continue. Thus the concept of the responsible prisoner involves recognising that though prisoners may have been criminally irresponsible they nevertheless retain social responsibilities, which on release we expect them once again to exercise. The prison should be organised in such a manner as to assist prisoners to meet those social responsibilities, and to foster, to the extent that security permits, prisoners' community ties rather than undermine them.

OPERATIONALISING JUST PRISONS FOR RESPONSIBLE PRISONERS

What should all this mean in day to day practice? It needs fundamental reassessment of prisons policy at two levels – strategic planning at a national level and operational practice locally. Some fundamental sea changes in policy direction are required. Since the Woolf Report was published I have written a number of pieces taking up the policy issues which need to be addressed (Morgan, 1992a, 1992b; Morgan and Maguire, 1994). Let me illustrate briefly. Despite the philosophical demise of the 'treatment and training' paradigm in the 1970s it was not operationally replaced by a new philosophy. Without elevating his approach to the status of a rival philosophy, Woolf has through various proposals – agreements or contracts between prisoners and governors about programmes, facilities and routines, the idea of the community prison, due process requirements for all decisions affecting the quality of prisoner lives, and so on – cut away the assumptions implicit in the 'treatment and training' paradigm which has dominated prisons policy in England since the 1940s. The paradigm was implicitly inequitable, paternalistic at best, authoritarian at worst, and unjust. It was inequitable because those prisoners deemed untrainable or untreatable – the unconvicted and unsentenced who were legally ineligible, the short-term sentenced not in prison long enough to make the effort worthwhile and the recidivist recalcitrants deemed to be beyond redemption – were excluded from the noble enterprise and consigned to the local prisons, which, as the pressures on the system increased, were allowed to become overcrowded, ill-resourced, insanitary sinks (Morgan, 1994). It was the training prison sector on which the energy and resources in the system were concentrated. The system was paternalistic because within this framework the Prison Service, strongly supported by the courts, insisted that prisoners enjoyed 'privileges' not 'rights' and because decisions were made for the prisoners on the basis of criteria that were seldom revealed. They were assessed, allocated and dispatched to the institutions that prison staff decided best met their training needs. The system was unjust because the quality of life provided for prisoners bore little or no relation to any legal theory informing the use of imprisonment, decision making lacked due process, the untried, subject to the presumption of innocence, suffered the most oppressive conditions, and because, as overcrowding got worse, executive release mechanisms were introduced thereby creating a progressively more complicated disjunction between sentences passed and sentenced served. All the remnants of this legacy – I say remnants because there *have* been piecemeal reforms over the past decade – need to be dismantled centrally and systematically.

Ideally, most prisoners – certainly the untried and unconvicted, the short- and medium-term sentenced, and a high proportion of the long-sentenced also – should be held in multi-functional community prisons or clusters of more or less specialised institutions that are physically proximate to their prisoners' community ties. This is the community prison principle spelt out by Woolf – geographically local institutions with walls that are much more permeable than they have been in the past, so that prisoners can maintain better contact with their families and those agencies with whom they dealt prior to incarceration and with whom they will have to deal again on release. It also means prisoners' relatively free access to telephones, relatively unrestricted use of the mails, more frequent visits in better conditions and enhanced home leave entitlements.

The development of community prisons is not, as the Government has rightly pointed out (Home Office, 1991, ch. 5; Morgan, 1992a, pp. 239–41), without its difficulties, and it will take time to shift the traditional emphasis on relatively specialised institutions organised nationally or regionally towards more comprehensive establishments clustered locally. As the data emerging from the recent prisoner surveys in both England and Scotland are revealing (see Wozniak in this volume, ch. 8; Walmesley, Howard and White, 1992), the regional distribution of prison places poorly matches prisoners' community ties and the concept of the community prison does involve the reconciliation of competing operational objectives – maximising the efficient use of resources and the prevention of overcrowding with the maximisation of the locality principle. But the task of reconciling the potentially irreconcilable is not a task best done by prison headquarters staff by fiat on behalf of both local management and prisoners. Nor in England will the problem best be solved within the administrative framework most recently devised by the Prison Service.

First, prisoners need to be involved in decision making. This is a central message of the Woolf Report and Lord Justice Woolf set an example on this question by the manner in which he conducted his inquiry (see Morgan, 1992a). For example, if the choice is between prisoners remaining in establishments relatively close to their homes, with all the advantages that that involves for visits, but having to live in relatively overcrowded conditions with few educational or recreational programmes and facilities, as opposed to being transferred to a relatively well-resourced establishment some distance from home then, wherever possible, prisoners and their families should make the decision. That would be a practical exercise in prisoner responsibility.

There are obvious difficulties with seeing prisoners as consumers of prison services and given the impoverishment of many prison facilities, it would be insulting as well as dangerous to advocate that prisoners be asked to make consumer choices in a market place monopolistically controlled by powerful providers offering limited and untenable choices. That is where enforceable minimum standards and prisoner rights have a part to play. Nevertheless, there is no reason why, given minimum standards, prisoners should not be given more opportunity to choose how they spend their time in prison and where they spend it. A 'facilitative' prison environment would involve prison staff professionally advising prisoners on their options and assisting them to make positive choices. These should be the watchwords of the future prison service – a well-informed 'professional staff' advising 'responsible prisoners' within a more open system which sets a high priority on maintaining prisoners' community ties and equipping them for release; providing prisoners, as the Scottish Service puts it, with 'opportunities' to match their 'responsibilities' (Scottish Prison Service, 1990).

The corollary of involving prisoners in decision making must be the devolution of management decision making within the Prison Service. Woolf had a good deal to say about the leadership of the Prison Service and its relationships with ministers as well as the organisation, role, recruitment and training of prison officers. But he avoided the topic of the administrative structure of the Service principally because in the middle of his inquiry, the Minister implemented a reorganisation of headquarters and the regional offices, which had been agreed prior to the events at Strangeways. Lord Justice Woolf left well alone. He had no practical basis for commenting on the new organisation and the structure that it replaced had already been abandoned. That topic must now be addressed, however.

I would pose two questions. Is it defensible that of the 34,200 staff employed by the Prison Service, no fewer than 2,550 of them, including many of the more highly paid, are employed in Headquarters and other national offices (HM Prison Service, 1991, p. 44)? Though the number of headquarters staff has grown less sharply in recent years compared to out-stations staff, the number has nevertheless continued to grow, as has the number of aspirational documents headquarters staff produce. Further, more and more complex monitoring exercises are being set in place whereby the centre measures what the institutions deliver (see Morgan, 1992c, pp. 8–9). The organisation of the Prison Service still has the feel of a centralised apparatus in which policy is made at headquarters and delivered top-down to the troops, as opposed to having a top tier of management whose function it is to support out-stations as they make the decisions devolved to them. If prisoners are to be given greater responsibility then it makes sense that decisions over the allocation of resources and the setting of priorities be made as close to the units in which they live as possible. There is a case for substantially reducing the share of resources eaten up by headquarters and it is no doubt partly with this outcome in mind that the Government has recruited someone with a background in the commercial world to head up the new Prison Service agency.[4]

Second, does the new area organisation of the English Prison Service – fifteen areas, each comprising an almost identical number of establishments headed by an Area Manager – fit well with the aim of developing the concept of the community prison? I think not. The areas comprise more or less geographically grouped establishments. But this is not invariably the case and the groupings are not self-sufficient in the sense that they include a range of institutions capable of accommodating – either now or, if re-categorised, in the future – all the prisoners generated by the area in which they lie. In this case the areas and their managers will be incapable of genuinely taking devolved responsibility for the creation of the range of community facilities from which their prisoners might choose. Further, none of the Prison Service areas are coterminous with the administrative areas in which other criminal justice agency services are sub-divided

– the courts, the police, the Crown Prosecution Service, probation, and so on. Indeed, the September 1990 Prison Service reorganisation represents precisely those insular centralised and bureaucratic features of which critics complain. All that needs changing. The regional organisation of prisons must comprise groupings of institutions capable of being self-sufficient so that regional managers can assist governors to rethink their priorities and allocation of resources.

THE FUTURE

The Government claims largely to be committed to implementing the Woolf package (Home Office, 1991). A number of Woolf's recommendations – enhancing the ease with which prisoners can maintain contact with their families and reform of the prison disciplinary system – have already been implemented. Others are to be implemented. Further developments, particularly privatisation and the shift to agency status, with which there is not space to deal here (see Morgan, 1992b), may signal important changes in the capacity of the system to deliver defensible regime standards. Over all of this welter of change, however, the spectre of prison overcrowding continues to hang. The latest prison population projections predict a prison population for the year 2000 of 57,500, some 10,000 more than at present (Home Office, 1992). The massive prison building programme of the 1980s is coming to an end. If the prison population rises as predicted – and most commentators anticipate that the short-term impact of the implementation of the Criminal Justice Act 1991 will mean a fairly substantial increase – and if no new prison-building programme is instituted then there will still be considerable system overcrowding at the end of the century. It is worth noting that Woolf prepared his report at a time when the prison population and projections suggested that system overcrowding would shortly be a thing of the past. Had he known what we know today then I believe he might have emphasised more the need for a population reductivist agenda.

Without embarking on the complex analysis needed to penetrate the arguments as to whether the Prison Service has suffered from a shortage or a plenitude of resources (including staff) with which to deliver a better quality of life for prisoners, it is clear that improved prison conditions are most likely to be achieved if the prison population can be held constant or reduced. The Prison Service then has room to manoeuvre. Everything hinges, therefore, on the Government having the will effectively to control the size of the prison population

for, as has repeatedly been pointed out, the prison population is
politically determined. At the time of writing (January 1993) the signs
are good. The prison population is below 44,000 and the prison
system has a capacity of over 46,000. For the first time in half a
century there is no system overcrowding, though most of the local
prisons remain overcrowded. It is by no means certain that this improving situation will be sustained, however.

It is in this context that I think it may be helpful to conceptualise
the modes of governance for prison systems, in order, pragmatically,
to see in which direction we should move in England and Wales.
Prison systems can be predominantly 'administrative' or 'statutory'. In
an administrative system the legal framework within which prison
managers work is only lightly sketched. Managers are granted a large
measure of discretion. In a statutory system, by contrast, the legal
requirements are detailed. The law may specify the types of institutions
in which prisoners with given characteristics must be held, may prescribe the conditions to which they will be subject, may circumscribe
their eligibility for an entitlement to visits, home leave, parole,
remission, etc. This is the constitutional dimension. But constitutional
frameworks do not determine operational practice. The latter we can
characterise as 'autonomous' or 'interventionist'. In the former prison
managers are quietly left to get on with the job, sometimes to the
extent that the requirements of the law are effectively ignored. In
the latter either politicians or the courts adopt a hands-on involvement
in prison administration. We can portray these possibilities on two
dimensions.

	MODE OF GOVERNANCE	
	Administrative	Statutory
OPERATIONAL PRACTICE		
Autonomous	Discretionary	Legalistic
Interventionist	Political	Judicial

This framework suggests four outcomes which I have labelled 'discretionary', 'legalistic', 'political' and 'judicial'. In fact the possibilities
are more complex. We can envisage systems in which there is intervention by both politicians *and* the courts. Moreover, judicial
intervention may arise out of a written constitution or judicial review
and not because prison statutes are detailed and prescriptive. There
are no mechanical pairings. Relationships depend on the prevailing

political and legal cultures. Thus operational practice may change, as it did in the United States in the 1960s, without the basic constitutional parameters changing. In the United States, as a result of the civil rights movement, litigation for prisoners' rights was embarked on in the 1960s, the 'iron curtain drawn between the Constitution and the prisoners'[5] was pulled back, and, ever since, US prisons administration has been dominated by a degree of legal intervention unparalleled in any other jurisdiction (Morgan and Bronstein, 1985).

In England and Wales there have also been significant shifts, both in the constitutional framework and in operational practice. In the nineteenth century, when the prisons were administered largely by local government, the constitutional framework comprised detailed statutes and the central problem was held to be one of non-compliance by local administrators. In the twentieth century the prison statutes have only lightly sketched what administrators are required to deliver. Managers enjoy enormous discretion and for the first half of this century they found that condition to be favourable. Lionel Fox took pride in the fact that the Prison Commissioners had been left in peace for fifty years by both the politicians and the courts, and had thereby been able to achieve enormous changes in the way prisons were run (Fox, 1952, p. 3). I doubt that senior prison administrators would write in that vein today. For the past forty years the English Prison Service has been fettered by an absence of law rather than the reverse. There has been nothing to protect administrators from the overcrowding which has been the bane of the system since the 1950s. Further, there has been a creeping form of interventionism, from the courts as a result of judicial review and, less well publicised, from ministers. Privatisation and the current Home Secretary's plans to throw some of the administrative cards in the air again are a manifestation of this tendency.

I do not believe there is a blueprint for achieving decent prison conditions and proper accountability for prisons administration in all jurisdictions for all time. Solutions must be tailored to the prevailing circumstances. In England and Wales, however, I believe there is now an overwhelming case for a more prescriptive statutory framework and a more active judicial hand on the tiller. Such a constitutional framework would fit well with the management accountability mechanisms which Woolf proposed and which the Prison Service is already developing.

Notes

1 Industrial disputes led to the setting up of the Inquiry in 1979 under Sir John May, May Committee (1990).
2 The last follows a recommendation in the Woolf Report and is heralded in the Government's White Paper response to the Woolf Report, Home Office (1991).
3 See Beccaria (1770); for estimates for the rate of attrition see Home Office (1991a), p. 31.
4 Mr Derek Lewis, Chief Executive-designate, was appointed in December 1992; his previous career was in television management.
5 *Woolf* v. *McDonnell* 418 US 539 (1974).

References

Beccaria, C. (1770), *An Essay on Crimes and Punishments*, Newbery, London.

Bottoms, A. E. (1990), 'The aims of imprisonment', in *Justice, Guilt and Forgiveness in the Penal System*, Edinburgh University Centre for Theology and Public Issues, Paper No. 18, Edinburgh.

Brody, S. (1976), *The Effectiveness of Sentencing*, Home Office Research Study No. 35, HMSO, London.

Council of Europe (1991a), *Report to the United Kingdom Government on the Visit to the United Kingdom carried out by the European Committee for the Prevention of Torture and Inhuman or Degrading Treatment or Punishment from July 29 1990 to August 10 1990*, Council of Europe, Strasbourg.

Council of Europe (1991b), *Response of the United Kingdom Government to the Report of the European Committee*, Council of Europe, Strasbourg.

Fox, L. W. (1952), *The English Prison and Borstal Systems*, Routledge & Kegan Paul, London.

Garland, D. (1990), *Punishment and Modern Society*, Oxford University Press, Oxford.

H. M. Prison Service (1991), *Report on the Work of the Prison Service, April 1990-March 1991*, Home Office, London.

Home Office (1984), *Managing the Long Term Prison Population: The Report of the Control Preview Committee*, HMSO, London.

Home Office (1988), *Punishment, Custody and the Community*, Cm 434, HMSO, London.

Home Office (1990), *Crime, Justice and Protecting the Public*, Cm 965, HMSO, London.

Home Office (1991a), *A Digest of Information on the Criminal Justice System*, HMSO, London.

Home Office (1991b), *Custody, Care and Justice: The Way Ahead for the Prison Service in England and Wales*, Cm 1647, HMSO, London.

Home Office (1992), *Projections of Long Term Trends in the Prison Population to 2000*, Statistical Bulletin 10/92, Home Office, London.

King, R., and Morgan, R. (1980), *The Future of the Prison System*, Gower, Aldershot.

May Committee (1990), *Report of the Committee of Inquiry into the United Kingdom Prison Disturbances*, Cmnd 7673, HMSO, London.

Morgan, R. (1994), 'An awkward anomaly: remand prisoners', in Player, E. and Jenkins, M. (eds.), *Prisons After Woolf*, Routledge, London.

Morgan, R. (1992a), 'Following Woolf: the prospects for prisons policy', *Journal of Law and Society*, XIX, pp. 231–50.

Morgan, R. (1992b), 'Prisons accountability revisited', unpublished paper presented at an Institute of Advanced Legal Studies Workshop, University of London, June.

Morgan, R. (1992c), 'Regime monitoring with prisoners', *Prison Report*, Spring, pp. 8–9.

Morgan, R. (1992d), 'Woolf: in retrospect and prospect', *Modern Law Review*, 54, pp. 713–23.

Morgan, R. and Bronstein, A. (1985), 'Prisoners and the courts: the US experience', in Maguire, M., Vagg, J. and Morgan, R. (eds.), *Accountability and Prisons: Opening Up a Closed World*, Tavistock, London.

Morgan, R., and Maguire, M. (1994), 'Accountability and justice in the English Prison System', in Stenning, P. (ed.), *Accountability for Criminal Justice*, Toronto Press, Toronto.

Morris, N. (1974), *The Future of Imprisonment*, University of Chicago Press, Chicago.

Prison Service (1991), *Treatment Programmes for Sex Offenders in Custody: A Strategy*, Directorate of Inmate Programmes, London.

Richardson, G. (1985), 'The case for prisoners' rights', in Maguire, M., Vagg, J. and Morgan, R. (eds.), *Accountability and Prisons: Opening Up a Closed World*, Tavistock, London.

Ruck, S. K. (ed.) (1951), *Paterson on Prisons: Being the Collected Papers of Sir Alexander Paterson*, Muller, London.

Scottish Prison Service (1990), *Opportunity and Responsibility: Developing New Approaches to the Management of the Long-Term Prison System in Scotland*, Scottish Prison Service, Edinburgh.

Scraton, P., Sim, J. and Skidmore, J. (1991), *Prisons Under Protest*, Open University Press, Milton Keynes.

Walmesley, R., Howard, L. and White, S. (1992), *The National Prison Survey Main Findings*, Home Office Research Study No. 128, HMSO, London.

Webb, S., and Webb, B. (1932), *English Prisons Under Local Government*, Longman Green, London.

Wood, C. (1991), *The End of Punishment: Christian Perspectives on the Crisis in Criminal Justice*, St. Andrews Press, Edinburgh.

Woolf Report (1991), *Prison Disturbances April 1990*, Report of an Inquiry by the Rt. Hon. Lord Justice Woolf (Parts I and II) and His Honour Judge Stephen Tumim (Part II), Cm 1456, HMSO, London.

Zellick, G. (1978), 'The case for prisoners' rights', in Freeman, J. C. (ed.), *Prisons Past and Future*, Heinemann, London.

8

A customer-focused prison service in Scotland

ED WOZNIAK

It is clear that the old objectives of 'treatment and training' are out-moded. A new approach is required which will recognise the mutual responsibilities of the prisoner and the prison authorities and ensure that the long term prisoner is encouraged to address his offending behaviour and offered an appropriate range of opportunities to use his time in prison responsibly for personal development.
(Malcolm Rifkind, Foreword, Scottish Prison Service (1990), *Opportunity and Responsibility*, p. 4)

INTRODUCTION

The use of the term 'customer' when applied to prisoners evokes considerable negative feeling: notions of the customer always being right, or the customer being able to take his or her 'custom' elsewhere in the event of dissatisfaction clearly cause problems for many and not just those working outside the Scottish Prison Service (SPS).

Such opposition to the use of the term is, however, not simply anecdotal: it is a view which is widely held in the SPS amongst both uniformed and senior staff. In two recent studies only 24 per cent of middle grade prison managers thought the idea of a 'customer' focus relevant to the SPS, and although marginally more encouraging, only 37 per cent of uniform staff think the idea of the prisoner as a customer appropriate.

These findings aside, what do I understand the SPS to mean by the term customer? *A customer is quite simply any person who relies upon me for the provision of a service.* Given this definition, it is possible to my mind for the organisation to develop a heightened awareness of who they serve and, therefore, how the organisation's internal services should be designed. In addition, I would go further and argue that for the term customer to have real meaning in creating and developing a customer culture it is necessary to introduce the notion of 'quality' as an integral part of customer service. How does one define quality? Haywood-Farmer (1990, p. 3) usefully defines quality as 'services that meet customer preferences and expectations', an approach which importantly emphasises the need for a match between any customer's perceptions of service and the actual service which is delivered. In this scheme, the role of research as the appropriate method for discovering what customer expectations actually are is apparent.

The remainder of this paper is devoted to understanding the processes that have been developed in the SPS in recent years to improve not only the management of establishments but also the level of service, conditions and facilities experienced at the ground level by prisoners and, for that matter, by staff. Uniquely, this process of change in the SPS is grounded in a system of strategic planning that involves staff and prisoners as central players in the planning process. More specifically, the paper is about the part that research has played and can play in such a process by informing and supporting change, by assisting in the 'prioritising' of competing claims for change and, at times, by driving the process of change forward.

THE PROCESS OF CHANGE

The change process that is currently underway in Scottish prisons is driven forward on two related fronts: one management focused, the other philosophical. The management initiative is centred around the application of the principles of strategic planning to the management of all Scottish establishments. Strategic planning is recognised in the Scottish Prison Service (SPS) as the managerial process of achieving the organisation's objectives by developing and maintaining a balance between resources and the changing demands of the environment. It is a system that makes no real attempt at understanding the use and purpose of imprisonment in society; it is a business system designed to provide better and more effective organisational management. Yet, despite this reservation, it is an approach to change which makes substantial efforts to involve two groups, both with a significant involvement in the business of imprisonment, but who have previously been largely ignored, namely staff and prisoners. The ultimate goal of the strategic planning initiative in Scottish prisons is the delivery of a quality service through a more directed and focused management system.

While the strategic planning initiative has been conducted without fuss and publicity, the same cannot be said for the philosophical shifts that have been occurring in Scotland. The recasting of a new philosophical approach to imprisonment can be demonstrated in a public discourse that began in Scotland in March 1988 with the appearance of the policy document *Custody and Care*, continued with *Assessment and Control* (1988) and *The Business Plan* (1989), and most recently, in 1990, was followed by *Opportunity and Responsibility*.

Central to these documents is a developing thread that seeks to revise the traditional notions of imprisonment by redefining the position of both staff and prisoners. The most recent of these documents, *Opportunity and Responsibility*, reviews the purpose of imprisonment and outlines a philosophy which:

(i) presents a view of the prisoner as a person who is responsible for his actions;
(ii) argues for the need to provide a range of opportunities to permit prisoners to accept responsibility for their behaviour and enable change and personal development;
(iii) acknowledges the resource value of staff;
(iv) recognises the critical role staff will have to play in implementing the new strategy; and
(v) acknowledges the need for staff training and development in this enhanced role.

The links between the notion of the responsible prisoner, the responsible prison service and the notion of a customer-focused prison service are to my mind fundamental and have not been fully developed or discussed in the SPS. It is this failure to articulate these links which has much to do with the inability of the SPS to enter into the vision of prisoners – and staff for that matter – as customers and to tailor services to meet their expectations.

The SPS, in *Opportunity and Responsibility*, recognises that the process of change is dynamic, far from complete and that the precise direction of future change is not as yet fully developed or certain. Indeed, it acknowledges that at certain points there may be a need for realignment, a need to revise and alter the direction of particular initiatives in the light of experience or comment. A striking example of this need to rethink strategy is the significant reworking, in the light of critical comment, of many of the ideas which were contained in *Assessment and Control* in the later document *Opportunity and Responsibility*. As a consequence, each new document is expressly seen as building on and developing the ideas of earlier initiatives and to use a phrase from *Opportunity and Responsibility*, simply takes the process 'some further steps along the road of change' (SPS, 1990, p. 7).

Even a cursory reading of the various SPS policy documents reveals the enormity of both the scale of the changes proposed by the SPS and the task which management faces in effecting and managing the change process. However, the ultimate success of the change programme will depend greatly on how staff and prisoners respond to the challenge. The programme has already created expectations of change among staff and prisoners; positive change is anticipated and the time-scale of expectation is that improvements will be delivered quickly. In a world of limited finance and resources this will not always be possible. Indeed, while certain services and facilities can be improved within a short time-scale others will, understandably, take a considerable period of time to implement fully. Faced with such competition for scarce resources a system of prioritisation is essential; research has come to play a critical part in assisting in the prioritisation process by discovering 'customer' views and relaying them to management teams so that, where possible, the aspirations of staff and prisoners can be incorporated into future plans.

Consultation at all levels is seen as essential to the process of change in the SPS and one of the major mechanisms by which consultation has taken place has been the development of research directed specifically at gauging 'customer' views about service delivery and organisational performance. Over the past two or three years some dozen or so surveys have been conducted as a means of 'consulting' customers – staff and prisoners – to establish their views on a range of topics (see References).

In the main part of this paper I want to consider some of the principal findings arising from the most significant of these pieces of work – *The Prison Survey* (1992). My purpose in doing this is twofold: first, to illustrate where we in the SPS stand, at present, in relation to progressing change, and secondly to show fully the nature and extent of the consultation programme.

THE PRISON SURVEY

To the survey itself: what was it about; who was involved; what did it cover, and, importantly, how did it deliver and how does other work fit in to the on-going programme?

The prison survey offered all staff and all prisoners in Scotland the opportunity to comment on facilities, conditions, cleanliness, prisoners' access to family and friends, the direction of change, the quality of relationships, prisoners' preparation for release and so on. The survey was also intended to tap the atmosphere or 'feel' of the prisons and was, in many ways, an attempt to examine and measure the degree of customer satisfaction or otherwise with service delivery in individual establishments and regimes.

Staff and prisoner views were sought through questionnaires administered on an establishment-by-establishment basis. A questionnaire was preferred to individual face-to-face interviews because it was hoped that wide 'ownership' could be developed if all 'customers' of the SPS were given the chance to participate in the exercise. In the distribution process an attempt was made to speak to all staff and prisoners before administering the questionnaire. This was meant to serve as a form of explanation as to what the survey was about, to explain its part in the planning process and to allay possible anxieties, especially in relation to how the findings would be used.

Each establishment's senior management team received the report on their 'customers' no later than one month from the time the survey was completed. Subsequently, all staff and prisoners received copies of the survey's main findings and the researchers returned to each establishment and made presentations to staff and prisoners detailing the findings.

MAIN FINDINGS FROM THE SURVEY

Having spent some time detailing the wider aspects of the change programme and the role of research in that process it would be useful to acquaint readers with the main findings of the work. In this way not only will the scope of the work become apparent but so perhaps also the enormity of the task of change within Scottish prisons. For ease of presentation the survey findings as they relate to staff and prisoners have been dealt with separately. However, as close inspection of the two sections will reveal, on a substantial number of items the views of staff and prisoners are in broad accord.

THE PRISONER FOCUS

Visits and access

The recurring and dominant theme that emerges from prisoners' responses is the request for closer and improved access to family. This request takes various forms among different groups of prisoners; a large number, mainly longer term prisoners, suggest family/conjugal visits, although there is also a demand for an increase in the volume of home leave and weekend leave, again principally among longer term prisoners. However, most prisoners think that family/conjugal visits are goals for the future. For the present, they feel that the current visiting facilities and arrangements are bad and in need of improvement. Uppermost in their concerns for improvement are facilities for children at visits: 76 per cent see these as poor at present. Given the geographical remoteness of a large number of Scottish prisons, hence the difficulty of access, it is not surprising that the length of visits is also criticised: 67 per cent express dissatisfaction with the present arrangements. Privacy at visits is also severely criticised: 78 per cent express dissatisfaction.

Relationships and atmosphere

The Scottish Prison Service experienced unprecedented prisoner unrest during much of the late 80s, including a series of violent prisoner rooftop demonstrations and several hostage-taking incidents. Against such a background a central part of the survey was directed at measuring the general atmosphere and quality of relationships in the prison. The large majority of prisoners, some 82 per cent, feel they have a good relationship with uniform staff. Indeed, 12 per cent describe it as 'very good'. A smaller number (73%), similar to the staff figure in fact, feel that the relationship with governor grades is reasonable. In respect of relationships with their fellow prisoners the percentage who feel they have a reasonable relationship increases to 95 per cent.

While fewer than one in five prisoners feel that they do not get on well with officers, more than a quarter feel that they do not get on well with governors: 27 per cent saying that they do not get on with those governors responsible for running their accommodation unit, and 28 per cent with other governors in the prison.

Interestingly, and perhaps surprisingly, 41 per cent of prisoners think that it is a good idea for prison officers and prisoners to have more contact with each other about personal problems. Reasons given in support were that staff have an understanding of the prison environment and any problem raised is likely to be solved more quickly. The primary reasons for not wanting more contact with staff are: poor relationships, lack of trust and not wanting to divulge personal details for fear that they will be more widely broadcast in the prison.

Physical safety
The often-made statement that prison is essentially an unsafe environment is in part supported by the survey results. Almost one in five prisoners (19%) worry about being assaulted by staff and a marginally higher number (20%) worry about the prospect of being assaulted by another prisoner. When asked if they have been assaulted during their present sentence 15 per cent say they have been assaulted by a member of staff (although this includes incidents of control and restraint), 13 per cent by another prisoner and a further 6 per cent by a group of prisoners.

Standards and services
While the majority of prisoners are content with the general standards of cleanliness in the prison, there is a sizable minority who think they are bad: 37 per cent feel the toilets and showers are dirty; 35 per cent think the clothes are dirty. Almost one half of those responding to the survey (47%) think the way in which the food is served is bad; 62 per cent feel the same way about the choice of menu and 64 per cent are critical about the quality of the food itself.

Overall, relationships with the specialists (psychologists, social workers and education staff) are seen as good (less than one in five express negative views). However, a large number (35%) say that they do not get on with medical officers. Relationships aside, the standard of care provided by the specialists in the prison is seen by prisoners as variable. Of particular concern is the level of dissatisfaction with medical (57%) and psychological (54%) care. The majority of prisoners are content with the standard of both social work and dental care but a large minority, almost one third (31%), feel that social work care/advice is bad and 35 per cent that dental care is bad. However, prisoners are more satisfied with the standard of education in the prison, with 27 per cent describing it as either fairly good or very good and a further 43 per cent as OK.

Changes
Prisoners were asked to identify what changes they would like to see introduced to the prison in which they are presently held and, also, to the Scottish Prison Service. In both of these areas the principal change that emerges is quite clear – better access to families. Specifically, the change that prisoners wish to see in prison is for better visiting arrangements: longer, more frequent and more private. In relation to changes in the Scottish Prison Service, the central thrust

is again for improved visiting arrangements inside, though a sizable number of prisoners (some 18%) feel that consideration should be given to the introduction of family/conjugal visits in prison and the extension of Home Leave schemes.

THE STAFF FOCUS

Facilities and conditions
At a very basic level, prison staff express considerable dissatisfaction with the conditions in which they are asked to work and the facilities which are provided to carry out their job. More than two-thirds (70%) express strong negative views about the lack of space and privacy provided in prisons to allow them to carry out aspects of their enhanced role (for example, writing reports on prisoners' progress and staff appraisal interviews). Broadly similar numbers express negative views about facilities for changing clothing before and after work (70%); eating facilities at the prison (66%), and showering (66%). Just over one-third feel that the standards of cleanliness are poor in the prison (hall, 32%; toilets and showers, 37%), and that the overall state of repair of the prison estate is poor (39%). Almost one-quarter (24%) express dissatisfaction with the quality of the food provided for prisoners.

Aspects of the prison officer's job
Eighty-one per cent of officers state that they enjoy their job (43% of whom most enjoy the security that the job guarantees). However, almost half (48%) of the uniformed staff feel that senior staff have little grasp of what goes on in their prison and, further emphasising a gulf between senior management and uniformed officers, 44 per cent feel that any suggestions they might make about the running of the prison will not be listened to by senior management grades. This seems to be part of a general discontent with communication arrangements in the Scottish Prison Service, particularly communication between headquarters and individual prisons.

Despite the many recently introduced developments in the Scottish Prison Service designed to involve staff and prisoners in closer liaison, just over half the staff (57%) say that prison officers are not equipped to handle prisoners' personal problems. However, staff responses to several other questions in the survey indicate that they *do* want to be able to deal with this area of work in the future, but feel that before assuming such a role they need to be given adequate time and training for the task.

An important part of any stressful job is the effect which it has on personal relationships and particularly one's family. When asked how they imagine their family feels about their job the major concern that staff raise is the problem of compulsory transfer between establishments. Although they clearly recognise that when they joined the service they signed on as a mobile grade, liable to transfer anywhere in Scotland, in practice only 43 per cent say that they would move willingly if transferred. The problems are obviously more acute for married staff, as they express greater concern than single staff. More than half (52%) of the respondents who had moved (45% of respondents had moved at least once during their career) had experienced severe problems (emotional, personal or financial) as a result of the move.

Current and future initiatives in the Scottish Prison Service
Encouragingly, staff appear to be broadly in favour of extending current initiatives and introducing many of the new ones currently being discussed in Scottish Prison Service documents such as *Opportunity and Responsibility* (1990). They particularly want to see the introduction of integral sanitation for all prisoners (96%); the introduction of the national sentence planning scheme for prisoners (92%); an extension of the personal officer scheme (79%); family visits for prisoners (74%), and increased Home Visits (63%). While some sixty-five per cent are in favour of introducing a prisons' ombudsman, by contrast, only 17 per cent of staff want to see a system of legal representation for prisoners at grievance procedures. Just over half (58%) want to see the introduction of electrical power sockets in cells. Those against such a proposal either fear for their personal safety from possible electrocution; worry about the cost to prisoners' families of purchasing TVs, etc.; or feel that it will lead to prisoners spending too much time 'behind their door' and detract from their participation in other programmes intended for their personal development.

Relationships in prison
A major aspect of the survey was to assess the quality of relationships in the prison. Overall, staff feel that relationships are good between themselves and prisoners (92%) and among officers (95%). By comparison, there is greater concern expressed about relationships with governors, although it must be said that this is relative – 75 per cent describe the relationship as good. A broadly similar number feel that

the relationships with specialists working in the prison setting are good: psychiatrists, 74 per cent; psychologists, 73 per cent and social workers, 72 per cent. Eighty-eight per cent think relationships with the medical officers are good.

Atmosphere
By any account the Scottish Prison Service experienced an unprecedented amount of prisoner unrest in the mid- and late 80s. An important part of the survey was to determine the atmosphere of prisons at the present time. Less than one in ten staff feel that there is any tension in the prison (8% in the prison generally; 11% in the halls and 9% in the workshops/workparties). Working in a prison environment presents many threats to an individual's personal and physical safety. This is borne out by the survey: 60 per cent of staff state that they have worried at some point about their physical safety at work and almost half (48%) report that they have been assaulted at some time during their career.

Response to current prison and to the Scottish Prison Service
Staff were asked a series of questions about their local management and headquarters management. In response to questions about the way the Scottish Prison Service as a whole is run, the single most important observation made by staff is the poor standard of communication at virtually all levels within the Service. As we saw earlier, staff are broadly in agreement with those initiatives being introduced (sentence planning, Home Leave, etc.) but feel they should be kept better informed and, where appropriate, consulted. Only 8 per cent of staff agree with the statement that everyone in the Scottish Prison Service is clear about where the Service is going in the next five years. Furthermore, only 17 per cent feel that as an organisation the Scottish Prison Service is good at communicating its new ideas to staff.

On a more positive note, 41 per cent feel that the Scottish Prison Service places a high value on staff participation; 45 per cent agree that the Scottish Prison Service places a great deal of emphasis on staff development and training, and 52 per cent agree that the Service is constantly committed to improving its performance. However, while marginally more than half the staff feel that the Service is committed to improving its performance, 80 per cent feel that there is a lot of criticism among staff about the way the Service is run and 36 per cent agree that conflict between staff and management is high.

Changes

Staff, like prisoners, were asked two questions about change: first, what changes they would like to see in the prison where they work and, secondly, what changes they would like to see in the Scottish Prison Service. In respect of change in the prison where they work the most frequent suggestion is for the introduction of integral sanitation. This is followed, but with less overall support, by suggestions for tightening regimes for prisoners and alterations in the management structure of the prison to reduce the number of governor grades.

As far as changes to the Scottish Prison Service are concerned staff want to see higher wages, better promotion prospects and the employment of more staff. Large numbers of staff want to see an end to compulsory transfers, better communication between the Prison Service headquarters and prisons and a reduction in the number of governor grades. Staff also want to see changes in the prison estate, with a definite move towards the introduction of smaller prisons and more semi-open and open prisons in the system.

CONCLUSIONS

The prison survey was the first systematic customer audit conducted by the SPS. It was conducted with the clear purpose of informing senior staff about their customer base and in this way giving a clearer understanding of the obstacles and resistance to change. Not surprisingly, this audit produced some unexpected findings: on the whole staff and prisoners rate relationships positively (and subsequent surveys have confirmed these findings); staff want to see those initiatives currently in preparation or under discussion implemented, and major initiatives such as Home Leave are supported by staff as well as prisoners. Prisoners wish to see the levels of contact with family improved; physical improvements such as integral sanitation are on the prisoners' agenda, but it is not *the* priority by a considerable margin.

However, the news from *The Prison Survey* is not all good: there are obvious pockets of concern. There are prisons where relations are not good; prisons where visiting arrangements are strongly criticised; prisons where food delivery, food quality and the variety of menu (each important concerns to the majority of the prisoner population) give cause for concern to staff and prisoner alike and are clearly in need of overhaul. Basic items such as clothing and footwear are seen by staff as well as prisoners as poor. It is vital to realise that while some of these areas may seem trivial and mundane when contrasted with the prisoner's loss of freedom, for many prisoners the true acid test of change in the SPS will be measured by improvements in areas such as food and laundry, and not in the implementation of major schemes such as Sentence Planning or Personal Officer Schemes.

If the prison survey was simply an isolated piece of research designed to 'test the water' then it would be of interest, but of little practical value. The fact that it is allied to the planning process, and that it has led to innovations such as a prisoner satisfaction index is indication that there is a commitment to creating change and developing a 'quality' organisation. The survey has provided a comprehensive and candid view of the task facing the SPS, and subsequent repeats of the survey are planned to plot the success of the process.

However, the prison survey can be no more than a 'snapshot' in time: relationships, atmosphere, standards and so on change with time, and sometimes rapidly. As well as answering questions the survey raises many more. A number of subsequent smaller scale pieces of work have been conducted to answer some of these questions but it must be recognised that many other areas need to be explored and, for particular groups of staff and prisoners, we need to develop a more sophisticated means of tapping into their needs and experiences. The value of the survey and other subsequent research to the planning process has been substantial, but to quote the former Director General of the English Prison Service: 'We must not make the mistake of talking loudly and proudly about fancy improvements while a prisoner sharing a cell with uncongenial companions has more fundamental grievances on his mind. We only deepen the frustration which makes him think he has to bring us to our senses' (Joe Pilling, Eve Saville Memorial Lecture, 1992).

References
Bruce, A., Phillips, R., and Dobash, R. P. (1992), *Physically Disabled Prisoners in Scotland*, Scottish Prison Service Occasional Paper No. 4, Scottish Prison Service, Edinburgh.
Cooke, D. (1992), *Mentally Disturbed Offenders*, Scottish Prison Service Occasional Paper No. 2, Scottish Prison Service, Edinburgh.
Cooper, D., and Wozniak, E. (1993), *Training for Freedom and Community Placements in the Scottish Prison System*, a research report commissioned by Her Majesty's Chief Inspector of Prisons for Scotland, Scottish Prison Service, Edinburgh.
Ferrant, E., and Wozniak, E. (1992), *A Survey of Employment Skills and Aspirations Among Young Offenders*, Central Research Unit Working Paper 4, Scottish Prison Service, Edinburgh.
Haywood-Farmer, J. (1990), 'A conceptual model of quality service,' in G. Clark (ed.), *Managing Service Quality*, IFS, London.

McAllister, D. and Wozniak, E. (1992), *Uniform in the Scottish Prison Service*, Central Research Unit Working Paper 1, Scottish Prison Service, Edinburgh.

McManus, J. (1992), *Mentally Disturbed Offenders*, Scottish Prison Service Occasional Paper No. 3, Scottish Prison Service, Edinburgh.

Power, K., Markova, I., and Rowlands, A. (1993), *HIV/AIDS in Scottish Prisons*, Scottish Prison Service Occasional Paper No. 1, Scottish Prison Service, Edinburgh.

Scottish Prison Service (1988), *Assessment and Control*, Scottish Prison Service, Edinburgh.

Scottish Prison Service (1988), *Custody and Care*, Scottish Prison Service, Edinburgh.

Scottish Prison Service (1989), *The Business Plan*, Scottish Prison Service, Edinburgh.

Scottish Prison Service (1990), *Opportunity and Responsibility: Developing New Approaches to the Management of the Long-Term Prison System in Scotland*, Scottish Prison Service, Edinburgh.

Shewan, D., Gemmell, M., and Davies, J. (1992), *Drug Use and Prison*, Scottish Prison Service Occasional Paper No. 5, Scottish Prison Service, Edinburgh.

Walker, D. (1990), *Customers First: A Strategy for Quality Service*, Gower, Aldershot.

Wozniak, E. (1992), *A Pilot Survey of Visitors' Views on Service in Three Scottish Establishments*, Central Research Unit Working Paper 3, Scottish Prison Service, Edinburgh.

Wozniak, E. (1992), *Plated Meals: An Examination of a Pilot Exercise in Perth Prison*, Central Research Unit Working Paper 2, Scottish Prison Service, Edinburgh.

Wozniak, E. (1992), *A Survey of Industrial Customers*, Central Research Unit Working Paper 5, Scottish Prison Service, Edinburgh.

Wozniak, E., and McAllister, D. (1992), *The Prison Survey*, Scottish Prison Service Occasional Paper No. 1, Edinburgh.

Wozniak, E., Cooper, D. and Whyte, D. (1992), *A Review of Regimes*, Scottish Prison Service Occasional Paper No. 6, Scottish Prison Service, Edinburgh.

PART FOUR

Non-custodial punishments

[9]

Changing aims of the English probation system

BILL McWILLIAMS

Forty years ago Erving Goffman (1952) published a paper under the title 'On cooling the mark out', with the sub-title 'some aspects of adaptation to failure'.[1] Goffman describes typical confidence tricks, or 'plays' in which the 'marks' or suckers are fleeced of their money:

> The typical play has three phases. The potential sucker is first spotted, and one member of the working team... arranges to make social contact with him. The confidence of the mark is won, and he is given an opportunity to invest his money in a gambling venture which he understands to have been fixed in his favour. The venture, of course, is fixed, but not in his favour. The mark is permitted to win some money and then persuaded to invest more. There is an 'accident' or 'mistake', and the mark loses his total investment. The operators then depart in a ceremony that is called the... sting. They leave the mark but take his money. The mark is expected to go on his way, a little wiser and a lot poorer. Sometimes, however, a mark is not quite prepared to accept his loss as a gain in experience and to say and do nothing... He may complain to the police or chase after the operators... From the operators' point of view, this kind of behaviour is bad for business... [and] in order to avoid this... an additional phase is sometimes added at the end of the play. It is called cooling the mark out. After the... [sting] has occurred, one of the operators stays with the mark and makes an effort to keep the anger of the mark within manageable and sensible proportions. The operator stays behind... in the capacity of what might be called a cooler and exercises on the mark the art of consolation. An attempt is made to define the situation for the mark in a way that makes it easy for him to accept the inevitable and quietly go home. The mark is given instruction in the art of taking a loss.

(pp. 451–2)

In a sting what the mark loses is not simply money but also face or a conception of self and thus, as Goffman says, 'the cooler has the job of handling persons who have been caught out on a limb – persons whose expectations and self-conceptions have been built up and then shattered' (p. 452). Of course, as Goffman points out, 'persons who participate in what is recognised as a confidence game are found in only a few social settings, but persons who have to be cooled out are found in many. Cooling the mark out is one theme in a very basic social story' (p. 453). In a society, whole classes of persons may be marks in this broader sense, and certainly some offenders, those from backgrounds of poverty, deprivation and inequality of opportunity, may be seen in this way. They have been stung by the societal operators and, if future trouble is to be avoided, need cooling out rather than punishing.[2]

Since the end of the nineteenth century it has been customary in the criminal justice system to cool some marks out, and arguably the probation service has existed for the purpose of pursuing that enterprise. The alterations which the 1991 Criminal Justice Act brings about and the rapid, concomitant changes which are taking place in the aims of the probation service mean that marks will no longer be cooled. This paper seeks to answer the question of why that should be so. The answer is complicated, but appears to be rooted, in large part, in changing conceptions of the ontology of the offender.

The desirability of cooling out at least some offender-marks began to be recognised in the nineteenth century. As fear of the mob began to recede it became possible to consider dealing with offenders in ways less savage than the traditional harsh punishments. The scope of capital punishment was substantially reduced, especially between the years 1827 to 1837 (D. A.Thomas, 1978) and, as one Member of Parliament, Sir Francis Powell (1897), remarked:

> the diminution of sentences had arisen not only from a change of public feeling and increase of sympathy and consideration for the weaker brethren, but also from a feeling that crime had diminished and that, therefore, there was not the same necessity for sharp punishment as a deterrent. There could be no doubt that judges and justices of the peace had diminished sentences because they believed that there was now greater order in society than formerly, and that property was in greater security.

> (p. 25)

First in the field as professional coolers were the police court missionaries and they were followed later by statutorily appointed probation officers. Probation was a process of cooling because, instead of being punished, selected marks were not sentenced, but rather conditionally released under benign supervision in order that they might be defined again as honest citizens.[3]

In a recent review, Howard Parker (1992) notes that 'change is routinely inflicted on the probation service rather than being created by the service's own ideology or agenda' (p. 59). Historically that is correct, but it has also been the case, at least until very recent times, that the service has played a part in defining the nature of offenders and hence the appropriate responses to them. Aims follow ontological understandings and thus the nature of probation has been defined by the perceived nature of the offenders deemed suitable for it, and this defining process has been carried out largely by members of the service. Traditionally, although it is not the case now, the government has been less inclined to define offenders, although there has often been an acceptance of service-generated definitions. Arguably, it is only in recent years with the collapse of the treatment ethic that the service has lost its powers of definition.

So far as the missionary officers were concerned, the ontology of the offender was simple: offenders were sinners whose offences, ultimately, were against God, and the probation officer's task was to aid in redemption and reconciliation. As one missionary officer put it, probation represented 'the grace of God combined with sensible treatment accorded by the State' (Holmes, 1913, p. 2). Goffman (1952) says of the cooling process that:

> For the mark, cooling represents a process of adjustment to an imposs-
> ible situation – a situation arising from having defined himself in a way
> which the social facts come to contradict. The mark must therefore be
> supplied with a new set of apologies for himself, a new framework in
> which to see himself and judge himself. A process of redefining the self
> along defensible lines must be instigated and carried along; since the
> mark himself is frequently in too weakened a condition to do this,
> the cooler must initially do it for him.

(p. 456)

Religious inspiration and conviction provided the missionary with ideal tools for the cooling task of redefining offenders; ultimately, the ambition was that they might be brought to a state of grace and hence totally transformed (McWilliams, 1983).

I have suggested in an earlier paper (McWilliams, 1987) that there have been three phases of understanding of the English probation system: a phase of 'special pleading' extending from roughly the 1870s to the 1930s and coinciding with the full flowering of the police court missionary endeavour; a phase of 'diagnosis' extending from the 1930s to the 1970s, and characterised by an attachment to a version of psychological science; and finally a phase of pragmatism extending from about 1970 to the mid–1980s, and characterised by a splitting of the unity of the service and the development of management thought. So far as the cooling of marks was concerned, the phase of diagnosis can be seen as a continuation of the phase of special pleading. At the same time there were important changes. The ontology of the offender was reconceptualised from that of an individual unique in the sight of God, a sinner in need of grace, to that of an individual with unique psycho-social traits who stood in need of accurate diagnosis, treatment and ultimately cure. The phase of diagnosis brought with it new understandings of the nature of the offender, and, concomitantly, of the aims of the probation service. It also brought new batteries of techniques to aid in the cooling process. Goffman (1952) noted a modern tendency to:

> shift certain losses of status from the category of those that reflect upon the loser to the category of those that do not. When persons lose their jobs, their courage, or their minds, we tend more and more to take a clinical or naturalistic view of the loss and a non-moral view of their failure. We want to define a person as something that is not destroyed by the destruction of one of their selves.

(p. 455)

This method of relocation of blame as part of the process of cooling offenders was greatly helped in the phase of diagnosis by the embracing of a determinist ontology; offenders were no longer to be seen as responsible for their actions but rather as the prey of psycho-social forces beyond their control. In view of this it is worth noting, parenthetically, that one of the curiosities of the diagnostic phase was that 'positive motivation' was frequently cited as a reason for recommending probation (McWilliams, 1986).

In the phase of pragmatism, cooling the mark out became attenuated and lost energy. The service split into three schools of thought: the radical school, the managerial school, and the personalist school. The radical school, which found its most forthright expression in the book by Hilary Walker and Bill Beaumont (1981), *Probation Work: Critical Theory and Socialist Practice*, had a central concern with societal change and class struggle which left little room for cooling marks out. As the authors said, there should be 'a shift away from the position of unqualified support for clients towards a more rounded concern with crime in so far as it is a problem for the working class' (p. 167). The managerial school also had little time for individual offenders.

The members of that school, the chief probation officers who began to conceive of themselves as managers in the 1970s, gradually cut themselves off from all professional work with offenders and work with the courts,[4] and their interest in cooling marks was minimal. They were concerned with the development of systems, rational efficiency and the application of social control mechanisms.

The school of thought which continued the tradition of cooling out offender-marks was the personalist school, but it was also the school of thought which had the most profound theoretical problems to contend with. The collapse of the diagnostic-treatment ethic had severe effects on the probation service as a whole. As Colin Thomas (1978) put it, 'the certainties of our traditional knowledge base have gone' (p.30). Whilst the radicals could retreat into a version of Marxism, and the managers into the bureau-managerial ideal, the personalists had no such bolt-holes. They remained committed to the enhancement of offenders as persons in the existing social order, but they had little in the way of support for their position. They could hang on to insights such as that provided by David Millard (1979): 'don't worry too much about what . . . you've been calling professionalism. Trust the clients. Believe what they say about their experience and trust the immediacy of your own responses' (p. 86), but their theoretical rationales were severely curtailed and hence their ability to justify the cooling enterprise was weakened.

Although because events are so near at hand it is difficult to be certain, it does appear that the probation service has now moved into a further, fourth phase of understanding of its purposes, and it seems appropriate to give it the title of the phase of social control. It is characterised by two important developments. First, management, which in the third phase of understanding had achieved a position of importance, is now the completely dominant influence, an influence which penetrates all aspects of agency life (McWilliams, 1992). The implications of this change have been summed up in the wider context of the penal system as a whole by A. A. G. Peters (1986); he says:

> The new [social control] approach is characterised by a withdrawal from the idea that the problem of crime can be eliminated, or even

can be brought under complete control. Emphasis has shifted from maintenance of the criminal code and the other criminal statutes to more general control of volumes of delinquent activity. Criminal policy is no longer occupied primarily with concrete offenders ... but with the management of aggregate phenomena of social activity, with criteria for selective law enforcement, with quantitative regulation in the organisational processing of offenders.

(p. 32)

Managers in the probation service have abandoned the idea that effective probation can cure individual offenders of their offending, and effectiveness now is seen as related to the success of imposed social control. Effectiveness, of course, is not the morally neutral ideal which managers strive to convey. As Alasdair MacIntyre (1981) points out: 'the whole concept of effectiveness is inseparable from a mode of human existence in which the contrivance of means is in central part the manipulation of human beings into compliant patterns of behaviour; and it is by appeal to his own effectiveness in this respect that the manager claims authority within the manipulative mode' (p. 71). MacIntyre concludes that management represents 'the obliteration of the distinction between manipulative and non-manipulative social relations' (p. 29). If that is a correct conclusion, then it is clear that the management model fits badly with any idea of cooling out marks. Additionally, as may be seen, the ontology of the offender has again changed: the offender is now but a unit in a central policy process.

The second important development in the fourth phase of understanding is the importation of desert theory into the probation service. Traditionally, the focus of the probation officer has been on the offender as a person rather than on the offence; in desert theory, that concern is turned on its head. According to desert theory, there are four essential types of offences: serious offences, offences of intermediate seriousness, less serious offences, and non-serious offences. Custodial sentences are seen as appropriate for serious offences; for intermediate offences and less serious offences, intermediate sanctions (community service, probation and so on) are seen as appropriate, and for non-serious offences, nominal penalties are in order. In the 1991 Criminal Justice Act the probation order is transformed from being a conditional release under benign supervision to a sentence of the court to be imposed as a community-based punishment; it becomes an intermediate sanction. This change was foreshadowed by desert theorists; for example, Martin Wasik and Andrew von Hirsch

(1988), in a paper on non-custodial penalties and the principles of desert, suggested that:

> traditionally, probation has been regarded not as a sentence in its own right but as a period 'on trust' which, if successfully completed by the offender, will result in no penalty being given for the offence . . . For our purposes, however, it seems preferable to regard the various conditions of a probation order as constituting the offender's penalty . . . Whilst probation supervision has historically purported to emphasise treatment, it could instead stress *surveillance*. Here, the idea is more special-deterrent than rehabilitative: surveillance will make it more difficult for the offender to offend, or intimidate him from doing so.
>
> (p. 569, emphasis in original)

The form of probation envisaged in the 1991 Act follows this line, and there is small scope left for cooling marks out. In terms of the ontology of the offender, desert theory is akin to management. Management's stress on systems, the manipulation of aggregate phenomena, and the techniques of social control leaves little room for the offender as a person. Similarly, desert theory, because of its stress on offences rather than offenders, tends to make the offender as a real person disappear. The specific link between desert theory and management, albeit not at the level of ontology, has been provided by Anthony Bottoms (1989) in a paper prepared for probation committee members. He says:

> The tasks of the probation service in . . . [a desert-based] structure would, of course, focus especially upon the middle band of penalties ('intermediate sanctions'), probably with a particular emphasis upon the more serious penalties within the intermediate band (because they are the ones most likely to be used to divert offenders from custody). Within this essentially offence-based framework, the probation service's role would be *effectively to manage within the community those offenders who had been awarded certain intermediate sanctions by the courts.*
>
> (Bottoms, 1989, p. 42, emphasis in original)

The problem with desert theory, of course, is that despite its apparent rationality and its technical presentation we do not know, ultimately, who deserves what. For example, Wasik and von Hirsch (1988), in discussing the potential which desert theory provides for substitution as between penalties, say that 'if A is a sanction that is appropriate for crimes of a given degree of seriousness, and B is a sanction of another type that is approximately of equal severity, then B can be substituted for A without infringing desert constraints' (p. 558). Quite so, but what the authors fail to provide is a justification for determining the appropriateness of A. This is a very old problem, of course. As was noted in the Seventh Report of the Commissioners on Criminal Law in 1843 (cited in D. A. Thomas, 1978): 'There is no real or ascertainable connexion or relation existing between crimes and punishments which can afford any correct test for fixing the nature or extent of the latter, either as regards particular offences or their relative magnitude' (p. i). As Shakespeare said: 'use every man after his desert, and who shall 'scape whipping? Use them after your own honour and dignity: the less they deserve, the more merit is in your bounty' (*Hamlet*, II. ii).

In conclusion, it may be said that the combination of modern managerialism in the probation service and the adoption of desert theory in the criminal justice system is bad news indeed so far as cooling marks out is concerned. Ironically, the combination is settling into place when the number of offender-marks is increasing and their plight is being more widely recognised. Sir Peter Imbert (1992), the Commissioner of the Metropolitan Police, in his annual report says: 'The continuing growth of crime is a fundamental concern which, in part, I attribute to the marginalisation of some elements in our society. The notion that there is a link between crime and social deprivation is compelling. There is a need to offer hope to those most disadvantaged if we are to see a reduction in crime' (p. 6). Would that such a message were to come from probation managers. It must be a cause for profound sadness that in our society offender-marks still stand in need of cooling out, but stand in such need they do. Of course, we should be working towards a juster society in which cooling out marks becomes unnecessary. Until that is achieved, it is vital that the probation service should continue to apply itself to the task.[5]

Notes

1 I am grateful to Dr Anne Celnick for drawing this paper to my attention.

2 Goffman (1952) points out that:

> although the term, mark, is commonly applied to a person who is given short-lived expectations by operators who have intentionally misrepresented the facts, a less restricted definition is desirable in analyzing the larger social scene. An expectation may finally prove false, even though it has been possible to sustain it for a long time and even though the operators acted in good faith.
>
> (p. 452)

3 Under the original legislation (1907 Probation of Offenders Act), those given probation orders were not convicted, rather the order was made 'without pro-

ceeding to conviction'. This substantially aided the cooling process because, so long as the mark committed no further offence and kept the requirements of the recognizance, the stigma of conviction was avoided altogether. This was changed by the 1948 Criminal Justice Act, but not without substantial protest. For an account see McWilliams (1990).

4   An important area of practice in which principal probation officers were heavily involved was that of acting as liaison officers to courts of assize and quarter session. In the late 1960s roughly 70 per cent of principal officers were thus involved, underlining the importance attached to the service's relationship with the courts. Today, not a single chief officer is liaison officer to a higher court, although the rhetoric of the value of close contacts with the courts remains *in situ.*

5   I am grateful to Mrs Fiona Hammond for discussions of a draft of this paper.

References

Bottoms, A. (1989), 'The place of the probation service in the criminal justice system', in I. Miles (ed.), *The Madingley Papers*, London (mimeo).

Goffman, E. (1952), 'On cooling the mark out: some aspects of adaptation to failure', *Psychiatry*, XV, pp. 451–63.

Holmes, T. (1913), 'Youthful dishonesty: how to deal with it', Howard Association, London.

Imbert, P. (1992), Annual Report of the Metropolitan Police, reported in *The Independent*, 30 July 1992.

MacIntyre, A. (1981), *After Virtue*, Duckworth, London.

McWilliams, W. (1983), 'The mission to the English police courts 1876–1936', *Howard Journal*, XXII, pp. 129–47.

McWilliams, W. (1986), 'The English social enquiry report: development and practice', Ph.D. thesis, University of Sheffield, unpublished.

McWilliams, W. (1987), 'Probation, pragmatism and policy', *Howard Journal*, XXVI, pp. 97–119.

McWilliams, W. (1990), 'The case against probation as a sentence', *NAPO News*, XX, May/June, pp. 8–9.

McWilliams, W. (1992), 'The rise and development of management thought in the English probation system', in R. Statham and P. Whitehead (eds.), *Management Issues in Probation*, Longman, London, pp. 3–29.

Millard, D. (1979), 'Broader approaches to probation practice', in J. F. S. King (ed.), *Pressures and Change in the Probation Service*, Cropwood Conference Series No. 1, University of Cambridge Institute of Criminology, Cambridge, pp. 84–99.

Parker, H. (1992), 'Saving community penalties: remaking sentencing tariffs', *Probation Journal*, XXXIX, pp. 58–62.

Peters, A. A. G. (1986), 'Main currents in criminal law theory', in J. van Dijh *et al.*, *Criminal Law in Action*, Gouda Quint, Arnhem, pp. 23–39.

Powell, F. S. (1897), 'Discussion of the Rev. W.D. Morrison's paper', *Journal of the Royal Statistical Society*, pp. 25–6.

Thomas, C. (1978), 'Supervision in the community', *Howard Journal*, XVII, pp. 23–31.

Thomas, D. A. (1978), *The Penal Equation: Derivations of the Penalty Structure of English Criminal Law*, University of Cambridge Institute of Criminology, Cambridge.

Walker, H., and Beaumont, B. (1981), *Probation Work: Critical Theory and Socialist Practice*, Basil Blackwell, Oxford.

Wasik, M., and von Hirsch, A. (1988), 'Non-custodial penalties and the principles of desert', *Criminal Law Review*, pp. 555–72.

10

Community service: progress and prospects

GILL McIVOR

Community service by offenders has now been available as a sentencing option in Britain for almost twenty years. Although its modern origins can be traced to California, where in 1966 certain traffic offenders were required to perform socially useful work for the community, community service was first introduced on a legislated basis in England and Wales and the British model has served as a blueprint for many schemes which were subsequently developed elsewhere.

The development of community service in England and Wales was greeted with a mixture of enthusiasm and (less commonly) scepticism. Much of the criticism directed at community service has centred on its confused penal philosophy and uncertain location on the sentencing tariff. The Wootton Committee (Advisory Council on the Penal System, 1970), which first proposed the introduction of unpaid work by offenders, was attracted by the notion that the community service order could appeal to a variety of philosophies and fulfil, though not necessarily simultaneously, a number of sentencing aims. Community service could punish offenders by depriving them of their leisure time while offering a cheaper and more constructive alternative than imprisonment; it could enable offenders to pay back something to the community; and it might, through bringing offenders into contact with non-offender volunteers and others more disadvantaged than themselves, help to effect a positive change in offenders' attitudes and behaviour.

There subsequently emerged conflicting views over what should be construed as the primary penal objective of this innovative sentencing option. The belief that community service was best conceptualised in reparative terms appears to have gained the widest currency (e.g. Thorvaldson, 1978). Young (1979), however, argued that the community service order was reparative only in a symbolic sense since society in general rather than the victims of crime benefit from such unpaid work. Symbolic reparation could not, moreover, be readily distinguished from retribution since both are ultimately concerned with restoring balance to the social order. Pease (1985) likewise questioned the appropriateness of extending the concept of reparation to a sanction which does not provide redress directly to the victims of crime and suggested instead that community service was best conceptualised in retributive terms.

Few, it seems, would regard community service as an explicitly rehabilitative sentence, though rehabilitation has often been identified as at least a secondary aim or a potential consequence of performing valued tasks for disadvantaged members of the community. If any broad consensus can be discerned, it is that community service should be regarded first and foremost as a retributive sanction, but one which has the added advantage of simultaneously benefiting the community and, perhaps, under appropriate circumstances, effecting reductions in subsequent offending behaviour.

These arguments are not, however, simply academic, since the perceived theoretical or conceptual underpinning of community service will influence the way in which schemes are administered and the manner in which the sentence is used by the courts. The Wootton Committee proposed that the new community service order might appropriately be used instead of short sentences of imprisonment (both at the point of first sentence and for fine default), but did not preclude its use even if an immediate custodial sentence was unlikely. Though the government appeared to be in favour of restricting community service to offenders who would otherwise receive immediate sentences of detention or imprisonment, the subsequent legislation required only that orders be imposed for offences that were punishable by imprisonment. The resultant confusion was clearly manifest in the six experimental schemes which were introduced prior to the extension of the community service scheme to other parts of England and Wales in 1974: while some probation staff regarded the new order as a sentence in its own right which might appropriately be imposed instead of other non-custodial penalties, others viewed community service exclusively as an alternative to imprisonment (Pease *et al.*, 1975).

Opinions have continued to be divided over whether community service should be conceptualised as an individualised or tariff sentence. Adherents to the view that, as with probation, the appropriateness of a community service order should properly be determined with regard to the needs of individual offenders, would advocate its use across a broad spectrum of offenders and offences. Those who emphasise the retributive nature of community service, on the other hand, are divided over where it should be located on the sentencing tariff. Some have argued that because of its relatively demanding nature, and to maximise its potential to reduce the courts' reliance on imprisonment, community service should be available only for those offenders who would otherwise receive a custodial sentence. Others, such as Pease (1978), prompted by the inappropriateness of fines for certain offenders, have favoured the extension of community service to offenders who would not necessarily be imprisoned if this option were not available. Recognising the adverse consequences for offenders which could result from inconsistencies in the use of community service orders across courts, Pease (1978) proposed the introduction of a split tariff, with shorter orders serving as substitutes for fines and longer orders as replacements for custodial sentences.

Community service was initially introduced in Scotland in 1977 on an experimental basis, pending the implementation of the Community Service by Offenders (Scotland) Act 1978. Despite its later introduction, however, the legislation failed to indicate unambiguously how this new option should be used, and thus failed to avoid the confusion which had characterised the operation of community service schemes south of the border. Scottish community service staff have tended to be more united in the view that the sentence should function explicitly as an alternative to custody (McIvor, 1992). But as Vass (1984) found in England, Scottish sentencers too have chosen to interpret and implement the legislation in different ways (Carnie, 1990).

Notwithstanding the lack of conceptual clarity which has surrounded the community service order, the use of this measure in Britain has increased steadily over the past two decades. In England and Wales, for example, community service orders were imposed for 7 per cent of indictable offences in 1989 (just over 34,000 orders), compared with only 3 per cent ten years earlier (Home Office, 1990). Scotland has similarly witnessed a growth in the use of community service over recent years, from 2,905 orders in 1984 to 4,190 in 1989. In that year community service orders accounted for 2.3 per cent of sentences imposed upon persons against whom a charge was proved in Scottish courts (Social Work Services Group, 1990).

BENEFIT TO THE COMMUNITY

Part of the appeal of the sentence clearly lies in its ability to provide valued services to individuals and groups in the community who otherwise would have difficulty getting certain essential tasks carried out. Voluntary or statutory placement agencies whose views have been sought have generally expressed satisfaction with the contribution made by offenders on community service orders, in terms of the quality of the work or its direct usefulness to the agency and its clients or users (e.g. Allen and Treger, 1990; Godson, 1980; Leibrich *et al.*, 1984; McIvor, 1992). Several of these studies have highlighted the not uncommon tendency for offenders to continue to work in a voluntary (and sometimes paid) capacity for their placement agency after completing the hours ordered by the court.

On the negative side, the negotiation of placements and supervision of offenders on community service can place an additional burden upon agency staff, and absenteeism has often been highlighted as a problem (e.g. Godson, 1980; McIvor, 1992), serving as a source of frustration to staff and diverting their time from other important activities. On balance, however, the willingness of agencies to continue offering placements to their local community service scheme would appear to indicate that, on the whole, the benefits outweigh the costs. Many Scottish agencies suggested that undertaking unpaid work for the community could enhance offenders' self-esteem, improve their social skills and increase their self-reliance and responsibility. Moreover, a community service order was more likely than a prison sentence to effect a positive change in offenders' attitudes and behaviour (McIvor, 1992).

Although team placements are at least as common as individual agency placements in Britain the only study, as far as the author is aware, which has systematically sought to document the experiences of members of the public who have had work carried out by supervised work teams is McIvor's (1992) Scottish survey of over 500 individual beneficiaries. With few exceptions, the respondents were happy with the standard of the work, believing it to have been well supervised and of considerable benefit to them. The attitudes of the offenders were often praised, problems were rarely reported and most people were willing, if the need arose, to make use of their local community service scheme again.

The possibility of offending against the beneficiaries is an ever-present risk and was the explanation most often offered by agencies for excluding offenders who had been convicted of certain types of crimes. Fortunately, however, the incidence of offending in placements appears to have been low, especially in work teams, which generally consisted of higher proportions of 'risky' offenders but in which closer oversight could usually be provided (McIvor, 1992).

OFFENDERS' EXPERIENCES AND VIEWS

Offenders have generally described their experiences of undertaking community service in positive terms (e.g. Polonoski, 1980; Varah, 1981). It has been compared favourably with imprisonment (McDonald, 1986) and with fines or probation (Flegg, 1976). Several studies have challenged the widely-held assumption that placements in voluntary or statutory agencies are inherently preferable to placements in work teams. McIvor (1991), for example, found that most offenders considered their community service placements to have been interesting, enjoyable and of likely value to the beneficiaries; many believed that they had acquired practical or interpersonal skills; and most believed that they had gained something from the experience. However, no clear preferences emerged for agency placements or for placements which engaged offenders in the provision of direct personal services; if anything, there was least support for agency placements involving routine practical chores.

The importance of the relationship between community service workers and their supervisors has been consistently highlighted. Offenders appreciate supervisors who reinforce their confidence, who exercise authority in a firm but friendly way and who provide personal support when required (Flegg, 1976). More generally, good relationships with their supervisors can help maintain offenders' motivation and commitment to their work (McIvor, 1992).

The literature is, however, divided over how offenders perceive the purpose of community service. Thus while Thorvaldson (1978) found that offenders identified most readily with reparative or rehabilitative objectives and few regarded their sentence as primarily punitive, most offenders interviewed by McDonald (1986) defined the community service order in retributive terms. Though McIvor (1992) found that most offenders had experienced community service as a punishment, because of its intrusion into their leisure time and the discipline and commitment that completion of an order required, some engaged in the type of syllogistic thinking described by McDonald (1986): prison was equated with punishment, and since community service was not imprisonment, then it could not be a punishment. Others found it difficult to conceptualise community service in punitive terms because they had enjoyed their placements and had not been particularly inconvenienced by undertaking unpaid work. As one offender, who appears to encapsulate the spirit of community service, commented: 'I found that I benefited more than I would have done if I had been sent to prison as I found something I really like doing. I wouldn't have got a chance to work for the elderly in prison. For minor crimes, community service would be a more beneficial sentence to both criminal and society' (McIvor, 1992, p. 103).

CHANGING ATTITUDES AND BEHAVIOUR

The Wootton Committee believed that the process of performing unpaid work for the community might, in some cases, contribute to 'a changed outlook on the part of the offender' (Advisory Council on the Penal System, 1970, para. 34), though Harland (1980) later argued that 'all claims about its rehabilitative efficacy continue to be perpetrated by impressionistic and anecdotal accounts by judges and probation officers, more than by the results of rigorous evaluation' (p. 457).

Even though community service is not generally regarded as an expressly rehabilitative sanction, there is nonetheless a widespread belief even among sentencers that it may in some instances be rehabilitative in effect. Carnie (1990), for instance, likewise found that, although sheriffs considered punishment and reparation to be their primary sentencing objectives when imposing a community service order, it was often suggested that a challenging and constructive placement experience might have a positive impact upon offenders' attitudes and behaviour:

> Working with those less fortunate than themselves, such as the disabled and the handicapped, even for a short time, could give some offenders a fresh perspective on the scope and scale of their own perceived problems. Through helping others their sense of self-worth and self-respect could improve. This was considered vital to the success of any rehabilitative process and was repeatedly endorsed. One sheriff managed to convey this sentiment rather eloquently, 'from my point of view I am looking for the offender to glimpse his own dignity and for the community to say that it was fitting; that's the ideal'.
>
> (Carnie, 1990, p. 30)

Harland (1980) was correct in highlighting the lack, at that time, of empirical evidence in support of such a view. The Home Office evaluation of the experimental schemes in England and Wales (Pease *et al.*, 1977) suggested that reconviction rates were no better after community service than following alternative non-custodial or custodial sentences, a conclusion echoed by a later analysis of reconviction among offenders given community service orders in 1979 (Home Office, 1983). Several more recent studies have produced similar results (e.g. Berk and Feeley, 1990) while others (e.g. Ervin and Schneider, 1990), have reported lower rates of recidivism among offenders sentenced to community service.

Reconviction appears, moreover, to be influenced by the quality of work placements. McIvor (1992) found that offenders who had been on community service were less frequently reconvicted, and were less often reconvicted of offences involving dishonesty, if their experience of community service had been particularly rewarding and worthwhile. Such placements, which were also associated with higher levels of compliance while orders were completed, were characterised by high levels of contact with the beneficiaries; by the provision of tasks which enabled offenders to acquire new skills; and by work which could be readily recognised by offenders as being of benefit to the recipients.

Further evidence that community service may have some impact upon crimes against property has been provided by a Dutch study (Bol and Overwater, 1986) cited by Bishop (1988). The largest differences in reconviction between offenders given community service and those sentenced to short-term imprisonment were found among a sub-group of young offenders who had been convicted of thefts and burglaries. These findings, which indicate that community service may have a particular impact upon premeditated crimes involving loss to victims, are consistent with the suggestion offered, among others, by the Wootton Committee, that contact with those who are more disadvantaged than themselves may provide offenders with greater insight into the practical and emotional consequences of their offending on other people. Ervin and Schneider (1990), on the other hand, have attributed the superiority of restitution over traditional juvenile programmes largely to 'the opportunity it presents for positively rewarding the juvenile for actions taken' (p. 204). This explanation is consistent with McIvor's (1992) finding that the quality of placement experience was most clearly associated with reductions in the rate and frequency of reconviction among offenders who may have had less opportunity for personal fulfilment or achievement in the past.

UNFULFILLED PROMISE

Some worrying inconsistencies, which have been most comprehensively documented by Pease (1985), have nevertheless plagued the community service scheme in Britain from the outset. The proportionate use of community service orders has varied from area to area, as have the types of work offenders are required to perform and the criteria employed by schemes to assess offenders' suitability to undertake unpaid work. Women have been under-represented on community service, schemes have differed both in the manner in which absences from placement are categorised (as acceptable or not) and according to how stringently the requirements of orders are enforced, and Vass (1984) has documented the 'creative' recording of hours worked.

However, it is perhaps the limited diversionary impact of community service which has proved the greatest source of disappointment to those who enthusiastically welcomed this innovative sentencing option. The tendency for courts to impose community service orders as alternatives to other non-custodial penalties at least as often as they are used to replace sentences of imprisonment is by now well documented (McIvor, 1990; Pease *et al.*, 1977; Willis, 1977); in Scotland the community service order appears, if anything, to have become increasingly used instead of other community-based sentences such as fines (Social Work Services Group, 1990). However, this is understandable given the ambiguous legislative basis of community service, the inappropriateness, for many offenders, of the current system of financial penalties and the tortured logic that the imposition of so-called 'alternatives to custody' involves (Pease, 1985).

THE SHAPE OF THINGS TO COME

Recent legislative and policy developments in England and Wales and in Scotland have been aimed at achieving increased consistency both in the operation of schemes and in the use of community service by the courts. In both jurisdictions, national objectives and standards for community service schemes were introduced by central government in 1989. Both documents contained detailed operational guidance on such issues as enforcement and the reckoning of hours worked; both identified punishment, reparation and benefit to the community as primary purposes of the community service order; and both were aimed in large part at enhancing the credibility of community service with the courts. But while the Scottish Office guidance placed particular emphasis on maximising the value to offenders, as well as to the community, of community service work, and encouraged schemes to ensure that work placements were characterised by work which 'is within the capacity of the offender and capable of enhancing his/her social responsibility and self-respect' (Social Work Services Group, 1989, para. 1.2.8.c), the Home Office introduced a requirement (now rescinded) that most offenders sentenced to orders of sixty hours or more should complete the first twenty-one hours engaged in demanding manual work – such as clearing waste ground, picking up litter or cleaning graffiti – which visibly improves the appearance or amenities of a neighbourhood. A circular accompanying the national standards indicated that community service schemes should 'try to provide offenders with work which they find personally fulfilling, *provided that it is also demanding*' (Home Office, 1989, para. 10; emphasis added).

The Home Office standards (and especially the first draft which contained several unworkable requirements) were widely criticised and it was argued that rigid adherence to the guidance on initial placement allocation and enforcement would result in substantial increases in the numbers of offenders returned to court for failure to comply (McWilliams, 1989). Although the use of community service throughout Britain has increased since national standards were introduced (and quite dramatically so in Scotland), this growth in the number of orders has been accompanied by increases in the proportions of orders breached. Lloyd (1991), who attributed the increased breach rate in England and Wales at least partly to the national standards, has cautioned that the government's attempts to increase the diversionary potential of the community service order could backfire if higher proportions of offenders end up in custody as a result of their orders being revoked, and if sentencers become frustrated and disillusioned by the large numbers of breached offenders appearing before the courts.

The introduction of national standards alone was, however, likely to have only a limited effect, if any, upon the manner in which community service was perceived and utilised by the courts. Few of the sentencers who were interviewed by Carnie (1990) shortly after the Scottish guidance was introduced had seen the document, and none were familiar with its detailed contents. Sheriffs were clear that they would not be significantly influenced by the national standards and considered it inappropriate that they should be. The Law Reform

(Miscellaneous Provisions) (Scotland) Act 1990 afforded the government an opportunity to amend the existing legislation by requiring that from 1 April 1991 the courts impose community service orders only upon offenders who would otherwise receive sentences of imprisonment or detention. There is, however, no guarantee that the new provision will universally have its intended effect: ways can be found to side-step legislative reforms, and if some sentencers continue to use community service as they have done in the past then the potential for inequities to occur may be heightened rather than reduced.

The change in the legislative basis of community service in Scotland coincided with the introduction by central government of national objectives and standards for statutory social work services to the criminal justice system (Social Work Services Group, 1991), aimed at increasing the range and quality of community-based social work disposals. The implementation of the standards and the simultaneous introduction of full central funding of these services should result in community service becoming more closely integrated with other statutory social work services to offenders and their families. It is also likely, if the new arrangements have their intended effect, that the courts will make increased use of probation, with or without additional requirements. The proportionate use of community service as a stand-alone option may decline as greater use is made of unpaid work as a condition of probation.

In England and Wales the fate of community service has been more clearly subsumed within broader developments in penal policy culminating in the Criminal Justice Act 1991. Since the Act came into effect in October 1992, courts in England and Wales have been able for the first time not only to combine community service and probation in a new 'combination order', but in addition to attach an array of requirements imposed alongside community sentences such as compensation orders and curfews. However, as Wasik and Taylor (1991) have commented:

> It may, perhaps, be doubted whether this 'cafeteria' style of sentencing can achieve very much, except further to confuse sentencing principles. It seems to owe more to the rather old-fashioned belief that a precise form of sentence can be selected to achieve a specific rehabilitative effect, than to the coherent grading of community orders. It seems to run contrary to the government's own stated preference for penalty scaling and tends to undermine recent official moves to standardise the operational and breach arrangements for community orders.

(p. 4)

In practical terms, these new community sentences may come to resemble the intensive supervision programmes developed in the United States during the 1980s in response to record levels of imprisonment and prison crowding. The effectiveness of these programmes, which place considerable emphasis upon surveillance and control, has increasingly been called into question (see, for example, Morris and Tonry, 1990). Doubts have been expressed about their diversionary impact, leading to concern on ethical grounds about imposing such restrictive sanctions upon offenders who would otherwise have been dealt with by means of some other less intrusive penalty. Revocation rates have been high and though most have been prompted by technical violations rather than by continued offending by the probationer, revocations have usually resulted in offenders being imprisoned for the original offence.

With the advent of the Criminal Justice Act 1991 the courts are likely to make increased use of community service as only one part of a package of measures imposed upon an offender. But if the experience in the United States is anything to go by, it can be anticipated that these new community sentences will be associated with high levels of breach. The quality and breadth of placement provision in community service schemes would almost certainly suffer, since agencies would be reluctant to commit themselves to offering placements to the higher numbers of offenders on short community service orders, many of whom, for reasons unrelated to their community service requirement, are unable to complete the work ordered by the court.

CONCLUSIONS

Community service has achieved a great deal in its first twenty years. Despite its confused penal philosophy and the inequities that this has engendered it has proved to be a popular and enduring sentencing option with British courts. It appears, moreover, that the community service order is able to fulfil simultaneously what might appear to be incompatible or conflicting aims. The community can clearly benefit both directly – from the receipt of unpaid work – and indirectly if, through the use of carefully chosen and imaginative work placements, offenders can gain from their experiences while undertaking what is first and foremost a punishment of the courts. There is a risk, however, that the benefit of community service to the community and to offenders will be eroded, and that elements of the 'penalisation' scenario envisaged by McWilliams and Pease (1980) will come increasingly to the fore following the implementation of the 1991 Criminal Justice Act.

Looking back over the first five years of the community service order, Baroness Wootton (1977, p. 112) observed that 'fashions in sentencing come and go; and it will largely be the recommendations of probation officers which determine whether the rising popularity of community service is just a flash in the pan, or whether this new sentence becomes a powerful and lasting addition to our armoury'. The challenge to probation officers over the next few years will be different, but no less important: first, to resist the allure of 'designer' sentences and ensure, through their recommendations, that community service remains, as far as possible, a distinctive and credible sentencing option; and second, to publicise more widely the achievements of community service to a public who appear not unsympathetic to its aims and who may, as a consequence, increasingly come to perceive those who have offended against society in other than a wholly negative light.

References

Advisory Council on the Penal System (1970), *Non-Custodial and Semi-Custodial Penalties*, HMSO, London.

Allen, G. F., and Treger, H. (1990), 'Community service orders in federal probation: perceptions of probationers and host agencies', *Federal Probation*, LIV, 3, pp. 8–14.

Berk, R., and Feeley, M. M. (1990), *An Evaluation of the Community Service Order Scheme in the US District Court for the Northern District of California*, Center for the Study of Law and Society, University of California at Berkeley.

Bishop, N. (1988), *Non-Custodial Alternatives in Europe*, Government Printing Office, Helsinki.

Carnie, J. (1990), *Sentencers' Perceptions of Community Service by Offenders*, Scottish Office Central Research Unit, Edinburgh.

Ervin, L., and Schneider, A.L. (1990), 'Explaining the effects of restitution on offenders: results from a national experiment in juvenile courts', in B. Galaway and J. Hudson (eds.), *Criminal Justice, Restitution, and Reconciliation*, Criminal Justice Press, Monsey, pp. 183–206.

Flegg, D. (1976), *Community Service: Consumer Survey 1973–76*, Nottingham Probation Service, Nottingham.

Godson, D. (1980), *Community Service by Offenders: The Agencies' Experiences in Hampshire*, Department of Sociology and Social Administration, University of Southampton.

Harland, A. T. (1980), 'Court-ordered community service in criminal law: the continuing tyranny of benevolence?', *Buffalo Law Review*, XXIX, pp. 425–86.

Home Office (1983), 'Reconvictions of those given community service orders', *Home Office Statistical Bulletin*, HMSO, London.

Home Office (1989), *National Standards for Community Service Orders*, Home Office Circular 18/89, London.

Home Office (1990), *Criminal Statistics England and Wales 1989*, Cm 1322, HMSO, London.

Leibrich, J., Galaway, B., and Underhill, Y. (1984), 'Survey of people connected with the community service sentence', in J. Leibrich, B. Galaway and Y. Underhill (eds.), *Community Service Orders in New Zealand: Three Research Reports*, New Zealand Department of Justice, Wellington, pp. 27–156.

Lloyd, C. (1991), 'National standards for community service orders: The first two years of operation', in *Home Office Research and Statistics Department Research Bulletin No. 31*, Home Office Research and Planning Unit, London, pp. 16–21.

McDonald, D. C. (1986), *Punishment Without Walls: Community Service Sentences in New York City*, Rutgers University Press, New Brunswick.

McIvor, G. (1990), 'Community service and custody in Scotland', *The Howard Journal*, XXIX, pp. 101–13.

McIvor, G. (1991), 'Community service work placements', *The Howard Journal*, XXX, pp. 19–29.

McIvor, G. (1992), *Sentenced to Serve: The Operation and Impact of Community Service by Offenders*, Avebury, Aldershot.

McWilliams, W. (1989), 'Community service national standards: practice and sentencing', *Probation Journal*, XXXVI, pp. 121–6.

McWilliams, W., and Pease, K. (1980), 'The future of community service', in K. Pease and W. McWilliams (eds.), *Community Service by Order*, Scottish Academic Press, Edinburgh, pp. 136–43.

Morris, N., and Tonry, M. (1990), *Between Prison and Probation: Intermediate Punishments in a Rational Sentencing System*, Oxford University Press, New York.

Pease, K. (1978), 'Community service and the tariff', *Criminal Law Review*, pp. 546–8.

Pease, K. (1985), 'Community service orders', in M. Tonry and N. Morris (eds.), *Crime and Justice: An Annual Review of Research*, VI, University of Chicago Press, Chicago, pp. 51–93.

Pease, K., Durkin, P., Earnshaw, I., Payne, D., and Thorpe, J. (1975), 'Community service orders', *Home Office Research Study No. XXIX*, HMSO, London.

Pease, K., Billingham, S., and Earnshaw, I. (1977), 'Community service assessed in 1976', *Home Office Research Study No. XXXIX*, HMSO, London.

Polonoski, M. (1980), *The Community Service Order Programme in Ontario (2): Participants and their Perceptions*, Ontario Ministry of Correctional Services, Scarborough, Ontario.

Social Work Services Group (1989), *National Standards and Objectives for the Operation of Community Service by Offenders Schemes in Scotland*, Scottish Office, Edinburgh.

Social Work Services Group (1990), *Statistical Bulletin: Community Service by Offenders in 1987, 1988 and 1989*, Government Statistical Service, Edinburgh.

Social Work Services Group (1991), *National Standards and Objectives for Social Work Services in the Criminal Justice System*, Scottish Office, Edinburgh.

Thorvaldson, S. A. (1978), 'The Effects of Community Service on the Attitudes of Offenders', unpublished PhD thesis, University of Cambridge.

Varah, M. (1981), 'What about the workers?: offenders on community service orders express their opinions', *Probation Journal*, XXVIII, pp. 121–3.

Vass, A. A. (1984), *Sentenced to Labour: Close Encounters with a Prison Substitute*, Venus Academica, St. Ives.

Wasik, M., and Taylor, D. (1991), *Blackstone's Guide to the Criminal Justice Act 1991*, Blackstone Press, London.

Willis, A. (1977), 'Community service as an alternative to imprisonment: a cautionary view', *Probation Journal*, XXIV, pp. 120–6.

Wootton, B. (1977), 'Some reflections on the first five years of community service', *Probation Journal*, XXIV, pp. 110–12.

Young, W. A. (1979), *Community Service Orders: The Development and Use of a New Penal Measure*, Heinemann, London.

11

Putting a price on harm: the fine as a punishment

PETER YOUNG

My aim in this paper is to advance discussion of a topic and a penal sanction both of which I hope to show are of importance but which, rather strangely, are largely ignored. The penal sanction is the fine and the topic is the broader one of the relationship between the social institutions of judicial punishment and money. Their importance derives from the central place that the fine occupies in the criminal justice system. As I think is well known, the fine is by far the most commonly used of all penal sanctions in most western penal systems, with the possible exception of the USA. In Scotland, for example, in a typical year the fine, in combination with other monetary sanctions, will be used to dispose of approximately 83 per cent of all the crimes and offences which appear before the criminal courts. Although it is used most to deal with minor offences and trivial crimes, it is also used to a very considerable extent as a punishment for many crimes of middling seriousness and each year there will be a number of very serious crimes, such as culpable homicide, serious assault or robbery, which are fined. In comparison, the other penal sanctions are rarely used; all custodial sentences together account for only about 8 per cent of sanctions, probation and community service orders each for 2 per cent and admonition and caution added together for approximately 9 per cent (all 1989 figures, see Figure 11.1). Two important observations follow from this: first, that a sentence to fine is probably the most common sentencing decision taken, which means, secondly, that sentencers are intimately and regularly involved, in effect, in putting a monetary value or price on the harms caused by crime. Viewed in the round, it thus can be argued that the penal system is best understood as working through a cash nexus; to put it quite

Figure 11.1 Average fine and per cent fined by type of crime in Scotland, 1989

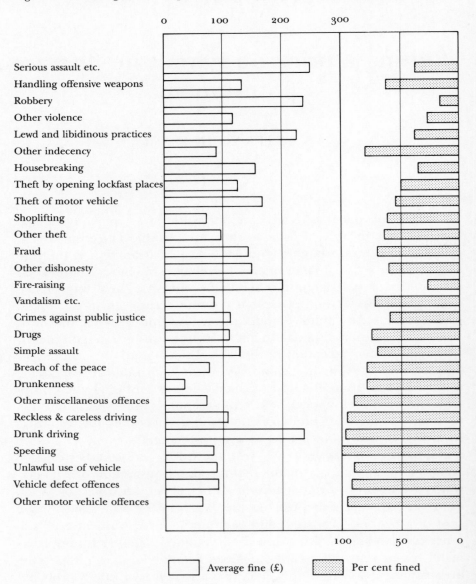

Source: Scottish Office Statistical Bulletin (Criminal Justice Series), December 1991.

simply, the most common act of judicial punishment revolves around the calculation of a cash exchange.

My intention in what follows is to try to throw some light on how these calculations are made and also to discuss the significance and relevance of this for our theoretical and practical understanding of punishment. These are very ambitious objectives, the full realisation of which calls for detailed, empirical and theoretical study. I cannot pretend to achieve this here, but I do hope to make some headway in the more modest task of trying to open up discussion of this neglected area. I shall do this by advancing an exposition of my own account of the processes that I claim to be at the heart of the monetary calculations upon which fines are based. I call my account the cultural estrangement of punishment and money. This concept is meant to refer to the ambivalent, even contradictory, set of cultural values that form the context in which money is used as a judicial punishment. My suggestion is that the judicial use of money-as-punishment is underscored by values which pull at one and the same time in opposing directions. At one level there exists a view of the nature of fines which makes them, in certain circumstances, an inappropriate sanction, even though their use may be perfectly legally permissible. In such circumstances, fines are seen as inappropriate, not so much, I shall suggest, because they fail to deliver an adequate quantum of pain or suffering to the offender, but because they fail to fulfil wider cultural expectations of what punishment ought really to be like. And, I argue, they fail in this way because there are certain harms or crimes which we see as being beyond the reach of money. When this happens, which is rarely, the values associated on the one hand with punishment and on the other hand with money are said to be estranged.

At another level, however, punishment and money are regularly and routinely brought into contact with one another, as they must be if the fine is to remain the most common penal sanction in use. In the common round of sentencing in the busiest criminal courts (in Scotland, the Sheriff Courts and District Courts), sentencers regularly put a monetary price on harm and thereby bring the values associated with punishment into some sort of relationship with those we associate with money.

The relationship between these two levels of use is of great significance. Although, as was said, punishment and money are rarely fully estranged, the occasions on which they are are nevertheless of great importance. Their importance lies in their wider cultural and symbolic resonance. As I show below, on these occasions the central values of what we understand by punishment are exposed, open to question and have to be reinforced if the criminal justice system is to maintain its legitimacy. The rarity of these occasions thus should not be thought to deny their importance; it is on these occasions that the central values which govern the use of money-as-punishment are raised to a structural principle of the sanctioning system as a whole. Although, at the second and lower level of the use of fines, the values associated with punishment and money are routinely brought together, they do so only in the shadow of the circumstances in which this is seen as inappropriate and wrong.

This completes my first general exposition of what I mean by the cultural estrangement of punishment and money. I am aware, however, of its rather abstract and formalistic nature. To bring it down to earth, I intend to analyse, as a sort of test case, an example of one of those rare occasions on which money and punishment are estranged. Although my example thus necessarily describes a situation in which fines are not used, I trust that my comments above make it clear that I see it as having a relevance for the opposite situation, the far more common one, in which fines are used as punishments. It is not just that the use of fines lies in the shadow of those circumstances in which punishment and money are estranged, but also that the wider scale of values intrinsic to the sentencing and sanctioning system is touched by similar considerations as well.

The example I have in mind is the deep reluctance that exists to use fines to deal with rape. I regard this as a test case because it fulfils the conditions hinted at above; that is, although the fine is technically a perfectly legal sanction by which to punish a guilty rapist, it is rarely used. My question is: why is this so? Why are sentencers reluctant to use fines for rape and why, on the odd occasions when this does happen, is there such a public outcry?

PUNISHMENT, MONEY AND RAPE

That the fine is generally seen as an inappropriate punishment for rape is clear. Although in Scots and English criminal law the fine can theoretically be used, there exist well-known and entrenched sentencing practices in both jurisdictions which make this a near impossibility. A sentencer who used the fine to 'punish' a rapist would risk being perceived as incompetent. The public and judicial furore that follows the very rare use of fines in these cases shows both how deeply this sentencing practice is embedded and how closely it resonates with public opinion. For example, the infamous English case of *R.* v. *Allen* (January 1982; not officially reported), in which a judge fined a man for raping a hitch-hiker, confirms these points. In the media coverage that followed public recognition of what had happened, the judge was pilloried. Indeed, questions were asked in the House of Commons, this in turn causing the then Lord Chief Justice, Lord Lane, to comment. As a result of this case and others in which inappropriately 'light' sentences had been seen to be given (not all fines), Lord Lane issued sentencing guidelines which declared the normal punishment for rape to be a lengthy prison sentence. (The Scottish 'practice' is the same: for a description see Nicholson (1985, pp. 52–3); for comments see *Conlon* v. *H.M.A.* 1982 S.C.C.R. 141, *Allen* v. *H.M.A.* 1983 S.C.C.R. 182, and *Barbour* v. *H.M.A.* 1982 S.C.C.R. 195.)

Now why should this be the case? Why do these sentencing practices exist which make the fine for all practicable purposes an entirely inappropriate punishment for rape, although, as has been said, it is a theoretical possibility?

One answer would be that the fine is not used because to do so would upset the scale of values implicit in the system by which the seriousness of crime and punishment is assessed. This scale can be broadly characterised thus: for crimes which harm the body or person of the victim the appropriate sanction is one which, within strictly defined legal limits, does the same in return. As the prison comes closest in the British legal systems to doing this, it is seen as the appropriate sanction. For those wrongful actions which are not perceived to harm the body or person of the victim, other less serious punishments can be brought into play. Quite clearly, within current conceptions the fine exists near the bottom end of this scale. Other considerations, of course, affect the scale, such as conceptions of what are *mala in se* as contrasted to *mala prohibita*, as do notions of dangerousness and public safety. In addition, another very important reason rapists and other dangerous criminals are 'locked up' is because they are seen to pose a threat to the public and this is generally seen as a legitimate and important consideration to take into account.

As sentencers are required to make their decisions in terms of this scale of values all seems to fall neatly into place. On this view, the fine is inappropriate in cases of rape because it belongs to the wrong end of this spectrum. To be plain about it, the fine is perceived to be inappropriate because it does not deliver an adequate quantum of pain. Ideas of proportionality are quite central to sentencing practice;

a serious harm, intentionally inflicted on the innocent, has to be met with an equivalent one equally intentionally inflicted. If any of these considerations are upset, the scale of values is compromised and the legitimacy both of the actor who caused the upset and of the system as a whole is potentially threatened.

But I suggest that the issue cannot be left here. This scale of values is not a neutral mechanical device. It is not simply, I contend, about the degree of harm and pain caused to victims and offenders, but also about the type. If it were just about the former then there is no convincing reason why fines should not be used in rape cases or, at the other extreme, why motoring offenders should not be imprisoned for parking offences. The levying of a very large fine can cause considerable pain to the offender. Depriving an individual of money – a commodity seen as essential in our society – can be extremely damaging. It limits choice, it restricts social intercourse and social interaction. While it does not literally 'lock someone away', the fine, if large enough, can cause destitution and penury and thereby restrict the effective exercise of liberty. But, I suggest, even if the rapist were fined his total income for a very long period – if the court were, in effect, and to borrow a phrase from Morris and Tonry (1990, p. 112), to impose 'financial capital punishment' – it would still be perceived as an inappropriate sanction; why?

The answer I propose is that the fine is seen to be the wrong sort of pain and suffering for the type of harm rape is regarded to be. It seems wrong to deal with a crime which so devastates the victim with a commodity like money. It appears morally repugnant to suggest that everything about a person can be translated into a monetary equivalent. Rather, I suggest, in contemporary perceptions there exists a core set of values and personal attributes which we resist being brought into contact with money or any other material resource. There are, in other words, certain facets of being a person which are reserved – those considered to be constitutive of personhood and individuality. We invest these facets with deep emotional intensity because to do otherwise would threaten our sense of moral integrity and wholeness. Sexuality is now seen as one such facet and this is why we balk at the idea of the rapist being fined. It appears tantamount to declaring that 'the person' can be bought and sold like a commodity in the market.

The reasons why it is seen as wrong to fine a rapist thus are essentially moral ones. Not just in the obvious sense that rape is morally wrong, but also because we see it as morally wrong to use money in these circumstances. Our moral sentiments are offended by the very notion. It upsets our natural sympathy.

This argument can be expressed in a more analytical way. Recently both Judith Jarvis Thompson (1986) and Robert Nozick (1974) have argued for the existence of what they call 'uncompensatable for harms'. What they have in mind is this. For most of the time and for most harms committed against us, we are happy to accept a 'principle of compensation'. That is, the harm committed by the offender is analogous to a debt and as long as payment is made to settle this debt, the relationship is restored or at least patched up. The payment need not be in money but usually is; as Thompson argues, we conventionally accept sums of money as the price individuals have to pay for damaging us. According to her, the law of delict or tort is based on this 'principle of compensation'. However, there are some types of harm, committed in certain circumstances, which we exclude from these arrangements. These harms Thompson and Nozick call the 'uncompensatable for harms'. How does this second category of harms differ from the first? Nozick's answer is that the difference lies mostly in the extent to which they are seen to affect the individual and also in the degree of culpability with which the 'offender' is seen to have acted. He asks us to imagine the individual as being surrounded by a 'line' or a 'hyper plane' drawn in moral space. The line is a boundary which other individuals are prohibited from crossing or transgressing. If they do they cannot compensate us. Rather in these circumstances they are punished.

Judicial punishment is a special case of this more general process. In the criminal law, however, the task of maintaining certain of these moral boundaries or hyper-planes is turned over to the state, which becomes, through its legal system, the agency which administers the punishment. (Why it becomes the duty of the state to patrol some of these boundaries and not others, indeed why the state has absorbed this job, are interesting and important questions but not central to my argument here.)

If we stretch matters slightly we can describe the way the criminal justice system works in terms of this distinction between those harms for which compensation is allowed and those for which it is not. My suggestion is that for most of the time and in most circumstances a principle of compensation is, in effect, at work in the criminal justice system. By this I do not mean that, in the technical legal sense, Compensation Orders as defined, for instance, by the 1980 Criminal Justice (Scotland) Act, are handed out in dozens, but that the heavy reliance on the fine is analogous to the principle of compensation. For most harms, the offender is allowed to pay a sum of money and matters end there (provided payment is made). At this level, the relationship between crime and punishment is a sort of 'trade-off' in which a monetary equivalence is struck between the harm caused by the crime to the victim and that which is to be imposed on the offender. However, there are some harms, like rape, which cannot be dealt with by this principle, by this 'trade-off'. These harms, the serious crimes, are punished, which means two things. First, that the harm has been evaluated in such a way as to rule out the calculation of a monetary equivalent. It is not, I claim, that the disutilities suffered by the victim are so high as to make them, for all practical purposes, incalculable in money terms. Rather, I contend, at this point there is a reluctance, perhaps even a refusal, to allow an economic vocabulary or calculus to be used at all. At this point the values associated with money and those associated with punishment are in conflict, and in consequence it becomes artificial to conceive of one in terms of the other. The second implication of requiring the guilty offender to be punished (rather than to pay compensation) is that the victim has effectively declared that the relationships involved cannot be patched up or restored but have been shattered beyond repair. It follows thus that the meanings associated with punishment become inherently hostile and non-utilitarian. This can be seen in the judicial vocabulary used to describe both crime and punishment in these circumstances. The vocabulary becomes increasingly moralistic and value-laden, as epitomised by grand, solemn judicial pronouncements before the passing of sentence. One aspect of this is that particular words and expressions are increasingly made to serve other than purely descriptive purposes; they take on a symbolic force which functions also to communicate a wider set of values, standards and norms. This simultaneously exposes this set of values to public view and also reinforces them. Justice is thus seen to be done, and one very important aspect of this is the conscious creation of a 'special' vocabulary of punishment that is made ever-distant and separate from the terms associated with compensation and money, except in the idea of offenders having to pay back their debt to society. Punishment can still be conceived of as an exchange or a transaction, but now in a context set by morality rather than economics.

This shift in vocabularies between the compensatable for harms and the non-compensatable for harms is related to the wider functions of estrangement within the criminal justice system. Earlier I argued that although punishment and money are fully estranged only in rare instances, such as in cases of rape, this nonetheless has a wider impact on the criminal justice system as it colours the scale of values used to evaluate crime and punishment more generally. The shifts in vocabulary alluded to above become part of this wider process because the openly moralistic vocabulary used to talk of punishment when it is estranged from money comes to be seen as characteristic, and thus may be said to constitute what can be seen as its focal meaning. By this I mean that our knowledge of the penal system comes to be largely modelled on what happens in serious crimes and punishments. And as the 'normal' practice at this level is to deal with crime by the use of the prison, it is the prison which comes to symbolise best what we understand by punishment. One consequence of this is that monetary sanctions, including the fine, come to occupy a 'second-best' position. Although at the lower end of the penal hierarchy the fine is the 'natural' punishment for sentencers to use, this use is always evaluated against the symbol of the prison, as it is this institution which best carries the meaning of punishment. As a result the monetary calculations in fines are always set against the broader cultural back-drop of a vocabulary that is expressly non-economic. Hence although the full estrangement of punishment and money is a rarity, its influence is systematic and profound.

I hope my analysis of the non-use of fines in cases of rape helps to illuminate what I mean by the cultural estrangement of punishment and money. As I see it, the phenomenon of estrangement is an active ingredient in penal practice as it is centrally concerned with the ranking of those values by which harms are evaluated, both by sentencers in court and within wider cultural perceptions of punishment as an institution. More specifically, I have tried to show how estrangement affects the monetary calculations that lie at the base of fines. I am very conscious that my analysis is brief and incomplete and that many important questions have been left untouched. Perhaps the most significant of these is a detailed discussion of how sentencers use fines at the lower end of the scale of crimes and punishments, especially in the light of my comments on the generalised effects of estrangement. However, I have dealt with this question in another paper (see Young, 1989 and forthcoming) and feel that the detail of the analysis makes it unsuitable for presentation in a summary form here. Another very important, but more general, sociological question concerns the broader social context of estrangement – why do we perceive money in such a way as to make monetary penal sanctions inappropriate in the sense outlined? Equally, why is it that we seem predisposed to define punishment essentially in terms of the deprivation of liberty? These are, as they say, 'big' questions, but the simple act of posing them, I hope, suggests lines of research to be explored (see Young, forthcoming).

I wish to conclude by very briefly considering two broad issues that I feel are implicit in my analysis. The first takes up one aspect of one of the 'big' questions I have just mentioned. One reason why I first became interested in research on fines and other monetary sanctions is that there seemed to me to be a central explanatory paradox in the sociology of punishment, indeed in the way that most relevant academic disciplines approached the study of the penal system. This is that there appears to be an almost inverse relationship between the amount of attention various literatures devote to the study of penal sanctions and their actual use in penal practice. While there are volumes on the study of the prison and other 'bodily' punishments, sanctions which are rarely used, there is still very little work on the fine, the most common of sanctions. We possess, of course, some very interesting and valuable administrative analyses of the fine, particularly from the point of view of problems in its enforcement, but there are remarkably few general studies of it. I do not claim to be the first to notice this.

In 1939, for example, Herman Mannheim made very much the same point. He wrote: 'both as regards the public interest it arouses as well as in the amount of scientific study devoted to it, the fine is the Cinderella among penal methods. We should not, however, overlook its great social significance' (Mannheim, 1939, p. 127). Mannheim did not go on to demonstrate either its 'great social significance' or to devote much time to the study of it, and this seems peculiar in a book explicitly on 'the economic factor' in the penal problem. Rather, he retreated by employing what I understand to have been one of his rarer traits – humour – to defuse the point. Talking of the fine, he said: 'there is an entire lack of sensation, mysticism and romance around this method of punishment. It is said to be not too difficult to make money out of prison memoirs, but who would buy a book with the title, "How I paid my fines"?' (Mannheim, 1939, p. 127)

The important analytical point that such comments raise is, why this imbalance in the literature? Why is our 'knowledge' of punishment so centred on the prison? There are, of course, many good reasons to study the prison and I am not suggesting that we ought to ignore it. But I do feel there is a genuine problem here. It seems dangerous to me to take a body of literature centred on the prison and assume that it can be applied to the study of another sanction, particularly when that other sanction differs so markedly in terms of the 'commodity', the deprivation of which will constitute the punishment. To state the obvious, the prison deprives individuals of their liberty; the fine deprives individuals of their money. Why should it be assumed that an explanation centred on the first has purchase upon the second? But so many explanations of punishment seem to me to make just this assumption implicitly or explicitly. Surely attention needs to be paid to the content of sanctions, for, as I have tried to show here, this must inevitably affect how they are used?

This suggests that what is required is a sociology of punishment which examines how both liberty and money are related to penal practice. And a first step in this, I suggest, is to think again about how our basic questions are set; there is a need to shift the explanatory agenda away from the prison and enrich it by a recognition of the importance of, in particular, the fine.

The other broad issue I wish to mention concerns the way in which the study of punishment can be approached. There has been a good deal of literature produced, particularly in the USA, within what is loosely known as the 'law and economics' school, and one of its foci of attention has been the economics of crime and punishment. The broad thrust of this approach is to apply economic concepts to the analysis of law, crime and punishment. One of the most interesting analyses of criminal law has been produced by Judge Posner. The originality of Posner's analysis is that he tries to analyse what he calls the 'passionate' crimes in economic terms, the particular example he takes being that of rape. He endeavours, in economic terms, to show (a) why laws on rape exist, and (b) why rape is punished in certain ways. Without going into great detail, I believe his argument can be reduced to these main points. He argues that laws on rape can be understood as a market regulator; his suggestion is that there exists an implicit market in sexuality which is regulated by marriage and other legitimate conventions. The law on rape endeavours to deter what he calls 'market by-passers' – that is, those who wish, as it were, to take a short cut by working outwith the particular market conditions that in this case regulate sexuality. As he puts it, 'the prohibition against rape is to the marriage and sex "market" as the prohibition against theft is to explicit markets in goods and services' (Posner, 1985, p. 1199). His analysis of sanctions aims to show why fines are not used to deal with rape and why the standard punishment is a long sentence of imprisonment. The essence of his argument is that fines are not used (a) because the disutilities suffered by the victim are so high they cannot be practically costed, and (b) because, he claims, the fine is economically less efficient as a punishment than the prison (see Posner, 1985, pp. 1193–1232).

Posner's arguments are clearly relevant to my own and also pose, in some respects, a challenge to it. The two differ, however, in a fundamental way. Posner assumes that all forms of behaviour can be understood in economic terms in the sense that he believes that such an analysis delivers the best type of explanation. My analysis implies that there are limits to the application of an economic vocabulary. This, I feel, comes out most clearly in the differing accounts of why fines are not applied in rape cases. For Posner this is a matter of disutilities; in my account it is because an economic calculus is seen as inappropriate. Of course, lying behind Posner's approach is an assumption that behaviour is best understood, and hence can be described, in terms of a series of transactions in a market setting. In contrast, the idea of estrangement implies that there are some things which are market inalienable, that is, are not exchanged in market situations at all. I am not arguing that sexuality *per se* is market inalienable because this is manifestly wrong, as such institutions as pornography, prostitution and bride-price show. What I am saying is that there is a deep-seated cultural resistance to applying an economic vocabulary in particular contexts, and one of these is the criminal law when it deals with certain very serious crimes.

I fully realise that my comments will not stop economists applying their vocabulary to all situations. The question is, however, whether it makes sense to do so.

References

Mannheim, H. (1939), *Dilemmas of Penal Reform*, Allen & Unwin, London.

Morris, N., and Tonry, M. (1990), *Between Prison and Probation: Intermediate Punishments in a Rational Sentencing System*, Oxford University Press, New York.

Nicholson, C. G .B. (1985), *The Law and Practice of Sentencing in Scotland*, W. Green, Edinburgh.

Nozick, R. (1974), *Anarchy, State and Utopia*, Basic Books, New York.

Posner, R. (1985), 'An economic theory of the criminal law', *Columbia Law Review*, LXXXV, pp. 1193–1231.

Thompson, J. J. (1986), *Rights, Restitution and Risk: Essays in Moral Theory*, Harvard University Press, Cambridge, MA.

Young, P. (1989), 'Punishment, money and a sense of justice', in P. Carlen and D. Cook (eds.), *Paying for Crime*, Open University Press, Milton Keynes, pp. 46–65.

Young, P. (forthcoming), *Punishment, Money and Legal Order*, Edinburgh University Press, Edinburgh.

PART FIVE

Violence against women

12

Criminal justice responses to violence against women

MARJORY D. FIELDS

INTRODUCTION

Wife beating has been the subject of sporadic reform movements and faded into the background as accepted behaviour several times in the last two centuries in the United States and the United Kingdom (Dobash and Dobash, 1979). To see the bias against protecting women from male violence, however, one must look outside the criminal assault laws because they are written to be gender neutral. The sexist underpinnings of our criminal laws are most visible in the rape laws (Burt, 1980; Burt and Albin, 1981; Estrich, 1986; Sanday, 1990).

Rape is unique among all crimes: historically, women were the only victims.[1] Yet women did not participate in the definition of rape, or in the legal procedures required to prove the crime (Estrich, 1986; MacKinnon, 1991). Thus male perceptions of women's credibility and sexuality are revealed in the definition and prosecution of the crime of rape (Bienen, 1983). Rape laws have been drafted and enforced in ways that protect rapists and exacerbate the harm to victims (Estrich, 1986; LeGrand, 1973; Quenneville, 1979; Robin, 1977; Schwartz and Clear, 1980).

The influential Model Penal Code rape provisions demonstrate this effect. The Model Penal Code is promulgated by the prestigious American Law Institute. The American Law Institute develops model laws used for reference by state legislatures, and cited by state appellate courts. The statutes and commentaries it publishes are written by legal practitioners, academics, and judges in the United States. The Model Penal Code drafters proclaimed their rape provisions 'balanced', 'enlightened', and 'objective'.[2] They were adopted by the American Law Institute in 1962 with Revised Commentaries published in 1980. The commentators quote Lord Matthew Hale's pronouncement, made in 1680, that 'Rape is an accusation easily to be made and hard to be proved, and harder to be defended by the party accused, tho never so innocent'.

Although the commentators deny adherence to the concept of the devious, vengeful, or fantasizing woman, the language of the Commentaries shows the opposite.[3]

> Often the woman's attitude may be deeply ambivalent. She may not want intercourse, may fear it, or may desire it but feel compelled to say 'no'. Her confusion at the time of the act may later resolve into non-consent. Some have expressed the fear that a woman who subconsciously wanted to have sexual intercourse will later feel guilty and 'cry rape'.[4]

The Model Penal Code has a corroboration requirement. This in effect preserves the requirement of victim resistance, because the 'objective evidence' of compulsion and lack of consent are provided best by the injuries and torn clothing which result from a victim's resistance.[5] No other crime of violence in the Model Penal Code, or in any state statute in the United States, has corroboration or resistance requirements.

Furthermore, it has been impossible to obtain repeal of the laws exempting from prosecution husbands who rape their wives ('the marital rape exemption').[6] Supporters of the marital rape exemption claim there are uniquely difficult proof problems and extraordinary motives to fabricate marital rape claims (Augustine, 1991). Some states have extended the marital rape exemption to unmarried people living together, and even to 'voluntary social companions' (Augustine, 1991; Buckborough, 1989; Lincoln, 1989).

Compared to the failures of the rape and marital rape law reform efforts, the domestic violence law reform campaign has achieved substantial successes (Dobash and Dobash, 1992). There are several technical reasons for this. Ostensibly, wife beating was included in the definition of the crime of assault before the reform efforts began. Domestic violence, unlike rape, usually has physical injuries to 'corroborate' the claim of assault. 'Consent' was never an issue in the crime of assault, therefore there was no 'resistance' requirement. Thus domestic violence law reforms did not require revising traditional legal theories and procedures.

The legislative response to domestic violence included creation of new, civil legal remedies for battered women. 'Orders of protection', which are injunctions, have been enacted in nearly every state in the

United States. They may contain provisions directing abusive spouses to cease beating and threatening their spouses and children, to remove themselves from family homes, and to stay away from their spouses and children. Child custody may be awarded to victims, and visitation by offenders prohibited or limited to supervised settings. This relief is available on an immediate, temporary basis prior to the time set for a full hearing, and before notice is given to accused spouses. Most state statutes authorize the police to arrest spouses alleged to have violated these civil orders on the same basis that persons alleged to have committed crimes may be arrested (Finn and Colson, 1990).

CRIMINAL JUSTICE RESPONSE TO VIOLENCE AGAINST WOMEN

Legislatures and courts also addressed wife beating as a crime of violence. They responded to pressure from the women's movement to stop domestic violence, thus the criminal justice system became involved in protecting battered women. In spite of these successes, the sexist attitudes so visible in the rape laws continue to affect the criminal justice response to violence against women (Dobash and Dobash, 1979, 1992).

Judges
Sentencing is exclusively within the power of judges, therefore judicial attitudes toward crimes against women will affect their sentencing practices in wife-beating cases. There is little empirical research on judicial attitudes toward domestic violence. The limited literature focuses on the criminal justice system, without specific attention to the judicial component (Fagan, 1988; Parnas, 1973). Anecdotal evidence, however, is available (New York State Task Force on Women in the Courts, 1986). I have seen judicial prejudice against domestic violence victims when I represented battered women in New York City courts, and now that I am a judge.

Judges assume that threats and minor violence by one family member against another are not serious, and will not be prosecuted beyond the arraignment stage. Court statistics show that 50 per cent of the battered women will seek to drop charges. Although it seems high, this attrition rate is no greater than the attrition rate for all felonies in New York City (Vera Institute, 1977).

Judges do not consider the attrition rate in other types of cases, yet judges believe the perceived attrition rate in domestic violence cases is an indication that battered women are misusing the court system. Judges find this offensive. Ironically, given the overwhelming volume of cases in the courts, attrition of all types of cases is essential to the continued functioning of the criminal justice system. The attrition rate for a type of crime is not a legal basis for dismissal or diversion of an individual case. Yet predictions of victim lack of co-operation and high court volume are reasons judges give for diverting domestic violence cases away from court. Judges, however, fail to assess the risks to victims when they divert or dismiss domestic violence cases (Goldsmith, 1990; Eisikovits and Edleson, 1989; Murphy, 1992).

Judges ignore the reasonable explanations for abandoned domestic violence cases. Some women do not return to court because arrests and arraignments resulted in the defendants ceasing their violence or terminating their relationships. Other women, unable to obtain protection from continued violence while waiting for trial dates, move away to be safe, or return to other remedies, such as divorce.

Another unwarranted judicial assumption is that criminal complaints of domestic violence are manoeuvres in pending or planned divorce actions, to bolster the cause of action for cruel treatment, and to get the husband out of the marital home prior to the divorce judgment (New York State Task Force on Women in the Courts, 1986). This assumption has several defects. A criminal prosecution requires proof beyond a reasonable doubt to succeed. A divorce action requires that the plaintiff establish her case for ultimate and preliminary relief by a preponderance of the evidence only. Thus, it is much easier to obtain relief in the divorce court.

Judges prefer adjournments in contemplation of dismissal (ACD), which are pre-trial compromises, because they take less court time (Fields, 1978; Murphy, 1992; Parnas, 1971, 1973). An ACD is a postponement of the trial on condition that the defendant is not convicted of a crime. In addition, the defendant may be required to participate in mediation or counseling programs. The complaint is dismissed automatically at the end of six months, without a trial, if the defendant complies with the conditions. The penalty for the defendant's failure to comply with the ACD conditions is restoration of the case to the court calendar for trial. This is well known to be an empty threat, because the prosecutors do not monitor compliance with the ACD conditions, and cannot reassemble the evidence to try a case four to five months stale (Harrell, 1991).

After conviction, sentences of probation supervision or incarceration are rare in domestic violence cases, even though the same types of rehabilitative-program conditions may be imposed in conjunction with probation, or a split sentence of brief incarceration followed by a period of probation (Fagan, 1989). A common disposition in domestic violence cases after a conviction is a conditional discharge (CD). Judges order the offender to attend counseling programs, receive drug or alcohol treatment, or comply with other conditions in lieu of imposing a sentence. If the offender violates the conditions, then the case may be returned to court for imposition of a sentence.

The threat of returning to court for sentencing is potent because there has been a conviction. The sentencing process does not require reassembling stale evidence. Only the probation pre-sentence report must be prepared. Even this procedure is ineffective, however, when the prosecutor fails to invoke the sentencing process for violation of the conditions.

ACDs or CDs with referrals to counseling and mediation are detrimental to the safety of battered women. Mediation is inappropriate in cases in which the parties do not have equality of bargaining power. Mediation ignores the past violence, and has the goal of preventing future problems between the parties through modification of the behaviour of both parties. Crime victims are thereby made responsible for the violence of the offenders. Offenders escape responsibility for their violence. The violence which brought the parties into the criminal justice system is ignored (Dobash and Dobash, 1992; Ellis, 1990; Fields, 1978; Geffner and Pagelow, 1990).

After conviction, judges do not impose sentences of incarceration for domestic violence cases at the same rate that they do for stranger violence cases. Judges adhere to the notion that domestic violence is the outgrowth of interpersonal problems, not amenable to criminal justice intervention. They resist ordering violent husbands or live-in companions out of the family home, although there is statutory authority for this, and no case law invalidating this power (Eaton and Hyman, 1992; Fagan, 1988; Fields, 1978; New York State Task Force on Women in the Courts, 1986). In the sentencing process judges focus on individual offender guilt, but mitigated by victim blaming: 'why does she stay with him?' 'why does she provoke him?'. Sentences or CDs which require wife beaters to attend programs designed to teach them anger control without addressing domestic violence as a method to enforce male dominance in the family, ignore the social context of domestic violence (Levinson, 1989). Thus psychological abuse continues, even when physical abuse stops (Bohm, 1986; Dobash and Dobash, 1992; Harrell, 1991).

Decisions in family law cases often contain judicial conclusions regarding family relationships, frequently without any basis in social science or the evidence presented in the case being decided. The effect of this style of decision making, which appears to be more common in family law matters than in other types of cases, is that social policy is made by courts in the guise of noticing social reality (Perry and Melton, 1983–84). This type of decision making is clear in the history of domestic violence in the courts.

The solution of judicial 'education' by women's advocates has not been successful (Eaton and Hyman, 1992). Judges have greeted these programs with scepticism. On the other hand, legal training from other judges and law professors, integrated into criminal law educational programs, has had some impact in increasing orders for victim protection (Carter, Heisler and Lemon, 1991). Several cities have assigned judges interested in domestic violence to hear all domestic violence cases (Smith, 1988; Gamache et al., 1988).

Those emphasising social and psychological services ignore the efficacy of legal services for battered women. Lawyers for battered women pressure the police to arrest, and convince prosecutors to try cases and to request orders of protection. Lawyers marshal evidence for prosecutors to use for trial and to present in support of sentencing requests. Lawyers represent battered women in civil proceedings to obtain orders of protection and divorces, title to or possession of the family home, child custody and support, restrictions on visitation or access by violent fathers, division of joint or marital assets, and money damages for injuries. Women who have overcome the emotional attachment to their abusive partners, on their own or through treatment, need legal representation to obtain protection.

Another indicator that domestic violence continues to be regarded as not 'real' crime, is the separation of domestic violence research from research on other violent crimes. A unified analysis of family and stranger violence would test the validity of the separate theory of family violence and improve policy analysis (Fagan, 1988, 1989). The criminal justice system should merge the information gained from empirical studies of family violence offenders and non-family violence offenders to develop better measures of offender dangerousness, and appropriate sanctions and interventions in all cases of violence. Longitudinal studies of the violent careers of wife beaters should be done using the model used for other types of criminal careers. Using information from family violence literature, the criminal justice system should assess which sanctions, treatments, and social responses work best for wife beaters, and other violent criminals (Fagan, 1988, 1989).

Treatment for domestic violence offenders
The criminal justice system relies heavily on treatment programs for domestic violence offenders, therefore an analysis of these programs is necessary. Early in the current movement to protect women from the violence of their male partners, referrals of both parties for couple, group, and individual psychotherapy were popular alternatives to police and court intervention. This preference for treatment continues today as an adjunct to police and criminal court intervention. One may conclude that the reason treatment programs, rather than traditional criminal justice solutions of probation supervision or incarceration, are preferred is that this lenient, unproven disposition corresponds with the social perception that assault of one's wife or female companion is not a crime, but tolerated social behaviour. Otherwise, one would expect treatment to be proposed also for offenders who assault strangers or rob banks (Fagan, 1988, 1989).

Levinson analysed anthropological studies of ninety societies to test the cross-cultural validity of the most common theories of family violence and to identify the correlates of wife beating (Levinson, 1989). He found that wife beating occurs in 84 per cent of those societies with considerable frequency. He found that although no family members are immune from family violence, adult women are most likely to be the victims, and adult men are most likely to be the perpetrators and least likely to be the victims. Women are more likely than any other category of family member to suffer 'severe and debilitating injuries', usually at the hands of their husbands (Levinson, 1989, p. 81; Gondolf and Fisher, 1991, pp. 278–9). It may be inferred, therefore, that since wife beating is so common, it is normal behaviour (Dobash and Dobash, 1979, 1992; Levinson, 1989; Parnas, 1978; Stanko, 1988). Thus the feasibility of treatment programs for wife beaters must be questioned, because their goal is to have men cease a normal behaviour.

Much of the early treatment literature is based on clinical experience from which generalizations are drawn concerning the characteristics of wife beaters and battered wives. The more recent literature contains descriptions and empirical evaluations of programs. The evaluations vary in the number of subjects, length of follow-up period, type of informants, use of control groups, and measures of success. They cover programs with divergent methods of intervention and different clients: men; women; and couples (Eisikovits and Edleson, 1989; Hotaling and Surgarman, 1986; Pirog-Good and Stets-Kealey, 1985; Saunders, 1988a; Yllo, 1988; Tolman and Bennett, 1990). The inconsistent measures and conflicting methods provide no basis for determining what types of treatment or combinations of interventions stop violent behaviour in which types of offenders.

The weakness of many current treatment programs is that they lack any theoretical bases for client selection, program form and content, treatment methods, and evaluation design (Eisikovits and Edleson, 1989). Each type of common therapeutic intervention has defects. The individual psychotherapeutic method views domestic violence as caused by the psychological problems of the individual patient. It relieves the individual of responsibility for his violence because of psychiatric illness, or finds the cause in the personality of the victim.

Although in individual instances wife beaters and their victims may have diagnosable personality disorders or mental illnesses, basing a general theory of domestic violence on the mental illness of offenders or victims ignores the widespread prevalence and social acceptance of wife beating. The logical extension of this theory is that there is a massive epidemic of mental illness. Significantly, the empirical literature fails to show that traditional psychotherapeutic or cognitive-behavioural approaches eliminate violence (Dobash and Dobash, 1992; Ptacek, 1988; Stanko, 1988).

Couples therapy based on the family systems theory places equal responsibility for the violence on the victim. Family systems practitioners focus on the violent couple, and do not recognize the concept of abusers and victims (Geffner and Rosenbaum, 1990; Lehr and Fitzsimmons, 1991). Their goal is to improve and preserve the relationship. The man's violent behaviour is usually ignored; responsibility is placed on the victim to stop provoking her companion's violence (Ptacek, 1988; Saunders, 1988b). Eisikovits and Edleson (1989) point out that the couples treatment literature fails to link theory and practice. The studies of outcomes of couples therapy lack control groups and consistent follow-up periods. The definitions of success in these studies are inconsistent. Some programs have the unsatisfactory goal of a 'decrease' in violence rather than cessation of violence (Eisikovits and Edleson, pp. 391–2).

The family systems premise of equal responsibility for domestic violence is refuted by the results of a study of 'risk markers' for husband to wife violence done by Hotaling and Sugarman (1986). They evaluated ninety-seven potential risk factors using fifty-two case-comparison studies; 'these studies identify factors associated with violent men compared to nonviolent men as well as the factors that differentiate female victims from non-victims' (p. 101). Hotaling and Sugarman use the term 'risk markers' to refer to factors associated with husband violence because they conclude that it is not possible to differentiate factors which are causes, coincidences, or results of domestic violence. Tolman and Bennett (1990) agree that traits such as depression, noted commonly in men who beat their wives, do not cause men to batter, but may result from the consequences of their violence – arrest, jail, or separation.

Hotaling and Sugarman (1986) found 'There is little current evidence that women with particular personality characteristics contribute to their own victimization ...' (p. 111). The only one of forty-two characteristics of women victims which was a consistent risk marker, as defined by Hotaling and Sugarman, was witnessing violence between parents during their childhoods (p. 106). No other characteristic examined in the fifty-two studies they reviewed could be used to discriminate victims of domestic violence from women who are not victims.

'Identifying female victims of violence is not possible if only her characteristics are considered ... It appears that personality and symptomological differences are a consequence of battering rather than a cause of it'. Low self-esteem, high anxiety, psychosomatic illness, alcohol and prescription drug abuse develop in response to chronic victimization. 'This review of victim characteristics makes it clear that the most influential victim precipitant is being female. The victimization of women may be better understood as the outcome of male behaviour' (Hotaling and Sugarman, p. 118). Diana E. H. Russell came to the same conclusion in her study of marital rape (1982, pp. 169–89).

Although Hotaling and Sugarman (1986) found the studies showed that batterers have many similarities to men with borderline and antisocial personality disorders (as defined in DSM III, 1980), they could not find 'direct evidence' that wife beaters have clinical character disorders to a greater extent than men who do not beat their wives (p. 118). Tolman and Bennett (1990), in their literature review, also found a high proportion of men in treatment programs with personality and psychological problems, especially those men with alcohol problems. They theorize, however, that there is an over-representation of psychopathology in treatment programs because men with greater pathology are more likely to be arrested, to be referred by social agencies, and to seek treatment for their multiple problems. They conclude that there is no clear causal connection between psychopathology and wife beating (p. 89).

Witnessing and experiencing violence during childhood was found to be common to men who batter their wives and men who do not batter their wives. 'Witnessing parental violence is more consistently related to husband and wife violence than experiencing parental violence in childhood.' Wife beaters also were found to exhibit a broad pattern of violence against other family members and strangers (Hotaling and Sugarman, 1986, pp. 119–20). Hotaling and Sugarman concluded that research should focus on male characteristics. Even though wife beating has complex causes, it is predominantly a male behaviour, thus men rather than women should be studied to find causes and solutions (p. 120).

Men's treatment groups have been promoted as the best solution to domestic violence. They are certainly the most cost effective, treating several individuals at one time for short periods. Eisikovits and Edleson (1989) noted more than fifty books and articles on this method of intervention in domestic violence. The many different techniques and structures are each advanced as effective. Varieties of combinations make it impossible to describe them all or to determine which are successful, or what elements account for success (pp. 392–5).

Men's groups which emphasize anger control and ignore social influences and sex-role stereotyping have been much criticized. Critics point out that anger is not the sole cause of wife beating. Anger, like jealousy, can be self-generated and is used as an excuse for violence, and claimed loss of control. Wife beating is often instrumental. Violence is used to maintain control. It is not the result of lost control. In addition, wife beaters have negative attitudes towards women. These issues should be addressed to change behaviour (Dobash and Dobash, 1992, pp. 240–50; Eisikovits and Edleson, 1989, p. 395; Holmes and Lundy, 1990; Tolman and Bennett, 1990, pp. 92–3).

The many empirical studies which show that men's groups are effective in stopping violence against women suffer from serious methodological defects. Furthermore, the definitions of 'success' are vague and inconsistent among the studies. Some programs claim success if violence decreases, but does not end (Rosenbaum and Maiuro, 1990). Decreased violence is not defined. It may mean frequent, but less severe beatings, or severe beatings administered less frequently. This is an unacceptable result for the victims, who must live with continued violence and psychological terror (Eisikovits and Edleson, 1989; Saunders, 1988a; Tolman and Bennett, 1990; Yllo and Bograd, 1988).

Acceptance of reduced severity of violence is condonation of continued criminal behaviour (Edleson and Grusznski, 1988; Holmes and Lundy, 1990). It would not be deemed satisfactory if a drug treatment program measured its success by decreased frequency of drug sales or frequent sales of smaller quantities of drugs. Once violence has been used, cessation of violence and psychological abuse is the only successful outcome for any intervention (Eisikovits and Edleson, 1989; Poynter, 1989; Saunders, 1988a).

A study conducted in the state of Maryland compared 81 men who completed one of three group treatment programs after being ordered to do so by a court, with 112 men who had been to court but were not ordered to enter treatment. Men who were ordered to attend treatment, but did not complete the program were not included in the comparison (Harrell, 1991). The results show:

Among cases with a history of physical aggression in the 6 months before court (157 cases), treated offenders were less likely to stop physical aggression during the treatment period: 43 percent of the treated cases exhibited acts of physical aggression across the treatment period compared to 12 percent of those not ordered to treatment. This result remained after controlling for differences in the amount of time the victim and offender lived together.

(Harrell, 1991, p. 5)

Threats continued in about half the cases without regard to treatment. Psychological abuse continued in all cases, without regard to treatment, although with reduced frequency among those who completed treatment (Harrell, 1991, p. 5). Other studies of men's programs also found that threats continued after treatment (Edleson and Grusznski, 1988; Hamberger and Hastings, 1988; Poynter, 1989).

Harrell (1991) was not able to identify those offenders more likely to benefit from treatment or to complete treatment. Personal characteristics identified in other studies as related to success or completion were not confirmed in her study. Criminal justice disposition, ACD or CD, also did not appear to have an impact on treatment effectiveness (Harrell, 1991, p. 7).

Victim safety, as measured by injuries to victims, and the probability of getting hit by the offender during the year following the court disposition, was not improved by offender participation in treatment.

There was no difference in victim perception of safety between those whose offenders went to treatment and those not ordered to enter treatment. This lack of perceived improvement in safety was realistic given the failure of the treated offenders to alter their beliefs regarding the appropriateness of wife beating, as measured in post-treatment tests (Harrell, 1991, p. 7).

Harrell concluded 'there was no discernible deterrent effect of treatment participation, despite its educational value in conveying an understanding of the consequences of violence. This outcome suggests that offenders were well aware that the risk of facing consequences for future violence from the court and police, as well as from acquaintances, was relatively low' (p. 7). Harrell stated further that her evaluation design and implementation problems 'increase the probability of observing positive treatment effects'. Judges tended to order treatment for those without prior criminal records and for those who appeared motivated to change. The slightly shorter follow-up period for those who completed treatment would also distort treatment effects in a positive direction. In addition, attrition removed from the treated group those least likely to stop their violence (p. 9). Chen, Bersani, Myers and Denton (1989) found similarly that the empirical evidence of success of court-sponsored abuser treatment programs was not clear.

The studies also fail to correct for the periodic nature of much wife beating, the impact of arrest or court action, or the effect of separation from the former partner on the absence of violence in the follow-up period. Follow-up periods not long enough to include those who are violent a few times a year or those who are without partners, fail to measure success meaningfully. Furthermore, short evaluation periods do not take into account that violence varies over time and in changing situations. (Edleson and Grusznski, 1988; Eisikovits and Edleson, 1989; Tolman and Bennett, 1990). Saunders (1988a) suggests follow-up periods of two to five years to correct for these variables.

Other defective evaluations are based on project staff self-evaluation and offender self-reports of success (Edleson and Grusznski, 1988; Eisikovits and Edleson, 1989; Saunders, 1988a; Tolman and Bennett, 1990). Many researchers have found that wife beaters are likely to under-report their continued violence, as well as the severity and frequency of their violence (DeMaris and Jackson, 1987; Edleson and Grusznski, 1988; Saunders, 1988a). Victims may under-report from fear of retaliation, or because they block unpleasant memories. Over-reporting by victims may occur from over-estimation of painful

events (Saunders, 1988a). Evaluations must thus have additional information from police and court records.

CONCLUSION

Refuges for battered women and their children are essential because
the criminal justice system in most instances cannot restrain wife
beaters for more than short periods. Programs for victims must receive
first preference when allocating limited resources. They are the best
assurance of safety for battered women and their children.

Criminal prosecution of wife beaters remains the only available
method for ending specific incidents of wife beating immediately. The
police must form a protective alliance with battered women to assure
their safety, even when arrest is not feasible. There must be co-ordination among police, social services, refuges, prosecutors, probation,
and parole. This co-ordinated effort should be organized to protect
battered women, to warn them of threats by their husbands, and to
notify them of their husbands' release from custody (Fagan, 1989).

Treatment programs for wife beaters must be improved significantly
to justify continued support. There must be a theoretical basis for
men's programs and a standardized evaluation design. Programs
for violent men must address violent behaviour on multiple levels:
individual; interpersonal; institutional, and cultural. Programs must
adapt to the heterogeneity of batterers, and provide services to satisfy
their diverse needs. Issues of misogyny and social supports for domestic violence must be confronted in treatment programs. Men must
be held responsible for their violence and emotional abuse, and made
to recognize the criminal nature of their actions (Bohm, 1986; Dobash
and Dobash, 1992; Eisikovits and Edleson, 1989; Fagan, 1989; Gondolf and Fisher, 1991; Tolman and Bennett, 1990)

The programs must operate on the premise that violence against
women is criminal conduct, and that the only successful program
outcome is cessation of violence and threats. Even minor violence,
threats, harassment, and menacing must be seen as more dangerous
in a family setting than in the street. These acts against family members
are recurrent and precede more serious violence. They create an
atmosphere of terror for all family members. Unless treatment programs address these issues, and incorporate victim notification and
protection into their practice, treatment programs increase the risks
to battered women by creating false expectations of change and safety.
These expectations can cause women to remain with or return to

dangerous men (Dobash and Dobash, 1992; Eisikovits and Edleson, 1989; Gondolf and Fisher, 1991).

Levinson concluded that 'violence is not an inevitable consequence of family life, as evidenced by the 16 societies . . . in which family violence is largely nonexistent' (1989, p. 82). In those societies women have economic power, equality in the home, and access to divorce. There are non-violent dispute settlement styles, and immediate intervention when a beating occurs. In the United States, police response, criminal justice intervention, and refuges are the most practical ways to stop wife beating.

Notes

1 The Crime of Rape, United States Department of Justice, Bureau of Justice Statistics (March, 1985).
2 Model Penal Code 213.1 comment at pp. 303–07 (1980).
3 Model Penal Code 213.1 comment pp. 302–03; 213.6 comment pp. 427–30 (1980).
4 Model Penal Code comment pp. 302–03 (1980).
5 Estrich (1986), p. 1139; Model Penal Code comment pp. 303–07.
6 D. E. H. Russell (1990), pp. xviii-xxii, 21–26, Appendix II, pp. 375–82; Finkelhor and Yllo (1985).

References

American Psychiatric Association (1980), *Diagnostic and Statistical Manual of Mental Disorders*, (DSM III) (3rd edn), Washington, DC.

Augustine, R. (1991), 'Marriage: the safe haven for rapists', *Journal of Family Law*, XXIX. pp. 559–84.

Bienen, L. B. (1983), 'A question of credibility: John Henry Wigmore's use of scientific authority in section 924a of the Treatise on Evidence', *California Western Law Review*, XIX, pp. 235–7.

Bohm, R. M. (1986), 'Crime, criminal and crime control policy myths', *Justice Quarterly*, III, pp. 193–214.

Buckborough, A. L. (1989), 'Recent developments in the law of marital rape', *1989 Annual Survey of American Law*, pp. 343–52.

Burt, M. R. (1980), 'Cultural myths and support for rape', *Journal of Personality and Social Psychology*, XXXVIII, pp. 217–27.

Burt, M. R., and Albin, S. (1981), 'Rape myths, rape definitions, and probability of conviction', *Journal of Applied Social Psychology*, XI, pp. 212–22.

Carter, J., Heisler, C., and Lemon, N. K. D. (1991), *Domestic Violence: the Crucial Role of the Judge in Criminal Court Cases*, The Family Violence Prevention Fund, San Francisco.

Chen, H., Bersani, C., Myers, S. C., and Denton, R. (1989), 'Evaluating the effectiveness of a court sponsored abuser treatment program', *Journal of Family Violence*, IV, pp. 309–22.

DeMaris, A., and Jackson, J. K. (1987), 'Batterers' reports of recidivism after counsel-ling', *Social Casework: The Journal of Contemporary Social Work*, October, pp. 458–65.

Dobash, R. E., and Dobash, R. P. (1992), *Women, Violence and Social Change*, Routledge, London.

Dobash, R. E., and Dobash, R. P. (1979), *Violence Against Wives*, The Free Press, Macmillan, New York.

Eaton, S., and Hyman, A. (1992), 'The domestic violence component of the New York Task Force Report on Women in the Courts: an evaluation and assessment of New York City courts', *Fordham Urban Law Journal*, XIX, pp. 391–534.

Edleson, J. L., and Grusznski, R. J. (1988), 'Treating men who batter: four years of outcome data from the domestic abuse project', *Journal of Social Service Research*, XII, pp. 3–22.

Eisikovits, Z. C., and Edleson, J. L. (1989), 'Intervening with men who batter: a critical review of the literature', *Social Service Review*, pp. 384–414.

Ellis, D. (1990), 'Marital conflict mediation and post-separation wife abuse', *Law and Inequality*, VIII, pp. 317–39.

Estrich, S. (1986), 'Rape', *Yale Law Journal*, XCV, pp. 1133–61.

Fagan, J. (1988), 'Contributions of family violence research to criminal justice policy on wife assault: paradigms of science and social control', *Violence and Victims*, III, pp. 159–86.

Fagan, J. (1989), 'Cessation of family violence: deterrence and dissuasion', in L. Ohlin and M. Tonry, *Family Violence*, University of Chicago Press, Chicago, pp. 377–425.

Fields, M. D. (1978), 'Wife beating: government intervention policies and practices', *Battered Women: Issues of Public Policy, United States Commission on Civil Rights*, Washington DC, pp. 228–87.

Fields, M. D. (1987), *Municipal Liability for Police Failure to Arrest in Domestic Violence Cases*, State of New York, Governor's Commission on Domestic Violence, Albany, NY.

Finkelhor, D., and Yllo, K. (1985), *License to Rape: Sexual Abuse of Wives*, Holt, Rinehart, New York.

Finn, P., and Colson, S. (1990), *Civil Protection Orders: Legislation, Current Court Practice, and Enforcement*, US Department of Justice, National Institute of Justice, Washington DC.

Gamache, D. J., Edleson, J. L., and Schock, M. D. (1988), 'Coordinated police, judicial, and social service response to woman battering: a multiple-baseline evaluation across three communities', in G. T. Hotaling, D. Finkelhor, J. T. Kirkpatrick, and M. A. Straus, (eds.) (1988), *Coping with Family Violence*, Sage, Newbury Park, California, pp. 193–209.

Geffner, R., and Pagelow, M. D. (1990), 'Mediation and child custody issues in abusive relationships', *Behavioral Sciences and the Law*, VIII, pp. 151–59.

Geffner, R., and Rosenbaum, A. (1990), 'Characteristics and treatment of batterers', *Behavioral Sciences and the Law*, VIII, pp. 131–40.

Goldsmith, H. R. (1990), 'Men who abuse their spouses: an approach to assessing future risk', in N. J. Pallone and S. Chaneles (eds.) (1990), *The Clinical Treatment of the Criminal Offender in Outpatient Mental Health Settings: New and Emerging Perspectives*, Haworth, New York, pp. 45–6.

Gondolf, E. W., and Fisher, E. R. (1991), 'Wife battering', in R. T. Ammerman and M. Hersen (eds.) (1990), *Treatment of Family Violence*, John Wiley, New York, pp. 273–92.

Hamberger, L. K., and Hastings, J. E. (1988), 'Skills training for treatment of spouse abusers: an outcome study', *Journal of Family Violence*, III, pp. 121–30.

Harrell, A. (1991), *Evaluation of Court-Ordered Treatment for Domestic Violence Offenders, Final Report*, Urban Institute, Washington DC.

Holmes, M., and Lundy, C. (1990), 'Group work for abusive men: profeminist response', *Canada's Mental Health*, December, pp. 12–17.

Hotaling, G. T., and Sugarman, D. B. (1986), 'An analysis of risk markers in husband-wife violence: the current state of knowledge', *Violence and Victims*, I, pp. 101–24.

LeGrand, C. E. (1973), 'Rape and rape laws: sexism in society and law', *California Law Review*, LXI, pp. 919–29.

Lehr, R. F., and Fitzsimmons, G. (1991), 'Adaptability and cohesion: implications for understanding the violence-prone system', *Journal of Family Violence*, VI, pp. 255–65.

Levinson, D. (1989), *Family Violence in Cross-Cultural Perspective*, Sage, Newbury Park, California.

Lincoln, J. A. (1989), 'Abolishing the marital exemption: the first step in protecting married women from marital rape', *Wayne Law Review*, XXXV, pp. 1219–31.

MacKinnon, C. A. (1991), 'Reflections on sex equality under law', *Yale Law Journal*, C, 1281–308.

Martin, D. (1976), *Battered Wives*, Glide, San Francisco.

Murphy, S. M. (1992), 'Pre-trial services, diverting abuse cases before they clog courts', *Human Rights*, XIX, pp. 20–21.

New York State Force on Women in the Courts Report (1986), *Fordham Urban Law Journal*, IV, pp. 11–198.

Ogloff, J. R. P., Wong, S., and Greenwood, A. (1990), 'Treating criminal psychopaths in a therapeutic community program', *Behavioral Sciences and the Law*, VIII, pp. 181–90.

Parham v. J. R., 442 US 584 (1979).

Parnas, R. I. (1971), 'Police discretion and diversion of incidents of intra-family violence', *Law and Contemporary Problems*, XXXVI, pp. 539–49.

Parnas, R. I. (1973), 'Prosecutorial and judicial handling of family violence', *Criminal Law Bulletin*, IX, pp. 733–69.

Parnas, R. I. (1978), 'The relevance of criminal law to inter-spousal violence', in J. M. Eekelaar, and S. N. Katz, *Family Violence*, Butterworth, Toronto, pp. 188–92.

Perry, G. S., and Melton, G. B. (1983–84), 'Precedential value of judicial notice of social facts: Parham as an example', *Journal of Family Law*, XXII, pp. 633–76.

Pirog-Good, M., and Stets-Kealey, J. (1985), ' Male batterers and battering prevention programs: a national survey', *RESPONSE to Violence in the Family & Sexual Assault*, VIII, pp. 8–12.

Poynter, T. L. (1989), 'An evaluation of a group programme for male perpetrators of domestic violence', *Australian Journal of Sex, Marriage and Family*, X, pp. 133–42.

Ptacek, J. (1988), 'Why do men batter their wives?', in K. Yllo and M. Bograd (eds.) (1988), *Feminist Perspectives on Wife Abuse*, Sage, Newbury Park, California, pp. 133–57.

Quenneville, K. (1979), 'Will rape ever be a crime of the past? A feminist view of societal factors and rape law reforms', *Golden Gate University Law Review*, IX, pp. 581–91.

Robin, G. D. (1977), 'Forcible rape, institutionalized sexism in the criminal justice system', *Crime and Delinquency*, XXIII, pp. 136–46.

Rosenbaum, A., and Maiuro, R. D. (1990), 'Perpetrators of spouse abuse', in R. T. Ammerman and M. Hersen (eds.), *Treatment of Family Violence*, Wiley, New York, pp. 280–309.

Russell, D. E. H. (1982), *Rape in Marriage*, Macmillan, New York.

Sanday, P. R. (1990), *Fraternity Gang Rape: Sex, Brotherhood and Privilege on Campus*, New York University Press, New York.

Saunders, D. G. (1988a). 'Issues in conducting treatment research with men who batter', in G. T. Hotaling, D. Finkelhor, J. T. Kirkpatrick, and M. A. Straus (eds.), *Coping with Family Violence*, Sage, Newbury Park, California, pp. 145–56.

Saunders, D. G. (1988b), 'Wife abuse, husband abuse, or mutual combat? A feminist perspective on the empirical findings', in K. Yllo and M. Bograd (eds.), *Feminist Perspectives on Wife Abuse*, Sage, Newbury Park, California, pp. 90–113.

Schwartz, M., and Clear, J. (1980), 'Toward a new law on rape', *Crime and Delinquency*, XXVI, pp. 129–39.

Smith, B. E. (1988), 'Victims who know their assailants: their satisfaction with the criminal court's response', in G. T. Hotaling, D. Finkelhor, J. T. Kirkpatrick, and M. A. Straus (eds.), *Coping with Family Violence*, Sage, Newbury Park, California, pp. 183–92.

Stanko, E. A. (1988), 'Fear of crime and the myth of the safe home: a feminist critique of criminology', in K. Yllo and M. Bograd (eds.), *Feminist Perspectives on Wife Abuse*, Sage, Newbury Park, California, pp. 75–88.

Steinmetz, S. K., and Straus, M. A. (1974), *Violence in the Family*, Harper & Row, New York.

Tolman, R. M., and Bennett, L. W. (1990), 'A review of quantitative research on men who batter', *Journal of Interpersonal Violence*, V. pp. 87–118.

Vera Institute (1977), *Felony Arrests: Their Prosecution and Disposition in New York City's Courts*. Vera Institute of Justice, New York.

Yllo, K. (1988), 'Political and methodological debates in wife abuse research', in K. Yllo and M. Bograd (eds.), *Feminist Perspectives on Wife Abuse*, Sage, Newbury Park, California, pp. 28–50.

Yllo, K., and Bograd, NM. (eds.) (1988), *Feminist Perspectives on Wife Abuse*, Sage, Newbury Park, California.

13

Confronting domestic violence: an innovative criminal justice response in Scotland

DAVID MORRAN AND MONICA WILSON

INTRODUCTION

The CHANGE Project came into being in September 1989 with the principal objective of establishing a criminal justice-based re-education programme for men who had been violent to their wives or female partners. The project aims to complement the work of Women's Aid in combating domestic violence by challenging men to take responsibility for and to end their violence against women.

CHANGE is funded by the Urban Renewal Unit (a government aid programme), and sponsored by the Central Regional Council Social Work Department. (Central Regional Council is the regional authority for the central area of Scotland, covering Stirling, Falkirk and other smaller towns.) The project comprises the practice element of a practice and research exercise aimed at examining the effectiveness of particular intervention strategies in dealing with male domestic violence. The research element is separately constituted and jointly funded by the Home and Scottish Offices (Dobash and Dobash, 1989). This paper describes the origins and perspective of the CHANGE Project and how it has gone about undertaking its task.

ORIGINS OF THE CHANGE PROJECT

Since the early 1970s women's movements in the UK and elsewhere have campaigned for recognition of the extent and impact of the problem of domestic violence on women's lives and have worked to provide safety and support for the victims of men's violence. This has involved the provision of refuges for women and their children, challenging institutional and community tolerance of men's violence against women and campaigning for social change and legal reform (Dobash and Dobash, 1992; Schechter, 1982).

Research into the nature and extent of this problem has established that women are predominantly the victims and men predominantly the perpetrators of what is alternatively called wife abuse, woman abuse or domestic violence (Dobash and Dobash, 1979; Levinson, 1989; Saunders, 1988; Smith, 1989). The burden of dealing with the outcomes of men's violence has fallen almost entirely on women, forcing them to leave their homes and, through organisations such as Women's Aid, to take on the state and its agencies to establish the legitimacy of the problem and develop effective responses to it.

Research also indicates that while campaigns for changes in practice by statutory agencies and for legislative reform have resulted in some real benefits for abused women, little has been done to confront men's violence directly or to deal with their responsibility for it. Social work and medical agencies, for example, have often dealt with abused women by redefining the abuse as symptomatic of other underlying welfare or medical problems. Responses such as these effectively ignore or minimise the issue of violence and men's responsibility for it, thus reducing the likelihood of women seeking further assistance (Johnson, 1985b; Kurz and Stark, 1988; Pahl, 1985).

The criminal nature of men's violence to their partners has often been underplayed by criminal justice agencies – the police, prosecutors and sentencers. For their part, the police have traditionally treated domestic violence as primarily a private affair between a man and his wife and marginal to the real task of policing (Faragher, 1985). Smith (1989) cites several examples of unsatisfactory practices by police in dealing with domestic violence. Despite considerable time spent responding to domestic incidents and assaults, record-keeping has often been poor or non-existent. Police have been seen to be slow to respond to domestic incidents, and reluctant to arrest men who have assaulted their partners, often against the stated request of the woman to do so.

Police have been reported as unsympathetic to battered women, often viewing them as unreliable and likely to withdraw their complaint. However, several studies point to a considerable variation in the extent to which women actually do withdraw complaints, and Wasoff (1982) found that women's reputation for being reluctant to have partners charged is not borne out by evidence. Pioneering US practitioners in this field, such as Pence and Paymar (1990), have argued that women will be less likely to ask for charges to be dropped where they receive both practical support and a sympathetic criminal justice response.

The 1980s have seen moves to demonstrate that the police are responding to this criticism and have taken steps to treat the problem more seriously. More emphasis is now given to the police response in training, with organisations such as Women's Aid contributing to courses. In 1985 the London Metropolitan Police Force's Working Party into Domestic Violence acknowledged that violence against women in the home was a 'significant problem', but concluded that their response had often been inappropriate and unhelpful. The lack of training was highlighted, as was the fact that current terminology – 'domestic dispute' – helps to trivialise wife abuse rather than treating it as an allegation of crime. In 1990, in a further move to improve the police response to domestic violence, the Home and Scottish Offices issued circulars to Chief Constables emphasising the need to treat domestic assaults as seriously as all other forms of assault (Police (CC) Circular No 3/1990).

Despite these changes, some officers still feel that their efforts are often frustrated by women's reluctance to testify against their partners. Intervention may be geared more to the chances of a successful legal action than to the behaviour of the perpetrator or the needs of the victim, the decision to charge resting on the officer's evaluation of the likelihood of the woman to follow through on the charge (Dobash and Dobash, 1992). For their part, women are often reluctant to call on the police, believing they will not take the violence seriously.

Women also have good reason to be mistrustful of the way their position has been perceived and responded to by prosecutors and sentencers within the courts. Domestic violence was long seen as a private matter or as an issue for the civil rather than the criminal courts. Difficulties in proving and processing domestic violence cases, the vulnerability of the woman victim and the fact that she has often been perceived unfairly as an 'unreliable witness' have perpetuated intransigence within the courts (Moody and Tombs, 1982).

Courts may also have felt frustrated by the limited and ineffective options at their disposal in dealing with the small proportion of men whose violent offences actually came before them. Admonishing an offender is likely to leave the man feeling justified in his use of violence and the woman feeling more vulnerable. It also fails to provide the wider community with a clear indicator that all forms of violence, including that directed at women in the home, are unacceptable and will not be ignored by agencies of the state. While a fine may provide the symbolic statement of rejecting violence, providing its size is not so small as to counteract the message, it also has the effect of fining the whole family. Imprisonment might provide temporary protection for the woman and register society's disapproval, but it does little to change the man himself who, in due course, will return to the community, and in most cases to the woman who has been abused.

The message given by the criminal justice system to women, men and the community is a vital part of the response to male violence and may either serve to reinforce the idea that wife abuse is a private matter, or that violence against any member of the community is an offence deserving an effective response from the justice system in co-ordination with other agencies of the state and the community.

PERSPECTIVES ON DOMESTIC VIOLENCE

Initial theories that gained currency following the exposure of the problem explained domestic violence as stemming from the pathologies of either the men or women concerned (cf. Smith, 1989; Stordeur and Stille, 1989). Men who used violence were described as neurotic, mentally ill or disturbed; female victims were similarly labelled, implying that they invited the violence upon themselves. Current evidence about the extent of domestic violence has highlighted the problem of pathological explanations. They seek to propose an 'exceptionalistic explanation to a universalistic problem' (Freeman, 1979). Although they may apply to a few cases, they do not provide a broad theory of the general phenomenon (Smith, 1989).

Also implicit in these pathological explanations is the notion that solutions lie in treating 'sick' individuals rather than addressing the need for wider social or institutional changes. Such explanations are politically attractive as they marginalise the problem as belonging to a few deviant individuals rather than stemming from social structural factors.

Other perspectives have explained male violence as a response to social structural factors, resulting in frustration and stress. As pathological explanations blamed individual abusers and victims, so these approaches indicted society. They fail, however, to explain why violence to women is seen as the appropriate response to these tensions. They tend also to imply erroneously that wife abuse is confined to those groups or strata of society who may be under particular stresses (Adams, 1988; Bograd, 1988; Smith, 1989; Stordeur and Stille, 1989).

Another model widely employed to explain domestic violence is the interactionist perspective, stemming from family systems theory. Here violence is seen as one extreme of a variety of coercive and encitement tactics used in dysfunctional relationships (Adams, 1988; Stordeur and Stille, 1989). This model ignores the importance of the power differential in relationships and thus views women as equal contributors to their victimisation. By concentrating on the 'violent couple' and looking at what provokes the violent response, responsibility for causing or provoking violence is attributed as much to the victim as to the perpetrator (Eisikovits and Edleson, 1989).

A pro-feminist perspective sees men's abuse of and violence towards women as intentional behaviour (Dobash and Dobash, 1992; Yllo and Bograd, 1988). By placing domestic violence in its historical and cultural context, a pro-feminist perspective offers a broad theory of the problem which can account for the question 'Why do men beat their wives/partners?' (Bograd, 1988). Such a perspective views domestic violence as stemming from an historical legacy of men's power over women. The development of Western civilisation in the Judaeo-Christian tradition defined woman's status as separate from and inferior to man. Women rarely had any identity outside the family. They were defined by their relationships to men or children: wife, daughter, mother. The seeds of wife beating lie in the subordination of women to male authority and control. This subordination was institutionalised in the structure of the patriarchal family and supported by economic and political institutions, and by a belief system which made women's subordination seem natural, morally just and sacred (Dobash and Dobash, 1979).

This historical legacy is at the root of the problem we still face today. There is still currency in the notion that a man's home is his castle, that a woman's place is at home and that what goes on in the home is essentially private even if it does contravene the law. The very rituals which we use to change single women into wives, with their emphasis on unviolated property (the white wedding), on the woman adopting the man's name and in the traditional wording of the wedding ceremony – 'love, honour and obey' – signify the inequality of the partners. From such a perspective the nature of male violence in the home is directed at establishing and maintaining the dominance of the man over his female partner and may extend beyond the use of physical violence to encompass other behaviour aimed at imposing his will on her.

A pro-feminist perspective has informed the approaches of many of the intervention programmes upon which CHANGE has drawn (Edleson, Miller and Stone, 1985; Pence and Paymar, 1985; Sinclair, 1989). Adopting a pro-feminist perspective requires that an intervention strategy for solving the problem of domestic violence should involve all those organisations and individuals concerned. Effective intervention needs to tackle both individual offenders, the way domestic violence is treated by the institutions of the criminal justice system (the police, courts and social work); and to challenge community tolerance for domestic violence by questioning social attitudes to the problem. At the same time it is crucial that refuge and support services for women are maintained, and that women are consulted by organisations undertaking intervention work with men. In order to highlight the criminal and unacceptable nature of men's violence to women, a pro-feminist perspective would also suggest that any programme aimed at changing men's violence should operate as a sanction of the justice system.

THE CHANGE MEN'S PROGRAMME

The CHANGE men's programme was set up to work with abusers who have been processed through the justice system. Men are referred to the programme by the courts and attend as an additional requirement of a probation order. By working with the police, courts, social work and voluntary agencies, CHANGE aims to encourage collaborative interagency responses which acknowledge the criminal nature of violence against women in the home. Both the operation of the men's programme and training of other professionals are oriented to influencing practice so that wife abuse is no longer treated as trivial or a private matter, but as serious and of public concern. In this way CHANGE hopes to play its part in changing general cultural norms and values which have long condoned domestic violence.

REFERRALS TO THE PROGRAMME

Through negotiations with courts and social work in Central Region an agreed process by which men are referred to the programme has been established. Where men appear before courts and have pled or been found guilty on a charge where domestic violence has been identified, sheriffs (judges) may call for CHANGE to assess a man's suitability for the programme.

CHANGE therefore conducts an assessment interview, which is concerned with a number of areas: the type of violence the man has used to his partner; the history, frequency and severity of that violence; whether and to what extent he takes responsibility for his violence and his motivation to stop it, and the safety of the woman involved. As admission to CHANGE is a condition of a probation order the man remains in the community. It is therefore necessary to ensure as far as possible that this does not endanger his partner.

It is recognised that at the time of the interview a man will have his own reasons for wanting to come on to the programme. He may be remorseful, anxious to stay out of prison, to stop his partner from leaving him or to get his partner back if she has already left. He is advised that acceptance onto the programme offers no such guarantees and that his partner will be contacted to be given details of the programme. The woman concerned is contacted at this stage to ascertain her safety needs, discuss her willingness to talk to CHANGE about the past violence and to offer the advice and support of Women's Aid. She in turn is advised that the sanction on her partner places no obligations on her and that her safety and wishes are paramount.

Where men are recommended for the programme they must agree to a contract, which is a specific requirement of the probation order. The man is made aware of its terms during the assessment and once the probation order has been made the document is signed by the man, in the presence of a representative of CHANGE and his social worker or probation officer. Men are also aware that non-compliance with the terms of their contract will be reported to the social work department, who in turn may refer them back to the court.

During the time that a man is on the programme, CHANGE liaises with the social worker holding the probation order, submitting written reports at the midway and completion stages, and attending probation reviews to discuss men's progress. Written completion reports are also submitted to the courts. Partners of men on the programme are consulted, where they consent to this. Where women do not wish this contact with the programme, they are still given information about the work undertaken with the man and are informed if he fails to comply with the programme requirements.

PROGRAMME STRUCTURE

CHANGE has drawn on the experiences of programmes already in operation in North America (Edleson, Miller and Stone, 1985; Pence and Paymar, 1985; Sinclair, 1989) and has been able to tailor the programme content and style to early findings about their effectiveness (Dobash and Dobash, 1992; Edleson and Syers, 1989; Eisikovits and Edleson, 1989; Pence and Shepard, 1988). While it is still too early for such research to be conclusive, it has nonetheless been helpful in shaping the CHANGE men's programme, as well as many of its specific components. In particular, Edleson and Syers' research (1989), which compared a number of different group-based programmes, found that comparatively short, structured educational programmes appear to have the most impact on ending men's physical violence and other abuse.

The CHANGE men's programme has therefore been designed as a short, structured group-based re-education programme, working with cohorts of four to six men at any one time. The sixteen-week curriculum comprises two-hour weekly sessions which are held in local community premises on weekday evenings. Men understand that they may be required to attend for longer than sixteen weeks, and that upon completion they have still only undergone a basic programme which has introduced them to some of the ideas and skills they need in order to understand why they use violence and how they can stop. One of the advantages of working with men who are on probation is that they can continue the work begun in the programme in the context of the individual contact they have with their social worker/probation officer. CHANGE influences this work through regular reports and liaison meetings with social workers, during which specific difficulties and outstanding issues for men can be discussed.

PROGRAMME CONTENT

The programme encourages men to take personal responsibility for their violent behaviour by increasing their awareness of the dynamics involved in its use; by challenging their attitudes and beliefs around both the use of violence and relationships between men and women, and by developing skills for relating non-violently to others. The methods employed include brainstorming, written work, including weekly homework, small group work, didactics, video, self-reporting, self-assessment and role play.

The programme begins by extending men's definition of what constitutes violent and abusive behaviour. Violence is defined as a range of physical, sexual and psychological actions, the purpose of which is getting and keeping control over others. Usually men will either deny their violence or try to blame it on someone or something else such as alcohol or a sudden loss of control, such as a 'blind rage'. Sometimes they seem frightened and confused by the apparent mystery of this behaviour and want to understand it for themselves. Men are therefore encouraged to examine in what circumstances and why they have used violence, and over the course of several weeks various incidents where men have been violent and abusive are broken down, including those which resulted in them being charged. Men may thus come to see that in these situations their violence had the purpose of maintaining or re-establishing authority, or of getting something they wanted, be it 'peace and quiet', an evening meal, obedience or sex.

Men often seek to excuse their unacceptable behaviour by blaming it on the woman involved. She is often portrayed as being culpable in some way or having provoked a justifiable retaliation on the man's part. While these are recognised by the programme as mere excuses, the fact that some men may live in relationships where there is conflict is nevertheless acknowledged. However, it is suggested to men that despite the quality of their relationship with their partner, the use of violence is solely their responsibility and that failure to accept this will inevitably nullify their promises to stop. Quite simply, they cannot refrain from behaviour which they do not accept as their own. Only by recognising and accepting that violence has been their *choice* can men refrain from behaving in this way in the future. Men must learn to deal with conflict without resorting to violence. They also need to examine the ideas and prejudices which 'justify' their behaviour and define it either as acceptable or 'only natural', thereby condoning its recurrence.

Men are encouraged to consider the consequences of their violence and the gains and losses it entails. The 'gains', which are short term, relate to the restoration of supremacy in the relationship or services rendered. The 'losses', however, are incurred at the expense of the 'gains' and are more long term. According to most men these include the loss of love, trust and respect from the woman and children alike. Usually men have not considered the effects of their behaviour, either through attributing blame to the woman and thus seeking justification, through 'forgetting' about the incident in order to cope with guilt or through straightforward lack of concern. The open acknowledgement that their behaviour has physically – and otherwise – damaged someone close to them often has a profound effect upon them.

Some men need to learn particular skills in order to rehearse situations in which in the past they have felt justified in becoming aggressive or violent. Many men report, for example, that they seem to have particular problems with anger or with jealousy and look for techniques which can keep them calm and rational. While the programme attempts to equip men with some of these skills, it is important to do this in a way which takes account of the context of their anger and jealousy, and emphasises that these are bound up with their notions of acceptable male and female behaviour.

Finally, in order to be accountable and effective, the programme must remain fully aware of the dangers in this type of work with men. Some men will continue to minimise their continuing abusive behaviour, and indeed some may flagrantly lie, secure in the knowledge that their partners will continue to protect them. The programme thus carefully monitors the effect it appears to be having on men's behaviour by confirming, if possible from sources other than the man, that participation is having the desired effect; where it clearly is not, appropriate prompt action results.

CONCLUSION

The CHANGE Project was established in 1989 to set up as a criminal justice-based programme for men who are violent to their wives or female partners. Operating from a pro-feminist perspective, CHANGE sees men's violence to their partners as intentional and as one aspect of a whole range of abusive behaviour which have the purpose of establishing and maintaining male dominance over women, and believes that male dominance is rooted in history and culture and is reflected in the responses of criminal justice agencies and traditional community tolerance of marital violence.

To be effective, CHANGE believes that intervention must go beyond confronting individual violent men by locating that work within the justice system in order to demonstrate to men, to women and to the community at large that violence to any member of that community is illegal and socially unacceptable and will be responded to accordingly.

References

Adams, D. (1988), 'Treatment models of men who batter: a pro-feminist analysis', in K. Yllo and M. Bograd (eds.), *Feminist Perspectives on Wife Abuse*, Sage Publications, London, pp. 176–99.

Bograd, M. (1988), 'Introduction', in K. Yllo and M. Bograd (eds.), *Feminist Perspectives on Wife Abuse*, Sage Publications, London, pp. 11–26.

Dobash, R. E., and Dobash, R. P. (1979), *Violence Against Wives*, The Free Press, New York.

Dobash, R. E., and Dobash, R. P. (1989), *An Analysis of Programmes for Violent Men*, a research proposal submitted to the Social Work Services Group of the Scottish Office and the Home Office.

Dobash, R. E., and Dobash, R. P. (1992), *Women, Violence and Social Change*, Routledge, London.

Edleson, J. L., Miller, D., and Stone, G. W. (1985), *Counselling Men Who Batter: Group Leader's Handbook*, Men's Coalition Against Battering, Inc., Albany, NY.

Edleson, J. L., and Syers, M. (1989), *The Relative Effectiveness of Group Treatments for Men Who Batter*, Domestic Abuse Project, Minneapolis, MN.

Eisikovits, Z. C., and Edleson, J. L. (1989), 'Intervening with men who batter: a critical review of the literature', *Social Service Review*, 63: 3, University of Chicago, pp. 384–414.

Faragher, T. (1985), 'The police response to violence against women in the home', in J. Pahl (ed.), *Private Violence – Public Policy. The Needs of Battered Women and the Response of Public Services*, Routledge and Kegan Paul, London, pp. 110–24.

Freeman, M. D. A. (1979), *Violence in the Home*, Saxon House, Farnborough.

Ganley, A. (1981), *Court Mandated Counselling for Men Who Batter*, Centre for Women's Policy Studies, Washington, DC.

Johnson, N. (ed.) (1985a), *Marital Violence, Sociological Review Monograph 31*, Routledge & Kegan Paul, London.

Johnson, N. (1985b), 'Police, social work and medical responses to battered women', in N. Johnson (ed.), *Marital Violence, Sociological Review Monograph 31*, Routledge & Kegan Paul, London, pp. 109–23.

Kurz, D. and Stark, E. (1988), 'Not so benign neglect: the medical responses to battering', in K. Yllo and M. Bograd (eds.), *Feminist Perspectives on Wife Abuse*, Sage Publications, London, pp. 249–66.

Levinson, D. (1989), *Family Violence in Cross-Cultural Perspective*, Sage Publications, London.

Moody, S. R., and Tombs, J. (1982), *Prosecutions in the Public Interest*, Scottish Academic Press, Edinburgh.

Morgan, P. A. (1985), 'Constructing images of deviance: a look at state intervention into the problem of wife battery', in N. Johnson (ed.), *Marital Violence, Sociological Review Monograph 31*, Routledge & Kegan Paul, London, pp. 60–76.

Pahl, J. (ed.) (1985), *Private Violence – Public Policy. The Needs of Battered Women and the Response of Public Services*, Routledge & Kegan Paul, London.

Pence, E., and Paymar, M. (1990), *Power and Control: Tactics of Men Who Batter*, Minnesota Program Development Inc., Duluth, MN.

Pence, E., and Shepard, M. (1988), 'Integrating feminist theory and practice: the challenge of the battered women's movement', in K. Yllo and M. Bograd (eds.), *Feminist Perspectives on Wife Abuse*, Sage Publications, London, pp. 282–98.

Pirong-Good, M., and Stets-Kealy, J. (1985), 'Male batterers and battering prevention programs: A national survey', *Response*, VIII, pp. 8–12.

Police (CC) Circular No 3/1990 (1990), *Investigation of Complaints of Domestic Assault*, Scottish Home and Health Department, Edinburgh.

Saunders, D. G. (1988), 'Wife abuse, husband abuse or mutual combat? A feminist perspective on the empirical findings', in K. Yllo and M. Bograd (eds.), *Feminist Perspectives on Wife Abuse*, Sage Publications, London, pp. 90–113.

Schechter, S. (1982), *Women and Male Violence – The Visions and Struggles of the Battered Women's Movement*, Pluto Press, London.

Sinclair, H. (1989), *Manalive: An Accountable Advocacy Batterer Intervention Program*, Marin Abused Women's Services, Marin County, CA.

Smith, L. (1989), *Domestic Violence: An Overview of the Literature*, HMSO, London.

Sonkin, D. J., and Durphy, M. (1989), *Learning to live without Violence*, Volcano Press, San Francisco, CA.

Stordeur, R. A., and Stille, R. (1989), *Ending Men's Violence Against Their Partners: One Road to Peace*, Sage Publications, London.

Wasoff, F. (1982), 'Legal protection from wifebeating: the process of domestic assaults by Scottish prosecutors and criminal courts', *International Journal of the Sociology of Law*, 10: 2, pp. 197–204.

Yllo, K., and Bograd, M. (eds.), (1988), *Feminist Perspectives on Wife Abuse*, Sage Publications, London.

PART SIX

Informal justice

14

Reintegration through reparation: a way forward for restorative justice?

JAMES DIGNAN

Reparation is one of several forms of informal dispute processing that flourished briefly in the United Kingdom during the 1980s, amid heady talk of a transformation of the entire criminal justice system.[1] Although its heyday was short-lived and quickly gave way to critical reviews, it has stubbornly refused to go away since then, and the time may now be ripe for an assessment of its principal shortcomings and prospects for recovery. In this paper I will argue, first, that one of the main reasons why reparation has failed to live up to the more optimistic claims made by some of its supporters is because until now it has lacked a coherent theoretical foundation;[2] second, that a convincing theoretical justification for the practice *is* now to be found in John Braithwaite's recent theory of reintegrative shaming (1989); but third, that if such a theory were to be adopted it would entail some major changes in the way reparation is currently performed. Finally, I will offer a brief sketch of the potential role that reparation might play in a criminal justice system that was reformulated around the goal of restorative rather than retributive justice.

REVIVAL OF REPARATION IN THE UK: PRINCIPAL SHORTCOMINGS

The revival of reparation in the UK during the 1980s excited a flurry of interest that briefly united penal reformers, policy makers and practitioners alike. One of its main attractions was that it appeared to offer a more humane way of bringing home to offenders the consequences of their wrongdoing, thereby retaining the possibility of reform (through moral education), while avoiding many of the disadvantages associated with prosecution. Another was the prospect of a better deal for victims than they had traditionally received at the hands of the courts. The concept also appeared to enjoy widespread popular appeal (Shaw, 1982; Hough and Mayhew, 1985), and could conceivably entail cost-savings as well. With support growing right across the penological spectrum, a variety of experimental schemes was established, including four which received financial support from the Home Office. 'Variety' was indeed an apt term to apply to these schemes, since they differed considerably in terms of their operational philosophy, practice, organisational context within the criminal justice system and much else besides. However, although its 'something for everyone' appeal may have been a source of strength in eliciting initial support – and funding – for the concept of reparation, it quickly became a source of weakness when attempts were made to put the idea into practice.

Among the many problems that have subsequently been encountered, the first and most important relates to confusion at a philosophical level over the *aims* and *objectives* of reparation. Is the emphasis mainly on reconciliation, or the provision of material restitution for *victims*, as in the majority of American Victim Offender Reconciliation Programs (VORP) for example; or is it seen primarily as a way of ameliorating the harshness of the conventional criminal process for the benefit of *offenders*, as some (but not all) of the British reparation schemes have interpreted the concept? Where this is the case diversion from prosecution or mitigation of sentence have tended to take precedence over the needs of victims (see in particular Davis *et al.*, 1989).

Secondly, problems have also been encountered at an *operational* level, though these have almost certainly been exacerbated by the philosophical confusion referred to above. This has engendered conflicting expectations on the part of different criminal justice agencies, project workers and their clients. It has also made it more difficult for reparation schemes to develop and defend a distinctive operating philosophy, thereby rendering them more vulnerable to marginalisation by other, more powerful, criminal justice agencies, such as the police and courts, on whom they continue to depend for the bulk of their referrals. Moreover, the sheer number and variety of such schemes, together with the absence of a common set of objectives and procedures, have added considerably to the *problems of evaluation* described by Marshall and Merry (1990).

Serious as these problems are, however, there are also 'success' stories. Elsewhere, I have reported (Dignan, 1991 and 1992) on a scheme which has shown that reparation can be made to work for both victims and adult offenders while operating in an inter-agency framework. What is distinctive about the Kettering Adult Reparation Scheme is that it adopted clear aims right from the outset; developed procedures that gave effect to these aims; worked hard with the relevant agencies to resolve potential conflicts in their expectations; and sought continuous monitoring and evaluation to determine whether its aims were being achieved. Nevertheless, it is fair to say that in general the failure to specify a clear set of aims and objectives has hampered the development of reparation and reduced its prospects for making it into the mainstream.

Finally, disagreement has also surfaced over the *institutional context* in which reparation is to take place. Should it be integrated within the existing criminal justice process, or should it provide an alternative mode of dispute resolution which might ultimately come to replace it, which would argue for an independent existence outside the mainstream agencies altogether?

RECENT THEORETICAL DEVELOPMENTS: REPARATION AS A MEANS OF
REINTEGRATION?

Although it appears to have been overlooked until now by reparation practitioners and commentators alike, Braithwaite's theory of reintegrative shaming appears to hold out the promise of a more coherent rationale for the practice of reparation, and is also compatible with the philosophical and normative impulses that helped to nurture it. Another advantage, according to Braithwaite (1989, p. 10 and 108–23), is that the theory's claims are empirically testable. Moreover, if its claims *were* substantiated, the theory appears to provide the most promising basis yet for a reformulation of the basic aims of the criminal justice system around the principles of *restorative* justice. The main price that would need to be paid for the increased theoretical coherence and renewed sense of purpose that is on offer would be a loss of diversity at the level of practice, but as this diversity is now a major source of weakness it may be a price worth paying. The theory of reintegrative shaming is therefore likely to be of critical importance if reparation is to be developed as an appropriate response to the manifest shortcomings (see Cavadino and Dignan, 1992) of the existing retributive system of criminal justice.

The theory is based on a detailed examination of shaming as a social response to crime, and draws a persuasive distinction between two very different kinds of shaming practice. One is associated with the conventional paradigm of retributive punishment and is based on the *stigmatisation* of offenders. This often involves an indelible and open-ended degradation of the offender as a person and so can often give rise to the negative effects identified by labelling theorists: namely the permanent out-casting of offenders on the part of society, accompanied by the adoption of a deviant self-image by offenders themselves. Because of this, Braithwaite suggests that shaming of this kind is likely to *increase* the risk of crime by offenders who are subject to it. 'Reintegrative shaming', on the other hand, is based on the practice of showing disapproval for what the offender has done while maintaining a relationship of respect and ultimate forgiveness. Since reintegrative shaming is finite in duration, and is normally terminated by 'gestures of reacceptance into the community of law-abiding citizens',[3] Braithwaite posits that it is more likely to result in a *reduction* of crime on the part of the offender concerned.

Supporters of reparative justice are unlikely to quarrel with the ontological assumption (p. 10) on which the theory is founded: namely that offenders are free agents, and thus capable of choosing how to behave – albeit against a background of societal pressures, one of which is the practice of shaming. Nor are they likely to disagree with the underlying normative assumption that a shift in the mechanism of social control away from repression and in favour of social control through moralising is a good thing. However, the theory does appear to generate a wide range of policy implications,[4] many of which would entail fundamental changes for the practice of existing reparation schemes, as we shall see in the next section.

REINTEGRATION THROUGH REPARATION: REMEDYING THE DEFECTS

One of the biggest problems facing reparation to date has been the lack of a *coherent philosophy*, resulting in confusion over its aims and ultimate objectives. As we have seen, there is even confusion over who is principally intended to benefit from reparation. Applying the principles of reintegrative shaming to the practice may help to resolve many of these difficulties. To begin with, Braithwaite makes clear in a later work that reintegration is not just for offenders. 'The most important target for reintegration is the victim of crime [who] has been devalued as a person' (Braithwaite and Pettit, 1990, p. 91). However offenders also need to be successfully reintegrated into the community if they are not to drift back into crime. In terms of their basic philosophy, therefore, the theory suggests that reparation schemes should seek to pursue a policy of 'even-handed reparation' with the aim of securing a *just* outcome between victim and offender. One of the reasons why the Kettering scheme appears to have been rather more successful than most may be that it consciously adopted such a philosophy at the outset. As a result, it appears to have gained respect and support not only from most victims and offenders but also, crucially, from the police and other criminal justice agencies. Conversely, those schemes that use reparation principally on behalf of offenders as an aid to diversion or mitigation of punishment clearly do not fit the model implied by the theory.

Reparation schemes have also agonised over two subordinate but closely related sets of issues, namely the *selection criteria* they employ and the *purposes of reparation*. Decisions about selection criteria are often constrained in practice by the attitudes of other agencies such as the police and courts, and are almost invariably defined with reference to offence-based or offender characteristics. In addition, certain schemes have excluded corporate or institutional victims as a matter of policy (Davis, 1992, p. 29). This reflects a widespread view (first propounded by Blagg, 1985) that any dialogue involving such victims would not be 'meaningful' for offenders. However, it also raises the broader and still unresolved question as to the purpose(s) to be served by reparation. A fiercely contested issue relating to this is whether the appropriate form of reparation is material or symbolic.

If 'even-handed reparation' *is* the ultimate goal of reparation, then the selection criteria adopted by most reparation schemes (including the one at Kettering) stand in need of revision. In principle, if the needs of victims are to be given equal consideration from the outset, then cases should be selected for referral whenever it appears likely that victims might benefit from such an approach – and not just when they happen to fit a pre-determined schedule of 'appropriate offences'.

As for the purpose to be served by reparation, the theory suggests that one of the primary aims should be to do all that is possible to reintegrate *both* victim *and* offender back into the community. One of the most effective and appropriate ways of attempting to reintegrate the victim might be to *combine* symbolic condemnation of the offence with material reparation. As Braithwaite and Pettit put it (1990, p. 91), 'symbolic reparation requires the tangible backing of compensation; otherwise it may come too cheap'. This, too, would require a change of practice on the part of those schemes (the majority in England and Wales) that only ever attempt to secure symbolic reparation. But since this is in line with what victims say they want (Shapland *et al.*, 1985;

Newburn and de Peyrecave, 1988), and is in any event more likely to engender respect in the eyes of other criminal justice agencies, there may well be sound policy reasons for moving in this direction. A similar conclusion is also reached if the matter is looked at from the offender's point of view. Where amends have been made by literally 'paying back the debt', this may help with the process of reintegration – particularly if the victim is then prepared to symbolically 'wipe the slate clean' by accepting an apology from the offender and expressing forgiveness.

So far, the discussion has assumed the involvement of individual as opposed to corporate victims. However, although the latter might be thought to be less in need of reparation, whether symbolic or material,[5] their involvement, together with that of other interested parties (see below), might still be helpful in reintegrating offenders following an offence. Accordingly, if reparation does indeed prove to be an effective way of achieving reintegrative shaming there seems to be no good reason for excluding such cases in the way that some schemes have done.

If the conclusions I have drawn from Braithwaite's theory are correct, it appears to offer a much more coherent rationale for reparation schemes. As for the practice itself, there has been much debate over the process by which reparation is negotiated (see Marshall and Merry, p. 107). Hitherto, schemes have mainly relied on one of two approaches. In the first, victim and offender are encouraged to meet one another face-to-face in the company of a mediator in order to discuss their feelings and hopefully reach a mutually acceptable outcome. Although favoured by many project staff, this procedure tends not to be that popular with the parties themselves, particularly victims.[6] Largely for this reason, the majority of cases are normally dealt with on the basis of 'shuttle diplomacy', with project staff acting as intermediaries and seeking to negotiate an outcome acceptable to both parties. In the Kettering scheme a minority of victims were willing to forego any claim to reparation and asked project staff to resolve the matter through informal negotiations with the offender. This often resulted in offenders being referred to a relevant agency on a voluntary basis for appropriate assistance, which could also be a way of reintegrating them back into the community.

If victims' wishes are to be respected when seeking to reintegrate *them* following an offence (as Braithwaite's theory requires), it won't always be possible for offenders to engage in face-to-face discussion with the person most directly affected by their behaviour, however effective this might be as a means of shaming them in a reintegrative way. From the victim's point of view, reintegration might well be accomplished most satisfactorily in such cases by asking a reparation bureau to negotiate indirectly with the offender on their behalf and, where this is the case, the theory would not imply any change in the current practice. In a number of other respects, however, the theory would entail some fairly fundamental changes, particularly regarding the way offenders are dealt with.

One of the main attractions of pre-trial reparation schemes for most offenders is that they not only avoid prosecution but also escape the unwelcome publicity and stigma that is normally associated with a trial, whatever its outcome. And although most offenders who are referred to such schemes end up being cautioned, this again is generally seen as preferable to being convicted and punished in court, however uncomfortable they might find the experience of being directly confronted by their victim. The question posed by Braithwaite's theory, however, is whether this existing procedure exploits the *shaming* potential of reparation to the full or whether it enables offenders to escape too lightly, even where some form of reparation is negotiated on behalf of the victim.

The process of shaming is seen by Braithwaite (1989, p. 10) as 'a means of making citizens actively responsible, of informing them of how justifiably resentful their fellow citizens are toward criminal behaviour which harms them'. Although one of the most effective ways of achieving this might well be to arrange a direct confrontation with an aggrieved victim, this clearly will not always be possible. In practice, therefore, as we have seen, it often falls to project staff to try to convey the sense of reprobation engendered by the offence. There may also be an element of shaming involved in a police caution, even though this is primarily intended to serve as a warning about future conduct. However, Braithwaite (p. 87) makes the point that shaming by 'significant others' – family, friends, or a personally relevant collectivity – is likely to be far more potent than shaming by an impersonal state or its representatives. Since an offender's intimates and close associates may also be in the best position to assist in his or her reintegration back into the community, there may be a strong argument for seeking to actively involve *them* in the process of reparation, whether or not the victim is also directly involved.

If Braithwaite is also right in thinking (p. 179) that 'visible shaming and reintegration are the real stuff of crime control', this raises two additional policy issues. The first has to do with media involvement in the process of reparation. If the media were to be given a role this would represent another major departure from current practice since, as we have seen, virtually all existing reparation schemes shield offenders from media exposure. The argument in favour of public shaming (Braithwaite, 1989, p. 82) is that it 'puts pressure on family and associates to ensure that they engage in private shaming'. On the other hand the kind of shaming indulged in by much of the media is highly stigmatising and might well hinder the process of reintegration. While reparation schemes are confined to relatively minor offences the arguments in favour of excluding the media are likely to prevail – at least where there is sufficient involvement on the part of either the victim or the close associates of the offender to ensure an appropriate degree of 'public shaming'. But if reparation schemes were to take on more serious offences in the future the pressure to allow increased media access would be likely to grow stronger; serious thought would then need to be given to the way in which this was handled if the prospects for successful reintegration were not to be seriously undermined.

A second policy issue concerns the need to think more seriously about how to *reintegrate* offenders once the shaming and reparation processes are completed. Involving 'significant others' in the process may be one way of working towards this, but as Braithwaite also points out (1989, p. 163) the traditional response to deviance in the West has been to '[give] free play to degradation ceremonies of both a formal and informal kind to certify deviance, while providing almost no place in the culture for ceremonies to decertify deviance'.[7] One of the most valuable services that reparation schemes could provide, therefore, might be to devise appropriate ceremonies or processes that would formally 'decertify' the offender as deviant on completion of the reparation. In many cases the victim may have an important part to play in such processes, but it may also be possible for the media to play a constructive role in this as well.

Another way of reducing the stigmatising effects that are currently associated with most pre-trial reparation schemes would be to drop the formal police caution that normally accompanies a referral. Arguably there would be little need of, or justification for, the practice if offenders were routinely obliged to make meaningful reparation to their victims, and if the informal offence resolution process was to become a more shameful and demanding experience, as implied by the theory.

A third and final area of contention for reparation schemes has to do with their *organisational context*, and in particular their relationship with the rest of the criminal justice system. Some have argued (e.g. Marshall and Merry, 1990, p. 201) that reparation should operate completely independently of the existing court system, though experience to date suggests that this would severely impair whatever potential it might have for further development, and would thereby perpetuate its marginalisation. Others (e.g. Watson *et al.*, 1989; Davis, 1992) have countered that a reparative element should be incorporated within the present broadly retributive criminal justice process by maintaining the centrality of the criminal courts and possibly involving victims more directly in their proceedings.

The theory of reintegrative shaming itself is silent on the precise context within which reparation might best take place. At times Braithwaite has argued in favour of this approach, but without specifically addressing the practice of reparation. However, he has also argued that 'a criminal justice system designed with sensitivity to the theory of reintegrative shaming would want to put shaming and reintegration up front as a common alternative to state sanctioning' (1992, p. 180). For my part, I find it difficult to envisage how this might be done without a radical rethink of the way the criminal justice system presently operates.

TOWARDS A RESTORATIVE SYSTEM OF CRIMINAL JUSTICE?

Figure 14.1 sets out an alternative model which seeks to combine the practical experience gained from existing reparation schemes with the theoretical insights offered by the concept of reintegrative shaming. This is an adaptation of a model which Braithwaite (1991) himself has proposed in a more recent work, albeit in a very different context.[8] The model is based on the notion of an enforcement pyramid, which sets out a gradation of sanctioning measures ranging from highly informal community-based measures to state-sanctioned mechanisms including prosecution and punishment. The standard response that is envisaged for the vast majority of criminal offences (including so-called regulatory offences)[9] would be for the matter to be referred by the responsible enforcement agency (or self-referred by one of the parties) to a local reparation centre. For minor property offences and most minor assaults recourse to the courts would not normally be allowed unless either the accused denied guilt, the parties were unable to reach agreement or the offender refused to make reparation as agreed; even then it would probably be appropriate to limit the sent-

Figure 14.1 Enforcement pyramid for a reparative system of criminal justice (The proportion of space at each layer of the pyramid represents the proportion of enforcement activity at that level.)

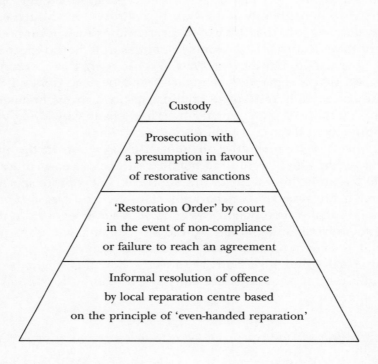

encing powers of the court to the award of compensation or the imposition of a community service order. Alternatively, courts might be required to refer a case back for informal resolution once the issue of guilt had been resolved or the amount of damage quantified.

The chief aim of the reparation process would be to resolve the matter informally by securing a negotiated settlement based on the principle of even-handed reparation, as outlined above. Even in the case of more serious offences it might still be desirable to at least explore the scope for informal resolution (provided guilt is admitted) before deciding whether or not to institute criminal proceedings. It would then be obligatory for the outcome of these negotiations to be taken into account by the prosecuting authorities when deciding whether or not to proceed, and by the court in passing sentence. Once again, there would be a presumption in favour of 'restorative penalties' such as compensation and community service orders for offenders who were prosecuted and convicted. While probation could still have a useful part to play within a penal system organised around restorative principles, both it and the community service order would need to be divested of the more overtly punitive elements that have recently been introduced. Finally, although custody would not be ruled out for very serious offences it would *only* be authorised on the grounds that the public are in genuine need of protection from probable future acts of violence that could not be prevented in any other way (see Bottoms and Brownsword, 1983).

TRANSITIONAL STRATEGY

A criminal justice system based on the principles of restorative justice is very far removed from the one that we are familiar with, and for that reason alone is liable to be dismissed as utopian. However, the existing system is facing such a crisis of confidence that it would be unwise to rule out even the possibility of fundamental change in the future. A number of radical blueprints for reform have appeared recently (Blom-Cooper, 1988; Sim, 1991; Wright, 1991), accompanied by a parallel upsurge of interest in the possibility of an impending 'paradigm shift' (see among others Barnett, 1977; Zehr, 1985) in favour of restorative justice. What is missing from most of these accounts is a transitional strategy that would indicate how such change might come about.

In developing such a strategy it is important not to overlook the progress that has already been made in developing restorative elements within the existing system of punishment. These include increased support for compensation orders, the introduction of community service orders, and the growth of a Victim Support network, quite apart from the more recent appearance of reparation and mediation schemes. If further progress is to be made in strengthening the principle of restorative justice in the short term there are at least three current sets of initiatives that could usefully be built upon.

The first would be to encourage the development of more reparation schemes (catering for both adult and juvenile offenders) along the lines of the Kettering model. This has already achieved a fair measure of success in promoting the concept of even-handed reparation within an inter-agency framework, a fact that is reflected in the recent decision to extend the scheme across the whole county of Northamptonshire.

A second possibility would be to gradually increase the range of offences dealt with by such schemes (as experience is gained) by adapting the principle of the guideline matrix that is used in certain American jurisdictions to assist in sentencing decisions. Such an approach might enable enforcement agencies to determine which cases should be referred to local reparation centres.[10] In other cases they could still be required to take into account any reparation agreement that had been negotiated between offender and victim when deciding how to proceed, since this might encourage the practice of self-referral by offenders before a prosecution gets under way.

Thirdly, for those cases still dealt with by the courts, a statutory presumption could be introduced in favour of restorative sanctions such as community service and victim compensation wherever possible. Likewise, the courts could also be required to take into account any reparation agreement that had been negotiated and performed when passing sentence.

CONCLUSIONS

One of the biggest failings with the recent crop of reparation initiatives in England and Wales is that until now they have lacked a coherent theoretical framework. This has encouraged a largely pragmatic response to the many shortcomings now being experienced on the part of the formal criminal justice system. As a result, a bewildering variety of schemes has been set up, usually on a highly localised basis, the aims and objectives of which are frequently ill-defined and contradictory. Braithwaite's theory of reintegrative shaming, although not specifically devised with this aim in mind, provides a convincing rationale for the practice, and suggests a way of resolving the confusion that has emerged at all three levels: philosophical, operational and institutional.

Applying the theory would mean abandoning some cherished beliefs and modifying much of the practice. But in doing so the movement would gain a clear sense of direction and purpose which hitherto it has lacked, and which has undoubtedly contributed to its marginalisation. Moreover, if the modest successes that have been achieved to date (for example with the Kettering scheme) can be built upon in ways that are suggested by the theory, the prospects for a restorative criminal justice system would also be considerably enhanced. Thus the theory of reintegrative shaming is worth taking seriously not simply in relation to reparation practice, but because it offers much the best prospect for replacing today's rather narrow preoccupation with securing 'punishment in the community' for offenders with the much more laudable aspiration of promoting 'justice in the community' for victims *and* offenders.

Notes

1   The term 'reparation' is used here to refer to the various ways in which offenders may seek to make direct amends (e.g. compensation, services, undertakings and 'symbolically' by apologising). The broader term 'restorative justice' is used to refer to these and other measures with a reparative element, including compensation orders, community service orders etc.

2   Harland, for example, predicted that 'whatever direction restitution does in fact take, there can be little doubt that its new-found impetus will take it into every part of the criminal justice system' (1977, p. 202). (NB The term restitution is commonly used, as here, synonymously with reparation.)

3   This aspect of the theory recalls Tony Bottoms' (1983) notion of 'juridical'-style punishments since these also result in the offender rejoining society as a 'requalified subject' once the penalty has been served.

4   Braithwaite himself makes little direct reference to reparation in his influential book *Crime Shame and Reintegration*. I cannot therefore be certain that he would endorse the conclusions I have drawn from his general approach, but I believe them to be relevant and of interest to the current debate on reparation and its future.

5   This wasn't always the case in Kettering, where many corporate victims were shop-keepers or small business proprietors who felt just as aggrieved as some individual victims.

6   Since most offences referred to pre-trial reparation schemes are relatively trivial there is often little at stake for victims.

7   In marked contrast to the position in Japan where 'a pattern of confession, repentance and absolution dominates each stage of the law enforcement process' (Harding, 1991, p. 640).

8   Originally developed in relation to business or agency regulation, Braithwaite has subsequently applied the model to the arena of domestic violence.

9   Indeed, one advantage is that it would harmonise the enforcement strategies used by different agencies, thereby redressing a systemic form of inequality in the way different kinds of offending behaviour are dealt with, regardless of the level of social harm that they cause (see Sanders, 1988).

10 Interestingly, such a scheme is currently under consideration in Northamptonshire (personal communication with Adrian Wright, who is director of the NARB).

References

Barnett, R. (1977), 'Restitution: a new paradigm of criminal justice', *Ethics: An International Journal of Social, Political and Legal Philosophy*, 87, 4, pp. 279–301.

Blagg, H. (1985), 'Reparation and justice for juveniles: the Corby experience', *British Journal of Criminology*, 25, pp. 267–79.

Blom-Cooper, L. (1988), *The Penalty of Imprisonment*, Prison Reform Trust and Howard League for Penal Reform, London.

Bottoms, A. E. (1983), 'Neglected features of contemporary penal systems', in D. Garland and P. Young (eds.), *The Power to Punish: Contemporary Penality and Social Analysis*, Heinemann, London.

Bottoms, A. E. and Brownsword, R. (1983), 'Dangerousness and rights', in J. W. Hinton (ed.), *Dangerousness: Problems of Assessment and Prediction*, George Allen and Unwin, London.

Braithwaite, J. (1989), *Crime, Shame and Reintegration*, Cambridge University Press, Cambridge.

Braithwaite, J. and Pettit, P. (1990), *Not Just Deserts: A Republican Theory of Criminal Justice*, Clarendon, Oxford.

Braithwaite, J. (1991), 'The political agenda of republican criminology', paper to the British Criminological Society Conference, York, 27 July.

Cavadino, M. and Dignan, J. (1992), *The Penal System: An Introduction*, Sage, London.

Davis, G., Boucherat, J. and Watson, D. (1989), 'Reparation in the service of diversion: the subordination of a good idea', *Howard Journal*, 27, pp. 127–32.

Davis, G. (1992), *Making Amends: Mediation and Reparation in Criminal Justice*, Routledge, London and New York.

Dignan, J. (1991), *Repairing the Damage: An Evaluation of an Experimental Adult Reparation Scheme in Kettering, Northamptonshire*, University of Sheffield, Sheffield.

Dignan, J. (1992), 'Repairing the damage: can reparation be made to work in the service of diversion?', *British Journal of Criminology*, 32, 4, pp. 453–520.

Harding, J. (1991), 'Japanese justice', *Justice of the Peace*, 155, pp. 640–1.

Harland, Alan T. (1977), 'Theoretical and programmatic concerns in restitution: an integration', in B. Galaway and J. Hudson, *Offender Restitution in Theory and Action*, D. C. Heath, Lexington. MA.

Hough, M. and Mayhew, P. (1985), *Taking Account of Crime: Key Findings from the 1984 Crime Survey*, Research and Planning Unit Study No. 85, HMSO, London.

Marshall, T. F. and Merry, S. (1990), *Crime and Accountability: Victim/Offender Mediation in Practice*, HMSO, London.

Newburn, T. and de Peyrecave, H. (1988), 'Victims' attitudes to courts and compensation', *Home Office Research Bulletin*, 25, pp. 18–21.

Sanders, A. (1988), 'The limits to diversion from prosecution', *British Journal of Criminology*, 28, pp. 513–29.

Shapland, J., Wilmore, J., and Duff, P. (1985), *Victims in the Criminal Justice System*, Gower, Aldershot.

Shaw, S. (1982), *The People's Justice: A Major Poll of Public Attitudes on Crime and Punishment*, Prison Reform Trust, London.

Sim, J. (1991), 'When you ain't got nothing you got nothing to lose: the Peterhead rebellion, the state and the case for prison abolition', paper presented at the British Criminology Conference, University of York.

Watson, D., Boucherat, J. and Davis, G. (1989), 'Reparation for retributivists', in M. Wright and B. Galaway, *Mediation and Criminal Justice*, Sage, London.

Wright, M. (1991), *Justice for Victims and Offenders*, Open University Press, Milton Keynes and Philadelphia.

Zehr, H. (1985), *Retributive Justice, Restorative Justice*, Mennonite Central Committee, US Office of Criminal Justice, Elkhart, Indiana.

15

Grassroots initiatives towards restorative justice: the new paradigm?

TONY F. MARSHALL

CRIMINAL JUSTICE SYSTEM OR COMMUNITY JUSTICE SYSTEM?

Job specialisation, professionalisation, ritualisation, and the ever-growing mountain of esoteric legal doctrine conspire to make criminal justice appear distinct and independent from the community. Although comparative studies of reported crime over historical periods of time are rife with methodological problems, I think we can be sure that we now, as citizens, have more precipitate recourse to the police in a far wider range of circumstances than ever before, and that the law is invoked in an increasingly large number of misadventures. Moreover, a vicious spiral is set in train, whereby community mechanisms for controlling and handling crime and justice issues are progressively run down by desuetude the more recourse to 'official' channels is relied upon. Increasingly, there are fewer and fewer alternatives to formal criminal justice.

A noticeable feature of the last few decades has been that this process has been recognised and steps taken to try to reverse it. A powerful driving force has been economics. Criminal justice is costly and it cannot go on expanding indefinitely. 'Diversion', especially through the growth of the police caution, has been the watchword from the 1960s onwards. The problem has been, however, that what is diverted tends either to remain in the hands of the same professions (so that the police take on functions previously the sole province of the courts, community service orders diverted from prison require battalions of probation officers, and lawyers start training themselves as mediators) or to require the evolution of new professions (for example, staff on community programmes). Internal savings of a minor nature have been made, but the criminal justice system has gone on expanding and becoming all the more indispensable.

This expansion of criminal justice has had a number of disadvantageous effects. Not only have natural community social control mechanisms tended to disappear, but readiness to accept responsibility for crime, misbehaviour, and the needs of others has similarly declined among citizens generally and in social institutions outside criminal justice. While people may feel faintly uneasy about the selfish 'take care of number one' culture that accompanies the decline in informal caring (although not so uneasy, generally, as to break away from the general mores), the present attitude of non-interference in issues of civility or behaviour (until they become too difficult to handle) is conveniently buttressed by notions of 'individual freedom' as a universal 'good' or 'right'.

Relying less and less on personal experience and more and more on mass media sensationalism, stereotypes are strengthened, fear is increased, and communities are reinforced in their attitude of 'leaving it to the professionals' by the seeming immensity of the task of crime control, represented in terms of acute danger, violence and brutishness. Not only are communities gradually losing the capacity for local social control, they are learning the rationales and skills for actively avoiding it. While Matza (1964) described offenders' 'neutralization' techniques for absolving themselves from responsibility for their behaviour, one can equally well suggest that the same process is occurring among citizens generally for absolving themselves of responsibility for the crime generated from within their own communities.

The escalation of overall costs reduces available expenditure on other services (schools, housing, social services, etc.) and the community infrastructure, further reducing their ability to contribute to crime prevention and control. The formal control system we have moved very close to in the last century is one which is distant from informal control mechanisms and everyday society. It is responsive to state concerns or those of professional groups staffing its agencies (corrections experts) rather than the public at large. Distance from other social control mechanisms leaves the formal control system totally reliant, in the last resort, upon the use of force. It cannot proceed by exhortation (although some, such as magistrates, may try) or shaming (Braithwaite, 1989), for example, because it is not part of the social world that those processed could recognise as their own. Its example, based on force, is in any case ambiguous. To many its chief message is that 'you get what you have the power to take'. It represents a world in which morality has failed as a force for order, a world which corresponds only too well to that of the value system of the thief or mugger.

There is little about such a system that can contribute to the reduction of crime. Those upon whom it has a direct impact, the offenders, have already been prepared to risk its unpleasantness, and are unlikely to be affected by its demonstration of fulfilled promise (especially as most will have experienced many more occasions on which they were not caught and the promise went unfulfilled). This serves to remind one that the major crime preventative is moral opprobrium, whether internalised or acting through community contacts. The court sentence does little to reinforce such morality; in fact, it may be counter-productive if it relays the message that the main reason for avoiding crime is its consequences for oneself rather than any *a priori* judgement of right or wrong, or consideration of the consequences for others.

Whatever the reason, the experience of formal criminal justice has been that official crime rates go on rising, increasing resort to punitiveness attempts (Canute-like) to stem the tide, and costs rise geometrically, driven not only by case-loads but also by the costliness of the increasingly frequent use of the ultimate punishment, incarceration.

THE BENEVOLENT CYCLE OF INFORMAL CONTROL

The vicious cycle of formal control contrasts with the 'benevolent' cycle of informal control. Informal control is not based on force, but on the implications for social relations of committing an unacceptable act. It assumes that individuals are dependent to a degree on social relations for economic support, esteem, association, security, affection, and so on. The existence of society itself is similarly predicated on such an assumption.

Unlike the formal cycle, where increased use of the process increases alienation, increased use of the informal cycle contributes to community- and relationship-building, so that it is positive in its results, helping both to incline individuals to accept the general morality and to reinforce the informal mechanisms of resolution themselves. In this way it is capable of being a 'benevolent' cycle.

The informal control system is very attenuated in contemporary society. The cohesive communities of the past are seldom replicated nowadays, and there is strong resistance to a return to such intrusive neighbourliness in a society that emphasises individual freedom and self-development. There are, however, other ways in which 'community' can be defined. There is no evidence that individuals have fewer social relationships than heretofore, or that interdependency is reduced. The change has been in the form these relationships take. In terms of individual self-control, the salient relationships – those which one is most concerned to preserve – are variable across persons. For some, association with members of the same ethnic group may be most important, for others it may be their church, their workplace, a voluntary organisation, a club, a political party or a common interest group. For others, it may, even now, be the local neighbourhood. If one is going to talk, therefore, in terms of returning control of crime to the community, one has to think in terms of multiple associational systems, only some of them neighbourhood-based, and each with variable degrees of control over different members.

RETURN TO COMMUNITY?

As a result we have seen a 'return to community' movement manifesting itself in many arenas of social life, not least that of criminal justice. Shonholtz (1987) has argued for community justice panels and school conflict resolution training, which would provide citizens with the experience of decision-making, responsibility and participation on the one hand, and with the skills for handling conflict at a local level, without bringing in outside 'experts' like the police, on the other.

Braithwaite (1989) similarly locates control in the community: 'Crime is best controlled when members of the community are the primary controllers through active participation in shaming offenders, and, having shamed them, through concerted participation in ways of reintegrating the offenders back into the community of law abiding citizens'.

A limitation to all such ideas, however, is that community tends to be defined on a purely geographical basis, although one sees other options in Shonholtz's advocacy of schools as one alternative base, and Braithwaite's (1989) similar references to schools and other organisations like business corporations.

One theory that manages to incorporate a wider sense of community is that of 'mediating structures' (Berger and Neuhaus, 1977). Such structures, which comprise membership groups of the kind listed above, provide real opportunities for social engagement, a feeling of worth and influence, the satisfaction of association, a sense of purpose and identification, and also, in modern complex societies, freedom of choice. They can also link in with wider social structures, including the state as a whole, and thus provide the individual with a readily identifiable 'place in society', moreover one which is chosen or achieved rather than ascribed. The role of the state, according to Berger and Neuhaus, would be to encourage such mediating structures and to work through them to ensure the commitment and participation of individual citizens. This theory contains the potential for resolving the fissile tendency in most pluralistic structures by identifying mechanisms for integration. The theory itself can be seen as a 'mediating structure' between those political theories which stress the role of the state (which tend towards authoritarianism) and those which stress the role of the individual (which tend towards the anarchy of de-construction).

The management of a society which emphasises the role of intermediate social structures, decreasing the dominance of the overarching state, while resisting the centrifugal pulls of self-centred individualism, poses special problems and calls for special techniques. Parallels can be drawn with the shifts in corporate management theory as organisations find themselves drawn by economic exigencies to place greater value on flexibility, change and innovation. The old organisational bureaucratic model of pyramidal hierarchical structures is now seen to have too much inertia and dead weight to survive in the present environment. The tendency now is towards flat structures emphasising 'sideways' communication and networks of semi-autonomous companies, worker involvement in decision-making and in generating change, teamwork, and recognition of conflict or friction as an opportunity for progress. The function of the executive is no longer 'direction' but co-ordination, ensuring that communication links are functioning, providing leadership stimulus, but no longer believing that the head of a large organisation can possibly lay down in advance optimal structures or procedures, which can only be evolved through consultation.

Transposing these post-Fordist ideas to societal structure, one can see 'mediating structures' as the equivalent of the functional workplace team and the state as the co-ordinating, enabling leadership which does not set policy but ensures its evolution through full democratic consultation. Within the 'new management', worker commitment is 'bought' by ensuring fair economic and social rewards (particularly concern for ensuring meaningful involvement and space for autonomous choice), while within a similarly 'flat' society, citizen commitment would be secured by precisely the same mechanisms (social justice, a 'caring' culture, and preservation of grassroots democracy as a major mechanism of social policy formation).

REFORMING JUSTICE?

Central criminal justice policy meanwhile has a number of options. It can accept that crime levels are determined by the success of *all* social institutions at all levels in generating personal commitment through mutually positive relationships, and thus endeavour to encourage all government departments and agencies, nationally and locally, to take responsibility for ensuring that their policies do not conflict with such achievement (recognising that, at least initially, some resource investment will be needed to improve the capacity of existing institutions to cater for 'quality' needs as well as 'productive' ones).

Meanwhile, the social casualties that have already evaded the informal control system and constitute the case-load of formal justice would continue to need dealing with, so that the second option, in no way excluding the first, is to build up mutually reinforcing links between the formal and informal systems and to attempt to introduce into the formal system some aspects of informal justice that might help to break down the vicious spiral of escalating cost. If successful, such reforms could release resources for bolstering the real crime preventative functions of other social institutions.

A number of criminological writers have recently explored the possibility of such reforms. Woodson (1989) explicitly employs the theory of Berger and Neuhaus to argue for mediating institutions which can incorporate natural social control mechanisms into criminal justice. He explores in detail the operation of one example, the House of Umoja in Philadelphia, one of a range of grassroots inner-city programmes for hard-core delinquents in which 'a structure of primary relations among members supports the possibility of cooperation and authentic mutual influence, as individual and community development proceed together' (Woodson, 1989, p. 58).

Both Marshall (1989) and Braithwaite (1989) refer to a 'family model' of punishment, where, in Braithwaite's terms, 'shame' is accompanied by social reintegration. Marshall refers to three phases of such a model of punishment: denunciation, justice (reparation), and reconciliation. Both contrast such a model of punishment with the state model, which fails to be socially reconstitutive, being remote and ineffective in terms of denunciation, marginalising reparation, and not at all concerned with reconciliation.

Just as the 'new management' theories appeal to values such as relationship-building, co-operation, win-win solutions, sensitivity to people and emotions – values more associated with women than with the traditional masculine culture – so de Haan (1990) claims that the new thinking on punishment leads to a value system closer to Heidensohn's (1986) 'caring' model of morality and justice, which employs essentially feminist values in opposition to the dominant masculine legal discourse of crime 'fighting' and adversarialism.

Lacey also approaches punishment as an attribute of society generally, not a purely legal construct. Her 'functional' conception 'emphasises the significance which punishment has for the citizens of a community, the place which it occupies in the development and cohesion of the community, rather than simply tangible goals such as deterrence or a particular desirable endstate' (Lacey, 1988, p. 186).

Similarly rejecting both retributivist and reformative philosophies of state punishment, Cragg (1992) derives a 'minimum force principle', by which punishment is seen as necessary to demonstrate that the law is viable and to be taken seriously, maintaining public confidence, but should be applied to the minimum extent possible if it is not to be itself perceived as 'both immoral and anti-moral', and thus seeking to bolster reform through persuasion rather than repression, as well as incorporating other social values.

The 'abolitionists' (see, for example, Bianchi and van Swaaningen, 1986; in this volume Sim, ch. 16; Rutherford, ch. 17, and Hudson, ch. 18) have long tried to deconstruct punitive state control, focusing chiefly on decarceration. There has been a tendency for opponents of 'repressive' social control to advocate minimal intervention to avoid problems of criminalisation and stigmatisation. While decriminalisation may at times constitute a rational policy, non-intervention has major costs in failing to denounce wrongdoing and reinforce norms of behaviour, apart from the fact that victims' needs are thereby ignored. Not all social control can be described as 'repressive'. Some forms of informal justice can be seen as offering the possibility of 'liberating' social control (Marshall, 1988), and this is essentially Braithwaite's argument (1989) in proposing 'reintegrative shaming' as an alternative to stigmatisation: 'moralizing social control is more likely to assure compliance with the law than repressive social control' (p. 5).

These ideas are reintroducing to criminal justice a variety of issues which had been squeezed out by its professionalisation and bureaucratisation, such as the interaction of crime and morality, problem-solving, individual feelings, social ties, and so on.

Another strand to this call for 'participation' was stimulated by Christie (1977), in his accusation of theft by the state from the people in the form of taking over their conflicts and crimes by professional agencies. He advocated returning such disputes to the community and the parties concerned, whose interests, particularly those of the victims, were not, he claimed, being met when the offence against an individual became reconstrued as a crime against society. Through the writings of a number of persons, from Barnett (1977) to Zehr (1990) in the United States, Wright (1991) in Britain, and Cragg (1992) in Canada, the concept of 'restorative justice' has been developed, which decries a 'retributive' (punishment-based) criminal justice system for its perceived failure to resolve crime satisfactorily, whether from the point of view of the victim, whose compensation is largely an afterthought if it is offered at all and who suffers from a lack of involvement and information; from the point of view of the offenders, who are neither made to face up to the consequences of their behaviour in person, nor given a chance to make up for it and to regularise their relationships with the community; or from the point of view of society, which fails to achieve a proper resolution of the problems and suffers from both a rising crime rate and an increasingly costly apparatus of justice. Instead, these writers argue, the aims of criminal justice should not be punitive for punishment's sake, but should rather be 'reparative' or 'restorative', seeking to mend the harm that has been caused by an offence in material, psychological and relationship terms, while giving the parties involved real responsibility and an opportunity for participation in all the decisions that are made affecting them. Criminal justice would become more than simply a reaction to crime.

These ideas have found a number of practical expressions throughout the world. The attempt to return crime prevention and justice processes to the 'community' in some way has been made frequently in Western societies, with Neighbourhood Watch Schemes, Neighborhood Justice Centres (USA), Community Justice Centres (Australia), community-based facilities for 'treating' delinquents (such as the House of Umoja referred to above), community-oriented policing, community service orders, and so on. Schemes to advance the needs of individual parties and to give them a chance of participation have included, for example, Victim Support and reparation schemes. Kelling and Moore (1987) describe American policing policy as having moved through three stages, of which the latest is 'community problem-solving', featuring decentralisation, community consultation, problem analysis, foot patrols, and teamwork, with the ultimate objectives of citizen satisfaction and improving the 'quality of life'.

Reference is often made to non-Western social systems that involve integrative processes of settling crime, from African village moots to native American customs. The most frequently cited case, however, is that of Japan, whose national system of justice places great emphasis on apology and reparation, reinforced by a culture which values family, community and interpersonal respect, and which is one of the few countries in the world where crime rates are falling and criminal justice costs are extremely low compared with Western nations (see for example, Haley, 1988).

One of the central planks of restorative justice theory has been experimentation with victim-offender mediation. The Canadian and American VORPS (Victim Offender Reconciliation Programs) were founded on the basis of healing relationships and reconstructing community, and the British and other European victim-offender mediation schemes share their aims (see Messmer and Otto, 1992).

The voluntary organisation MEDIATION UK has taken such thinking forward in its brief paper on 'Criminal justice policy' (1990), which attempts to apply the general principles of conflict resolution to the process of dealing with offending. There is a danger in restorative justice formulations based on the centrality of victim-offender mediation that emphases on personal involvement and negotiation will lead to a person-centred model of justice. While it may be an important advance to provide the opportunity and freedom for individual negotiation, this cannot be seen as a sufficient response to crime, which has community-wide social and moral implications. Wright (1991), for instance, argues for a 'civil' approach to most crime, which is criticised by the Jubilee Policy Group (1992), which chooses to replace the term 'restorative justice' with 'relational justice' to symbolise the fact that any suggested reform must pay attention to the wider social implications of crime. Similarly Mika (1992) argues that victim/offender mediation must learn to transcend the solely interpersonal and be ready to tackle wider and more basic social conflicts if it is to be capable of contributing to a radical transformation of criminality in our society.

It is interesting, and no doubt important, that these ideas are emerging out of practice – Zehr, Wright and Mika, for instance, are all mediators with local schemes as well as academic writers, and

MEDIATION UK is an umbrella membership body for British initiatives in mediation. It is dissatisfaction with the current state of criminal justice in local neighbourhoods and in local agencies that is leading to experimentation with new forms and their associated philosophies. Within the membership of MEDIATION UK alone there is a huge diversity of grassroots initiatives.

At the most established end there are the independent divorce conciliation services (which also have their own organisation, the National Association of Family Mediation and Conciliation Services), numbering nearly fifty. There are getting on for thirty community mediation schemes in MEDIATION UK's Directory, with numbers having increased in the last two or three years, as local authority housing and environmental health departments became aware of their utility. Their crime prevention potential has been appreciated by the police in many areas, and they are one of many referral sources. Some schemes have been funded under the Home Office's Safer Cities programme for this reason – Islington in its first year, Coventry and Bristol, for instance. Some community mediation services offer training for schoolchildren in conflict resolution skills and help schools manage better the multitude of conflicts they continually encounter.

Another large proportion of MEDIATION UK's membership comprises the victim-offender mediation schemes, which number around fifteen, one being county-wide with several local centres (the Northamptonshire Adult Reparation Bureau). In a few cases (Lambeth, Sandwell), victim-offender mediation is provided by community mediation schemes, while some victim-offender schemes have widened their remit to take referrals of neighbourhood disputes, thus emphasising the essential similarity of their work. In addition, a volunteer mediator with the Leeds Mediation and Reparation Service has set up a special service on one estate for mediating between mothers and difficult children, and the project has also set up a programme for lifers about to leave prison to mediate any conflicts likely to be awaiting them from their local communities, their victims or victims' families. Some agencies working with homeless youths are using mediation between them and their parents to enable them to return home by resolving family conflicts. In this way the idea of using mediation is being extended beyond offender and victim to include offenders and their communities.

The Alternatives to Violence Project was started in the USA, using trained volunteers to bring training into prisons for violent offenders. It uses direct involvement and discussion techniques (including a number of 'games') with groups of prisoners to teach them how they can handle conflict more constructively and control their own reactions in their own ultimate interests, a process seen by the project as personally empowering because the individual learns to exercise rational choice instead of giving in to violent instincts or habitual responses. A branch of AVP has now been started in England, offering training for prisons and other groups. Similar training has been available for some years for men who have been violent toward their wives. Such training is distinct from that traditional in therapeutic regimes in that it does not identify the violence as a fault in the offender so much as a failure to realise potentials and capacities already there. (See Morran and Wilson, ch. 14 in this volume, for a discussion of the criminal-justice-based programme in Britain which emphasises men's responsibility for their own behaviour.)

More general application of conflict resolution principles has been introduced into training for Metropolitan Police officers at various levels. Examples are described by Beckett (1992) and Oakley (1992) in Marshall (1992), *Community Disorders and Policing*, a book which gives many other examples of such applications, not only in connection with training. They include grassroots initiatives and intervention by mediation bodies as well as police activities.

DESIGNING A RESTORATIVE JUSTICE SYSTEM

These examples give a flavour of the many ways in which formal justice processes could be re-oriented to a problem-solving perspective based on collaboration rather than the present basis in a retributive philosophy, but it may be useful to give some idea of how a systematic restorative justice approach might look.

In essence, restorative justice rests on the principle that crime, like any other social problem, represents a disjuncture between the aims, aspirations, needs, feelings, and behaviour of different individuals and social groups, including society as a whole. Crime is a relationship problem that therefore should be approached in a rational problem-solving way. While recognising that crime may give rise to emotional feelings in individuals, especially those who have suffered from it directly, restorative justice asserts that policy cannot be adequately based on gut-reactions such as revenge, anger, hatred, or even righteous indignation. The fact that people find it difficult to relate to the idea of crime in a detached and objective manner is seen as a major reason for the crisis within the current formal control system. Such detachment can be achieved by applying conflict resolution principles that have been used with success in dealing with many other social problems.

Apart from these principles of internal operation, it is apparent that we need to recognise the importance of both informal and formal control systems. The former represents the primary forces for reduction of crime and incivility, as well as avoiding cost escalation, but the formal system is needed to address the inevitable failures of informal mechanisms, the problems that go beyond their reach, and the justice problems that may arise from the improper operation of community control.

The formal system needs to be able to interface with the informal and to play an enabling, reinforcing, co-ordinating and resourcing role in relation to it, functions which themselves demand changes in the present character of formal justice systems. The underlying principles of restorative justice and the types of institution needed to take them forward, both in the community and in statutory agencies, have been summarised in a MEDIATION UK discussion paper (1992), the main points of which are summarised below.

1.   Crime would be viewed as a social phenomenon, with loose definitions grounded in community experience, and not just as a set of artificial legal categories. In the context of a community, crime problems are inextricable from the more general problems of social justice, social disadvantage, social integration, social control, intergroup tolerance and understanding, and the development of collective standards.

2.   Crime emerges from, and is affected by, social conditions and is thus best resolved through general social processes rather than specialist crime-oriented processes. Crime prevention and control should, as far as possible, be integrated into community decision-making forums, the management systems of schools and other organisations, etc.

3.   The basic institutions (those of first recourse) would be community-based and community-run, relatively informal in nature, and would provide maximum potential for public participation. Development of these would need central state resourcing and encouragement.

4.   While individuals should be held to have, and be expected to exercise, responsibility for their behaviour, it must be recognised that society generally must also share such responsibility. It is important to a restorative justice system that those involved with it, formally and informally, are aware of, and adhere to, this con-

ception and the principles underlying the system, of collaborative problem-solving and helping individuals to reform by listening, discussion, persuasion and enabling.

5. The main role of the state would be to oversee local arrangements to ensure that fairness and justice are maintained, to deal with criminal matters – such as environmental crime – that may go beyond the boundaries and capacities of local systems, to enshrine the basic rights of individuals, groups, society and the environment in a system of exemplary laws, to exercise control over the ultimate coercive sanctions such as custody, and to help communities establish procedures for the prevention and resolution of crime.

6. The basic approach to dealing with offenders would not be, as at present, a retributive system which has precipitate recourse to what should be the ultimate sanction of punishment, but a restorative system which both denounces the offence and deals constructively with the victim and the offender.
Contributing objectives would be:

   • to encourage the offender's involvement and commitment;
   • to encourage the community, especially the offender's personal network, to share in this process;
   • to come to a decision (preferably consensual) on the responsibilities or restrictions to be imposed on the offender;
   • to encourage the offender to make amends with the victim(s) in whatever ways might be feasible, and to provide whatever additional assistance or support might be needed by the victim(s);
   • to reaffirm the values of the community and its expectations of individual members' behaviour.

7. The cost and bureaucracy of criminal justice should be kept to the minimum necessary to protect citizens and the environment from serious harm or undue fear. Courts should only be allowed to employ costly sanctions when the cost can be justified as a saving in relation to the economic and social costs of allowing a particular pattern of behaviour to continue.

8. At its basic informal level, justice would be a feature of everyday social life, with control exercised in a constructive way by families, neighbourhoods, schools, and other organisations. Such control (emphasising individual responsibility) would be balanced by communal responsibility for ensuring that all members receive respect, care and support, especially those who have difficulties adjusting to social expectations. Adequate education in the skills of handling conflict and problem behaviour, and in the duties and methods of citizenship, will need to be generally available.

These features are particularly lacking in those areas that have high rates of crime, and these areas should be given priority in building up local resources.

9. Basic community-level institutions would include victim support (including Women's Aid and Rape Crisis), dispute mediation, crime investigation, peace-keeping force, legal advice, support services for offenders and others with personal problems, victim/offender mediation and reparation service, and community justice panels.

10. There is currently some conflict between the roles of the police as community 'helpers' and as crime investigators. There is a case for considering the differentiation of police forces into two distinct professions. The first would comprise a peace-keeping force, with duties in the areas of emergency assistance, social order, crime prevention and patrolling. The second profession would comprise traditional policing functions of crime investigation and collection of evidence.

11. A combination of a police caution and voluntary reparation to the victim would normally be sufficient to warrant discontinuance of any further action. Only if the offence were relatively serious (i.e. causing community concern), or if the offender were persistent, unco-operative or needing help, would a case need to be referred to a community justice panel.

12. Formal courts would be invoked only for offences or offenders constituting a serious threat, and where the application of coercive sanctions was necessary because of a failure to achieve voluntary co-operation. Such courts would still operate in accordance with problem-solving and restorative principles as far as was feasible, but they would be able to impose reparation to the victim and/or society, and restrictions on liberty.

13. Detention would be ordered only where there was a clear risk to public safety, and not as a punishment. Places of detention would therefore be seen not as 'prisons', but as secure facilities for voluntary treatment, training and counselling with the aim, ultimately, of rehabilitation and reintegration into the community.

14. The probation service, already a 'mediating' institution between formal justice agencies and the community, would acquire a major role in a restorative justice system, resourcing, facilitating and co-ordinating the various strands.

Construction of such a system would require initiatives from both the grassroots (examples of which have already been described) and from the centre, to build up the necessary 'mediating structures', for neither local communities nor the state can solve the problem of rising crime on their own. The problem is that we tend only to be prodded into change by crisis, and the conditions of crisis themselves usually determine short-run, cost-cutting, unsystematic measures which are not conducive to the building of a purposeful system and long-term survival. While various observers see criminal justice in the UK as being close to crisis, it may not be helpful to conclude that we need to rush to solutions. It may be better to accept that we are not currently in crisis, although running conspicuously in the wrong direction, and that we need to start planning now for a more effective system, including investment in the types of institution and training that will lead to long-term improvement. If we allow a sense of crisis to overwhelm such rational planning and evolutionary change, for the sake of indiscriminate short-term cost-cutting, then we shall merely be getting further into crisis and ensuring that what we wish to avoid really will happen.

References

Barnett, R. (1977), 'Restitution: a new paradigm of criminal justice', *Ethics*, 87, pp. 279–301.

Beckett, I. (1992). 'Conflict management in the police: a policing strategy for public order', in T. F. Marshall, *Community Disorders and Policing*, pp. 129–40.

Berger, P., and Neuhaus, R. (1977), *To Empower People: The Role of Mediating Structures in Public Policy*, American Enterprise Institute for Public Policy Research, Washington, DC.

Bianchi, H., and van Swaaningen, R. (eds.) (1986), *Abolitionism*, Free University Press, Amsterdam.

Braithwaite, J. (1989), *Crime, Shame and Reintegration*, Cambridge University Press, Cambridge.

Christie, N. (1977), 'Conflicts as property', *British Journal of Criminology*, 17, pp. 1–15.

Cragg, W. (1992), *The Practice of Punishment: Towards a Theory of Restorative Justice*, Routledge, London.

de Haan, W. (1990), *The Politics of Redress: Crime, Punishment and Penal Abolition*, Unwin Hyman, London.

Haley, J. (1988), 'Confession, repentance and absolution', in M. Wright and B. Galaway (eds.), *Mediation and Criminal Justice*, Sage, London.

Heidensohn, F. (1986), 'Models of justice: Portia or Persephone?', *International Journal of Sociology of Law*, 14, pp. 287–98.

Jubilee Policy Group (1992), *Relational Justice: A New Approach to Penal Reform*, Jubilee Centre, 3 Hooper Street, Cambridge CB1 2NZ.

Kelling, G. I., and Moore, M. H. (1987), *The Evolving Strategy of Policing*, National Institute of Justice, Washington, DC.

Lacey, N. (1988), *State Punishment: Political Principles and Community Values*, Routledge, London.

Marshall, T. F. (1988), 'Out of court: more or less justice?', in R. Matthews (ed.) (1988), *Informal Justice*, Sage, London.

Marshall, T. F. (1989), 'Punishment in the dustbin', paper to British Criminology Conference, July 17–20, Bristol.

Marshall, T. F. (1992), *Community Disorders and Policing: Conflict Management in Action* (published on behalf of the Forum for Initiatives in Reparation and Mediation), Whiting and Birch, London.

Matthews, R. (ed.) (1988), *Informal Justice?*, Sage, London.

Matza, D. (1964), *Delinquency and Drift*, Wiley, New York.

MEDIATION UK (1990), *Criminal Justice Policy*, MEDIATION UK, 82a Gloucester Road, Bristol BS7 8BN.

MEDIATION UK (1992), *Working towards 'Restorative Justice'*, MEDIATION UK, Bristol.

Messmer, H., and Otto, H.-U. (eds.) (1992), *Restorative Justice on Trial*, Kluwer Academic Publishers, Dordrecht.

Mika, H. (1992), 'Mediation interventions and restorative justice: responding to the astructural bias', in H. Messmer and H.-U. Otto (eds.), *Restorative Justice on Trial*, Kluwer Academic Publishers, Dordrecht.

Oakley, R. (1992), 'Learning from the Community: facilitated police-community workshops at the local level', in T. F. Marshall, *Community Disorders and Policing*, pp. 217–28.

Shonholtz, R. (1987), 'The citizen's role in justice: building a primary justice and prevention system at the neighbourhood level', in T. F. Marshall (1992), *Community Disorders and Policing*, pp. 145–58.

Woodson, R. L. (1989), *A Summons to Life: Mediating Structures and the Prevention of Youth Crime*, American Enterprise Institute for Public Policy Research, Washington, DC.

Wright, M. (1991), *Justice for Victims and Offenders*, Open University Press, Milton Keynes.

Wright, M., and Galaway, B. (eds.) (1988), *Mediation and Criminal Justice*, Sage, London.

Zehr, H. (1990), *Changing Lenses: A New Focus for Criminal Justice*, Herald Press, Scottdale, PA.

PART SEVEN

Abolitionism

[16]

The abolitionist approach: a British perspective

JOE SIM

> Among social scientists there seems to be considerable disillusion-
> ment, and, indeed, a turning away from the goal of abolition –
> more or less as if it were a youthful and confused prank from the
> late sixties which the middle aged and wise can hardly uphold. I
> have, however, never understood why a negative political trend –
> be it increased armaments or expanded prison systems – should
> lead one to conclude that the trend in question no longer consti-
> tutes a point of fundamental attack and final abolition from a
> radical position.
>
> (Mathiesen, 1986, p. 84)

The title of this paper, 'The abolitionist approach: a British perspective',[1] will probably seem like an anachronism to many. For those
concerned with the daily grind of criminal justice and penal policy,
abolitionism is likely to be regarded as an esoteric, academic luxury
which is irrelevant to the delivery of penal services both to the confined and to the wider society. The British demand for 'facts' as
opposed to historically, theoretically and philosophically grounded
analysis, whether of an abolitionist nature or not, is as prominent in
the prisons debate as it is in other social policy debates. A number of
academics in the UK, no doubt, will have other, but no less critical
views. Abolitionists are now regarded as sociological dinosaurs, unre-
constituted hangovers from the profound but doomed schisms of the
late 1960s, who are marginal to the 'real' intellectual questions of
the 1990s. Like Marxism, abolitionism appears to have been left
behind on the sandbank of history while the river of modernity – or
as many intellectuals would have it, postmodernity – flows progressively
forward producing wave after consumerist wave of choice, opportunity

and desire. Social formations now need realistic economic and social policies in general, and penal policies in particular, to respond to the new times flooding the planet, which in turn require research that is relevant to the service orientation of the newly reformed state and its subject/customers both inside and outside the walls of the penitentiary.

Superficially, there appears to be strong sociological evidence to support this contention. Abolitionism, it seems, has failed to impact upon the direction of penal policy or the debate on crime and punishment. Indeed, the modern prison, despite 150 years of 'monotonous critique', as Michel Foucault put it, has not only endured but expanded to become materially and ideologically critical in the remorseless struggle to enforce law and maintain order. The institution's presence on the landscape of British society appears to be so deeply embedded that it has become almost naturalised in popular consciousness and state discourse as an immutable barrier, which despite crises and contradictions protects the law-abiding from the swamping encroachment of the desperate and degenerate in the same way that it was thought to protect the respectable from the ravages of first the parasitic delinquent, and then the dangerous classes in the nineteenth century (Garland, 1985). This conception of the prison has continued into the late twentieth century. Whatever social index is taken – the rate of imprisonment, numbers detained, expenditure, time served or judicial sentencing patterns – the prison, despite the occasional drop in the average daily population, is on a relentlessly expansionist course.

This perception was confirmed in 1991 by the former Home Secretary, Kenneth Baker. In an unwitting affirmation of Foucault's maxim that the prison 'is always offered as its own remedy' for its internal problems, Baker pointed to the steps involved in his government's 'programme of prison reform'. In England and Wales this included raising expenditure to £1.4 billion in 1992–93, recruiting an extra 4,100 prison officers and opening thirteen new prisons by January 1994 at a cost of £900 million (*Hansard*, 1991, col. 168). Expenditure on law and order in general was expected to rise by 11 per cent in 1992–93 taking it up to £6 billion, still a clear exception to the prudent monetarist axe which successive Conservative governments have taken to public spending as the austere prerequisite for the economic, political and ideological resurrection of the nation. There has been a parallel growth in the range of alternatives to custody, which was supplemented in October 1992 by curfew orders and the cybernetic electronic tag (Muncie, 1990; Vass, 1990). By the year 2000 the number of prisoners will have increased by 25 per cent, reaching 57,500 in England and Wales. This figure includes a 44 per cent increase in the remand population (Home Office 1992, Table 1).

Abolitionism also appears to have been further weakened by the state's strategy for reform, developed in the wake of the furious demonstrations by prisoners in the mid–1980s. Within this discourse the mistakes of the past have been recognised and prison regimes will be modified so that the disasters of the 1980s, such as those at Strangeways (in Manchester, England) and Peterhead (in Scotland) will never be repeated. Even those on the left who might be broadly sympathetic to abolitionists have been highly critical, describing their 'anarcho-communist' position as 'preoccupied with abolishing or minimising state intervention rather than attempting to make it more effective, responsive and accountable' (Matthews, 1989, p. 5).

This paper will challenge this pessimistic reading of abolitionism by exploring three themes. First, I want to analyse the theoretical and political contribution of British abolitionists and to illustrate the hegemonic impact of this contribution on the traditional, more conservative reform lobby in this country. Second, the paper will explore the specificity of abolitionist thought in Britain and will illustrate the sociological influences on abolitionists here which took them along a different theoretical and political path to abolitionists in other countries. Finally, the paper will focus on the state of British prisons today and will discuss the reforms now being proposed to alleviate the perennial and debilitating crisis in the system. I will argue that these reforms will do little to alter 'the fiasco' that is the prison system (Mathiesen, 1990, p. 140). The paper concludes by reasserting the need for an abolitionist perspective in which the starting-point for changing prisons is changing the inequality in power, both at the micro and macro levels, in a society that is deeply and increasingly divided along the fault lines of class, gender, race and sexuality.

ORIGINS 1970–80

Willem de Haan's recent overview of abolitionism provides a useful starting-point for tracing its development in Europe and North America. It emerged at the end of the 1960s as part of a destructuring movement whose main objective 'was to soften the suffering which society inflicts on its prisoners' (de Haan, 1991, p. 204). Since then abolitionism has developed along a number of different dimensions. Theoretically, it has rejected the claims made by defenders of the conventional criminal justice system that it protects people and controls crime. The prison is 'counter productive, difficult to control and [is] itself a major social problem', and crime should be understood as a complex, socially constructed phenomenon which 'serves to maintain political power relations and lends legitimacy to the expansion of the crime control apparatus and the intensification of surveillance and control'. Strategies such as redress, compensation and reconciliation need to be introduced into a decentralised criminal justice system. Politically, abolitionism has called for the 'fundamental reform of the penal system [which] presupposes not only a radical change of the existing power structure but also of the dominant culture'. Finally, social problems, conflicts and troubles should be taken seriously but not as crime. This means arguing for 'social policy rather than crime control policy' within a framework of 'decriminalisation, depenalisation, destigmatisation, decentralisation and deprofessionalisation' (de Haan, 1991, pp. 205–14).

This general history of abolitionism's development is, I think, well known. However, there has been much less discussion about how abolitionists have operated within the specific context of British politics, the issues they have confronted and perhaps most importantly, the nature of the interventions they and other radical prisoners' rights organisations have made in the last twenty years. Close examination of these issues highlights a number of significant theoretical, political and strategic differences between abolitionism in this country and elsewhere.

The first abolitionist group, Radical Alternatives to Prison (RAP), was established in Britain in 1970. As Mick Ryan has noted, RAP's initial position on prisons was straightforward: it was out to abolish them. For the group reform was highly problematic; 'by improving conditions prisons are made more acceptable, they are legitimised in the public mind' (Ryan, 1978, p. 138). It is important to recognise, however, that despite this hard-line position RAP was involved from the beginning in a series of campaigns around specific issues. As I noted above, this point has rarely been discussed in the literature on abolitionism, yet it is critical for understanding the influence of British abolitionist thought and the nature of its political and humanitarian concerns.

In May 1971, RAP convened a conference on women in prison. From this meeting a campaign was organised against the rebuilding of Holloway women's prison as a secure hospital which would have minimal custodial facilities. There were demonstrations and exhibitions and a pamphlet, *Alternatives to Holloway*, was published in May 1972. The pamphlet pointed to the facts of female crime and argued that too many women were remanded unnecessarily in custody, that many offences could be dealt with by other means, and that women should not be imprisoned for offences such as alcoholism, child cruelty and petty theft. Instead, RAP suggested that community-based projects should be introduced which would 'make prison for women seem irrelevant'. The new Holloway was a £6 million 'folly' which would detain women 'unnecessarily labelled as criminal and then treat them in an institutional setting which was almost bound to fail' (Ryan, 1978, pp. 102–5).

What is interesting, I think, is the outcome of the campaign. At one level, it could be judged to have failed as the prison was rebuilt, though it is worth noting that it did nothing to alleviate the problems of confined women in the ensuing years. The repressive nature of the regime, particularly the notorious C1 wing, the 'Muppet House', resulted in a series of gruesome self-injuries as women responded to the particular pains of imprisonment they endured and the patriarchal discourses which underpinned them (Padel and Stevenson, 1988, p. 72). At another level, 'there is very little doubt that the campaign made the problem of women in prison more visible that it had been in the past' (Ryan, 1978, p. 106). This visibility was to be reinforced and sustained over the next fifteen years, first in the proliferation of academic work in the area (Carlen, 1983; Dobash, Dobash and Gutteridge, 1986); second, through the formation of the pressure group Women in Prison in 1983; and finally in the impact that these early campaigns had on the traditional reform groups, who had previously ignored this issue.

Ryan also points to a second early campaign which was mounted against the notorious psychiatric Control Units, secretly opened by the Home Office in July 1974 to discipline those labelled as subversive trouble-makers. Removed from the general population, they were kept in strict isolation twenty-three hours a day for ninety days, followed by a second ninety-day period when they were allowed to mix with others in the Unit. If an individual prisoner broke any prison rule, however minor, he went back to day one, stage one, to start again.

It is important to recognise that RAP campaigned for the closure of the Units alongside other, more traditional reform groups, including the government-sponsored National Association for the Care and

Resettlement of Offenders and the Howard League for Penal Reform. In October 1975 it was announced that the Units were to be discontinued. In one sense, this could be seen as a victory both for interventionist politics and for RAP's uncompromising position. On the other hand, as Ryan notes, the extent to which the campaign's pressure moved government policy 'is genuinely difficult to say since what actually happens inside our prisons is surrounded by secrecy, a secrecy which is well-served by the ambiguity of official statements' (Ryan, 1978, p. 137).

These initial campaigns were followed by a number of others which took place against a background of an ever-deepening crisis in Britain's prisons (Fitzgerald and Sim, 1982). They included highlighting the use of drugs to control prisoners, pointing to the role of the Prison Medical Service in this control, defending the philosophy and practices of the Barlinnie Special Unit and establishing alternatives to custody such as the Newham Alternative Project, which showed 'the possibilities of achieving genuinely humane as well as potentially negating reforms with the most limited resources' (Cohen, 1980, p. 6). In January 1979 RAP began publishing its journal, *The Abolitionist*, which was to run until 1987. Its first editorial pointed out that while the organisation did not have a blueprint for the future, it did believe that its:

> ideas about and approach towards antisocial behaviour (as opposed to 'crime') are much more relevant and credible than the established logic which reflects and only serves to perpetuate an unequal and exploitative social system. It follows that we seek to remove such sentiments from the ephemeral regions they tend to inhabit and translate them into an effective force for social change.
>
> (*The Abolitionist*, No. 1, p. 1)

This editorial position, which came very close to that of European abolitionism, was not to be sustained. By the beginning of the 1980s RAP, while still maintaining that radical structural change was the key to dealing with crime and punishment, nonetheless underwent some important changes both in personnel and in its theoretical position, which in turn had repercussions for its political strategy. If the 1980s was to be the decade of law and order, arguably it was also the decade in which a more theoretically sophisticated and politically astute organisation made a significant impact on many traditionalists involved in the debates around penal policy.

INTO THE LAW AND ORDER DECADE

The refinement in RAP's position took place against an intensification in the prison crisis which I mentioned earlier. The interlocking nature of the crisis was apparent in the overcrowded and appalling conditions in short-term prisons, in the challenges to the state's definition of penal truth mounted by radical prisoners' rights organisations, in the violent confrontations in long-term male prisons, and in the vociferous, widespread industrial action taken by prison officers. These, in turn, were underpinned by a more general crisis of penal legitimacy (Fitzgerald and Sim, 1982). More widely, the election of the new Conservative government in May 1979 underlined the collapse of the social democratic consensus, the emergence of a strong state and the consolidation of the new right as the hegemonic bloc in society, held there by the ideological cement of authoritarian populism (Hall, 1988). At the same time, those social movements which emerged at the end of the 1960s and which stood outside of both organised left and state-defined political action had also consolidated their position, competing with and contradicting dominant discourses surrounding race, gender, sexuality and ecology (Gilroy, 1987).

RAP's response to these profound events was outlined in *The Abolitionist* by two members of its editorial collective. First, Tony Ward, the journal's editor, dealt with the perennial issue of reform and argued that the immediate priority was to 'gain support for reforms of the penal system which while making it more humane will also *show up its inherent limitations and contradictions*' (Ward, 1982, p. 22, emphasis in the original). Ward also wrote the editorial outlining the organisation's goals. He maintained that while many reforms amounted to 'a sugar coating on a toxic pill', it was nonetheless important to argue for the immediate reform and abolition of particular parts of the system, including the use of drugs as control mechanisms, solitary confinement, the system of security classification, secrecy and censorship. The Barlinnie Special Unit indicated, for Ward, what could be achieved by a 'less authoritative and restrictive approach'. He concluded by differentiating the politics of RAP from those in the traditional reform lobby, so that while many of RAP's medium term goals were shared by the traditionalists, they did not share 'our political outlook': 'RAP's fundamental purpose is, through research and propaganda to educate the public about the true nature, as we see it, of imprisonment and the criminal law; to challenge the prevailing attitudes to crime and delinquency; and to counter the ideology of law-

and-order which helps to legitimate an increasingly powerful State machine' (*The Abolitionist*, No. 12, p. 2).

The second article, written by Jill Box-Grainger, critically evaluated RAP's first ten years, pointed to the recent sociological and political influences on the organisation and outlined RAP's developing strategy for changing prisons and the wider criminal justice process. This strategy included supporting 'negative' reforms such as disbanding the Prison Medical Service, prohibiting the use of drugs to control prisoners, removing the disciplinary role from prison Boards of Visitors, abolishing parole and introducing greater accountability through ending prison secrecy and the censorship of mail. These reforms were underpinned by the demand for a moratorium on prison building, a reduction in maximum sentences, curtailing the power of sentencers, decriminalisation of certain offences and the implementation of radical alternatives to prison. Finally, and contrary to the ill-informed assertion that radicals have not been concerned about victims of crime, she pointed to RAP's call for a re-evaluation of the 'significance of criminal restitution [and of] the relationship between the offender and the victim' (Box-Grainger, 1982, pp. 17–18).

The article then moved on to discuss the perennial and key issues of serious offenders and dangerousness. This debate had been fuelled by two developments. First, there was the apparent bifurcation in British penal policy which was leading to an expansion in the numbers and rate of turnover in short-term prisons, and the simultaneous increase in the numbers and length of detention in long-term prisons. Second, the debate was increasingly influenced by the philosophical, epistemological and political questions raised by the women's movement, particularly the demand to be protected from 'oppressive and gratuitous street and domestic violence'. RAP therefore was '(quite healthily) . . . forced to consider "what should be done" with the serious offender if it is to be at all responsible to popular demands (albeit that RAP continues to underline the fact that serious offenders constitute a very small proportion of all offenders)' (Box-Grainger, 1982, p. 21).

The organisation also began to reassess its position on radical alternatives, particularly the place of 'the community' within the framework of an alternative model of justice. Constructing the problem of prison abolition through community alternatives assumed a homogeneity of values within society in general and in working-class communities in particular. It was therefore important to distinguish between the long-term interests of working-class people, where there 'may be enormous similarity', and short-term interests, which were 'frequently antagonistic'. This had serious implications for women: '[community] has always involved the re-assertion of the role of the family, the basic unit of the community and ultimately the containment of women in the home. That in the short term the interests of a son may be in conflict with a mother's own interests is not only a theoretical problem but potentially a barrier against "community" support for radical alternatives' (Box-Grainger, 1982, p. 16).

RAP's consideration of this issue was underlined by the formation of a Sex Offences Group within the organisation. The group maintained that it was hazardous to attempt to construct a definition of dangerous individuals. Rather it argued for a policy of exemplary or retributive punishment 'as an appropriate response to *some* offences. The important thing then is the viciousness of the act not the actor . . .' (*The Abolitionist*, No. 10, p. 4, emphasis in the original). It also argued for a radical restructuring of both sentencing policy and wider social relationships. Again influenced by the impact of feminism, the group confronted the sentencing issue in its evidence to the Criminal Law Revision Committee's Working Paper on Sexual Offences. It asked 'how can the law emphasise the unacceptable nature of rape and indecent assault without resorting to excessively long prison sentences for rapists who are not representative of the majority of those who rape?' Additionally, could sentencing protect women from rape at all? The group made ten proposals to deal with sentencing and imprisoned rapists and concluded:

> RAP recognizes that the above proposals are only a brief outline of a possible sentencing practice for convicted rapists, where all custodial sentences are shorter and where custody is not so debasing and destructive as at present. And again we would stress that this type of sentencing can only be effective if it is used against a background of real equality of opportunity for women – an equality that offers women economic independence, political, ideological and sexual determination.
>
> (*The Abolitionist*, No. 10, pp. 6–7)

THEORETICAL UNDERPINNINGS

It is important to recognise that the change in RAP's strategy and political orientation was mirrored in a series of more general theoretical debates that occurred at the beginning of the 1980s. In particular, the question of reform as initially discussed in Mathiesen's seminal *Politics of Abolition* (1974) was addressed as a theoretical and political problem. In 1982, Mike Fitzgerald and I, while arguing for an abolitionist position as the answer to the enduring crisis in British prisons, also maintained that the 'positive' and 'negative' distinction made by Mathiesen did not address the subtleties and ramifications of particular reforms. For us 'reform *by its very nature* contain[ed] both positive and negative possibilities' (Fitzgerald and Sim, 1982, p. 164, emphasis in the original). In 1985, Dave Brown and Russell Hogg developed a similar critique. Pointing to the issue of legal rights, they asked if introducing due process was a positive or negative reform. The answer was not straightforward:

> reform measures or lines of advance cannot necessarily be adequately specified or evaluated *a priori* by reference either to some positive/ negative calculus or to some general theory of law ... state ... capital ... legitimation ... legal right etc. It is not necessary to embrace the ambiguous assumptions of 'the justice model' ... or 'rights' discourse ... to recognise that the introduction of legal representation, procedural and appeals rights into internal disciplinary hearings presents a possibility of 'bringing power to particular account' ... On the other hand detailed practices of discipline and normalisation, surveillance, differentiation, classification, assessment, segregation, deprivation within the site of the prison are not adequately contested simply through attempts to 'legalise' the prison.
>
> (Brown and Hogg, 1985, p. 73)

Brown and Hogg developed this analysis in a number of other papers which raised a series of theoretical questions about abolitionism. They pointed out that abolitionism tended to posit common political interests, usually built on class affiliation, between the unproductive (prisoners) and radical fractions of the working class. There were problems with constructing a unified class subject in this way in that this construction underestimated power networks which divided, differentiated and classified populations on the 'basis of sexual differentiation or grids of normality, age, health, etc.' (Brown and Hogg, 1992). This differentiation had real effects: 'the success of the prison and other agencies such as the police at constituting an "alien and dangerous" criminal class is real and cannot be reversed by a simple assertion of common class interests. It is always a question of *constructing* alliances often in very specific, localised and short-term ways. There is no necessary underlying unity waiting to be recognised' (Brown and Hogg, 1992, pp. 154–5, emphasis in the original).

Tony Ward has also argued that within the specific context of Britain, struggles around and resistance to penal power are better understood by reference to Foucault's 'oppositional model of action' rather than Mathiesen's concept of 'contradiction'. He points to the strategy of opposition developed in the probation service and maintains that the clear division within abolitionist thought between control and welfare agencies, while 'theoretically attractive', is 'politically untenable in Britain'. The largest support for abolitionism has come from the voluntary agencies, social workers and probation officers whose everyday activity 'inescapably involves mixing care and control. To present these people with a stark choice between providing "pure" control within the penal system or "pure" help outside it could simply play into the hands of those in authority who are eager to reassert the importance of control as the system's primary role' (Ward, 1991, p. 161).

Along with Mick Ryan, Ward has also highlighted other theoretical currents which influenced abolitionism in the 1980s, including feminist theory and the campaign around rape launched by Women Against Rape. It was from this 'difficult but productive debate' that a range of other questions arose concerning the role of the state, the relationship between capitalism and patriarchy and, following Foucault, the problem of defining the nature of power and crimes of the powerful:

> No longer did the world appear to be neatly divided between the 'powerful' and the 'powerless', nor were 'crimes of the powerful' the sole prerogative of the ruling class, once the concept was extended to take account of the power of men over women, of white people over black and of adults over children. (RAP was one of the first groups in the lobby to engage seriously with the issue of child sexual abuse).
>
> (Ryan and Ward, 1990, p. 7)

CRIMINOLOGY FROM BELOW

The theoretical debates outlined above were reflected in RAP's interventionist strategy in the 1980s. As in the previous decade, the organisation was involved in a series of campaigns, often with other mainstream groups, to lobby for 'an agreed programme of reform' (Ryan and Ward, 1990, p. 9). This meant supporting those in the traditional lobby who argued for a reductionist strategy as a response to the prison crisis. At the same time, RAP also pointed to issues which until then had been neglected by traditional reformers. The scandal surrounding deaths in custody is a good example of this process. RAP was involved in the formation of the pressure group Inquest, established in 1980 to draw attention to those who had died 'suddenly, violently or inexplicably in police and prison custody' (Benn and Worpole, 1986, p. 1). Twelve years on, the work of the group has become central to this debate. The issue has also become a cause for concern in the mainstream lobby and for the Chief Inspector of Prisons himself. It also inspired the formation of a similar group in Australia in 1984, which was concerned with the general question of deaths in custody and the disproportionate number of Aboriginal deaths in particular (Hogan, Brown and Hogg, 1988). Inquest's work extended across a range of areas throughout the 1980s and can be seen as part of the hegemonic process mentioned earlier. Its members picketed police stations and coroner's courts, organised meetings, arranged legal support for the families of the deceased, who scandalously were and are denied legal aid, highlighted the unaccountable and often unacceptable practices of the coroner's courts and helped to sponsor a number of legislative changes, including the Administration of Justice Act 1982 and the Coroner's Juries Act 1983. This work also began to raise broader theoretical questions, particularly around the nature of state power and the processes of institutionalised violence (Sim, Scraton and Gordon, 1987, pp. 14–15). Both Inquest and RAP worked closely with a number of other radical prisoners' rights organisations, including Women in Prison, whose goal was 'to redress the injustices presently suffered by Britain's hitherto neglected women prisoners'. In 1986 these organisations gave evidence to the House of Commons Social Services' Committee on the Prison Medical Service which was directly linked to the Committee's recommendation which 'called for the abolition and complete replacement of Holloway's C Wing' (Sim, Scraton and Gordon, 1987, pp. 15–16).

The ongoing campaign for the abolition of the Prison Medical Service (PMS) in England and Wales provides another example of this joint endeavour. As I noted above, it was RAP and the National Prisoners' Movement who, because of their close contact with the confined, first raised this issue in the 1970s. Both groups pointed to the role of medicine inside, not as a neutral dispenser of medical care but as a set of interlocking, disciplinary discourses built on 'less eligibility', control and regulation (Sim, 1990). By the mid–1980s the issues involved had become so contentious that they were taken up by a range of mainstream groups, including the Howard League for Penal Reform, The National Association for Mental Health, The Royal College of General Practitioners and The Royal College of Psychiatrists (Sim, 1990, pp. 122–3). In April 1991 the National Association of Probation Officers and Inquest introduced into the House of Com-

mons the Health Care of Prisoners Bill, which contained provisions
for the abolition of the PMS. As I have noted elsewhere, this Bill could
be seen as a 'highly symbolic measure for achieving radical change . . .
which if accepted will not solve all of the problems concerning the
psychological and physical health of prisoners but is a realistic starting
point for raising other, more fundamental questions regarding the
treatment of the confined' (Sim, 1991, p. 38). Similar themes can be
identified in relation to the campaign around the privatisation of
prisons, where abolitionists have supported the moves by groups as
diverse as The National Association of Probation Officers, The Civil
and Public Servants' Association and The Prison Officers' Association
to prevent further spread of the privatised network in Britain. The
points raised by this campaign, which include the unethical nature of
privatisation in relation to punishment and the non-accountability
of those operating private prisons, directly parallel the issues raised
by two of the leading members of the abolitionist movement in Britain
in the book they published on the subject in 1989 (Ryan and Ward,
1989).

These campaigns, seen alongside those discussed earlier, indicate
that abolitionism has not been the marginalised and irrelevant discourse claimed by its critics. Rather, it should be understood as a
hegemonic force which has been generated by and responded to the
'contingent [and] fundamentally open-ended nature of politics'. In
that sense it can be seen as part of the struggle to develop a radical
discourse around penality, in Gramscian terms attempting to replace
'common sense' with 'good sense' in relation to crime and punishment (Hall, 1988, p. 109). In making this argument I am not positing
a simple, uni-dimensional, causal relationship between abolitionist
thinking and penal reform, particularly in terms of policy as 'the
emergence of policy reforms from below (as with those from above)
is the result of a complex and often fractious process' (Sim, 1991,
p. 33). Nor am I idealising the impact of abolitionism on the increasing authoritarianism of state power. Rather I am pointing to the
specificity of the abolitionist project in Britain, which in utilising a
complex set of competing, contradictory and oppositional discourses,
and providing support on the ground for the confined and their
families, has challenged the hegemony around prison that historically
and contemporaneously has united state servants, traditional reform
groups and many academics on the same pragmatic and ideological
terrain. In a number of areas discussed in this paper, such as deaths
in custody, prison conditions, medical power, visiting, censorship and

sentencing, these groups have conceded key points in the abolitionist argument and have moved onto a more radical terrain where they too have contested the construction of state-defined truth around penal policy. What this process means for the future is the subject of the last section of this paper.

The debate about the future of the prisons and the criminal justice system in general is now dominated by the issue of state-inspired reforms. It is important to recognise, however, that the movement for reform has been generated not by state benevolence but by the demands made by prisoners in different demonstrations, by grassroots organisations unwilling to accept the 'truth' surrounding the appalling miscarriages of justice that have occurred in the last twenty years, and by pro-feminist organisations demanding changes in the definitions of – and responses to – male brutality towards women. In the light of the major disruption in the prisons during the 1980s two significant reports have been published, *Opportunity and Responsibility* (Scottish Prison Service, 1990) and the Woolf Report (1991). These documents appear to herald a new beginning for prisons in this country. In recognising that change is needed if the deeply damaging events of the 1980s are to be avoided, they propose a number of reforms, including establishing a framework of justice for prisoners, improved conditions, increased contact with the outside, better staff training and, crucially, making the confined responsible for their behaviour through introducing prisoners' contracts. Both documents have been almost uncritically endorsed in the media, and by academics and politicians as the panacea for alleviating the crisis inside.

From an abolitionist perspective there are some serious theoretical and political problems in utilising these proposals as the basis for future penal arrangements. Space does not permit me to provide an in-depth analysis, although I have done this elsewhere (Sim, 1991; 1993). However, I want briefly to point to four distinct areas which would form part of an abolitionist critique of the rhetoric of reform contained in these reports.

First, both documents either marginalise or heavily qualify the experiences of the confined. This means that alternative definitions of penal reality remain hidden and subservient to orthodox and state definitions of events. This is important because it allows both reports to transform questions of power, domination and institutionalised intimidation, which have been central to the abolitionist position, into more benign problems of administrative malpractices or individual deviance. There is a classic passage in the Woolf report which illustrates this point. Woolf points out that after the demonstration in Pucklechurch Remand Centre (near Bristol) in April 1990, surrendering prisoners were told that their arms and legs would be broken. The report notes:

> There is no doubt that at the time the inmates were very frightened (I use that word advisedly) and even if the remarks made to them when waiting on the lawn were made in jest, they could, and did, cause considerable fear to the inmates. When considering these criticisms the long hours that management and staff had been on duty should be taken into account. Each member of staff must have been extremely tired and . . . close to exhaustion.
>
> (Woolf and Tumim, 1991, p. 271)

The second problem also relates to the politics of marginalisation, in this case the failure to deal with or respond to a number of key prison issues that have arisen in the last twenty years: the unfettered discretion of staff, prisoners' rights, the accountability of prisons within a liberal democracy, the financing and cost of the service, women in prison and the sentencing process. For both documents the alleviation of the crisis lies not in confronting these issues but in the development of the responsible prisoner/customer, tied to each establishment by an agreed individual contract. Through this construction the debate is shifted onto the narrow ledge of individualism and social administration and away from wider structural questions concerning power, collective rights and democratic control (Sim, 1993).

Third, the increasing emphasis on coercion and militarisation as strategies for maintaining order means that the proposed reforms, even if they are accepted on their own terms, are unlikely to marginalise the ideological and material support within the state for these strategies. Prisoners will now receive an extra ten years for what is quaintly described as 'prison mutiny'. As Kenneth Baker has maintained, they must learn that rioting is not a 'cost-free option' (cited in Sim, 1993).

Finally, current reformist rhetoric misses a central issue raised by abolitionists and others in the last two decades, namely that unconditional support for limited change mystifies broader structural questions around the prevailing definitions of criminality that operate in this society, and who is punished as a result of these definitions. The first national survey published by the Prison Reform Trust in December 1991 showed that unemployment, homelessness, lack of education and psychiatric disorders were prevalent in the prison population, that prisoners were overwhelmingly males aged 17–40, that 16 per cent of males and 26 per cent of females came from Afro-Caribbean backgrounds, and that this group was serving substantially longer sentences than white prisoners, in the case of the women over twice as long. The report concluded that imprisonment 'exacerbates those very disadvantages which . . . led the person into crime in the first place' (Prison Reform Trust, 1991, p. 6).

Historically and contemporaneously, the prison has overwhelmingly contained the detritus generated by this society's hierarchical arrangements. In making this point I am not denying the impact that crimes committed by many of the imprisoned can have, nor am I positing a model of behaviour in which human beings are propelled in a positivist sense by forces outside of their control. Clearly, there are important philosophical and social psychological questions to be discussed concerning free will, responsibility and personal accountability, although given the abject recidivism rate in prisons the institution's supporters can hardly defend its track record in encouraging responsible behaviour in the confined. Having said that, I do want to make the point that today's age of penal improvement is simply reinforcing conventional definitions of criminality, and that the prison of the twenty-first century is likely to operate at an ideological and symbolic level in the active construction and reconstruction of very precise and narrow definitions of criminality and social harm. As abolitionists like Mathiesen have maintained, the prison has to be understood both as a material place of confinement and as an ideological signifier. Not only does the institution encourage and reinforce bifurcation, powerlessness and stigmatisation, but it also establishes 'a structure which places members of one class in such a situation that the attention we might pay to the members of another is diverted' (Mathiesen 1990, p. 138). Distracting attention away from crimes of the powerful and actively constructing particular images of criminality, however fragmentary and contradictory that process might be is, in Mathiesen's view, central to the continuation of the prison and to the reinforcement of a 'pervasive ideological mystification' around crime (Mathiesen, 1990, p. 141). This argument is particularly relevant to the debates around dangerousness. One of the most depressing elements in recent academic debates in criminology, which in my view can be directly linked to the reformist rhetoric of the state, is that in the rush to take crime seriously and to rediscover aetiology, the symbolic place of institutions like prisons as cultural signifiers has been neglected. This continually allows the debate on dangerousness (and crime in general) to take place on a conventional terrain clearly marked out in the discourses of state servants, government ministers, most media personnel and in the common sense of popular consciousness. Consider the brief passages below, describing two events separated by only eighteen months that occurred in the late 1960s:

> Tex's final thrusts were suddenly interrupted by a frantic shout from Katie. While Tex and Sadie had been focusing their attention on Frykowski, Folger had freed herself from the noose and was making an effort to escape. Katie caught her, but was losing the battle until Tex got there. He clubbed Folger with the pistol and then stabbed her until he thought she was dead. Between his dash from Frykowski to Katie, Tex saw Sebring moving, and paused long enough to make several knife thrusts into Sebring's body. Once Folger was down and apparently dead, Tex returned to finish the job on Frykowski.
>
> (Emmons, 1988, pp. 244–5)

> When children came running to them for sweets, they scythed them down with automatic fire. They herded mothers and babies into bunkers and threw grenades in after them. They raped and sodomised Vietnamese girls and then sliced open their vaginas with bayonet or knife. They scalped old men and women, beheaded others, slit throats, cut out tongues, sliced off ears, and hacked off limbs . . . Some wanted the dubious honour of being a 'double veteran' – American army slang for raping a woman and then murdering her.
>
> (Knightley, 1992, p. 40)

The first passage describes the murders committed by the Manson family, the second those committed at My Lai in March 1968. Despite the appalling brutality of both actions, the response to them was (and is) very different: Charles Manson is still serving a life sentence, William Calley, one of 'C' company's officers, served four-and-a-half months. There are a number of significant sociological questions to be raised here, not least of which relates to the culture of masculinity within which these actions can be contextualised and perhaps understood. For the purpose of my argument it is important to recognise that twenty years on, the Manson case reverberates symbolically as a chilling example of how serious crime and dangerousness continue to be defined in conventional and narrow positivist terms, while the

Calley case is effectively closed. As Barbara Hudson has noted, 'serious crimes and crimes which are taken seriously are not necessarily the same . . . seriousness of law enforcement . . . does not relate to seriousness of crime if the latter is to be judged by any rational calculus of harm as suggested by the more liberal justice model theorists' (Hudson, 1987, p. 126). This argument can clearly be extended to other activities that remain effectively unpoliced and unpunished: large-scale commercial fraud (Levi, 1987), the criminality of the state in terms of espionage, assassination and conspiracy (Barak, 1991; Gill, 1994); and at more micro levels, violent male behaviour underpinned by power, militarisation and the culture of masculinity (Tift and Markham, 1991). Even when fraud cases are prosecuted, poorer and powerless offenders 'are more likely to be imprisoned, pound for pound stolen, than is a fraudster' (Levi, 1989, p. 107).

Critics of this position will no doubt say (as they always do) that even if the definition of crimes of the powerful is extended and recognised, abolitionists and other radical critics still fail to confront the fact that there are some dangerous individuals, overwhelmingly men, who in the conventional sense need to be confined. This view can be challenged at two levels. First, as I have already noted, many of those involved in the abolitionist movement in Britain have been confronting the issue of violence at least since the early 1980s and have been pointing to the problems that those defined as conventionally dangerous, for example, male rapists, have brought to the lives of particular groups. Second, British abolitionists have never advocated simply 'tearing down the walls' of the penitentiary. Rather they have maintained that incapacitating conventionally dangerous individuals such as rapists through detention does not necessarily guarantee an alleviation of violence, either at an individual or collective level. Imprisoned rapists are likely to be confronted by a prison culture which will do little to change their behaviour, heighten their consciousness or the consciousness of those in the wider society concerning the 'intimate intrusions' which face women on a daily basis (Stanko, 1985). The first major study of imprisoned rapists in the UK supports this argument. It showed that only 32 out of 142 men believed that raped women had been harmed, while less than half displayed any compassion for their victims (*The Guardian*, 5 March 1991). While some exemplary work has been done with sex offenders in institutions such as Grendon Underwood and Wormwood Scrubs, supported by individually well-motivated prison officers, which perhaps will be consolidated by the newly formed national system for the treatment of sex offenders, it could be argued that there is a danger that at an ideological level this work and reform simply reassert the 'therapeutic discourse', which conceptualises 'male violence as an irrational act of emotional ventilation' rather than as behaviour based on intentional motivation and the will to dominate (Dobash and Dobash, 1992, p. 248). A similar point has been made in relation to the most recent proposals for reforming police practices concerning domestic violence, which are based on the reassertion of traditional family values (Radford and Stanko, 1991).

My scepticism towards these reforms does not mean resorting to incarcerating the powerful as a way forward. Clearly that would defeat the politics and the objectives of abolitionism by implying that the phenomenon of a 'fair incarceration rate' exists (Thomas and Boehlefeld, 1991, p. 249). It does mean, however, recognising that the operationalisation of power, its interpersonal and structural abuse and its mediation by social class, gender, race and sexuality needs to be responded to; it is *how* we respond that remains the key question for abolitionism. I believe that current reformist proposals, because of their marginalisation of the issue of power, do not come close to addressing the philosophical, sociological, psychological *and* political nuances generated by this question.

CONCLUSION

This paper has quite deliberately covered a lot of sociological ground, because I wanted to illustrate the importance of abolitionist thought in this country and the diverse range of concerns of its supporters. I do not therefore take the pessimistic view that abolitionism has offered nothing or continues to offer nothing towards the prison debate. As Jim Thomas and Sharon Boehlefeld have noted: 'struggle is as long as history . . . the outcomes of our resistance to unjust forms of social control are rarely immediately visible' (Thomas and Boehlefeld, 1991, p. 249). Indeed, the abolitionist argument remains a powerful one, as Willem de Haan's critical dissection of traditional forms of punishment has indicated (de Haan, 1990). Similarly, Pat Carlen's cogent argument for the abolition of women's prisons as 'one small step towards giving the criminal justice and penal systems the thorough shake up they so desperately need' also provides a clear theoretical and pragmatic view of the way forward in this still neglected area (Carlen, 1990, p. 125). As Thomas and Boehlefeld point out, a theoretically refined abolitionism can offer a new way of thinking about the world *and* a vision of the future which contrasts sharply with traditional methods of penality based on incapacitation, deterrence, punishment and rehabilitation. It directly confronts the 'cynicism and anomie' of postmodernism, it reaffirms the argument that prisons don't work 'either as punishment or as a means of ensuring the safety and stability of the commonweal' and it recognises that predatory behaviour needs to be responded to and dealt with within the structural and interpersonal contexts of power and politics (Thomas and Boehlefeld, 1991, pp. 246–49). That vision can be compared with the present situation here and elsewhere, which is evoked in the words of George Jackson: 'The ultimate expression of law is not order – it's prison. There are hundreds upon hundreds of prisons, and thousands upon thousands of laws, yet there is no social order, no social peace' (Jackson, 1975, p. 95). Jackson's posthumous thoughts provide a fitting description of both the politics of British prisons and the increasingly factious and divided nation they help to legitimate and sustain in the late twentieth century.

Note

1. Thanks to Anette Ballinger, Dave Brown, Jenny Burke, Russell Dobash, Paul Gilroy, Paddy Hillyard, Tony Jefferson, Mick Ryan and Tony Ward for discussing different aspects of this paper with me.

References

The Abolitionist Numbers 1, (January 1979), 10 (winter 1982) and 12 (1982); available from Radical Alternatives to Prison (RAP), 104A Brackenbury Road, London W6.

Barak, G. (ed.) (1991), *Crimes by the Capitalist State*, State University of New York Press, New York.

Benn, M., and Worpole, K. (1986), *Death in the City*, Canary Press, London.

Box-Grainger, J. (1982), 'RAP – a new strategy?', *The Abolitionist*, 12, pp. 14–21.

Brown, D., and Hogg, R. (1985), 'Abolitionism reconsidered: issues and problems', *Australian Journal of Law and Society*, 2, 2, pp. 56–75.

Brown, D., and Hogg, R. (1992), 'Law and order politics – left realism and radical criminology: a view from down under', in R. Matthews and J. Young (eds.), *Issues in Realist Criminology*, Sage, London, pp. 136–76.

Carlen, P. (1983), *Women's Imprisonment*, Routledge, London.

Carlen, P. (1990), *Alternatives to Women's Imprisonment*, Open University Press, Milton Keynes.

Cohen, S. (1980), 'Introduction', in L. Dronfield, *Outside Chance*, Radical Alternatives to Prison, London.

de Haan, W. (1990), *The Politics of Redress: Crime, Punishment and Penal Abolition*, Unwin Hyman, London.

de Haan, W. (1991), 'Abolitionism and crime control: a contradiction in terms', in K. Stenson and D. Cowell (eds.), *The Politics of Crime Control*, Sage, London, pp. 203–17.

Dobash, R. E., and Dobash, R. P. (1992), *Women, Violence and Social Change*, Routledge, London.

Dobash, R. P., Dobash, R. E., and Gutteridge, S. (1986), *The Imprisonment of Women*, Blackwell, Oxford.

Emmons, N. (1988), *Without Conscience*, Grafton, London.

Fitzgerald, M., and Sim. J. (1982), *British Prisons*, Blackwell, Oxford.

Garland, D. (1985), *Punishment and Welfare*, Gower, Aldershot.

Gill, P. (1994), *Policing Politics: Security Intelligence and the Liberal Democratic State*, Frank Cass, London.

Gilroy, P. (1987), *There Ain't No Black in the Union Jack*, Hutchinson, London.

The Guardian, 5 March 1991, 29 May 1992.

Hall, S. (1988), *The Hard Road to Renewal*, Verso, London.

Hansard (1991), 3 December.

Hogan, M., Brown, D., and Hogg, R. (1988), *Death in the Hands of the State*, Redfern Legal Centre Publishing, Redfern.

Home Office (1992), *Home Office Statistical Bulletin 10/92*, Research and Statistics Department, London.

Hudson, B. (1987), *Justice Through Punishment*, Macmillan, London.

Jackson, G. (1975), *Blood in My Eye*, Penguin, London.

Knightley, P. (1992), 'Review of *Four Hours in My Lai* by M. Bilton and K. Sim', *New Statesman*, 15 May, p. 40.

Levi, M. (1987), *Regulating Fraud*, Tavistock, London.

Levi, M. (1989), 'Fraudulent justice? Sentencing the business criminal', in P. Carlen and D. Cook (eds.), *Paying for Crime*, Open University Press, Milton Keynes, pp. 86–108.

Mathiesen, T. (1974), *The Politics of Abolition*, Martin Robertson, London.

Mathiesen, T. (1986), 'The politics of abolition', *Contemporary Crises*, 10, pp. 81–94.

Mathiesen, T. (1990), *Prison on Trial*, Sage, London.

Matthews, R. (1989), *Reflections on Recent Developments in Social Control*, paper presented at the British Criminology Conference, July, Bristol.

Muncie, J. (1990), 'A prisoner in my own home: the politics of electronic tagging', *Probation Journal*, June, pp. 72–7.

Padel, U., and Stevenson, P. (1988), *Insiders*, Virago, London.

Prison Reform Trust, (1991), *The Identikit Prisoner*, Prison Reform Trust, London.

Radford, J., and Stanko, E. (1991), 'Violence against women and children: the contradictions of crime control under patriarchy', in K. Stenson and D. Cowell (eds.), *The Politics of Crime Control*, Sage, London, pp. 188–202.

Radical Alternatives to Prison (Holloway Campaign Group) (1972), *Alternatives to Holloway*, Radical Alternatives to Prison.

Ryan, M. (1978), *The Acceptable Pressure Group*, Gower, Aldershot.

Ryan, M., and Ward, T. (1989), *Privatisation and the Penal System*, Open University Press, Milton Keynes.

Ryan, M., and Ward, T. (1990), 'The penal lobby in Britain 1950–1990: from positivism to poststructuralism – an autocritque', unpublished paper.

Scottish Prison Service (1990), *Opportunity and Responsibility: Developing New Approaches* to the Management of the Long-Term Prison System in Scotland, Scottish Prison Service, Edinburgh.

Sim, J., Scraton, P., and Gordon, P. (1987), 'Introduction: crime, the state and critical analysis', in P. Scraton (ed.), *Law, Order and the Authoritarian State*, Open University Press, Milton Keynes, pp. 1–70.

Sim, J. (1990), *Medical Power in Prisons*, Open University Press, Milton Keynes.

Sim, J. (1991), ' "When you ain't got nothing, you got nothing to lose": the Peterhead rebellion, the state and the case for prison abolition', paper presented at the British Criminology Conference, July, York.

Sim, J. (1993), 'Reforming the penal wasteland?: a critical review of the Woolf report', in E. Player and M. Jenkins (eds.), *Prisons After Woolf: Reform Through Riot*, Routledge, London.

Stanko, E. (1985), *Intimate Intrusions*, Unwin Hyman, London.

Thomas, J., and Boehlefeld, S. (1991), ' "Rethinking abolitionism: what do we do with Henry?", Review of de Haan's *The Politics of Redress*', *Social Justice*, 18, 3, pp. 239–51.

Tift, L., and Markham, L. (1991), 'Battering women and battering Central Americans: a peacemaking synthesis', in H. Pepinsky and R. Quinney (eds.), *Criminology As Peacemaking*, Indiana University Press, Indianapolis, pp. 114–53.

Vass, T. (1990), *Alternatives to Prison*, Sage, London.

Ward, T. (1982), 'Towards abolition', *The Abolitionist*, 12, pp. 20–2.

Ward, T. (1991), 'Rediscovering radical alternatives', in Z. Lasocik, M. Platek, and I. Rzeplinska (eds.), *Abolitionism in History*, Institute of Social Prevention and Resocialisation, Warsaw University, Warsaw.

Woolf Report, (1991), *Prison Disturbances April 1990*. Report of an Inquiry by the Rt. Hon. Lord Justice Woolf and His Honour Judge Stephen Tumim, CM 1456, HMSO, London.

17

Abolition and the politics of bad conscience: a response to Sim

ANDREW RUTHERFORD

> But all change in history, all advance, comes from the noncon-
> formists. If there had been no trouble-makers, no Dissenters, we
> should still be living in caves.
>
> (Taylor, 1985, p. 14)

Abolitionist theory (including the special contribution of RAP) occupies an honourable place at the hard end of the politics of penal
dissent in the United Kingdom. There is much in Joe Sim's excellent
review that I find compelling. As Sim makes clear, the dissent is of a
quality that opens the door to constructive ways of approaching complex issues, such as violence against women and child sexual abuse.
This positive vein of abolitionist thought is close to the tradition of
'founding fathers' such as Louk Hulsman and Nils Christie.[1] It is also
exemplified by others of the new generation such as Willem de Haan,
who has this to say:

> The term 'abolitionist' stands for a social movement; a theoretical
> perspective; and a political strategy; is devoted to a radical critique of
> the criminal justice system and committed to penal abolition. When we
> fully appreciate the complexity of a 'crime' as a socially constructed
> phenomena, any simplified reaction to crime in the form of punishment
> becomes problematic.
>
> (de Haan, 1990, pp. 9–10)

Sim follows de Haan in arguing that precedence be given to social
policy crime control, but he draws our attention particularly to the
operationalisation of power in terms of class, gender and racial factors.

Refreshingly, Joe Sim resists the temptation to pursue some exclu-
sive utopian adventure, or what might be called the Shining Path of

abolitionist criminology. He also carefully avoids retreating into an academic ghetto, preferring to confront the world as it actually exists. These considerations do, however, prompt a number of questions about the effects of British abolitionism at the level of both policy and practice.

POLICY

What has been the impact of British abolitionism at the level of policy-making, specifically upon those elites who determine the shape and direction of penal policy and its relationship to other aspects of social policy? There is little indication that abolitionist thought has had much impact at this level. Nothing in Sim's paper disturbs that conclusion. There has been, for example, no equivalent of the 'Utrecht School' which was so influential in The Netherlands during the 1950s and early 1960s. This was the small group of scholars at Utrecht University, consisting of Baan, Pompe, Kempe and one or two others, who had a distinctive impact on the reductionist course of Dutch penal policy for a generation.[2] As Willem de Haan observed, these scholars were 'motivated by a humanistic outlook and a deeply felt compassion for fellow human beings' and appealed 'to the conscience of the criminal justice authorities' (de Haan, 1990, p. 70). It is useful to fully set out de Haan's assessment:

> Central to their thinking was the notion that the convict is, on the one hand, a person needing help and, on the other hand, entitled to certain basic rights. In other words, compassion, co-responsibility and a deep sense of humanity supplied the main motives for the School's critique of institutions and conditions which do not do justice to the delinquent's basic rights.
>
> (de Haan, 1990, p. 69)

Members of the Utrecht School sought out opportunities to speak across the country and they enjoyed constant contact with elites within and beyond government circles. As de Haan concluded, the School helped to generate 'a shared community of values underpinning prosecution and sentencing'. They pioneered what de Haan was later to call 'a politics of bad conscience' about the criminal justice process. That this was so speaks not only to the effectiveness of the members of the Utrecht School but also, perhaps, to the political and social traditions of The Netherlands.

As David Downes has pointed out: 'The various pressure groups lock into politics of penal reform, and even advocates of extreme positions, such as abolitionists, take the business of participation seriously, avoiding the polarization so evident in Britain' (Downes, 1988, p. 75). Downes illustrates this difference with reference to two leading Dutch abolitionist scholars, Herman Bianchi and Louk Hulsman:

> Criminologists like Bianchi and Hulsman, whose views on criminal justice would tend to exclude them from advisory roles in Britain or the United States, have served on commissions of enquiry, are quoted by quite ordinary members of the judiciary as holding views that deserve to be taken seriously, producing 'green papers' as alternative policy proposals that are published along with official policy statements by the government, in short, operate perhaps to shift the axis of debate to more radical positions of compromise than would otherwise occur.
>
> (Downes, 1988, p. 75)

Most recently, Thomas Mathiesen, another of the 'founding fathers' of abolitionism, has drawn attention to the need to undermine the 'pretence' erected by the inner circle of elites that prison is a success, and thereby breaking down the wider 'non-recognition of the fiasco' of prison (Mathiesen, 1990, p. 140). This places upon these elites a responsibility to engage in 'communicative rationality' in penal policy discussions. Mathiesen points to the striking example of Alonso de Salazar Frias, an inquisitor in the Logrono tribunal in the Basque province in the early seventeenth century. It was Salazar's insistence upon truthfulness, relevance and sincerity (in short, communicative rationality) that was the turning point in the suspension of witch-hunts by *la Suprema*. As Mathiesen comments: 'A liberal inquisitor with support from above became instrumental in the subsequent abolition of witch burning and hunts, in a way interestingly reminiscent of the professionals involved in the prison reductions and abolitions of more recent times' (Mathiesen, 1990, pp. 156–9).

PRACTICE

Joe Sim usefully draws attention to Tony Ward's observation that much of the support for abolitionism in Britain has come from practitioners, including persons working within criminal justice agencies such as the probation service. It is therefore curious that he makes no reference to one of the more remarkable developments on the post-war penal scene in England and Wales: the dramatic reduction in the use of custodial sentences with respect to juveniles (and to a lesser extent, young adults). In 1980, 7,500 14 to 17-year-olds received custodial sentences. By 1990 this number had been reduced to 1,450, a decline of 80 per cent (for young adults, persons aged 17–21, the use of custodial sentences fell by 38 per cent). Much of the impetus for this reduction occurred at the coal face, driven by basic grade social workers working directly with youngsters and in a position to influence key decisions at various stages of the process. In 1986, these practitioners established their own national membership organisation, the Association for Juvenile Justice (AJJ), which soon had some 500 members. As its central goal, AJJ campaigned for the *abolition* of juvenile custody. As one practitioner turned policy maker recently recalled, 'AJJ was important in establishing this single ethos about keeping youngsters out of custody and keeping this at the forefront of people's minds' (Rob Allen, quoted in Rutherford, 1992, p. 22). This abolitionist working credo and its impact upon practice is graphically illustrated in the following episode recalled by Sue Wade, another practitioner.

> One morning I heard that two sixteen-year-olds, both with one previous conviction each, had been remanded to the local prison by a Saturday court. I decided to abandon caution but first of all it took me a day to find out the facts. That made me even more angry because it seemed no-one was particularly concerned that this had happened or was trying to sort it out urgently. Quite clearly somebody with one previous conviction should not be in prison. It was absolutely outrageous. They were both young men who over the summer had left school, not got work, had problems with their families and were living rough. It was clear that the court had been given incomplete information to make the remand decision and I decided to appeal to the justices' clerk's sense of justice. I was also quite worried as we had the suicide at Swansea prison so I phoned the clerk at home.[3] He said to telephone him the next day. I phoned him in the morning but he was in court all day and his clerks said that I should wait until Thursday when the case would be back in court. I said that we were not going to wait until Thursday. I went down and sat outside his court until he came out for lunch. He then gave me his office and telephone and said: 'Make all the phone calls you need, use my authority and we will pretend Saturday did not happen and rehear the case this evening. You must get the governor to let them go, because we can't do it without the two of them'. He said he would get a prosecutor and that I should get a solicitor.
>
> I first phoned up the probation service at the prison and they could not understand why I was getting involved in this, and said that it had nothing to do with them. I thought fine, thanks very much, and put the

phone down on them. I phoned the prison's discipline office and they said they were sorry they had far too much to do at the moment and all that sort of thing. I said thanks very much and put the phone down. I thought, right, I will have to go to the top and phoned the governor who was away at a conference. But I got the duty governor, an assistant governor. I explained to him that we really had to have these two bodies and that if we could do that I was sure the court would agree to a remand in care. He said it sounded like a good idea but he had no-one to transport them, which he had to do because they were in his custody. I said: 'Well how about if I said to you that social services transport people to secure units which is the same sort of thing. They could do all the transport'. He thought about it and said 'Let's have a go at it'. I asked: 'If I come at two o'clock we can then have them. I won't have any paperwork but can we have the two bodies?' He said that would be fine. We then went to get these two kids from the prison. I won't forget it ever. They brought us into the special visits area. It was me and a colleague, who was on his first day of the job. He must have wondered what he was getting into. I have never seen people so frightened in my life. They smelled to high heaven of sweat and fear and had obviously not slept at all. We explained to them what we were doing and they had to go to court. I got them in my car, and when we drove out they were both in tears. They had just had the worst experience of their lives, not just because they were incredibly vulnerable sixteen-year-olds . . . and so we got them out. It was the best thing I have ever done.

(Sue Wade, quoted in Rutherford, 1992, pp. 142–3)

The Utrecht School, at the level of policy and elite practitioners in The Netherlands thirty years or so ago, and more recently, probation officers and social workers in England and Wales at the level of every-day practice shared a humanistic crusading zeal that made a great deal of sense in the face of the immediate human situations facing them. It was not some abstract, theoretical ideal but a crucial part of an occupational credo – a set of beliefs and values that imbued all aspects of their work.[4]

It is this humanistic working philosophy that underscores the remarkable career of a policy maker, practitioner and working abolitionist, Jerome Miller. Appointed commissioner of the Massachusetts Department of Youth Services in 1969, by the time of his departure from the state a little over three years later, Miller had essentially shut down the custodial facilities for juveniles across the state. What Miller achieved in the early 1970s later served to inspire Mathiesen's observation: 'the attack on the prisons, should come *before* rather than after the alternatives . . .' (Mathiesen, 1990, p. 161).

In his remarkable account of the Massachusetts experience, Miller describes how he came to adopt his 'deep-end' strategy of closing down the most secure institution first. He writes:

> The rationale underlying corrections is the violent, irredeemable offender or intractable delinquent. The whole system rests on those difficult and dangerous youngsters at the deep-end. If they weren't there, there would be no need for the system. Violent and dangerous youth became my symbol. If I could do something decent and humane with these most threatening delinquents, then the whole system would be shaken. Doing things differently with these youngsters would demand that we address the values justifying our system. The strategy was to undermine the whole institutional system.
>
> (Miller, 1991, p. 91)

More broadly, Jerome Miller's strategy was to take actions that questioned the premises that sustained the institutions. 'Even questioning them created hyper-ambivalence, weakened norms, and blurred roles. It was no recipe for smooth management, but management was not my purpose' (Miller, 1991, pp. 90–91). Miller also has useful things to say about the 'real world of deinstitutionalization', where success 'has more to do with manipulating labels than with diagnosis, more to do with deflating stereotypes than with management techniques, more to do with mitigating harm than with proper rehabilitating models; more to do with swarmy politics than with human service planning' (Miller, 1991). But Miller makes it clear that he is no close adherent of any particular doctrine.

> I was not given much to worrying about class struggle. I had no grand scheme or ideology for reforming youth corrections and I was as wary of doctrinaire explanations for crime and delinquency as I was of recipes for treatment, whether concocted from the narrow nosologies of the psychiatric professions or derived from the grand social and economic theories in vogue amongst left-wing criminologists ... Radical sociologists pretty much dismissed what we were doing. Only after we had finally closed the institutions did they pay much attention, and then it was to discount as basically irrelevant whatever we might have accomplished, calling it a classic liberal reform that ignored the economic roots sustaining the institutional tradition.
>
> (Miller, 1991, p. 86)

In conclusion, it is worth pondering upon the sobering recollection by Jerry Miller of his early months in office, some two years before he shut the system down:

I was invited to speak to a citizen's group made up mostly of angry Harvard students and leftist hangers-on who, as was their wont in the early seventies, were briefly hobnobbing with the oppressed working class from the rowhouses of Somerville and outer Cambridge. The group wanted to know what I intended to do about the state's reform schools. When I said I wanted to do better by individual youngsters, the audience was in near riot. At my suggestion that by going kid to kid I hoped we might actually reduce the populations of some reform schools, I was all but hooted off the stage.

(Miller, 1991, p. 86)

Notes

1   See, for example, Hulsman (1986); Nils Christie (1982; 1989).
2   For assessments of the 'Utrecht School' see especially Downes (1988, pp. 88–97), and de Haan (1990), pp. 69–70.
3   Fifteen-year-old Philip Knight was found hanged in Swansea Prison in July 1990. He was one of three 15-year-olds who died in prison system institutions during 1990–91. For enquiries into teenage suicide in British prisons, see Grindrod and Black (1989) and Scrivener (1993).
4   For a recent study of working credos located across the criminal justice process, see Rutherford (1993).

References

Christie, N. (1982), *Limits to Pain*, Martin Robertson, Oxford.
Christie, N. (1989), *Beyond Loneliness and Institutions. Communes for Extraordinary People*, Norwegian Press, Oslo.
de Haan, W. (1990), *The Politics of Redress. Crime, Punishment and Penal Abolition*, Unwin Hyman, London.
Downes, D. (1988), *Contrasts in Tolerance. Post-war Penal Policy in the Netherlands and England and Wales*, Oxford University Press, Oxford.
Grindrod, H., and Black, G. (1989), *Suicides at Leeds Prison: An Enquiry into the Deaths of Five Teenagers during 1988–89*, report of an enquiry set up by the Howard League for Penal Reform, London.
Hulsman, L. (1986), 'Critical criminology and the concept of crime', *Contemporary Crises*, 10, pp. 63–80.
Mathiesen, T. (1990), *Prison on Trial – A Critical Assessment*, Sage, London.
Miller, J. (1991), *Last One Over the Wall*, Ohio State University Press, Colombus, OH.
Rutherford, A. (1992), *Growing Out of Crime. The New Era*, Waterside Press, Winchester.
Rutherford, A. (1993), *Criminal Justice and the Pursuit of Decency*, Oxford University Press, Oxford.
Scrivener, A. (1993), *Suicides in Feltham*, report of an enquiry set up by the Howard League for Penal Reform, London.
Taylor, A. J. P. (1985), *The Trouble Makers. Dissent Over Foreign Policy, 1792–1939*, Penguin, London.

18

Punishing the poor: a critique of the dominance of legal reasoning in penal policy and practice

BARBARA A. HUDSON

In this paper I will argue that current penal policy demonstrates preoccupations consistent with legal thinking about crime and punishment, and that the neglect and subordination of other perspectives on the appropriate response to crime means that penal policy will fail to fulfil both the goals that it has espoused for itself, and those that are expected of it by the wider society. Although not arguing for an abolitionist agenda as such, my perspective is close to abolitionist arguments which question the prevailing assumption that legal reasoning is necessarily the framework within which the response to crimes should be decided. I shall also draw on the wider body of critical sociology and critical legal theory to assist my discussion of penal policy and of the dominance of legal reasoning.

By 'current penal policy' I have in mind developments with which we are all familiar – the legislation, guidelines and other initiatives which have appeared during the 1980s and into the 1990s: federal sentencing guidelines in the USA and Canada; the new Swedish penal code and penal code revisions in Norway; innovations in Germany, and the 1991 Criminal Justice Act in England and Wales. Although of course there is considerable variation between these policy developments, there are some very important common features which together can be said to characterise contemporary penality in at least the Anglo-Saxon countries, Scandinavia and non-Latin northern Europe (Ashworth, 1989). The most important of these are consistency of sentencing derived from proportionality of punishment to seriousness of offences; reservation of imprisonment for serious crimes, and the development of community-based, but nonetheless punitive, sanctions. Fair punishment, rather than rehabilitation, is the overriding penal aim. The new policies, of which the 1991 Act is a paradigm case, mark in particular concern with acts rather than with people, and the influence of juridical rather than alternative discourse.

THE GROWTH OF LEGAL HEGEMONY

Ever since the emergence of the human sciences in their modern form – psychiatry, pedagogy, criminology – there has been tension between the purely legalistic approach to crime and the desire to treat, cure, prevent (Garland, 1985). Whether one conceptualizes this tension as that between punishment and welfare, rights and remedies, free will and determinism, law and social science, conservatism and socialism, there clearly have been ebbs and flows in the relative authority of what might broadly be termed penalizing and normalizing responses to crime.

Until the mid-1970s, it seemed that the normalizing discourses were in the ascendancy. By 'normalizing discourses' I intend Foucault's meaning of knowledges and technologies which seek to define and induce 'normality' of behaviour, attitudes and even desires, rather than the current penological sense of making penal circumstances more similar to non-penal circumstances (Cousins and Hussain, 1984; King and Morgan, 1980). Not only was rehabilitation in the ascendancy over retribution as a goal of penal sanctions, but the legal establishment and lay magistracy seemed to be losing power relative to other professionals. Sentence lengths actually served were determined by prison and parole authorities; social workers were given expanded roles in community treatment of offenders and in advising sentencers; inside the prison the proportion of educators and therapists grew relative to prison officers pure and simple. Even those who worried about the effects of all this 'soft machine' activity did not dispute its influence, and the 'disciplinary mode' rather than an incapacitating or deterrent mode was accepted as the penal character of the modern welfare-capitalist state (Cohen, 1985; Foucault, 1977).

As well as the influence of the normalizing discourses within the criminal justice system, there were moves to bypass formal law altogether. The diversion and informal justice movements gained adherents and influence, so that for a while it looked as though not only was the era of the use of segregative institutions as the usual way of dealing with problem populations over, but the authority of formal law itself could be diminishing (Unger, 1976, p. 204).

From around the mid-1970s, however, the tide began to turn. Not only were the normalizers criticised for their excesses as well as for lack of effectiveness, but legal discourse began to reassert its superiority. Apparently no longer seeking to curb the reach of formal law, erstwhile advocates of informal justice came to see it as second-rate law, something with which people who were denied access to 'proper' justice could be fobbed off. Informal justice provisions, such as the neighbourhood disputes centres in the USA and law centres in the UK, were said to be dealing with women, minorities, debt and domestic disputes: people and matters not of much concern to real lawyers (Abel, 1982; Harrington, 1985). Other informal diversion-from-court measures, especially those for juvenile offenders, were accused of widening the social control net (Lemert, 1981; Matthews, 1988).

This much discussed shift back to due process was achieved through self-denying ordinances on the part of non-legal professionals (no social inquiry reports on first offenders; gate-keeping to restrict entry to Intermediate Treatment projects and probation case-loads, etc.) as well as by legislation. The various determinate sentencing laws and parole guidelines in the USA restored power to judges and reduced the discretion of or even abolished parole authorities, whilst in the United Kingdom the 1982 Criminal Justice Act shifted power back to judges and magistrates, for instance by giving magistrates powers to make care orders residential rather than leaving the decision of whether a young offender subject to a care order should be at home or in an institution to social workers, and providing conditions of probation such as attendance at daycentres in probation orders.

The 1991 Criminal Justice Act is a landmark in the growth of dominance of legal reasoning. It is built upon the principle of proportionality, and any other considerations are clearly very subordinate to consistent apportioning of punishments commensurate with the gravity of the offence. More than this, however, there is reduction of the scope allotted to other discourses. Not only must probation officers present their reports in quasi-judicial terminology, but they are now being told they must not recommend a sentence. Even more significant are the 'fast-track' pre-sentence reports. In order to reduce delays in sentencing – it is claimed – one week rather than the customary three or four will be allowed for reports prepared between conviction and sentence. There are no corresponding curbs on procedures necessitating adjournments in other stages of court proceedings: lawyers will still be able to request such delays as they feel they need in order to assemble their cases. Clearly, legal facts are being accorded much more importance than social facts. Proportionate sentencing, substitution of automatic and 'good time' remission for parole, have been seen as parts of a movement to restrict professional discretion in criminal justice (Christie, 1982; Cohen, 1985), and the 1991 Act certainly seems to continue this trend, curtailing discretionary powers of probation officers as the 1982 Act curtailed those of social workers. Taken together with the introduction of national standards for the supervision of offenders in the community, probation discretion is much reduced. Sentencers can decide which elements of the various community sentences to impose; what conditions to include in probation orders, and national standards rather than their own professional judgement will dictate to probation officers when an offender should be brought back to court for breach of an order, how often he/she should be seen, and so on.

Judicial discretion, however, has not been curbed, so that the Act continues the trend to transfer criminal justice discretion from non-legal professionals back to lawyers. Increased powers of regulation of care and supervision orders, and now of community sentences, have not been matched by any corresponding restrictions on sentencing powers. A sentencing council has not been introduced, and although there are exhortations to observe seriousness thresholds when deciding between fines/discharges and community sentences, as well as between community sentences and custody, the legislation is facilitative rather than prescriptive. The courts in general, and the Court of Appeal in particular, have been left with the interpretation of the Act and the development of a body of case law (Ashworth, 1992, p. 231).

Restrictions on discretion of criminal justice professionals, then, have resulted in transfer of discretion from non-lawyers to lawyers. As well as these instances of rehabilitative professionals losing – or more accurately, giving – power back to the courts, another example is the introduction of the Crown Prosecution Service, which again is a transfer of decision-making powers from non-lawyers (police) to lawyers. Many critics and reformers support moves to transfer disciplinary powers over inmates from prison administrators to courts: we have argued that offences committed inside prisons should be subject to the same due process as offences committed on the outside. Right or wrong, such arguments illustrate the general willingness to trust legal processes, legal reasoning, rather than normalizing practitioners and precepts. Civil libertarian support for transfer of disciplinary proceedings from the prisons to the courts is mirrored by the solution to prison disturbances proposed by the political right, that is, creation of a new crime of prison mutiny, decisions about which will, one may suppose, be subject to legal processes of definition, investigation and adjudication.

LEGAL REASONING AND THE POLITICS OF LAW AND ORDER

Legal discourse is hegemonic, then, in the sense that not only do members of the legal establishment have more power than other participants in criminal justice processes, but also legal reasoning is seen as superior to other perspectives, even by non-lawyers. The presence of law is felt across more and more areas of social life: 'Law is now the accepted mechanism for resolving social and individual problems and conflicts from theft of a bottle of milk to individual conflict and genetic engineering' (Smart, 1989, p. 20).

Law is unrivalled not only in its power to hand down material judgements, but also in its power to define events. From inner-city and prison disturbances to deaths at football grounds, the judicial commission of enquiry is the accepted way of establishing 'what happened'; social problems, moral problems, relationship problems are translated into legal problems. Law is accepted as a discourse unique in its clarity, its impartiality, its wisdom – its judiciousness, in fact. Even when the activities of the judiciary itself come into question, as with the present enquiries into miscarriages of justice, it is particular instances, the judgement of individual lawyers, rather than the authority of law itself which is challenged. We may shift from a predominantly adversarial system to a more investigative system; we may institute some system of review of Appeal Court decisions; we may press for a sentencing council to reduce disparities, but the problems raised and the solutions proffered are internal to law. Was evidence withheld; was due process circumvented; was the tariff sentence ignored? – these are the questions asked, rather than whether the legal frame of reference itself is sometimes inappropriate or over-dominant. If review procedures are initiated for Appeal Court decisions, powers will in all probability be vested in the Lord Chief Justice rather than going right outside the system. As with disparity in sentencing, issues which are attended to are those which risk undermining respect for law, and the solutions adopted – Royal Commissions, policy initiatives to make sentencing more rational and therefore impregnable to criticism – are those which will reinforce dominance of law.

This growth of legal hegemony is symbiotically related to what sociologists have described as the 'drift to a law and order society' (Hall, 1980). Critical theorists of the state have described how the Reagan-Thatcher era was characterized by ideological promotion of crime as the most pressing social problem of the time, and how problems of inner-city decay, structural unemployment and withdrawal of welfare provisions have been played down by blaming the victims themselves for their problems rather than blaming the policies of governments and the unfettered activities of capital. With formulations such as the 'culture of dependency' and the 'underclass', the unemployed became the unemployable, the homeless became the feckless, and we were all induced to deplore the criminality of the poor rather than poverty itself. Neglect of social and material deprivation was accompanied by emphasis on the supposed moral shortcomings of the poor; deregulation of the City was accompanied by coercive regulation of the inner city. The twin strategies of economic libertarianism and social authoritarianism meant that tackling problems by structural investment was rejected in favour of containing them by legal regulation (Scraton, 1987).

The replacement of Thatcher/Reagan by Major/Bush did nothing to reverse these policies. In spite of Major's declaration that he wanted to promote a more caring society and Bush's assurance that his America would be a 'kinder, gentler society', the policies of economic non-intervention but greater regulation of sexuality and family life continued. At the time of writing there is another round of public expenditure reduction under way in the United Kingdom, withdrawal of unemployment benefit after six months is being considered, but the prison building programme continues.

Potential resistance to these policies continues to be deflected through criminalization of disadvantaged or disaffected groups. Those marginalized or expelled by economic and social decline, the so-called underclass, are projected as criminal. Striking miners, young men stealing or vandalizing cars, Third-World women carrying drugs, young people sleeping on the streets, 'New Age' travellers – we are encouraged to focus not on the problems of impoverishment and hopelessness that society has posed for them, but on the problems of lawlessness they pose for society. 'The problem' in these cases is not just dealt with by law, but it is also defined by law: illegal secondary picketing, aggravated car theft, trafficking, vagrancy and trespass; law is endlessly inventive in finding words to describe, proscribe and penalize the survival strategies of the poor.

Penal policy has readily filled the vacuum left by the withdrawal of governments from economic and social policy. This era of supposed rolling back the reach of the state has seen unprecedented levels of innovation in penal policy and practice. With 'realists' of left and right exhorting us to take crime seriously, it has been easy to see the new penal principles as the translation into policy and practice of the demands of the political climate. It is not my purpose here to describe the fit between just deserts penal policies and new right ideologies, but to note that the drift to law and order provided the ideological space in which penal policy and provision could be increased at the expense of health/welfare/education policy and provision, and further made it likely that penal policy and provision would be within a crime/punishment/individual wickedness frame of reference rather than a social problem/help and social investment frame of reference. It was the ideologically-driven criminalization of the poor and disaffected which facilitated the increase in authority of legal discourse, as the discourse which defines their crimes and apportions their punishments. The irony in all this, however, is that in so privileging legal discourse, a penal principle has become dominant which makes no claim to do anything about crime. Those who have been urging us to take crime seriously from the right have been arguing for incapacitative or deterrent punishments (van den Haag, 1975; Wilson, 1975), whilst left realists call for greater attention to social rather than penal policy:

> the endemic problems of society at large, namely, gross economic inequality and patriarchy – that is, *structural* problems – are of greater importance in the creation and control of crime than unfairness and injustice in the *administration* of justice. Intervention to control crime must, therefore, prioritize social intervention over criminal justice intervention.
>
> (Young and Matthews,1992, pp.3–4; emphasis in original)

It is important to note that deserts theorists themselves endorse this view that penal policy and practice are less important for crime reduction than policies in other spheres: 'more can probably be achieved through various techniques of situational crime prevention, social crime prevention, and general social and educational policies' (Ashworth, 1991, p. 13). Desert-based penal policy, then, aims to punish crime (fairly) rather than to prevent it.

The 1991 Act, moreover, contains no commitment to reduce prison populations. The aim is to reserve prison for serious offences, encouraging the use of community sanctions for non-serious offences. Given the longer sentences expected for serious crimes, this could well produce increases rather than decreases in prison populations, even if the policies lead to reductions in numbers of prison receptions, as has already happened in The Netherlands. In England and Wales, prison populations are expected to rise to 57,500 by the year 2000 (Home Office, 1992); in the USA, rises in prison populations which used to be blamed on lack of coherent penal policy are now attributed to the adoption of determinate and presumptive sentencing in a get-tough law and order climate (Walker, 1991).

Legal discourse, then, does not aim to reduce crime, and political discourse does not aim to reduce imprisonment. The two discourses meet (for the moment) on the ground of fair and consistent punishment, meaning imprisonment for serious offences. This legal-political alliance has resulted in the 1991 Criminal Justice Act, and although there has been considerable tension during the passage of the Act, the two discourses seem to be in some sort of equilibrium at the present. In following this strategy of legal regulation rather than social provision or economic intervention, promoting penal policy whilst neglecting social policy, and adopting the goal of twin-tracking rather than reductionism, however, politicians have ensured that they cannot satisfy the demands which they themselves have stimulated. By their criminalization of the poor and disaffected, they have aroused the demand that increased expenditure on police, courts and prisons will result in a reduction in the crime rate; on the other hand the allegiance of penal reformers to deserts policies, and the compliance of groups such as probation officers with the new practices required of them, has been obtained on the expectation that prison populations will fall.

What has happened, then, is that new right ideologies, in placing emphasis on crime rather than deprivation, explaining events such as the disturbances in 1991 in Tyneside, Oxford and Cardiff and in 1992 in Bristol, Carlisle and Darlington in terms of 'crime', 'professional criminal ringleaders', 'wickedness' and 'lawlessness', have given legal discourse unparalleled authority with regard to social problems. In giving it power to define events, however, it has also had placed upon it the expectation of providing solutions. The alliance between law and politics, then, is inherently unstable.

CLOSURES IN PENAL POLICY: (1) PUNISHMENT

Contemporary penal policy assumes that punishment is the axiomatic response to crime; that the judicial task is to decide how much punishment is appropriate in each case. This assumption of punishment causes several problems, which can broadly be grouped as problems of efficacy and problems of fairness. Whilst deserts theorists themselves may deny any concern of penal policy with reduction or prevention of crime, society as a whole most certainly expects that criminal law and penal practice as a whole ought to be such as to make socially intolerable behaviour less frequent. The general justification of criminal law and the penal sanctions behind it is that they should contribute to the good of society (Hart, 1968) and this can only be by making crime less likely, or by restoring balances of rights and advantages disturbed by crimes. In the first case, the consequentialist justification of punishment raises questions of efficacy; the second case, what I will call the pure law justification, raises questions of fairness.

It is generally claimed against abolitionists that criminal law definitionally entails punishment, and certainly criminologists often use the definition 'forms of wrongdoing about which proscriptions are backed by state punishments' to distinguish crimes from other forms of deviance or anti-social behaviour. Some abolitionists argue that a distinction between sanction and punishment can be maintained, so that criminal law could entail positive sanctions of redress rather than negative sanctions of punishment (de Haan, 1988). I would accept the definitional necessity of punishment, however, with the important proviso that it is the availability rather than the inevitability of punishment which is entailed by the idea of criminal law (Lacey, 1988). Whether punishment ought to be imposed in a particular case depends on several things, but amongst the first considerations should be whether a punitive response will be likely to reduce or increase the probability of reoffending.

In individual cases there may well be conflicts between imposing the tariff-appropriate penalty, and reducing the likelihood of further crime. Obvious examples from opposite ends of the penal spectrum are fines for crimes motivated by economic necessity or imprisonment which through brutalization, contact with more sophisticated prisoners, introduction of drugs, loss of employability and contact with families and so forth may make crime commission on release more rather than less probable. Sometimes it might be that the penalty with the best chance of preventing reoffending might seem inadequate on desert grounds, whilst at other times it might be that foregoing the right to punish altogether, in favour of treatment, restorative measures or recognition of changes already made in the offender's life, might be more effective in preventing reoffending than punishment.

Proportionality is most defensible as a setter of upper limits to punishment. Within the proportionality limit, considerations of efficacy and feasibility should guide the actual choice of sanction. The principle of feasibility developed by Pat Carlen (Carlen, 1989) relates not just to availability of penalties, but to their feasibility for the offender. As well as being physically feasible – availability of transport to probation venues, child-care or work commitments – sentences should not be so demanding that the offender is almost bound to fail; feasibility should also take into account such things as requirements on black offenders to attend day centres where they are likely to encounter racism, or female offenders to encounter sexism; curfew orders should take account of domestic relationships.

Proponents of 'realistic' community sanctions have too readily accepted that they should be punitively equivalent to short prison sentences, and proposals for disposals which minimise punishment have been said to lack credibility with sentencers. On the contrary, punishment, rather than its avoidance, needs justification in individual cases because it: involves deliberate infliction of pain by the state on individuals; may not be the most effective way to achieve ends such as prevention of further crime or restoration of social equilibrium; is an expensive resource.

CLOSURES IN PENAL POLICY: (2) FAIRNESS AND DIFFERENCE

Considerations of feasibility and efficacy involve apprehending the offender as an individual, appreciating that injustice can result as much from punishing different offenders similarly as from punishing similar crimes differently. We are led, then, to look at questions of fairness in contemporary penal policy. These questions are even more crucial than the questions of efficacy, firstly because lack of crime reduction effectiveness in penal policy could be compensated in actual penal practice or in other policy spheres whereas lack of fairness could not; secondly – and critically – because the adherents of deserts penality justify it in terms of its fairness to offenders (von Hirsch, 1990).

The claims of law to superiority over other discourses derive from its claims to universality – it can make rules which cover more than the present instance – and impartiality – all are treated the same. Individuality and difference, then, cannot but be problematic for legal reasoning, over and above the claims of any particular emphasis in penal policy to fair treatment of offenders.

Law's claims to universality have been challenged by the critical legal studies movement, and particularly by feminist legal scholarship. Constructions which are supposed to be general have been shown to be gender- or class-specific; the ideological nature of law is revealed in its blindness to its standpoint relativity (Kerruish, 1991). Current examples such as the law of provocation in murder trials have demonstrated that a supposedly gender-neutral formulation in fact correlates with male behaviour in its insistence on spontaneity, whereas female response to aggression or provocation is more usually to await a moment when the woman is not likely to be overwhelmed by the superior physical strength of a male violent response.

Of more general application, the notion of free will that is assumed in ideas of culpability and thus of desert is a much stronger notion than that usually experienced by the poor and powerless. That individuals have choices is a basic legal assumption; that circumstances constrain choices is not. Legal reasoning seems unable to appreciate that the existential view of the world as an arena for acting out free choices is a perspective of the privileged, and that potential for self-actualization is far from apparent to those whose lives are constricted by material or ideological handicaps.

Freedom of choice in the strong sense which is basic to law is a standpoint relative concept, and legal reasoning has no conception of standpoints. Not only does it not have such a conception, it could not – its claims to truth deny such a possibility. Law's claim to be a unitary, objective, rationally superior perspective would be undermined by admitting any notion of a plurality of valid perspectives. Law cannot concede that the meaning of 'the same' act could be different to people acting out of different motives, from within different social circumstances, with different degrees of power in social relationships, and at the same time be able to make judgements by deciding to which category of acts a particular crime belongs. Legal discourse has been remarkably successful in persuading us that whatever the unemployment rate, however rampant racism and sexism may be, however uncaring society seems to the marginalized, there is no excuse – the law is still the law, a crime is just a crime and must be punished. It is legal reasoning itself, not just the law-and-order ideology of the Reagan-Thatcher era, which persuades us of the urgency of clamping

down on crime, and which leads us to lose sight of the difference
between condoning the act and sympathizing with the actor.

Against the substantive inequalities which make it difficult to maintain that those who enjoy so few of society's benefits should endure
an equal portion of its pains if they transgress its laws, legal theory
gives us procedural equality. Legal theory does not accommodate to
actual subjects, but constructs the legal subject who is identical to all
other legal subjects. We are procedurally equal in that our relationships to the state in terms of rights and obligations are the same. By
defining the state as victim in criminal law, identity in state-subject
relationships displaces differences in subject-subject relationships, so
that material social equalities are irrelevant to law in the face of
abstract procedural equalities. Legal reasoning, in deciding which
cases fall under the same general rule, has the power to decide
which characteristics of act and actor are relevant: social inequalities
are normally ruled irrelevant, procedural and capacity equalities are
ruled relevant.

CONCLUSION: THE LIMITS OF LEGAL REASONING

The success of legal ideology in enforcing equality of obligation in a
grossly unequal society has led some critical legal theorists to question
the usefulness of the idea of rights to the powerless (Fitzpatrick and
Hunt, 1987). Formal legal rights, they argue, have no meaning for
people who have no power to define which rights should be guaranteed by law, to secure for themselves rights which are so guaranteed,
or to secure redress for violations of rights. Others maintain that even
in the most unequal society, the powerless are better off with the
existence of law than without it (Kerruish, 1991; Lacey, 1988) and so
there is a general obligation to uphold the law. I would accept this,
as long as it is correspondingly accepted in criminal justice decision-
making that just as rights are theoretically but not actually applicable
to all members of society, so punishment may be theoretically available
but not actually imposed on all offenders.

As the right to punish should be limited by considerations of efficacy, feasibility and inequality, so claims of fairness to offenders must
be limited by the realization that even though law may strive to treat
equally all those who come before it, the criminal justice system itself
is partial. Criminal justice, penal policy and practice form the system
which deals with forms of wrongdoing typically engaged in by the
poor and powerless; the wrongdoings of other groups are dealt with

by administrative circuits, or by health/welfare circuits. Whilst many forms of behaviour, perpetrated by all social groups, may be against the law, there is partiality in which are criminalized and penalized. There is not scope here to discuss the differences in penalization of crimes of the poor and crimes of the powerful, differences in the seriousness with which black-on-white, white-on-black and black-on-black crime are dealt with, but such issues are sufficiently well-documented for it to be accepted that the criminal justice/penal system is a homogenizing filter, filtering out the misdeeds of the rich and filtering in the misdeeds of the poor (Hudson, 1993; Shelden, 1982).

The partiality of the system as a whole is no reason, of course, why law should not treat fairly within its allotted sphere, and desert again works as a limiting factor, at best making sure that no new legal injustices are added to the social injustices already suffered by impoverished and powerless offenders.

A discourse of rights, a discourse developed to define the mutual powers and obligations of states and subjects towards each other, is, then, valid and valuable, but its closures are such that it cannot be the only discourse which has authority in criminal justice decision-making. Discourses which are centred on helping offenders refrain from reoffending, which insist on feasible as well as fair penalties, which reveal the offender's individuality and difference from other offenders, which appreciate constraints on choice and which understand the disadvantages which not only play their part in people's likelihood of wrongdoing but also of having their wrongdoing dealt with by the penal system, should be given their voice. Guidelines, judgements and the like may tell us the appropriate punishment for the type of crime committed, but they cannot tell us what is the just solution for the particular offender. Whilst legal reasoning might have an important role in penal policy and practice, what is wrong is the present imbalance between legal discourses and the other discourses which have bearing on the response to crime.

References
Abel, R.L. (ed.) (1982), *The Politics of Informal Justice*, Academic Press, New York.
Ashworth, A. (1989), 'Criminal justice and deserved sentences', *Criminal Law Review*, pp. 340–55.
Ashworth, A. (1991), *Principles of Criminal Law*, Clarendon Press, Oxford.
Ashworth, A. (1992), Editorial, *Criminal Law Review*, pp. 229–31.
Carlen, P. (1989), 'Crime, inequality and sentencing', in P. Carlen and D. Cook (eds.), *Paying for Crime*, Open University Press, Milton Keynes, pp. 8–28.
Christie, N. (1982), *Limits to Pain*, Martin Robertson, Oxford.

Cohen, S. (1985), *Visions of Social Control*, Polity Press, Cambridge.

Cousins, M., and Hussain, A. (1984), *Michel Foucault*, Macmillan, London.

de Haan, W. (1988), 'The necessity of punishment in a just social order: a critical appraisal', *International Journal of the Sociology of Law*, XVI, pp. 433–53.

Fitzpatrick, P., and Hunt, A. (1987), *Critical Legal Studies*, Basil Blackwell, Oxford.

Foucault, M. (1977), *Discipline and Punish: The Birth of the Prison*, Allen Lane, London.

Garland, D. (1985), *Punishment and Welfare*, Gower, Aldershot.

Hall, S. (1980), *Drifting into a Law and Order Society*, Cobden Trust, London.

Harrington, C. B. (1985), *Shadow Justice? The Ideology and Institutionalization of Alternatives to Court*, Greenwood Press, Westport, Conn.

Hart, H. L. A. (1968), *Punishment and Responsibility*, Oxford University Press, Oxford.

Home Office (1992), *Projections of Long Term Trends in the Prison Population to 2000*, Statistical Bulletin 10/92, Home Office Research and Statistics Department, London.

Hudson, B. (1993), *Penal Policy and Social Justice*, Macmillan, Basingstoke.

Kerruish, V. (1991), *Jurisprudence as Ideology*, Routledge, London.

King, R. D., and Morgan, R. (1980), *The Future of the Prison System*, Gower, Aldershot.

Lacey, N. (1988), *State Punishment*, Routledge, London.

Lemert, E. (1981), 'Diversion in juvenile justice: what hath been wrought', *Journal of Research in Crime and Delinquency*, XVIII, pp. 34–46.

Matthews, R. (1988), 'Reassessing informal justice', in R. Matthews (ed.), *Informal Justice*, Sage, London, pp. 1–24.

Scraton, P. (ed.) (1987), *Law, Order and the Authoritarian State*, Open University Press, Milton Keynes.

Shelden, R. G. (1982), *Criminal Justice in America*, Little Brown, Boston.

Smart, C. (1989), *Feminism and the Power of Law*, Routledge, London.

Unger, R. (1976), *Law in Modern Society: Towards a Criticism of Social Theory*, The Free Press, New York.

van den Haag, E. (1975), *Punishing Criminals*, Basic Books, New York.

von Hirsch, A. (1990), 'The politics of just deserts', *Canadian Journal of Criminology*, XXXII, pp. 397–413.

Walker, M. (1991), 'Sentencing system blights land of the free', *Guardian Weekly*, June 30, p. 10.

Wilson, J. Q. (1975), *Thinking About Crime*, Basic Books, New York.

Young, J., and Matthews, R. (1992), 'Questioning left realism', in R. Matthews and J. Young (eds.), *Issues in Realist Criminology*, Sage, London.

Appendix 1

Fulbright Colloquium – University of Stirling 1–4 September
1992
Penal theory and penal practice: tradition and innovation in
criminal justice

Colloquium programme

Plenary papers

Andrew von Hirsch, *The prospects for sentencing reform*
Hans Toch, *Arranging chairs on the Titanic: prison policy in the nineties*
Rod Morgan, *Just prisons and responsible prisoners*
Michael Tonry, *Proportionality, interchangeability and intermediate punishments*
Ian Brownlee, *Hanging judges and wayward mechanics: a reply to Michael Tonry*
Marjory Fields, *Criminal justice responses to family violence*
Russell Dobash, *Response to Marjory Fields*
Michael Moore, *Retributivism and proportionate punishment: the special case of double jeopardy*
Dudley Knowles, *Response to Michael Moore*
Joe Sim, *The abolitionist approach: a British perspective*
Andrew Rutherford, *Abolition and the politics of bad conscience: a response to Joe Sim*
Michael Cavadino, *The UK penal crisis: where next?*

Seminar papers

Andrew Ashworth, *What victims of crime deserve*
Paul Cooper, *Commensurability after the Criminal Justice Act*
Alan Norrie, *Contradictory sentences*
Paul Robinson, *Desert, crime control, disparity, and units of punishment*
T. Drummond Hunter, *The role of imprisonment*
Benedikte Uttenthal, *Prison as a means of managing anxiety*
Ed Wozniak, *Are they being served? A customer-focused prison service*
Gill McIvor, *Community service by offenders: progress and prospects*
Peter Young, *Putting a price on harm: the fine as a punishment*
Bill McWilliams, *The changing aims of the English probation system*
Roger Statham, *The growth of the management culture in probation and the practice ideal*

Barbara A. Hudson, *Punishing the poor: a critique of the dominance of legal reasoning in penal policy and practice*

Jim Dignan, *Reintegration through reparation: a way forward for restorative justice?*

Robert Mackay, *A humanist foundation for restitution*

Tony Marshall, *Grassroots initiatives towards restorative justice: a new paradigm?*

Ronnie Mackay, *Capping the length of detention of mentally disordered offenders*

Tony Ward, *Dangerousness, insanity and indeterminate detention: penal theory and psychiatric practice*

David Morran and Monica Wilson, *The CHANGE Project. Confronting domestic violence: an innovative criminal justice response in Scotland*

Neil Hutton, *Patterns of custodial sentencing in the Sheriff Courts*

Lord Morton, *Implementing and monitoring change*

Vinit Haksar, *Choice and punishment*

Uma Narayan, *Contrition and criminal punishment*

Panel discussion

Rebecca Dobash, Sandra Marshall, Betsy Stanko, Jacqueline Tombs, *Gender, crime and criminal justice*

Appendix 2

Colloquium participants

Ms Dorothy Anderson, CHANGE Project, University of Stirling
Prof. Andrew Ashworth, School of Law, King's College London
Mr Ian Brownlee, Department of Law, University of Leeds
Dr Michael Cavadino, Centre for Criminological and Legal Research, University of Sheffield
Prof. Juliet Cheetham, Social Work Research Centre, University of Stirling
Prof. David Cooke, Barlinnie Special Unit
Dr Paul Cooper, Department of Law, Liverpool John Moores University
Ms Anne Creamer, Department of Social Work, University of Dundee
Dr Joseph Curran, Central Research Unit, Scottish Office
Mr James Dignan, Centre for Criminological and Legal Research, University of Sheffield
Prof. Rebecca Dobash, School of Social & Administrative Studies, University of Wales College of Cardiff
Dr Russell Dobash, School of Social & Administrative Studies, University of Wales College of Cardiff
Prof. Antony Duff, Department of Philosophy, University of Stirling
Judge Marjory Fields, Bronx Family Court, New York
Dr Vinit Haksar, Department of Philosophy, University of Edinburgh
Dr Barbara A. Hudson, Centre for Criminal Justice Studies, University of Northumbria at Newcastle
Mrs Peggie Hunter, Howard League, Scotland
Mr T. Drummond Hunter, Howard League, Scotland
Dr Neil Hutton, School of Law, University of Strathclyde
Prof. Nils Jareborg, Faculty of Law, Uppsala University
Prof. Roy King, Centre for Criminal Justice Studies, University of Wales, Bangor
Mr Dudley Knowles, Department of Philosophy, University of Glasgow
Prof. Michael Levi, School of Social & Administrative Studies, University of Wales College of Cardiff
Dr Gill McIvor, Social Policy Research Centre, University of Stirling
Mr Robert Mackay, Department of Social Work, University of Dundee
Mr Ronnie Mackay, School of Law, De Montfort University, Leicester
Dr Bill McWilliams, School of Social Work, University of East Anglia
Mr Mike Maguire, School of Social & Administrative Studies, University of Wales College of Cardiff

Ms Sandra Marshall, Department of Philosophy, University of Stirling
Mr Tony Marshall, Research and Planning Unit, Home Office
Mr James Milne, Area Director, Scottish Prison Service
Prof. Michael Moore, Law School, University of Pennsylvania
Prof. Rod Morgan, Faculty of Law, University of Bristol
Mr David Morran, CHANGE Project, University of Stirling
Lord Morton, Scottish High Court
Dr Uma Narayan, Department of Philosophy, Vassar College
Dr Alan Norrie, Faculty of Law, University of Warwick
Mr John Pearce, Area Director, Scottish Prison Service
Ms Susan Rex, Division C1, Home Office
Prof. Paul Robinson, School of Law, Northwestern University
Mr Andrew Rutherford, Faculty of Law, University of Southhampton
Dr Joe Sim, Institute of Crime, Justice and Welfare Studies, Liverpool John Moores
    University
Dr Lorna Smith, Programme Development Unit, Home Office
Dr Betsy Stanko, Department of Law, Brunel University
Mr Roger Statham, Cleveland Probation Service
Mr David Stewart, Director of Strategy and Planning, Scottish Office
Mr Nigel Stone, School of Social Work, University of East Anglia
Prof. Hans Toch, School of Criminal Justice, University of Albany
Dr Jacqueline Tombs, Central Research Unit, Scottish Office
Prof. Michael Tonry, Law School, University of Minnesota
Mrs Benedikte Uttenthal, Polmont Young Offenders Institution
Prof. Andrew von Hirsch, School of Criminal Justice, Rutgers University
Mr Tony Ward, School of Law, De Montfort University, Leicester
Prof. Martin Wasik, Faculty of Law, University of Manchester
Ms Monica Wilson, CHANGE Project, University of Stirling
Dr Ed Wozniak, Central Research Unit, Scottish Office
Dr Peter Young, Centre for Criminology and the Social and Philosophical Study of
    Law, University of Edinburgh

Index